Communications
in Computer and Information Science   1359

More information about this series at http://www.springer.com/series/7899

Sergio Nesmachnow · Luis Hernández Callejo (Eds.)

Smart Cities

Third Ibero-American Congress, ICSC-Cities 2020
San José, Costa Rica, November 9–11, 2020
Revised Selected Papers

 Springer

Editors
Sergio Nesmachnow 🄳
Universidad de la República
Montevideo, Uruguay

Luis Hernández Callejo 🄳
University of Valladolid
Soria, Spain

ISSN 1865-0929 ISSN 1865-0937 (electronic)
Communications in Computer and Information Science
ISBN 978-3-030-69135-6 ISBN 978-3-030-69136-3 (eBook)
https://doi.org/10.1007/978-3-030-69136-3

This Springer imprint is published by the registered company Springer Nature Switzerland AG
The registered company address is: Gewerbestrasse 11, 6330 Cham, Switzerland

Preface

This CCIS volume presents selected articles from the 3rd edition of the IberoAmerican Congress on Smart Cities (ICSC-CITIES 2020), held on November 9–11, 2020 in Costa Rica as a virtual congress. This event continued the successful two previous editions of the congress, held in Soria, Spain in 2018 and 2019.

The main goal of the ICSC-CITIES 2020 congress was to provide a forum for researchers, scientists, teachers, decision-makers, postgraduate students and practitioners from different countries in Ibero America and worldwide to share their current initiatives related to Smart Cities. Articles in this volume address four relevant topics (energy efficiency and sustainability; infrastructures and environment; mobility and IoT; and governance and citizenship) covering several areas of research and applications.

The main program consisted of seven keynote talks, fourteen oral presentations and four poster presentations from international speakers highlighting recent developments in each of the areas. Over two hundred distinguished participants from 26 countries gathered virtually for this conference. The Program Committee of ICSC-CITIES 2020 received 99 manuscripts. 51 articles were accepted for oral presentation (21 selected for CCIS publication). All articles have undergone careful peer review by three subject-matter experts before being selected for publication.

We would like to express our deep gratitude to all the contributors of ICSC-CITIES 2020 and to the Conference Organizers, and also to the authors and reviewers for their endeavors that efficiently completed the paper-reviewing and publication process. We also thank the participants of the conference, our government and industry sponsors and the readers of the proceedings.

November 2020

Sergio Nesmachnow
Luis Hernández Callejo

Organization

General Chairs

Luis Hernández Callejo   Universidad de Valladolid, Spain
Sergio Nesmachnow   Universidad de la República, Uruguay

Organizing committee

Luis Hernández Callejo   University of Valladolid, Spain
Carlos Meza Benavides   Costa Rica Institute of Technology, Costa Rica
Orlando Murillo Alvarado   Colegio Federado de Ingenieros y de Arquitectos, Costa Rica
José Alberto Díaz   Costa Rica Institute of Technology, Costa Rica
Carlos Mauricio Segura   Costa Rica Institute of Technology, Costa Rica
Ángel L. Zorita   University of Valladolid, Spain
Daniel Moríñigo-Sotelo   University of Valladolid, Spain
Adriana Correa   University of Valladolid, Spain
Epifanio Díez   University of Valladolid, Spain
Manuel Á. González   University of Valladolid, Spain
Jesús M. Vegas   University of Valladolid, Spain
Teodoro Calonge   University of Valladolid, Spain
Oscar Duque   University of Valladolid, Spain
Lilian J. Obregón   University of Valladolid, Spain

Program Committee

Adolfo Ruelas Puente   Autonomous University of Baja California, Mexico
Adriana Correa   University of Valladolid, Spain
Albert Rego   Polytechnic University of Valencia, Spain
Alberto López Casillas   Diputación de Ávila, Spain
Alejandro Otero   Computational Simulation Center, CONICET, Argentina
Alejandro Paz Parra   Pontificia Universidad Javeriana Cali, Colombia
Alfredo Cristóbal Salas   Universidad Veracruzana, Mexico
Alina Rodríguez   Costa Rica Institute of Technology, Costa Rica
Ana Carolina Olivera   Universidad Nacional de la Patagonia Austral, Argentina
Ana Ruiz   San Jorge University, Spain
Andrei Tchernykh   CICESE Research Center, Mexico
Andrés Adolfo Navarro Newball   Pontificia Universidad Javeriana Cali, Colombia

Andres Felipe Fuentes Vasquez	Pontificia Universidad Javeriana Cali, Colombia
Ángel Luis Zorita Lamadrid	University of Valladolid, Spain
Ângela Ferreira	Polytechnic Institute of Bragança, Portugal
Belén Carro	University of Valladolid, Spain
Carlos Grande	Central American University "José Simeón Cañas", El Salvador
Carlos Meza	Costa Rica Institute of Technology, Costa Rica
Carlos Torres	CENIDET, Mexico
Carmen Vásquez	UNEXPO University, Venezuela
Claudia Patricia Murcia Zorrilla	Universidad Cooperativa de Colombia, Colombia
Claudio Risso	Universidad de la República, Uruguay
Cleonilson Protásio	Federal University of Paraíba, Brazil
Cristina Sáez Blázquez	University of Salamanca, Spain
Daniel Moríñigo-Sotelo	University of Valladolid, Spain
Daniel Rossit	Universidad Nacional del Sur, Argentina
Diego Alberto Godoy	Gastón Dachary University, Argentina
Diego Arcos-Aviles	Armed Forces University - ESPE, Ecuador
Diego Gabriel Rossit	National University of the South, Argentina
Diego Gonzalez-Aguilera	University of Salamanca, Spain
Diego Loaiza	University of Santiago de Cali, Colombia
Diego Vilches Antão	National University of La Plata, Argentina
Edgardo Aníbal Belloni	Gastón Dachary University, Argentina
Eduardo Omar Sosa	National University of Misiones, Argentina
Emmanuel Luján	University of Buenos Aires, Argentina
Esteban Mocskos	University of Buenos Aires, Argentina
Euler Cássio Tavares de Macedo	Federal University of Paraíba, Brazil
Fabian Castillo Peña	Free University of Cali, Colombia
Fabrício Carvalho	Federal University of Paraíba, Brazil
Fernando Velez Varela	University of Santiago de Cali, Colombia
Francisco Moya Chaves	Francisco José de Caldas District University, Colombia
Francisco Valbuena	University of Valladolid, Spain
Gregorio López	Polytechnic University of Madrid, Spain
Gustavo Richmond	Costa Rica Institute of Technology, Costa Rica
Hortensia Amaris	University Carlos III of Madrid, Spain
Ignacio Martín Nieto	Universidad de Salamanca, Spain
Ignacio Turias	Universidad de Cádiz, Spain
Irene Lebrusán	Harvard University, USA
Itziar Angulo	University of the Basque Country, Spain
Jaime Lloret	Polytechnic University of Valencia, Spain
Jamal Toutouh	Massachusetts Institute of Technology, USA
Javier Prieto	University of Salamanca, Spain
Javier Rocher	Polytechnic University of Valencia, Spain
Jesús Vegas	University of Valladolid, Spain

Jonathan Muraña	Universidad de la República, Uruguay
Jorge Mírez	National University of Engineering, Peru
José Aguerre	Engineering Faculty, Universidad de la República, Uruguay
José Antonio Ferrer	CIEMAT, Spain
José Díaz	Costa Rica Institute of Technology, Costa Rica
José-Ramón Aira	Polytechnic University of Madrid, Spain
Juan R. Coca	University of Valladolid, Spain
Juan Mauricio	Federal University of Paraíba, Brazil
Juan Espinoza	University of Cuenca, Ecuador
Knud Erik Skouby	Aalborg University, Denmark
Leonardo Suárez	Universidad Técnica Nacional, Costa Rica
Lilian Johanna Obregón	University of Valladolid, Spain
Liliana Gutiérrez Rancruel	Free University of Cali, Colombia
Luis Hernández Callejo	University of Valladolid, Spain
Luis García Santander	University of Concepción, Chile
Luis Marrone	National University of La Plata, Argentina
Luis Murillo-Soto	Costa Rica Institute of Technology, Costa Rica
Luisena Fernández	University of Zulia, Venezuela
Luiz Angelo Steffenel	University of Reims Champagne-Ardenne, France
Manuel Gonzalez	University of Valladolid, Spain
Manuel Alvarez-Campana	Polytechnic University of Madrid, Spain
Martín Draper	Universidad de la República, Uruguay
Mathis Hoffmann	FAU Erlangen-Nuremberg, Germany
Miguel Davila	Universidad Politécnica Salesiana, Ecuador
Mónica Alonso	University Carlos III of Madrid, Spain
Nestor Rocchetti	Universidad de la República, Uruguay
Noelia Uribe-Pérez	Tecnalia Research & Innovation, Spain
Noelia Soledad Pinto	Technological College, Resistencia Regional Faculty, Argentina
Óscar Izquierdo	CEDER-CIEMAT, Spain
Oscar Duque-Perez	University of Valladolid, Spain
Pablo Monzón	Universidad de la República, Uruguay
Paul Ayala	Armed Forces University - ESPE, Ecuador
Paulo Gondim	University of Brasília, Brazil
Pedro Moreno-Bernal	Universidad Autónoma del Estado de Morelos, México
Ponciano Jorge Escamilla-Ambrosio	Computing Research Center - IPN, México
Rafael Asorey Cacheda	Polytechnic University of Cartagena, Spain
Raquel Mejías Elizondo	Costa Rica Institute of Technology, Costa Rica
Renato Alejandro Andara Escalona	UNEXPO University, Venezuela
Renzo Massobrio	Universidad de la República, Uruguay
Rhonmer Pérez	UNEXPO University, Venezuela
Roberto Getino de Mano	Ente Publico Regional de la Energía de Castilla y León, Spain

Contents

Mobility and IoT

Infrastructure, Environment, Governance

Energy Efficiency and Sustainability

Low-Cost and Real-Time Measurement System for Electrical Energy Measuring of a Smart Microgrid

Oscar Izquierdo-Monge[1]([⊠]), Paula Peña-Carro[1],
Mariano Martín Martínez[1], Luis Hernández-Callejo[2]([⊠]),
Oscar Duque-Perez[3], and Angel L. Zorita-Lamadrid[3]

[1] CEDER-CIEMAT,
Autovía de Navarra A15 salida 56, 422290 Lubia (Soria), Spain
{oscar.izquierdo,paula.pena,mariano.martin}@ciemat.es
[2] University of Valladolid,
Campus Universitario Duques de Soria, 42004 Soria, Spain
luis.hernandez.callejo@uva.es
[3] University of Valladolid, Paseo del cauce 59, 47011 Valladolid, Spain
{oscar.duque,zorita}@eii.uva.es

Abstract. One of the most important things in a microgrid is the real-time measurement of all its elements, whether they are consumers or energy producers so that at the end of an established period, the total balance of production-consumption is carried out. It is at this moment when the energy distribution company and its costs become important. Focusing on it, a measurement system based on an infrared sensor and Arduino has been developed, to which a specific software is installed that allows obtaining the value of the instantaneous power consumed by the microgrid from the reading of the LED indicator of metrology of the meter of the distribution company with an error less than 1% daily. This means an important improvement in the knowledge of the energy consumption of the microgrid and implies an advance in the understanding of the electric bill allowing reducing its cost in the contracted terms.

Keywords: Electric smart microgrids · Arduino · Consumption · Measurement system

1 Introduction

A microgrid is a concept used to define a group of interconnected loads and distributed energy resources within clearly defined electrical boundaries that act as a single controllable entity regarding the distribution network. A microgrid can be connected and disconnected from the grid to allow it to operate in grid-connected or island mode [1–3].

To manage a microgrid properly, it is essential to have a system of measurement, communication, and control in real-time. This remote monitoring will help in the management of the load and generation of the whole set, making it a semi-autonomous or autonomous microgrid and significantly reducing the response time to supply problems that may arise. With its implementation, an evolution from a microgrid to an

© Springer Nature Switzerland AG 2021
S. Nesmachnow and L. Hernández Callejo (Eds.): ICSC-CITIES 2020, CCIS 1359, pp. 3–16, 2021.
https://doi.org/10.1007/978-3-030-69136-3_1

intelligent network is achieved, providing the system with two-way communication technologies, cyber-security, and intelligent software applications within its entire field of action.

In this way, greater security and knowledge of all the installed systems are achieved. After the study of the collected data, there is the possibility of modifying the management mode, to improve it [4, 5].

There are various communication technologies within this context, some of which are copper conductors, optical fibre, power line communication, and wireless communication. Among them, the most outstanding and most used today is the wireless one, due to its high monitoring accuracy, its tolerance to failures, and the capacity to cover large areas thanks to the remote control without the need of civil works [6].

In turn, several standard communication protocols provide remote control and protection of the critical components that make up the microgrid, such as the Modbus, Profibus, or Fieldbus Foundation protocol.

For the total control of the microgrid, measurement mechanisms must be installed in each of the loads/generation systems, or group them by transformer stations. But if what is sought is the generation or total consumption of the entire microgrid the point of interest is the PCC (Point of common coupling) or meter of the distribution company. Point where the sum of energy generated/consumed by the entire microgrid is collected [7–9].

Thanks to the knowledge of these readings, different management strategies can be defined [10], such as storing energy in situations where production is greater than consumption, or providing energy at times when generation does not cover all the needs of the different centres of consumption.

The introduction of smart meters have provided detailed information on customer energy consumption [11]. In Spain, the National Commission for Markets and Competition (CNMC) has among its functions to ensure that customers have access to their consumption data in an understandable, harmonized and rapid manner [12, 13]. However, at no time is indicated that access to data is in real-time.

The electricity distribution companies that own these smart meters allow access to the fifteen-minute average data used to prepare the electricity bill, which is not useful to carry out the real-time management of a smart microgrid.

The smart meters are technically prepared to perform instant queries [11] in real-time. However, communication can be slowed down by performing instant readings, generating a time lag that makes it difficult to perform in real-time on the microgrid.

In the case of the presented case study, after contacting the distribution company, they allowed access to this data for a brief period, less than a month, for testing purposes, but in no case did they grant access continuously. The only option to obtain the same measurements as the distribution company is to duplicate the measurement cell of the entrance substation or replace the current one with another double output measurement cell and in both cases install another meter. Either of these two options, apart from being costly (they can cost more than 3500€ between materials and installation work), are complex due to the reduced space available within the substation to install everything necessary.

For this reason, it is necessary to look for alternatives to know in real-time the value of the energy consumed by the microgrid or the energy injected into the distribution network from the microgrid.

This work aims to define an alternative measurement system for the intelligent meter of a microgrid, and of low cost that allows knowing in real-time the energy consumed from the distribution network or the one injected to it. The rest of the paper is as follows: Sect. 2 explains the case study, showing the consumption of the microgrid and how it is currently measured. Section 3 presents the proposed new measurement system, the elements used and its installation. Section 4 details the results obtained. Finally, the conclusions obtained and the cited bibliography is presented.

2   Measurement of Consumption in the CEDER Microgrid

The microgrid under study belongs to CEDER, which is the Centre for the Development of Renewable Energies. It is located in the municipality of Lubia, in the province of Soria and belongs to the Centre for Energy, Environmental and Technological Research (CIEMAT), which is a Public Research Organisation, currently dependent on the Ministry of Science and Innovation. It covers an area of 640 ha with more than 13000 m^2 built in three separate areas.

The CEDER microgrid starts from a 45 kV distribution line and serves a 45/15 kV (1000 kVA) substation. From this substation, it is distributed in medium voltage through an underground network to 8 transformer stations that adjust the voltage to 400 V three-phase low voltage. The network can be operated both in ring mode, which allows a medium voltage perimeter of 4,200 m and in radial mode.

At CEDER, the loads are the elements that make up the centre, being the different buildings and their equipment (motors, lighting, boilers, laboratories, etc.) the energy demanders for its operation and thanks to which the daily activity of the centre is carried out. All these loads are connected to the low voltage network and have different consumption profiles, which are similar to those that can be found in an industrial environment, in the service sector, or even in domestic consumption.

To measure consumption, apart from the meter of the distribution company, CEDER has eight power grid/energy quality analysers (PQube). There is one in each transformer station, on the low voltage side. These analysers are also connected to the CEDER data network through an Ethernet card, so we can access their readings from any point of the centre.

To obtain the real power consumption of CEDER, besides the sum of the values measured by the PQube, we would have to add the consumption of the transformation centres (given that the PQube are on the low voltage side and therefore do not measure their consumption or losses) that we obtain from the test protocols of each of the CEDER transformation centres and that vary according to their load, and the possible losses due to the more than four kilometres of cabling that form the CEDER microgrid.

Figure 1 and Fig. 2 show the comparison between the value obtained from the sum of the PQube and the value of CEDER consumption on April 5 and 25, 2020 respectively.

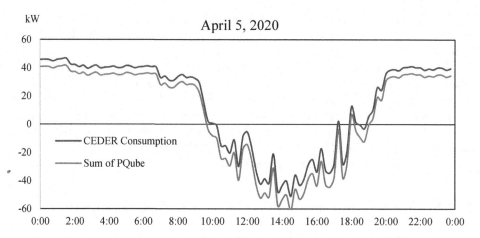

Fig. 1. Comparative CEDER consumption - Sum PQubes (05/04/2020).

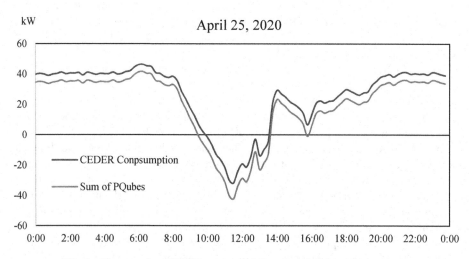

Fig. 2. Comparative CEDER consumption - Sum PQubes (25/04/2020).

The curves are parallel and the difference between both is due to the consumption of the transformer stations. It can also be observed that in low power values (close to zero), the curves are closer together.

If instead of one day, we see the data of a whole month, we get the results shown in Fig. 3.

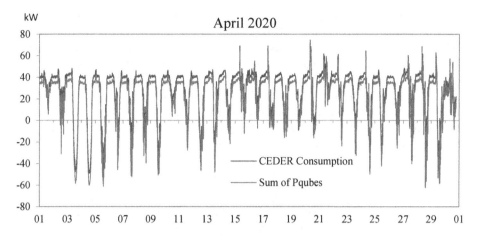

Fig. 3. Comparative CEDER consumption - Suma PQubes (April 2020).

The PQube equipment is very complete and robust, but they also have a high cost (more than 2000€ each equipment), so we are going to look for an alternative measurement system that allows obtaining similar results to those obtained with the PQube with a much lower cost.

3 Proposed Measurement System

To understand the measurement system to be used, it is necessary to know the smart meter installed by the distribution company. It is a meter model ACTARIS SL7000, it is a static meter, polyphase, in four quadrants, of multiple tariffs.

This counter has LED metrology indicators. The visible metrology pulses proportional to the active and reactive energy consumption are indicated by two LED indicators that blink according to the metrological constant marked on the front of the meter (imp/kWh or imp/kVAh).

This LED indicator is used by distribution companies to perform check readings in the field, in situations where automated reading fails, and temporarily perform manual readings through the optical reading port.

The direct connection specifications, as shown on the meter are nominal voltage 230 V, maximum voltage 400 V, nominal current 1 A, and maximum current 10 A.

Furthermore, the metrology constant for active energy is 10000 imp/kWh, that is to say, the LED light would flash 10000 times in an hour for every kWh imported or exported from the distribution network, provided that there was a direct voltage/current ratio.

In our case, there is no direct current-voltage ratio, but there is a transformation ratio for current 10/5 A and voltage 16500/120 V.

These three parameters, metrology constant, and the current and voltage transformation ratios will allow us to calculate, from the pulses of the LED light in a given period, the imported or exported active power recorded by the meter.

To measure these pulses, a measurement system based on an Arduino One will be used, with a microSD card where the operating system and software to be used are installed, connected to an optical sensor (an infrared meter that allows the measurement of the light pulses of the led light of the meter) and to an Ethernet card for Arduino. The cost of this equipment is less than 150 €.

Once the measurement system is installed, placing the optical sensor in front of the infrared communication port of the active power (see Fig. 4), it is necessary to develop the software that allows calculating the active power from the number of light pulses of the meter using the three parameters of the meter that we have seen previously.

Fig. 4. Mounting the measuring system on the counter.

By default, Arduino stores the measured data on a microSD card, but this would not allow us to see it in real-time from the control system, which is why the Ethernet card is used to connect it to the CEDER data network and communicate with it.

Data transmission from the Arduino to the control centre can be done in two different ways:

- Arduino can be programmed to work as a web server and publish the measured values on a web page from which our control system will read them.
- Arduino can be programmed to have Modbus TCP communication and the control system communicates directly with it, defining it in its configuration file.

After several tests with each of the two systems, it has been proven that Modbus communication is faster and more robust than the web server, so it will be the latter system that is used.

4   Results Obtained

Once the Arduino based measurement equipment is installed and programmed, and the communication with the CEDER microgrid control system is established, the data acquisition begins.

Comparing the data obtained with this measurement system based on Arduino with the consumption of CEDER obtained from the measurements of the PQube network analyzers plus the consumption of the transformer stations, it can be seen in Fig. 5 and Fig. 6 (for the 5th and 25th of April respectively), that the results are practically the same.

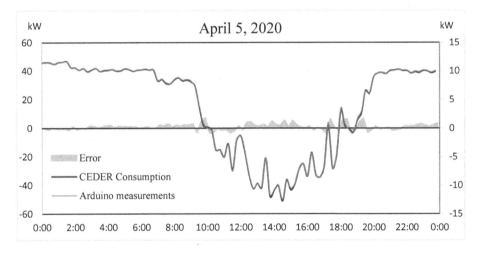

Fig. 5. Comparative CEDER consumption - Arduino measures (05/04/2020) and error

Graphically, it can be seen that the two curves are practically the same, there are hardly any differences between the two measurement systems. These variations can be somewhat higher in the proximity of zero kW and below −40 kW.

If we analyze the results numerically, averaging the measurements in real-time to periods of fifteen minutes, which is how the electricity distribution company accounts, we obtain the results shown in Table 1.

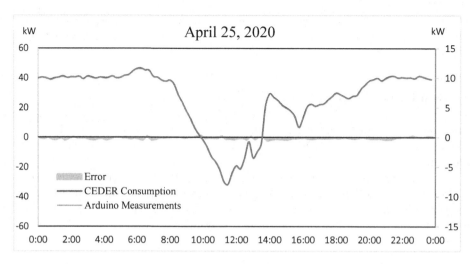

Fig. 6. Comparative CEDER consumption - Arduino measures (25/04/2020).

Table 1. PQube, Arduino and Real Consumption Data (25/04/2020).

Time	Measures PQube + consumption Transformer Substations		Arduino measures		Difference	
	CONSUMPTION (Wh)	INJECTED (Wh)	CONSUMPTION (Wh)	INJECTED (Wh)	CONSUMPTION (Wh)	INJECTED (Wh)
0:00	39641	0	39777	0	136	0
0:15	40128	0	40365	0	237	0
0:30	39909	0	39913	0	4	0
0:45	38639	0	39016	0	377	0
1:00	39492	0	39890	0	398	0
1:15	40203	0	40311	0	108	0
1:30	40671	0	41191	0	520	0
1:45	39959	0	40111	0	152	0
2:00	40690	0	40628	0	−62	0
2:15	40339	0	40470	0	131	0
2:30	40818	0	40945	0	127	0
2:45	39155	0	39267	0	112	0
3:00	40746	0	41103	0	357	0
3:15	40062	0	40522	0	460	0
3:30	39377	0	39682	0	305	0
3:45	40174	0	40369	0	195	0
4:00	39659	0	40149	0	490	0
4:15	39822	0	40136	0	314	0
4:30	41201	0	41191	0	−10	0
4:45	39964	0	39931	0	−33	0
5:00	40171	0	40256	0	85	0
5:15	41457	0	41584	0	127	0
5:30	41772	0	42068	0	296	0
5:45	44279	0	44420	0	141	0
6:00	45794	0	46104	0	310	0

(continued)

Table 1. (*continued*)

Time	Measures PQube + consumption Transformer Substations		Arduino measures		Difference	
	CONSUMPTION (Wh)	INJECTED (Wh)	CONSUMPTION (Wh)	INJECTED (Wh)	CONSUMPTION (Wh)	INJECTED (Wh)
6:15	45960	0	46469	0	509	0
6:30	45489	0	45263	0	−226	0
6:45	44522	0	44996	0	474	0
7:00	40575	0	40940	0	365	0
7:15	40247	0	40377	0	130	0
7:30	38322	0	38414	0	92	0
7:45	37600	0	37691	0	91	0
8:00	38436	0	38464	0	28	0
8:15	35475	0	35507	0	32	0
8:30	28547	0	28538	0	−9	0
8:45	23425	0	23596	0	171	0
9:00	17699	0	17709	0	10	0
9:15	12697	0	12719	0	22	0
9:30	6564	0	6415	0	−149	0
9:45	2257	0	1944	0	−313	0
10:00	0	1999	0	1800	0	−199
10:15	0	6701	0	6586	0	−115
10:30	0	13096	0	12953	0	−143
10:45	0	16597	0	16421	0	−176
11:00	0	21312	0	21516	0	204
11:15	0	30239	0	29895	0	−344
11:30	0	32089	0	31797	0	−292
11:45	0	24370	0	23983	0	−387
12:00	0	19393	0	19192	0	−201
12:15	0	21409	0	21262	0	−147
12:30	0	14532	0	14105	0	−427
12:45	0	2726	0	2891	0	165
13:00	0	14188	0	13810	0	−378
13:15	0	9719	0	9778	0	59
13:30	0	4406	0	4437	0	31
13:45	20396	0	20983	0	587	0
14:00	28862	0	29277	0	415	0
14:15	26628	0	26935	0	307	0
14:30	24526	0	24858	0	332	0
14:45	21314	0	21742	0	428	0
15:00	19569	0	19975	0	406	0
15:15	17618	0	17818	0	200	0
15:30	14034	0	14243	0	209	0
15:45	6539	0	6660	0	121	0
16:00	13150	0	13294	0	144	0
16:15	20361	0	20664	0	303	0
16:30	22077	0	22376	0	299	0
16:45	20838	0	20988	0	150	0

(*continued*)

Table 1. (*continued*)

Time	Measures PQube + consumption Transformer Substations		Arduino measures		Difference	
	CONSUMPTION (Wh)	INJECTED (Wh)	CONSUMPTION (Wh)	INJECTED (Wh)	CONSUMPTION (Wh)	INJECTED (Wh)
17:00	21962	0	22143	0	181	0
17:15	22431	0	22622	0	191	0
17:30	24965	0	25167	0	202	0
17:45	27476	0	27580	0	104	0
18:00	29664	0	29878	0	214	0
18:15	28709	0	28800	0	91	0
18:30	27227	0	27340	0	113	0
18:45	26031	0	26210	0	179	0
19:00	27460	0	27703	0	243	0
19:15	28202	0	28346	0	144	0
19:30	32758	0	32731	0	−27	0
19:45	35131	0	35304	0	173	0
20:00	37722	0	38001	0	279	0
20:15	38605	0	38879	0	274	0
20:30	39572	0	39810	0	238	0
20:45	37793	0	38157	0	364	0
21:00	39395	0	39820	0	425	0
21:15	40665	0	41043	0	378	0
21:30	41105	0	41193	0	88	0
21:45	39960	0	40021	0	61	0
22:00	40463	0	40408	0	−55	0
22:15	40014	0	40002	0	−12	0
22:30	40497	0	40266	0	−231	0
22:45	39595	0	39565	0	−30	0
23:00	41101	0	41160	0	59	0
23:15	40762	0	40706	0	−56	0
23:30	39859	0	39700	0	−159	0
23:45	39103	0	39053	0	−50	0

The consumption of the distribution network by CEDER's microgrid on 25 April 2020, measured with PQube network analyzers is 677 kWh, while that obtained with the Arduino based measurement system is 674 kWh. The difference between both measurement systems is 3 kWh, which is 0.44%.

If we look at what CEDER's microgrid injects into the distribution network, with the PQube there is 57.6 kWh, while with the Arduino we have 58.1 kWh. The difference is only 0.5 kWh, which represents 0.86%.

f we look at each of the periods averaged individually, we see that the biggest differences when there is consumption, have a value of less than 600 Wh (587, 520 and 509). In the case of injection into the grid, the greatest differences are barely 400 Wh (427, 387 and 378).

It can also be seen that the measurement with the Arduino is not always higher than the measurement with the PQube, but it changes from one period to another, thus compensating for the total daily value. Thus, the average difference between the two measurement systems is 0.119 kWh in the 96 fifteen-minute periods that a day has.

The total energy measured by Arduino during the day is 615.8 kWh while the sum of the PQube plus the consumption of the transformation centres and the losses in the cabling is 619.8 kWh, which means an error of 3.97 kWh which represents 0.409% during the whole day.

If we analyze the data of the 5th of April 2020, they are similar, although the differences are slightly higher. In the case of distribution network consumption, measured with the PQube, 558.6 kWh are obtained, while with the Arduino based measurement system, 563.8 kWh are obtained. The difference between both measurement systems is 5.2 kWh, which is 0.93%.

In the injection to the distribution network, with the PQube, 212.5 kWh are obtained, while with the Arduino, 211.2 kWh are obtained. The difference is only 1.3 kWh, which represents 0.61%.

If we compare each of the periods averaged individually, the greatest differences occur for values close to zero (1.89, 1.63 and 1.58) and values below −40, that is to say when the microgrid injects more than 40 kW into the distribution network (1.39, 1.58 and 1.25). For all other values, the differences are less than 1 kWh.

If we do the study for a longer period, and instead of a day, we analyze a full month, we will have the results shown in Fig. 7.

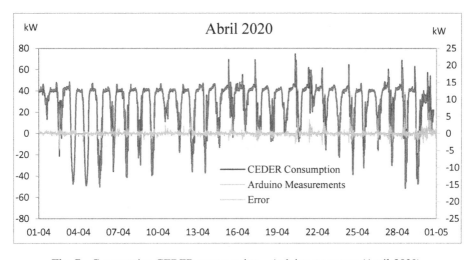

Fig. 7. Comparative CEDER consumption - Arduino measures (April 2020).

We see that the results obtained for one month are similar to the daily ones and no major differences are observed in Fig. 7 between the two measurement systems studied. Generally, it is observed that the greatest differences occur for values around zero and values below −40 kWh.

If we analyze the data numerically, we get the following results:

- The consumption of the distribution network during April 2020 by CEDER's microgrid, measured with PQube network analyzers is 21808 kWh, while that measured with the Arduino based system is 21825 kWh. The difference between both measurement systems is only 17 kWh, which is 0.077%.
- If we look at the injection of CEDER's microgrid into the distribution network, with the PQube we get 1650 kWh, while with the Arduino we get 1658 kWh. The difference is 8 kWh, which represents 0.48%.

Table 2 shows the average differences between the two measurement systems used for all days in April 2020.

Table 2. Average daily differences between the two measurement systems (April 2020).

Day	Consumption obtained from PQubes (Wh)	Consumption obtained from Arduino (Wh)	Difference (Wh)	Error (%)
01/04/2020	879.96	874.43	5.53	0.63
02/04/2020	778.97	778.26	0.71	0.09
03/04/2020	356.10	355.30	0.80	0.22
04/04/2020	302.32	306.26	3.94	1.30
05/04/2020	351.37	353.50	2.13	0.61
06/04/2020	636.82	635.36	1.46	0.23
07/04/2020	576.65	575.91	0.74	0.13
08/04/2020	649.26	651.20	1.94	0.30
09/04/2020	538.90	541.08	2.18	0.41
10/04/2020	825.46	823.32	2.15	0.26
11/04/2020	694.97	694.81	0.16	0.02
12/04/2020	531.42	524.82	6.60	1.24
13/04/2020	679.33	681.49	2.16	0.32
14/04/2020	735.24	733.88	1.36	0.18
15/04/2020	865.15	860.49	4.67	0.54
16/04/2020	865.79	867.00	1.21	0.14
17/04/2020	721.74	719.97	1.76	0.24
18/04/2020	696.69	700.77	4.08	0.59
19/04/2020	710.01	713.65	3.63	0.51
20/04/2020	768.87	767.06	1.81	0.24
21/04/2020	976.49	968.50	7.99	0.82
22/04/2020	805.00	801.66	3.34	0.42
23/04/2020	723.40	726.33	2.93	0.40
24/04/2020	617.25	616.55	0.70	0.11
25/04/2020	615.83	619.86	4.03	0.66
26/04/2020	717.06	718.61	1.55	0.22
27/04/2020	753.97	756.22	2.25	0.30
28/04/2020	655.46	653.73	1.73	0.26
29/04/2020	434.16	439.81	5.65	1.30
30/04/2020	703.79	694.87	8.93	1.27

The average difference in April 2020 is 2.94 kW and represents a measurement error of 0.44%. The maximum difference between the two measurement systems occurs on April 30, 8.93 kW (error 1.28%) and the maximum error occurs on April 4 and 29, reaching a value of 1.3%.

5   Conclusions

This paper proposes a low-cost measurement system that allows real-time readings of any meter with active and reactive energy metrology LEDs to know the instantaneous power consumed or injected into the distribution network by a microgrid. This measurement system avoids having to duplicate the measurement cell at the entrance of a microgrid connected to the distribution network with the consequent cost savings.

Its operation has been tested on the CEDER electric microgrid for validation and has allowed knowing the energy measured by the meter in real-time, that is to say, the energy consumed or injected into the distribution network by the microgrid with an error of less than 1% in the worst case.

In this way, greater control of the production of the microgrid generation sources and their consumption is achieved, which translates into better management of the total invoice of the system with the distribution company, eliminating ranges of contracted power and their respective costs.

Besides, this low-cost measurement system, based on an Arduino and an infrared sensor, obtains measurements that are practically the same as those obtained with the previous system used at CEDER, based on PQube, significantly reducing the cost of the system for recording the readings of the different generation and consumption elements of the microgrid.

References

1. Ton, D.T., Smith, M.A.: The U.S. department of energy's microgrid initiative. Electr. J. **25**, 84–94 (2012). https://doi.org/10.1016/j.tej.2012.09.013
2. Lasseter, R., et al.: The CERTS microgrid concept, white paper on integration of distributed energy resources. Calif. Energy Comm. Off. Power Technol. Dep. Energy, LBNL-50829, vol. 29 (2002). http://certs.lbl.gov
3. Sachs, T., Gründler, A., Rusic, M., Fridgen, G.: Framing microgrid design from a business and information systems engineering perspective. Bus. Inf. Syst. Eng. **61**(6), 729–744 (2019). https://doi.org/10.1007/s12599-018-00573-0
4. Teufel, S., Teufel, B.: The crowd energy concept. J. Electron. Sci. Technol. **12**, 263–269 (2014). https://doi.org/10.3969/j.issn.1674-862X.2014.03.006
5. Gharavi, H., Ghafurian, R.: Smart grid: the electric energy system of the future. Proc. IEEE **99**, 917–921 (2011). https://doi.org/10.1109/JPROC.2011.2124210
6. van Leeuwen, G., AlSkaif, T., Gibescu, M., van Sark, W.: An integrated blockchain-based energy management platform with bilateral trading for microgrid communities. Appl. Energy **263**, 114613 (2020). https://doi.org/10.1016/J.APENERGY.2020.114613

7. Khavari, F., Badri, A., Zangeneh, A.: Energy management in multi-microgrids considering point of common coupling constraint. Int. J. Electr. Power Energy Syst. **115**, 105465 (2020). https://doi.org/10.1016/j.ijepes.2019.105465

8. Vargas-Salgado, C., Aguila-Leon, J., Chiñas-Palacios, C., Hurtado-Perez, E.: Low-cost web-based Supervisory Control and Data Acquisition system for a microgrid testbed: A case study in design and implementation for academic and research applications. Heliyon. **5**, e02474 (2019). https://doi.org/10.1016/j.heliyon.2019.e02474

9. Khan, K.R., Siddiqui, M.S., Saawy, Y. Al, Islam, N., Rahman, A.: Condition monitoring of a campus microgrid elements using smart sensors. Procedia Comput. Sci. **163**, 109–116 (2019). https://doi.org/10.1016/j.procs.2019.12.092

10. Hernández Callejo, L.: Microrredes eléctricas. Integración de generación renovable distribuida, almacenamiento distribuido e inteligencia. Publicaciones, Ibergarceta (2019)

11. Ministerio de Industria Turismo y Comercio: Reglamento de Puntos de Medida del Sistema Eléctrico 2007 Real Decreto 1110/2007, de 24 agosto. ELECTRICIDAD. Aprueba el Reglamento unificado de puntos de medida del sistema eléctrico, vol. 28 (2007)

12. CNMC: DEL ÚLTIMO HITO DEL PLAN DE SUSTITUCIÓN DE CONTADORES (2019)

13. CNMC: CONTADORES ELÉCTRICOS (2016).

A Prototype of Classroom Energetically Efficient

Diego A. Godoy$^{(\boxtimes)}$ ⓘ, Santiago H. Bareiro ⓘ, Fabián E. Favret ⓘ,
Juan P. Blariza ⓘ, and Guillermo Colotti ⓘ

Centro de Investigación en Tecnologías de la Información y Comunicaciones
(CITIC), Universidad Gastón Dachary, Av. López y Planes 6519,
3300 Posadas, Argentina
{diegodoy, hbareiro, efabianfavret}@citic.ugd.edu.ar,
juanblariza@gmail.com, gui.colotti@gmail.com

Abstract. Various organizations have reported that buildings (among them, educational institutions) are responsible for the consumption of 40% or more of all the primary energy produced worldwide. The control of temperature and lighting in said institutions is carried out manually. That means that every time a classroom is used, people must turn on lights and air conditioners, and then take care of turning them off whenever they are not required. Faced with this scenario, the alternative proposed in this work allows efficient automatic control of lighting and temperature preferences for each professor and each class.

That is why a Prototype of Classroom Energetically Efficient was built in this paper. It has three modules: The one is the web application that was developed using the Laravel framework for the backend and Vuejs for the frontend. Its main function is to send commands to devices. The second is the IoT framework, which fulfills the function of communicating the web application with the hardware, providing the necessary endpoints, and making the registered data available. And finally, the hardware that was built using NodeMCU ESP8266 boards. Its function is to be an actuator i.e. receive the data from the IoT framework and executes commands. We also build a classrom mockup to show the prototype in action.

Also, the performance tests of different scenarios were carried out, being satisfactory, and allowing the development of the planned functionalities.

Keywords: Internet of Things · Smart classrooms · Energy efficiency

1 Introduction

A modern educational institution has a large number of classrooms, each with many lighting and cooling devices (air conditioners). "Various organizations, committed to the efficient use of energy and the conservation of our environment, have reported that buildings are responsible for the consumption of 40% or more of all the primary energy produced worldwide..." [1]. For this reason, it is reasonable to say that the energy consumed in a school day during peak hours is very high.

© Springer Nature Switzerland AG 2021
S. Nesmachnow and L. Hernández Callejo (Eds.): ICSC-CITIES 2020, CCIS 1359, pp. 17–29, 2021.
https://doi.org/10.1007/978-3-030-69136-3_2

That is normal (as well as in any, or most, educational institutions) considering the daily use and movement of students and professors. As well, it is also normal that the temperature control (by turning on/off and regulation in air conditioners) and lighting (by turning on/off lights) in the classrooms, is carried out manually. This means that every time a classroom must be used, one person must take care of turning on the lights and air conditioners (if necessary), and turning them off when they are not required. And if we take into account that the people who perform these tasks are the same janitors and secretaries, responsible for many other tasks. Several devices may be turned on unnecessarily for several hours.

Likewise, it is observed that each professor usually has a lighting requirement in the classroom. For example, while there are professors who require the maximum possible lighting (all classroom lights on), others do not use the headlights (near the blackboard), since they use projectors with presentations and/or slides. In this way, the visualization of slides showed by projectos are more clear. So also other professors prefer all lights completely off for the same reason. The temperature will depend on the weather conditions. For example, days with extreme temperatures (hot or cold), will require more use of air conditioners.

Therefore, it is extremely important to find the method to manage efficiently the energy consumption, not only to reduce the institution's expenses but also to help preserve finite resources and thus mitigate the environmental impact due to its unnecessary use.

Consistently and because the technology advances it is necessary to design a solution to that problem through the use of an IoT Framework evaluated in [2], a Web application and specific hardware [3], which allows each professor to independently configure their desired lighting and temperature profile for the classroom to be used, and that this is applied automatically in the right time.

2 Related Works

Educational institutions are one of the main responsible for the amount of energy consumed, for the number of activities carried out in classrooms, offices, libraries, and also for the waste of energy due to the inefficient use of electricity [4], but also, by the mobilization of people using vehicles [5].

In [1] a line of action is established regarding customs and policies for the good use of energy that not only promotes the development, implementation, and adaptation of software and hardware. Instead, they serve as tools to save money at the National University of Misiones. In [6] the research process for the development of an IoT system is presented, which has been designed to promote an intelligent lighting service in an academic environment. The IoT system orchestrates a series of sensors, monitoring systems, and controlled actions, based on the principle of making available the functions of the system and the record of consumption in real-time through web services. Likewise, in [7] the design and implementation of an intelligent automated system based on Ethernet for the conservation of electrical energy using a second-generation INTEL GALILEO development board are proposed. The proposed system works on automation so that electrical devices and switches can be remotely controlled and monitored without any human intervention. The project developed in [8] uses IoT-based technology to achieve automation in classrooms and proposes an approach to control and manage electrical equipment such as fans and lights based on the presence of people.

3   Methodology

This section presents the hardware and technology used in this research project

3.1   Used Hardware

The hardware used is the NodeMCU ESP8266 (Fig. 1). NodeMCU is an open source IoT platform. Includes firmware that runs on Espressif Systems ESP8266 WiFi SoC (System on Chip) and hardware that is based on the ESP-12 module [9].

Fig. 1. Node MCU ESP8266.

The ESP8266 is a low-cost WiFi chip with a full TCP/IP stack and a microcontroller. The firmware can be programmed using the Lua scripting language, although currently the Arduino IDE also supports programming in C language [10].

3.2   Used Web Applications Technologies

In the web application development, different frameworks were used such as Laravel, VueJs, and Postman.

Laravel is an open source PHP framework for developing web applications and services through layered architecture, providing multiple functionalities required for any web application.

VueJs is a progressive JavaScript framework for creating user interfaces. It is an alternative to frameworks like Angular or React [11].

Postman is a tool that allows you to make HTTP requests to any REST API, whether third-party or your own, to test the operation of the API through a graphical interface.

3.3   Framework IoT Ubidots

Ubidots [12] is a platform for building, developing, testing, learning, and exploring the future of applications and solutions connected to the Internet [12].

Regardless of whether one or one thousand devices are connected, the same effort is required with all types of Ubidots devices. The creation of the new device in Ubidots can be replicated by automatically setting the variables, the device properties, and the appearance each time a new piece of hardware is detected. Some of its characteristics can be seen in [13]. The Ubidots service stack can be seen in Fig. 2.

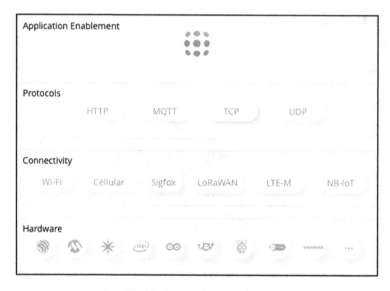

Fig. 2.   Ubidots service stack

4   Proposed Solution Architecture

The technological solution to the problem consists of using an IoT framework that fulfills the function of carrying out communication between the parties(Web Application and Hardware), providing a method to store the information and make it available to read, to be consumed at the required time. The Web Application defines all the behavior to be followed and the hardware is only an executor of actions, ordered by the Web Application. Examples of this would be the web application reads the information from the temperature sensor sent by the hardware, and tells when to switch on or off an air conditioner. The proposed solution is shown in Fig. 3.

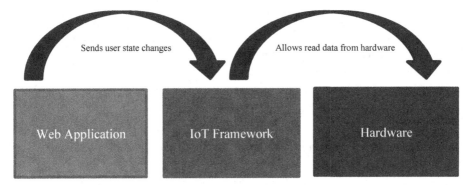

Sends user state changes

Allows read data from hardware

Web Application

IoT Framework

Hardware

Fig. 3. Proposed solution architecture

Each arrow in the previous graphic represents an HTTP request performed by the web application and the hardware respectively. Based on this, we have four situations:

1. The web application sends state change data to the IoT framework. These changes of states refer to changes in the profiles according to the preferences of each professor. For example: If the air conditioning in classroom 1, at a certain time, should be turned on. The IoT framework stores this data and makes it available to be consumed. It should be noted that the IoT framework, in this case, does not handle the logic of when an air conditioning should be turned on or not, it simply receives the data. For example, "Air1: 1" data, already generated by the web application, and makes it available to be consumed by who requires it.
2. The available data is consumed by the hardware. The latter reads the data, through an HTTP Request, and just executes the action. For example, if the hardware read that the lights in classroom 1 should be on and they are off, it will turn them on.
3. There are certain times when the hardware needs to feed information to the system, for example, with the temperature sensor. In this case, it will take the ambient temperature and send it to the IoT framework, so that it is available to those who require it. As in previous cases, the IoT framework will only be in charge of storing and making the information available, without processing it.
4. Finally, there will be cases where the web application requires feedback from the system, such as, for example when the hardware reports the current temperature of a certain classroom. In this way, the Web Application will know what information to produce and send it to the IoT framework again.

5   Test Scenarios

The following scenarios will be used for testing the prototype.

1. A professor is far from the institution and has classes at that time.
2. A professor is at the institution and has classes at that time.
3. Functioning with different personalized professor profiles.

The activation condition of each profile includes the following three variables:

1. The professor is in the institution (position simulated by the marker on the map)
2. The professor has classes at that time.
3. The professor attends classes.

The actors involved are specified in each test. Also, if necessary, a different lighting and/or cooling profile is specified.

5.1 Scenario 1: A Professor is Far from the Institution and Has Classes at that Time

Actors Involved: Web Application.
In this test, the framework did not participate, because the one who sends the orders to later be read by the hardware, is the web application. In this case, with any lighting and cooling profile activated, and being class time for the professor, no request was sent to the IoT framework since the professor was far from the institution. Figure 4 shows in the "Network" tab how simulating any location of the professor on the map outside of the profile activation field, no request is sent.

Fig. 4. Scenario 1

5.2 Escenario 2: A Professor is at the Institution and Has Classes at that Time

Actors Involved: Web Application, IoT Framework and Hardware.

Test Profile: All lights on and air conditioning on. Being the teacher's class schedule, the teacher being in the activation zone and marking that he attends classes in Fig. 5 we can see how the Web Application sent 10 requests correctly, corresponding to the 10 variables used.

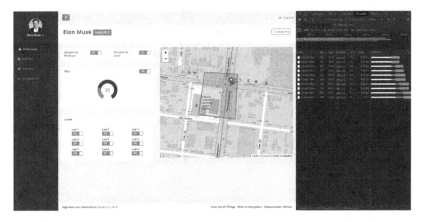

Fig. 5. Web application sending power signal for lights and air conditioning using Ubidots IoT Famework.

When clicking on the first request sent by the Web Application, corresponding to the first variable "led1" of Ubidots, the request details are observed in Fig. 6:

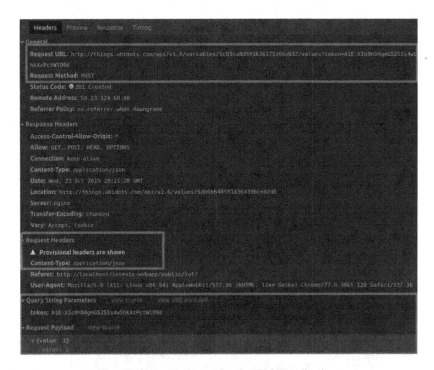

Fig. 6. first request sent by the Web Application.

The Request URL shows the endpoint to which the request was sent, corresponding to the first variable ("led1"). Other important data are observed, such as:

- Status Code 201: The request was successfully sent.
- Content-Type application/json: One of the headers required by the framework.
- Token
- Variable ID in the URL.

In the following requests corresponding to the other lights and air, the same results were obtained. As seen in Fig. 7, it is verified that the data was written correctly in the Framework, using Ubidots Dashboard created for quick visualization.

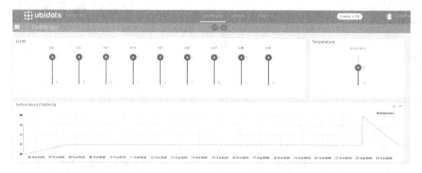

Fig. 7. Public Ubidots dashboard, showing widgets of all variables.

In the Classroom mockup where the hardware is installed, all the lights and the engine were turned on, as we can see in Fig. 8:

Fig. 8. A classroom mockup with all light and engines turned on.

5.3 Scenario 3: Functioning with Different Personalized Professor Profiles

Actors Involved: Web Application, IoT Framework and Hardware.

Test Profile: Only the last three lights turned on (in the classroom back) and air conditioning turned off.

The new profile with only the lights at the back of the classroom on (LEDs 7, 8, and 9) and the air conditioning off as we can see in Fig. 9.

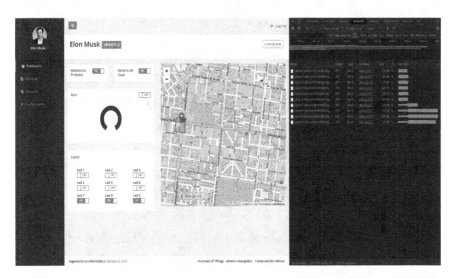

Fig. 9. Web application sending on signal only for the last three lights and air conditioning off, using Ubidots.

The profile was configured, to leave only the lights in the background of the classroom on, and you can see how the web application sent ten requests correctly. For the lights that should be on, he sent "value": 1, and for those that should be turned off, he sent "value": 0. The air conditioning, with a temperature lower than 24° C, turns off.

In the first request, it is observed that the Request Payload has the value of false (Fig. 10)

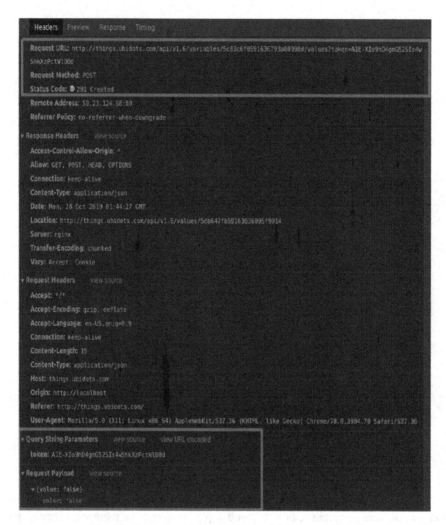

Fig. 10. Request with signal to turn off "led1" variable.

The same happens with the requests for all the lights in the first two rows. On the other hand, for the last row of lights, we can see light turned on. To do this, we observe the request, the variable "led9" and Request Payload has true value, as we can see in Fig. 11:

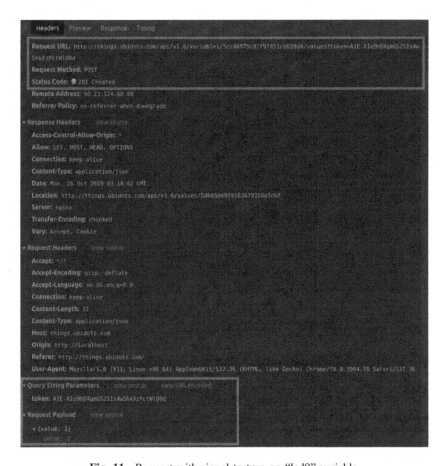

Fig. 11. Request with signal to turn on "led9" variable.

As seen in Fig. 12, everything worked as we expected in the Ubidots Dashboard.

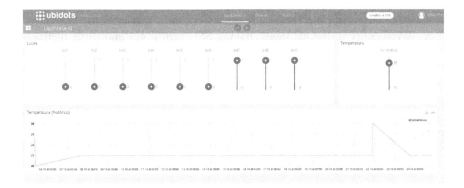

Fig. 12. Ubidots dashboard, showing the devices that must be turned on.

The hardware in the same way, it correctly read the framework data and executed the action (Fig. 13).

Fig. 13. The classroom mockup in the dark with only the last three lights are on.

6 Conclusions and Future Works

The use of the IoT Ubidots framework for the development of a Prototype of Classroom Energetically Efficient allowed to increase the implementation speed and the time saved in the construction of systems that need the interaction of devices connected to the internet. This is mainly due to the fact that it has the communication already resolved, having to focus only on the construction of the parts that must communicate.

Taking into account that all the packages that allow communication between the parties over the internet, using HTTP, the framework must guarantee the tools to give the necessary security to the packages, having SSL certificates and some method of authentication for the requests, either a token or an API_Key.

Finally, an efficient optimization in the time that lighting and cooling devices are on, avoiding idle time, translates into lower consumption, lower costs, and therefore less environmental pollution and greater energy efficiency.

Future work includes: Implement the prototypes with the MQTT protocol and later make the comparison against HTTP protocol used in this work.

Refactor the Ubidots firmware code for the NodeMCU ESP8266, improving the data reading and writing algorithms, to get better operations performance.

Design and implement fully functional versions of the web application which allow executing in a real way the change of teacher profiles as well as the dynamic configuration of the same, for each subject and schedule. Use the geo-positioning of a mobile device, for example, a cell phone, to locate the teacher, no just simulating the localization. Implement the prototype, in real classrooms of an educational institution to be used as a living laboratory.

References

1. Sosa, E.O., Godoy, D.A., Benítez, J., Sosa, M.E.: Eficiencia Energética y Ambientes Inteligentes. Investigación y Desarrollo Experimental en la UNaM, Posadas, Misiones, Argentina (2015)
2. Godoy, D., Bareiro, H., Fabret, F., et.al.: Propuesta de métricas para comparación de Framewoks IoT. In: Workshop de Investigadores en Ciencias de la Computación., El Calafate (2020)
3. Godoy, D., Bareiro, H., Fabret, F., et.al.: Análisis de componente de hardware para la utilización con Frameworks de IoT. In: Workshop de Investigadores en Ciencias de la Computación., El Calafate (2020)
4. Frimpong, E.A., Appiah, F.: Energy efficiency awareness and preparedness among students (2017)
5. Perez, J.A.: Proyectos de Eficiencia Energética para Instituciones de Educación Superior
6. González-Amarillo, C.-A., C.-G.-A., C.-L.: Smart lumini: a smart lighting system for academic environments using IOT-based open-source hardware. Revista Facultad de Ingeniería **29**(54) (2020)
7. Gupta, A., Gupta, P., Chhabra, J.: IoT based power efficient system design using automation for classrooms. In: Third International Conference on Image Information Processing (ICIIP), Waknaghat, India (2015)
8. Ani, R., Krishna, S., Akhil, H., Arun, U.: An Approach towards building an IoT based smart classroom. In: 2018 International Conference on Advances in Computing, Communications and Informatics (ICACCI), Bangalore, India (2018)
9. NodeMCU: Wikipedia. In: NodeMCU. https://www.nodemcu.com/index_en.html. Accessed 2020
10. Programar facil.. https://www.programarfacil.com/esp8266/como-programar-nodemcu-ide-arduino/
11. Vuejs. https://vuejs.org/v2/guide/. Accessed Aug 2020
12. Ubidots. https://ubidots.com/docs/. Accessed Aug 2020
13. Hernandez, M.: Ubidots Basics: Devices, Variables, Dashboards, and Alerts. https://help.ubidots.com/en/articles/854333-ubidots-basics-devices-variables-dashboards-and-alerts. Accessed Aug 2020

REMOURBAN: Evaluation Results After the Implementation of Actions for Improving the Energy Efficiency in a District in Valladolid (Spain)

Cristina de Torre[1(✉)], Javier Antolín[1(✉)],
Miguel Á. García-Fuentes[1(✉)], Jaime Gómez-Tribiño[2(✉)],
José Cubillo[3(✉)], María Luisa Mirantes[4(✉)], and Isabel Tome[5(✉)]

[1] Fundación CARTIF,
Parque Tecnológico de Boecillo 205, 47151 Valladolid, Spain
{critor, javant, miggar}@cartif.es
[2] VEOLIA Servicios LECAM,
Avenida del Euro 7, Ed B, OF312, 47009 Valladolid, Spain
jaime.gomeztribino@veolia.com
[3] ACCIONA Ingeniería, C/Anabel Segura 11 Ed D, 28108 Alcobendas, Spain
jaimejose.cubillo.capuz@acciona.com
[4] Xeridia, Av del Padre Isla 16, 24002 León, Spain
ml.mirantes@xeridia.com
[5] Iberdrola, C/Tomás Redondo 1, 28033 Madrid, Spain
ites@iberdrola.es

Abstract. REMOURBAN is a large-scale demonstration project whose main objective is to accelerate the urban transformation towards the smart city concept considering all aspects of sustainability. For this purpose, an Urban Regeneration Model has been developed and validated in the three lighthouse cities of the project (Valladolid-Spain, Nottingham-United Kingdom and Tepebaşı-Turkey). REMOURBAN has carried out different interventions in the city of Valladolid with the aim of transforming it in a more sustainable and smarter city. These actions have been evaluated using the evaluation framework developed within the project, to know the real impact of these interventions in the project area and to transfer the knowledge to other cities that want replicate these solutions for improving their sustainability and smartness. This paper is focused on showing the evaluation results after the application of the evaluation framework to the energy actions in a district in the city of Valladolid (Spain).

Keywords: Smart city · Near zero energy district · District heating · Biomass · Evaluation · Sustainability · Photovoltaic

1 Introduction

The sustainable development of urban areas is a key challenge for Europe where the retrofitting of its buildings and, more specifically, its thermal retrofitting takes on special importance. In Spain, more than half of the buildings are built without adequate

S. Nesmachnow and L. Hernández Callejo (Eds.): ICSC-CITIES 2020, CCIS 1359, pp. 30–41, 2021.
https://doi.org/10.1007/978-3-030-69136-3_3

thermal insulation, which means very high energy consumption and mostly from fossil fuels which exacerbates the problem of external energy dependence. In order to deal with this situation, projects such as REMOURBAN are demonstrating innovative, efficient and accessible technologies and processes in districts whose energy problems are evident in order to achieve Near Zero Energy Districts that serve as a reference and allow the replicability of this type of actions in other similar neighborhoods, improving the environment and the quality of life of citizens.

In order to help other cities to identify their needs and to establish the most suitable interventions for covering that demand and replicate the success of the project, REMOURBAN has designed a methodology, the Urban Regeneration Model, which covers all the phases of the transformation process. Within this model, the evaluation is sought as the main supporting mechanism throughout the deployment of this process. REMOURBAN evaluation framework considers two levels of evaluation: city level, to assess both sustainability and smartness of the city as a whole, from a comprehensive and integrated perspective, and project level, to provide a clear identification of the impact of implementation of technologies and solutions on the three key priority areas (sustainable districts and built environment, sustainable urban mobility and integrated infrastructures and processes) aimed at achieving the city high-level goals.

The objective of this paper is to present the evaluation framework at project level developed in REMOURBAN and to show the results of the final evaluation of the energy interventions implemented in the FASA district in Valladolid.

2 Description of the Interventions Implemented

In Valladolid, one of the lighthouse cities of the project, the FASA neighbourhood was selected for the implementation of a set of interventions designed in order to become a Near Zero Energy District and contribute to the city transformation to a more sustainable environment. This neighborhood was built during the 60 s for the workers of the Renault factory in Valladolid, and it is composed by 19 blocks, a tower and a building that contains the thermal power station that supplies heating to the 398 homes that make up the neighborhood. These buildings presented severe deficiencies in their thermal insulation that resulted in lack of habitability and comfort, as well as low energy efficiency.

The heating system consisted of a district network supplied by two fossil fuel boilers (natural gas and gasoil) and it was divided into three different circuits that provided the 398 dwellings with space heating, whereas the domestic hot water (DHW) was individually produced in each dwelling with different technologies depending of the energy source in each particular case: natural gas, butane and electricity.

In REMOURBAN, with the aim of turning the neighbourhood into a Near Zero Energy District, a set of actions have been designed and those are described in following sub-sections:

2.1 Passive Measures: Façade and Roof Insulation

One of the main objectives considered for the design of the interventions, was the reduction of the energy demand. For achieving the aim of decreasing it, it was needed to improvement the thermal isolation of the building envelope, including roof and façade.

For the thermal insulation of the façades, it was taken into account the least intrusive solution that could solve the thermal bridges completely. The external insulation was the final solution chosen, which consists of fixing an insulation board to the external side of the façade and later applying a finish over the board.

In FASA district, the installed insulation consisted of a four-layer scheme, based on a 60 mm expanded polystyrene (EPS) board fixed on the brick wall, a first layer of mortar, followed by a glass fiber mesh and a second layer of mortar. Finally, a surface finish was applied for aesthetical reasons.

Regarding the insulation of the blocks roofs, among the available options for their insulation, an intermediate insulation was chosen for the blocks and external insulation for the tower. The intermediate insulation offers a combination of best performance, easy installation and no disturbance on the tenants. 60 mm of sprayed foam (SPF) insulation were laid under the roof and over the last slab of the block.

The tower roof insulation was improved by adding an external insulation over the existing asphaltic layer. The scheme was an inverted roof system consisting of 60 mm of extruded polystyrene (XPS) insulation, a geotextile layer and gravel.

2.2 Active Measures

Once the energy demand was reduced thanks to the passive measures implemented, the next step was to retrofit the thermal facilities in order to improve their energy efficiency and integrate renewable sources to the system.

The existing district heating system was renovated, on one hand the fossil fuel boilers were replace by biomass ones with occasional support from natural gas and on the other hand the 20 substations of the district were renovated together with the distribution network which was updated with pre-insulated pipes to minimize heat losses.

With this new system, the dependence of the system on fossil fuels has decreased given that now the system depends fundamentally on a renewable energy source. Other relevant advantage is the decrease in the CO_2 emissions from the district heating to the environment because the CO_2 emissions factor for biomass is significantly lower than that for fossil fuels.

In addition to the new biomass boilers, with the aim of increasing the energy supply through renewable sources, a photovoltaic installation has been carried out. This new PV system was built on the south façade of the tower, which has a deviation of 12° and no shading obstacles, and the ventilation effect reduces overheating during summer improving the efficiency of the modules. The PV modules selected have a nominal power of 77.5 Wp. They were installed in two rows in the flat area of the façade avoiding interferences with the existing windows, finally adding up to a total aggregated capacity of 27.435 kWp.

The PV energy is fed into a circuit with 8 electrical resistors that heat up the water tank, which acts as a buffer. Then the hot water harnessed is used to preheat the DHW, and therefore reduce the biomass consumption.

Other intervention aiming to improve the energy efficiency of the district was the substitution of the incandescent lamps by LED in common areas of all buildings.

Last but not least, an Energy Management System (EMS) structured in three different levels has been implemented in the district. There are a District EMS that is responsible for managing the district heating as a whole, a Building EMS in charge of monitoring and controlling both the heating and DHW facilities in each of the 20 buildings and a Home EMS that has been installed in all 398 dwellings of the district. At this level there are two different kinds of devices: heat cost allocators installed in each radiator to measure the individual consumption of the dwellings and thermostatic valves to allow the tenants to adjust the temperature inside each room.

3 REMOURBAN Evaluation Framework

REMOURBAN Evaluation Framework establishes the basis of the evaluation mechanisms for the REMOURBAN Project. The framework defines two levels of evaluation: Project Level, to provide a clear identification of the project impact regarding interventions, and City Level, to assess both sustainability and smartness of participating cities and the impact of the Sustainable Urban Regeneration Model developed in the project on the sustainability and smartness goals.

This paper is focused on the evaluation at project level and more specifically in the evaluation of energy actions in Valladolid. For the evaluation at project level, a specific index was defined; the Demo Site Index (Ds) that is used to evaluate the actions described in the previous section and others interventions related to urban mobility, ICT and non-technical actions.

Although the Ds index is used for the evaluation at project level, the specific actions in each city can be evaluated through one or various measurable objectives or sub-indexes to assist the evaluation of the project impacts and assess the progress of the lighthouse cities interventions.

The basis for the evaluation process are the KPIs (Key Performance Indicators) which are normalized, weighted and aggregated to calculate the Ds global index. Project level indicators (showed in Table 1) are weighted to estimate partial indexes defined for each of the areas of intervention (Buildings and District, Urban Mobility, integrated infrastructures through ICTs and Non-Technical actions). This framework of indicators, sub-indexes and project evaluation index constitute a valuable supporting tool for the evaluation of the impact and expected result of the REMOURBAN project.

Table 1. Project level indicators

Measurable objective	Indicators	
Buildings and Districts	Energy demand	CO_2 emissions
	Energy consumption	Thermal comfort
	Primary energy consumption	Indoor air quality comfort
	Useful energy	Energy bill
	Renewable energy production	Investment
Urban mobility	Energy consumption (buses)	PM emissions (buses)
	Energy consumption (cars)	PM emissions (cars)
	CO2 emissions (buses)	EV penetration rate
	CO2 emissions (cars)	EV charging points
	NOx emissions (buses)	Total KWh recharged
	NOx emissions (cars)	Energy bill (buses)
	HC emissions (buses)	Energy bill (cars)
	HC emissions (cars)	Investment
ICT	Smart electricity meters	Indoor sensors
	Visualising real-time information	Web applications and services
	Modes of transport integrated on smart cards	Visits/Access to webs/Services
	Rate of trips using smart cards	Registered users
	Location tracker sensors	App downloads
	Meteorological sensors	Investment
	Air quality sensors	
Non-technical	Initiatives of public incentives	Initiatives of public incentives
	Awareness raising campaigns	Marketable products
	Learned solutions for non-technical barriers	Innovative/Green public procurement
	Channels used for citizen engagement	Papers for innovative actions
	Visits to project information	Cities interested to be followers
	Social media accounts	Investment

4 Methodology for the Evaluation at Project Level

This section presents the methodology of the project level assessment through the calculation of the Demo Site Index after the demonstration phase of the REMOUR-BAN project. This methodology requires of the following steps.

- Scope definition: It is each of the three demo-sites (Valladolid, Nottingham and Tepebaşi) including the four areas of intervention (energy, mobility, ICT and Non-technical).

- Baseline period definition: it is the timeframe chosen to represent the initial status of the project level indicators that is used as reference for comparison in order to measure the impact due to the implementation of the project interventions.
- Reporting period definition: it should encompass at least one complete normal operating cycle, in order to fully characterize the effectiveness of the actions. Depending on the specific implementation timings for each of the actions in each demo-site a specific reporting period has been defined for each one. In REMOURBAN, the reporting periods of the energy and mobility actions implemented cover at least the last year of the project, but in most cases this period is longer, exceeding 24 months.
- Data collection and analysis: the collection of data is one of the most challenging tasks of the process and at the same time the quality and amount of data used for calculating the indicators is one of the most critical issues to obtain a reliable index. Most of the data required for the calculation of the indicators at project level is gathered directly from direct measurement, statistical information and in some cases also from simulations. Data is collected and processed in each of the three Local ICT platforms deployed in each of the three lighthouse cities; and sent to the REMOURBAN Global ICT platform.
- Calculation of the index: the computer-based Evaluation Tool STILE has been defined and developed in the REMOURBAN framework to be used for the calculation of the established indices. STILE tool calculate and normalize the indicators, weights and aggregate them in order to calculate the Ds index in an automatic way based on the methodology and calculations implemented within the tool.
- Evaluation of the results. At this point it is possible to perform the comparison and detailed analysis of the reporting period index results and the baseline period index results.

5   Evaluation Supporting Tool: STILE

A valuable computer-based tool, named SmarTness and SustaInabiLity Evaluation Tool (STILE) has been developed as one of the core services that form part of the REMOURBAN ICT solutions. STILE was conceived as the service to support, automate and help to achieve the objectives set out in the Evaluation Framework. Therefore, in line with the Evaluation Framework, this tool allows for a quantified measurement of the cities' progress on the way to sustainability and smartness on one hand, and the performance of REMOURBAN project in terms of efficiency and effectiveness of its interventions on the other hand. This way, STILE arises as the cornerstone to reinforce the communication between stakeholders and decision-makers in the cities.

STILE enables to run evaluations for any of the REMOURBAN lighthouse cities at any moment. When an evaluation is launched, STILE takes the set of monitored variables stored in the Global ICT Platform for that city and the corresponding period of time.

The tool, at a first step, calculates a set of indicators taking those variables as inputs, by applying the formulas defined in the Evaluation Framework. Then, the set of formulas and calculations designed in the Evaluation Framework to obtain the Measurable Objectives from the indicators, were programmed as part of the tool and, finally, by implementing the corresponding formulas from the Measurable Objectives, the indices are obtained.

The key benefit of using STILE is not only the quantification of the indices, but a powerful presentation of the whole data set behind the final value of the index, that goes from the set of variables to an index value, with several intermediate calculation levels in between, all depicted in a graphical way, making it easier for the user to have full information at a glance.

The picture below let us find the direct relation of the general schema proposed by the Evaluation Framework for the Demo Site Index and its computer-based implementation (Fig. 1):

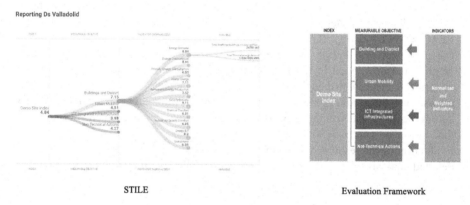

Fig. 1. Direct relation of the evaluation framework and the computer based implementation

STILE visualization solution to represent the whole data set from variables to the final index makes it easier information understanding, having all figures in just one screen, quantified and depicted in a hierarchical way for a deeper insight into grouping levels and dependencies (Fig. 2).

Besides, the user can dig into any level or branch to get more information, just by clicking on each of the elements in a fully interactive way, which helps to better understand the final value of the indexes, based on its indicators and measurable objectives.

This way, the main objective of STILE tool implementing the Ds index is to help in the assessment of the effectiveness of the demo site interventions in cities, supporting decision-making when some new interventions or improvement of the existing ones is being under discussion or evaluation in the city.

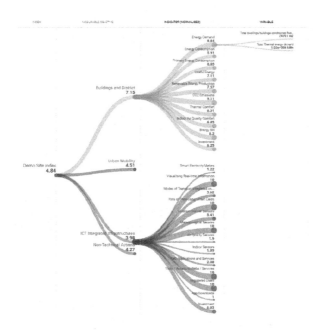

Fig. 2. Example of calculation and representation of Ds

6   Evaluation of Valladolid Demo Site

The Ds index is defined to assist on the assessment of the impacts of the overall project in each of the demo cities. This section presents the results of the calculation of the Demo Site Index (Ds) of the interventions in Valladolid.

The demo site index of Valladolid has increased from 1.89 to 4.84 showing the great impact of REMOURBAN interventions in the different areas of the city (Fig. 3).

Fig. 3. Valladolid Ds Index (Baseline (Green) vs. Reporting 2019 (Blue)) (Color figure online)

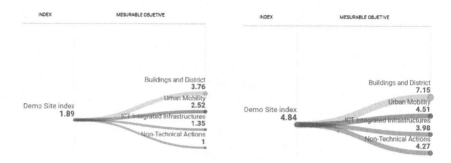

Fig. 4. Valladolid Ds Index. Baseline tree diagram (Left) vs. Reporting tree diagram (Right)

In Fig. 4 can be appreciated as all the interventions areas (Buildings and District, Urban Mobility, ICT and non-technical) have increased their values. Since this paper is focused on Energy Interventions, looking at the Buildings and District sub-index it possible to conclude that both active (such as the new district heating system and PV panels) and passive (façade and roof insulation) interventions in the Valladolid district have had a positive impact, it is possible to see how these actions have allowed Buildings and District measureable objective to move from a baseline of 3.76 to 7.15 in the after retrofitting situation doubling practically the value.

6.1 Evaluation of Buildings and District Indicators for Valladolid Demo Site

The main aim of the REMOURBAN project within the scope of Buildings and District is to improve the efficiency in the use of energy and to change the current energy sources by decarbonising the energy supplies and increasing the share of renewable at the same time that improving the users comfort and reducing energy bill.

The Buildings and District Sub-Index it is composed by a group of indicators which allow to assess the impact of the specific actions and interventions of the project i.e., Energy demand, Energy consumption, Renewable energy production, Thermal comfort, etc., comparing the situation before and after the interventions.

Calculation algorithms have been implemented in STILE tool to calculate the buildings and district indicators according to their definition. These indicators are weighted to estimate the "Buildings and district sub-index" and to evaluate the impact of the area of the project related to buildings and district.

Fig. 5 shows the comparison of the Valladolid demonstrator indicators' results in the baseline and the reporting periods of Buildings and District. It shows an overall improvement in the district.

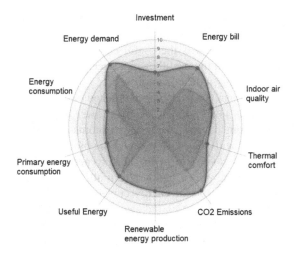

Fig. 5. Valladolid Ds Evaluation. Indicators related to the measurable objective "Building and Districts" Baseline (Green) vs Reporting 2019 (Blue) (Color figure online)

The most affected indicator is the renewable energy production. In the baseline period, the energy produced for the heating and the domestic hot water came from non-renewable sources. The heating was produced with natural gas and diesel sources and the DHW with individual heaters fed with natural gas, butane and electricity. The intervention meant the replacement of one of the existing natural gas/diesel boilers with two new biomass boilers (renewable) and the centralization of the DHW in 46% of the dwellings. Furthermore, a new PV system was installed as support for the thermal plant. These measures implied that the renewable energy production was over 70% during the reporting period, making the value of the indicator increase up to 7.57.

Both energy demand and energy consumption improved almost in parallel. The energy demand was reduced due to the improvement in the insulation of the buildings carried out during the retrofitting. It was reported a reduction of 30% in "Thermal Energy Demand" (mainly due to the façade insulation carried out), and a 28% reduction in "Energy Consumption" (mainly also as improved efficiency in DH system). As buildings now have lower energy losses, the energy demand was reduced and the indicator improved. Together with this indicator goes the energy consumption. A reduction in the energy demand means also a reduction in the consumption, which considering also the higher increase of the systems efficiency implies the improvement on this parameter.

Furthermore, as buildings now have better thermal response to thermal fluctuations, the parameter "Thermal Comfort" increased a 12% showing a better thermal behaviour of insulated dwellings.

The primary energy consumption is also related to the energy consumption. However, it involves the typology of fuel too. The use of biomass boilers and PV system implied a variation on the fuel share and, thus, a variation on the primary energy factors, as the primary energy factor for biomass and PV are lower than the one for natural gas/diesel and electricity from grid respectively. The combination of a lower (better) primary energy factor together with lower energy consumption implied an important improvement in the primary energy consumption indicator.

A parameter that improved too is the useful energy. As the energy demand was reduced during the intervention, the useful energy necessary to heat the dwellings was also reduced, meaning that this indicator improved.

The energy bill for the tenants has also been reduced due to several factors. On one hand, the energy demand is lower, which means a lower consumption. On the other hand, the fuel changed from natural gas/diesel to biomass/natural gas. The cost of biomass is lower compared with the other two and the biomass share is close to 80%. Also the PV contribution to cover part of the heating needs of the district should be considered as it is reducing the use of biomass/natural gas and therefore reducing the operational costs. These two factors of energy consumption reduction and RES contribution justify the improvement on this indicator.

Important to highlight also the great reduction in CO_2 emissions, where a reduction of 70% was achieved, mainly due to high increase in renewable energy use, and efficiency achieved with dwellings insulation.

7 Conclusions

Evaluation is one of the key frameworks of the Urban Regeneration Model defined and developed in the REMOURBAN project. This evaluation framework defines metrics and standards for implementing the evaluation mechanisms in the project.

The evaluation of the results is key to assess the achievement of the expected impacts but also it brings an essential mechanism to foster replication of the solutions developed which, indeed, is one of the strategic elements of the project. To ensure the replicability of the actions it is needed to create a consolidated and consistent reference of impacts.

For the evaluation of the actions, two levels have been considered within REMOURBAN evaluation framework: the Project Level, to provide a clear identification of the project impact regarding actions on the three key priority areas and the City Level, to assess both sustainability and smartness of participating cities.

The work presented in this paper is focused on the project level showing the Demo Site Index (Ds) which has been designed for this aim and more specifically the results achieved thanks to the actions implemented to reach a Near Zero Energy District in Valladolid.

The interventions carried out in the buildings (both passive and active) have reduced all forms of energy (demand, consumption, primary and useful). The increase of the use of renewable sources has considerable contributed to achieving a very low dependence on fossil fuels through the implementation of solutions such as biomass boilers and PV system. Interventions in buildings have not only reduced CO_2 emissions, but they have also improved indoor air quality and thermal comfort for people living in these buildings. From an economic perspective, the energy bill per household has been reduced considerably thanks to the combination of all the energy measures.

Acknowledgements. This research work has been partially funded by the EU through the European Union's Horizon 2020 Research and Innovation Programme under the research project REMOURBAN with grant agreement No 646511. The authors would like to thank the rest of the partners for their support. All related information to the project is available at www.remourban.eu.

.

References

1. REMOURBAN project Deliverable 2.2: Evaluation protocols and indicators. July 2016
2. REMOURBAN project Deliverable 2.3: Implementation of the Methodology of Evaluation of Sustainability and Smartness in Cities. November 2016
3. Bosch, P., Jongeneel, S., et al.: D1.4 Smart city KPIs and related methodology. CITYkeys Project. Co-funded by the European Commission within the H2020 Programme.Grant Agreement no: 646440 (2016)
4. European Committee for Standardisation, 2007. Ventilation for non-residential buildings - Performance requirements for ventilation and room-conditioning systems. European Standard EN 13779

Analysis of Residential Electricity Consumption by Areas in Uruguay

Juan Chavat$^{(\boxtimes)}$ and Sergio Nesmachnow

Universidad de la República, Montevideo, Uruguay
{juan.pablo.chavat,sergion}@fing.edu.uy

Abstract. Home electricity demand has increased uninterrupted and is expected in 2050 to doubles the demanded in 2010. Making reasonable use of electricity is increasingly important and, in that way, different policies are carried out based on knowledge of how it is used. This article presents a procedure for measuring the potential electricity consumption in Uruguay. The study takes as main axis the appliance ownership information revelled by a national survey about severe socioeconomic aspects, and combines it with data on the characteristics of appliances, collected from local shops with an internet presence. Based on this data, an index of potential electricity consumption is performed for different census areas. To validate the analysis, it uses electricity consumption data from the ECD-UY (Electricity Consumption Data set of UruguaY) dataset and performs OLS linear regressions to evaluate real consumption and index correlation. The implementation uses Jupyter notebooks, language Python version 3, and utils libraries such as Pandas and Numpy. Results indicate that the departments with the highest index score are located on the West/Southwest coastlines. About census sections and segments in Montevideo, results show that the highest score areas are located in the South/Southeast coastlines, while lowest score ones are located in the outskirts. The validation process was limited by the lack of real consumption data.

1 Introduction

Word Energy Outlook report, by the International Energy Agency [6], states that residential electricity demand has increased uninterrupted worldwide. It is expected to be double in 2050 than what it was in 2010 [7]. For that reason, it is important to make responsible use of electricity. In that way, multiple investigations have been carried on with the purpose of apply policies that motivate saving and reducing climate impact in factories, buildings, and homes [3,5,9,12].

The population of Uruguay is 3.4 million inhabitants. Electricity in country is provided by the state-owned company, UTE. In 2020, the company provides electricity to a total of 1,498,164 customers throughout Uruguay, where 1,355,995 (90.5%) are residential customers. About 1.5 million people live in the capital city, Montevideo. The city presents an electrification rate of 99.8%, including urban and rural areas, according to data of 2018. In average, and according

© Springer Nature Switzerland AG 2021
S. Nesmachnow and L. Hernández Callejo (Eds.): ICSC-CITIES 2020, CCIS 1359, pp. 42–57, 2021.
https://doi.org/10.1007/978-3-030-69136-3_4

to 2017 stats, UTE serves per month 246 kWh to each residential customer in Montevideo.

Energy consumption data analysis and characterization are needed to apply demand management techniques oriented to a better use of energy resources. A possible approach for demand management is to motivate behavioral changes in customers that lead to electricity savings. Data analysis provides precise information on how customers consume electricity, which can be used to elaborate effective policies to consider for promotion of behavioral changes, elaboration of new plans and tariffs, etc.

In this line of work, this article presents an index of residential electricity consumption based on statistics about appliance ownership. The data of the 2017 National Continuous Household Survey (ECH, by its Spanish acronym) is used in combination with appliance characteristics information collected from local shops with a presence on the internet. The index is calculated to three census area levels: by departments, by sections and by segments. Real electricity consumption data, gathered from a subset of the ECD-UY dataset [2], is finally used to validate the correlation of the index results with real data.

The study applies a data analysis approach [10] over appliance ownership statistics, together with appliance characteristics information, to evaluate the potential electricity consumption by census area. Also, a validation method is proposed for the index, using real consumption data.

Results show that the departments with the highest index score are located on the West/Southwest coastlines, while the ones with the lowest scores are located in the East of Uruguay. Regarding census sections and segments in Montevideo, results show that the highest score areas are located in the South/Southeast coastlines of the city, decreasing progressively as it approaches the outskirts of the city. Score at the segment level shows great differences, up to six times, between the highest and lowest extreme. The index validation process was limited by the lack of more real consumption data.

This work is developed in the context of the project "Computational intelligence to characterize the use of electric energy in residential customers", funded by the National Administration of Power Plants and Electrical Transmissions (Spanish: Administración Nacional de Usinas y Trasmisiones Eléctricas, UTE), and Universidad de la República, Uruguay. The project study how computational intelligence techniques can be used to process household electricity consumption data and characterize energy consumption. It also focuses on determining which appliances have the greatest impact on household electricity consumption and in the identification of patterns in residential consumption.

The article is structured as follows. Next section describes the problem of analyzing residential electricity consumption and reviews the main related work. The proposed approach for analyzing the electricity consumption in Uruguay is described in Sect. 3. The datasets and the processing are described in Sect. 4. The main results are reported and analyzed in Sect. 5. Finally, Sect. 6 presents the conclusions and the main lines of future work.

2 Analysis of Residential Electricity Consumption

This section describes the problem addressed in this article and reviews relevant related works.

2.1 Main Research Question and Hypothesis

This work analyzes the electricity consumption based on an index built from appliance ownership statistics. The statistics were obtained from a national survey implemented year by year by the National Statistics Institute (INE), Uruguay. The formulated question is: Can an index build from appliances ownership statistics model the electricity consumption per census area in Uruguay?

Some energy-intensive appliances, such as air conditioner or electric water heater, determine the electric consumption of a household. Some of these appliances are not a basic need, and therefore not every household count with them. If a degree of the appliances ownership is calculated for census areas, is expected to determine an average level of electricity consumption. From the previous question and considerations, and based on intuitive ideas, the following hypothesis was formulated to work on it.

Hypothesis: The more energy-intensive appliances owned, the higher the potential electricity consumption.

2.2 Related Works

The analysis of the related literature allowed identifying several approaches for electricity consumption characterization in several countries. Most of the approaches have applied statistical tools (e.g., multilevel and logistic regression), such as in this article. Some relevant related works are reviewed next.

Chévez et al. studied the electricity consumption in Great La Plata, Argentina [4]. Two relevant problems of the Argentinean electricity sector were identified: i) consumption peaks, that increased 5% per year, could not be satisfied, and ii) a poor diversification of the electricity generation matrix. 1010 census areas with similar electricity consumption were identified and clustered in eight groups applying the k-means algorithm. Results were related to sociodemographic variables and its relevance in electricity consumption was studied. The article concluded that electricity demands grow quickly as the ratio of people per home and people per room increases. The greater the presence of flats in the area, the lower the electricity consumption. In turn, the more precarious the buildings, the greater the electricity consumption. Concerning unsatisfied basic needs, at higher the index level, proportionally higher is the electricity demand.

McLoughlin et al. [11] analyzed energy consumption data from 3941 smart meters in Ireland, and socio-economic, demographic, and dwelling characteristics. Four parameters were considered in the study: i) total electricity consumed, ii) maximum demand, iii) load factor (the lower, the more "peaky" of the consumption), and iv) time of use of maximum electricity consumption. Linear regression algorithms were developed to study how the dwelling/occupant characteristics and how the owned appliances affect on the electricity consumption. The analysis concluded that electricity consumption was negatively influenced by a higher number of bedrooms, head of households between 36–55 years, and a higher presence of professionals. On the other hand, it is positively influenced by dwelling type apartments and lower/middle social classes. About appliances, households using electricity for water heating or cooking consumed more electricity than the rest. Load factor, a measure of daily mean to daily maximum electricity demand, was sensible to the dwelling type and the number of bedrooms. Time length of maximum demand is more by the number of occupants than the dwelling type. It occurs during the morning for older heads of households, and late in the day for middle age heads of households.

Anderson et al. [1] explored inferring household characteristics of census areas from electricity consumption and number of residents for Ireland too. Data was limited to three days (Tuesday, Wednesday, and Thursday) of October 2009. Indicators were generated to describe household electricity consumption, considering load magnitude, summary statistics, and temporal properties. First, household characteristics were identified to infer profile indicators, applying multilevel regression considering several explanatory variables: income, employment status of the household response person (HRP), presence of children, and the number of residents. Then, the most likely profile indicators to reverse the direction of the prediction model were selected by logistic regression. Results showed an accuracy close to 60% to classify the employment status of the HRP. The work concluded that, despite the accuracy achieved, it is a feasible approach to infer household characteristics from the electricity consumption profiles.

Villareal and Moreira [13] studied residential electricity consumption in Brazil in 1985–2013. Residential consumption represented 26% of the electricity used in country, and the most demanding appliances were electric shower (19%), refrigerator (18%), lamps (15%), TV (11%), air conditioning and freezer (5%). Elasticity values were obtained from processing explanatory variables into linear regressions, and used to relate variables to consumption behaviours. The follow variables were used for the analysis: number of households on the country, available family income, electricity tariffs, appliances ownership, and social/economic policies that affect electricity consumption directly. About extra factors, the following three social policies were chosen: restraining of electricity consumption, facilitate access to electricity for low incoming families, and energy efficiency programs. Three models were developed to describe the consumption: i) considering variables represented by time series only, ii) considering electricity restraints, and iii) considering all the extra factors. Authors concluded that a rise of 1% in the number of residences increases electricity consumption by 1.53%, a rises of 1% in family income increase consumption in 0.19%, and a rise of 1% in the tariff cause a decrease of 0.23% in the consumption. The models presented high coefficients of determination (0.968 the first, 0.989 the rest), showing a strong relationship between explanatory variables and electricity consumption.

In Uruguay, Laureiro [8] analyzed residential electricity consumption based on socioeconomic characteristics, dwelling characteristics, energy uses, and temperature. Ordinary Least Square (OLS) and Quantile Regression (QR) were applied on data from 2994 houses. A cursory analysis yielded that income per capita is a relevant factor but not the unique, owning certain appliances (electric water heater/air conditioner) directly impacts over electricity consumption, and thermal comfort appliances are more common in dwellings with high electricity consumption. The OLS analysis concluded that: i) per capita income has high elasticity, ii) an increment of 1% in the square meters of a dwelling, increments 0.06% the electricity consumption, iii) houses consume 10.8% more than apartments, iv) electricity consumption increases 8.2% for each extra air conditioner and 17.2% for each extra electric water heater, and v) regional variables do not impact significantly in the consumption. The QR analysis concluded that: i) the impact of income per capita over consumption is lower in high quartiles than in low/medium ones, ii) dwelling size impact more in higher than in lower deciles iii) the dwelling type impacts only in medium/high deciles while building materials do not impact at all iv) air conditioners impact more in lower deciles and electric water heaters impact equally in all deciles, vi) the impact of cooking, washing/dryer machines, and sanitary heating have an inverted 'U' behaviour (low in extreme deciles, high in medium deciles). The work concluded that although the income per capita is a determining variable, it is not the only one that impacts on electricity consumption, and other characteristics must be take into account (e.g., family composition, dwelling characteristics, and energy uses).

This article contributes by studying the electricity consumption based on appliance ownership data processed from national surveys in Uruguay.

3 Proposed Approach for Electricity Consumption Analysis

The proposed approach for the analysis consists of building an index that scores the electricity consumption degree, per census areas. For the construction, data provided by the ECH national survey from the year 2017 is used. ECH counts with several variables, described in the following section, that quantify the appliances ownership of the households. The surveyed households have geo-referenced information in at least three census levels: departments, census sections and census segments. Further details about the census areas are provided next.

Data is grouped by census area and the likelihood of owning the surveyed appliance is calculated. Besides, each appliances power consumption is collected from many local shops to weight the impact of each appliance in the final value. For example, owning an air conditioner affect more on electricity consumption than owning a flat TV. In the same way, each appliance is categorized by its frequency of use between low, medium or high. This represents a second weighting on the appliance consumption impact over the final result. Therefore, a fridge that is always on affects more than a notebook computer (sporadically used) on the final results. Frequencies are assigned as a rule of thumb guided by the authors own experience.

The index scores are calculated as shown in Eq. 1. Given a type of census area r with m different areas (e.g., $m = 19$ if $r =$ departments), $A^{(r)} \in \mathbb{R}^{m \times n}$ a matrix with one row per census area and one column per appliance likelihood information; $c^{(r)} \in \mathbb{R}^n$ a vector with the consumption of the n appliances; and $f^{(r)} \in \mathbb{R}^n$ a vector with quantified frequency of use for the n appliances. The result is a vector $index^{(r)} \in \mathbb{R}^m$ where each value in position i means the index score for the area i.

$$index^{(r)} = A_{m,n}^{(r)} \cdot c^{(r)} \cdot f^{(r)} \cdot \begin{bmatrix} 1 \\ \vdots \\ 1 \end{bmatrix} \qquad (1)$$

4 Data Collection and Processing

This section describes the data used for the analysis and how it was prepared to be processed.

4.1 Census Data

Used census data is provided by the National Institute of Statistics (INE, by its Spanish acronym). INE collect data of different index with monthly, quarterly, half-yearly and annual periodicity. The information is presented as a continuous household survey (ECH, by its Spanish acronym) every year. The ECH collects data about the labour market and income of households and individuals, from a representative set of households distributed around the country.

Information in ECH is georeferenced by, at least, the department, the census section, and the census segment. The definition of these georeferenced levels are provided next:

- *Department*: Coincides with the nineteen different political-administrative borders of the country.
- *Census section*: Corresponds to the first division level of the departments. Each section area can be cut into blocks or not. Its borders coincide with the ones used in the national census of 1963.
- *Census segment*: The segments are the subdivision of the sections. In census locations or areas cut into blocks, corresponds to a set of blocks, otherwise, the segments are a portion of territory that groups minor units with recognisable physical limits in the terrain and can include population centres.

Only a subset of the indexes in ECH was selected for the analysis. The selected indexes focus on georeferencing the data and quantifying appliance ownership. Table 1 list detailed information about the selected indexes.

Table 1. Description of data from ECH (2017) used to build the index

Name	Description	Type of value
dpto	Code of the department	Number (1–19)
nomdpto	Name of the department	String
secc	Census section	Number
segm	Census segment	Number
nombarrio	Name of the neighbourhood	String
d9	Number of residential rooms	Number
d18	Energy source for lighting	Number (1: electric; 2–4: other)
d260	Energy source for heating	Number (1: electric; 2–6: other)
d20	Energy source for cooking	Number (1: electric; 2-6: other)
d21_1	Electric water heater	Number (1: yes; 2: no)
d21_2	Shower water heater	Number (1: yes; 2: no)
d21_3	Fridge	Number (1: yes; 2: no)
d21_4	Tube TV	Number (1: yes; 2: no)
d21_4_1	Number of tube TVs	Number
d21_5	LCD/Plasma TV	Number (1: yes; 2: no)
d21_5_1	Number of LCD/Plasma TV	Number
d21_6	Radio	Number (1: yes; 2: no)
d21_8	Videocassette player	Number (1: yes; 2: no)
d21_9	DVD player	Number (1: yes; 2: no)
d21_10	Washing machine	Number (1: yes; 2: no)
d21_11	Clothes dryer	Number (1: yes; 2: no)
d21_12	Dishwasher	Number (1: yes; 2: no)
d21_13	Microwave	Number (1: yes; 2: no)
d21_14	Air conditioner	Number (1: yes; 2: no)
d21_14_1	Number of air conditioners	Number
d21_15	Notebook computer	Number (1: yes; 2: no)
d21_15_2	'Plan Ceibal' laptops	Number
d21_15_4	Other notebooks	Number

Data Preparation. Preliminary analysis showed that records outside Montevideo do not have census section nor segment values set. Therefore, the index for these areas is evaluated only for Montevideo. The Yes/No columns were transformed from {1, 2} values to {0, 1} to facilitate the multiplication by the columns that indicate the number of appliances. Additionally, columns with common and 'Plan Ceibal' laptops were merged into one with the sum of both and the lighting columns was multiplied by the number of residential rooms to represents a light per room. Also, to discriminate between the air conditioner and other electric heating sources, the column indicating source was set to 'No' if the column of the air conditioners has a 'Yes' value. The final transformation consisted of multiplying all the columns that indicate the presence of an appliance by the corresponding column that indicates the number of appliances in the household.

Finally, several validations were processed to assure the integrity of the information. For example, columns that indicate the number of an appliance in a household were checked that if the value is greater than zero, then the column indicating the presence of this appliance have the corresponding "Yes" value. No integrity errors were found in this last step.

4.2   Appliance Characteristics Data

ECH surveys gather data about the ownership of certain household appliances. Based on these appliances and using the information of local shops with presence on the Internet, power consumption data was collected. Up to five different appliance models were gathered to define the median power consumption of each appliance. Table 2 lists the result of the data collection process, and Fig. 1 presents a bar graph of the mean power consumption together with its standard deviation measure. It can be observed how some appliances are more energy-intensive than others.

Table 2. List of appliances information used to build the index

Appliance	Mean power (W)	Frequency of use	Power weighted by frequency of use
Lighting	11.8	Medium	8.85
Heating	1200.0	High	1200.00
Oven	1380.0	High	1380.00
Electric water heater	1600.0	High	1600.00
Shower heater	1810.0	Medium	1357.50
Fridge	199.4	High	199.40
Tube TV	124.8	Medium	93.60
Flat TV	85.6	Medium	64.20
Radio	20.2	Low	10.10
VHS player	10.0	Low	5.00
DVD player	10.5	Low	5.25
Washing machine	740.0	Medium	555.00
Clothes dryer	3154.0	Medium	2365.50
Dishwasher	1409.6	Medium	1057.20
Microwave	1068.0	Medium	801.00
Air conditioner	1290.0	High	1290.00
Notebook	57.0	Medium	42.75

4.3   Electricity Consumption Data

Real electricity consumption data is gathered from the ECD-UY dataset [2] and corresponds to the *electric water heater consumption* subset. The records

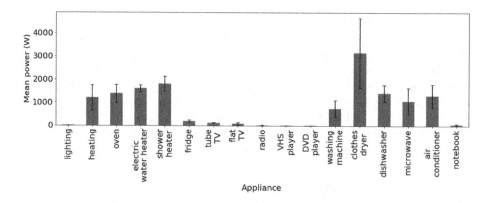

Fig. 1. Electricity consumption of the appliances used to build the index

originate from different clamp/meters installed by the National Electricity Company (UTE) in the households of their customers. The subset consists of mainly two parts, the records of the appliance consumption disaggregated and the total aggregated household consumption. The location of the households varies among the main Uruguayan cities. For this work, only the total aggregated consumption and the customer georeferenced information were used.

The subset contains the total consumption of 541 households on which only 242 are georeferenced. These georeferenced households are distributed into 6 departments. Household located in Montevideo are located along 12 census sections and 38 census segments. Figure 2 shows three maps at different area level. The marked areas in each map correspond to those for which electricity consumption data is available in the ECD-UY dataset.

The data preparation phase consisted of two steps. First, the electricity consumption of customers without georeferenced data was removed from the subset. Then, abnormal consumption values were filtered. For this task, the records with values lower than the 15th percentile and greater than the 85th percentile were removed.

4.4   Implementation

The implementation consists of the next main steps: the load of the datasets, matrices construction for power demand by appliance and appliance ownership likelihood, processing of the index score per census area, visualization of results, and validation of the index scores.

The processing was executed on a personal computer with average processing power. Code was implemented in a Jupyter notebook using Python language version 3. For the data loading and the matrices construction, the utility libraries Pandas and Numpy were used, and the GeoPandas extension was applied for maps generation. The resulting notebook with its processing results is available for download at https://bit.ly/3kGUfVO.

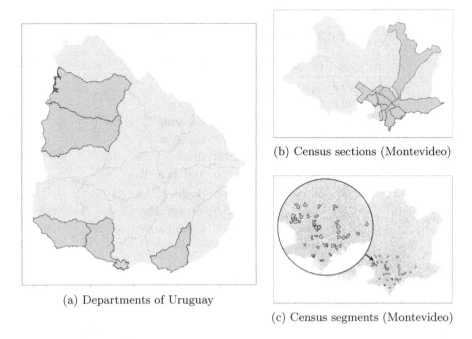

(b) Census sections (Montevideo)

(a) Departments of Uruguay

(c) Census segments (Montevideo)

Fig. 2. Maps where the marked areas represents the one that counts with real electricity consumption data in the ECD-UY subset

5   Results

This section present first the result of the proposed analysis by the three different census areas and then the results on the validation of the data using real consumption records.

5.1   Index Scores by Census Areas

Results of the index by department areas show a difference up to 65% between the first and the last position. The department that results with the highest score is Montevideo, while the one with the lowest score was Cerro Largo. In general, the departments that present higher scores index are located on the west and south-west coastlines. A visual inspection of the departments in the Uruguayan map, starting from Colonia at the most southwest and pointing to the northeast, shows a progressive increase of the index score. That is observed at the map presented in Fig. 3. The complete list of departments together with its resulting index score is shown in the Table 3

Results corresponding to the index score calculated by census section of Montevideo shows that the highest index score sections are located beside the southeast coastline of the city. The difference between the highest and the lowest index scores is up to 66%. The section with the highest score is number 10, and it covers the neighbourhoods Carrasco Norte, Buceo, Malvin, Malvin Norte, Punta

Table 3. Index score by departments

Score	Department	Score	Department
4505.8	Montevideo	3725.7	Flores
4139.5	Colonia	3695.0	Florida
4097.9	Salto	3559.0	Durazno
4008.6	Maldonado	3543.8	Lavalleja
3964.9	Paysandu	3427.0	Rivera
3915.5	Rio Negro	3385.0	Treinta Y Tres
3894.8	Soriano	3373.8	Rocha
3821.7	Canelones	3322.9	Tacuarembo
3804.3	Artigas	2950.7	Cerro Largo
3792.1	San Jose		

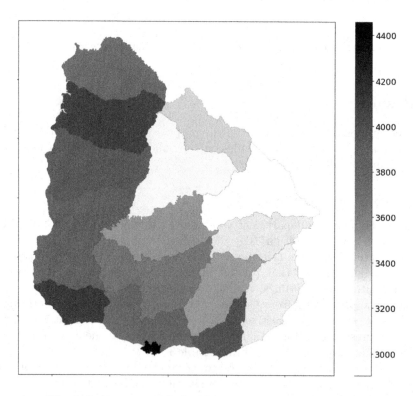

Fig. 3. Index scores calculated for departments of Uruguay

Gorda, Union, Las Canteras and Carrasco. In the opposite side, the section with the lowest score is number 16, it covers the neighbourhoods Tres Ombues, Victoria, Nuevo Paris, Paso de la Arena, Casabó, and Pajas Blancas. A visual inspection on the map shown in Fig. 4 shows that starting from the southeast coastline and pointing to the northwest, the index score decrease progressively. Table 4 list the resulting scores by census section, together with the list of corresponding neighbourhoods of each section.

Finally, the index calculated by census segments shows an accumulation of segments with highest scores on the south and southeast area of Montevideo, while lowest scores segments are located mainly in the outskirts of the city. Figure 5 shows a map of census segments in Montevideo, coloured by its index score. Results also reveal a big difference in the score among top and bottom scored segments, differing by more than six times in the most extreme cases. Table 5 shows a truncated list of the census segments ordered by its resulting index score.

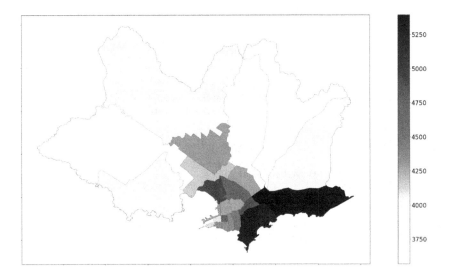

Fig. 4. Index score calculated by census sections of Montevideo

5.2 Validation of the Proposed Approach

For validating the proposed approach, the monthly average electricity consumption is calculated and compared with the index score results. Finally, the average consumption and the index scores are processed by an OLS linear regression to measure the correlation between real consumption and the index score.

Figure 6 shows the average monthly electricity consumption of departments with available consumption data in the ECD-UY dataset. The calculation of

Table 4. Index score by census sections

Score	Section	Neighbourhoods
5444.1	10	Carrasco Norte, Buceo, Malvin, Malvin Norte, Punta Gorda, Union, Las Canteras, Carrasco
5297.3	18	Punta Carretas, Pocitos, Cordon, Tres Cruces, Parque Batlle, V. Dolores, Parque Rodo
5284.1	24	Pocitos, Pque. Batlle, Villa Dolores, Buceo
4981.8	14	Prado, Nueva Savona, Reducto, Capurro, Bella Vista
4898.2	23	Tres Cruces, La Blanqueada, Larrañaga
4795.5	6	Centro (Norte)
4710.5	12	Reducto, Atahualpa, La Figurita, Jacinto Vera,Larrañaga, Brazo Oriental, Mercado Modelo, Bolivar
4549.0	15	Cordon, Palermo, Parque Rodo
4432.7	7	Cordon, Palermo
4428.4	4	Centro (Suroeste), Ciudad Vieja (Sureste), Barrio Sur
4414.0	5	Centro (Sur), Barrio Sur
4358.1	21	Peñarol, Lavalleja, Conciliacion, Sayago, Nuevo Paris Paso de las Duranas, Belvedere
4322.9	22	Cerrito, Brazo Oriental, Villa Española, Bolivar, Mercado Modelo, Castro, P. Castellanos
4313.7	8	Aguada
4305.6	19	La Comercial, Villa Muñoz, Retiro
4211.6	20	Aires Puros, La Teja, Prado, Nueva Savona, Belvedere, Nuevo Paris
4162.1	3	Ciudad Vieja (Sur)
4143.9	1	Ciudad Vieja (Noreste), Centro
3907.3	13	Casabo, Pajas Blancas, Paso de la Arena, La Paloma, Tomkinson, Cerro
3867.4	9	Colon Centro y Noroeste, Colon Sureste, Abayuba, Lezica, Melilla
3842.9	99	Flor de Maroñas, Maroñas, Parque Guarani, Union Bañados de Carrasco, Villa Garcia, Manga Rural, Punta Rieles, Bella Italia, Las Canteras
3693.1	17	Casavalle, Manga, Las Acacias, Villa Española, Piedras Blancas, Castro, P. Castellanos, Manga, Toledo Chico
3663.9	11	Ituzaingo, Jardines del Hipodromo, Flor de Maroñas, P. Rieles, Bella Italia, Manga, Toledo Chico, Manga, Piedras Blancas, Villa Garcia, Villa Española, Union
3621.2	2	Ciudad Vieja (Norte)
3616.8	16	Tres Ombues, Victoria, Nuevo Paris, Paso de la Arena Casabo, Pajas Blancas

Table 5. Truncated list of index scores by census segment

Score	Section	Segment	Neighbourhoods
9249.1	10	67	Carrasco
9120.0	10	246	Malvín
9020.2	10	75	Carrasco
9013.0	10	74	Carrasco
8687.8	10	64	Carrasco
...	...	...	...
2322.6	9	1	Leizica, Melilla
2235.4	2	3	Ciudad Vieja
2164.1	99	208	Bañados de Carrasco
2141.0	13	9	Cerro
1450.4	13	113	Casabó, Pajas Blancas

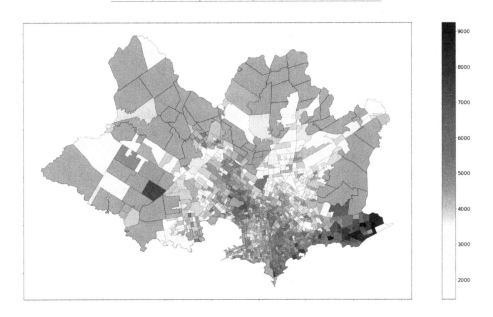

Fig. 5. Index score calculated by census segments of Montevideo

the consumption is based on 242 georeferenced customers unequally distributed in departments. The comparison of the real consumption and the index score results shows that only two of the six departments, Montevideo (72 customers) and Paysandú (152), are in the same order. These two departments are the ones with more real data available, and therefore, its calculated average consumption is more reliable than the rest (which accounts for just six or less customers each).

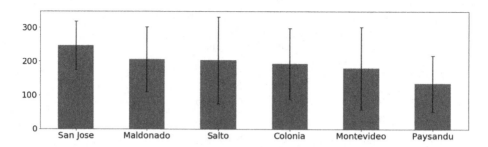

Fig. 6. Monthly average consumption from real data in ECD-UY dataset

OLS was performed with average real consumption and index score data. Results showed no correlation between the values but it should be taken into account the low number of samples that conform the calculation of average consumption. It is necessary to repeat the experiments with a more reliable calculation of real average monthly consumption.

Regarding the validation of the index by census section/census segment, the available real data is even more limited. For census sections, the available data is from 72 customers distributed in 12 sections, meaning an average ratio of 6 customers per section. For census segments, the 72 customers are distributed in 38 segments and its average ratio is lower than 2. Both cases are not statistically representative, and therefore, a full validation is not possible in this case.

6   Conclusions and Future Work

This article presented an electricity consumption analysis based on household appliance ownership data processed from national surveys in Uruguay. The proposed approach consists of building an index to score the potential electricity consumption in three different census areas: departments, sections, and segments.

Appliance information was collected from several sources and processed to build the proposed index. Results showed that departments located the Southeastern coastline have the highest index scores while departments in the north and northeast have the lowest ones. Regarding census sections and segments, the index was performed only for Montevideo and results show the highest scores in the south/southeast coastlines and lowest scores in the outskirts of the city. Census segments show great differences, up to six times, between extreme values. Validation of the index was limited by the lack of more real data.

The main lines for future work are related to study the relationship between the index and socioeconomic variables provided by the ECH, such as household incoming, education level, number of kids, among others. Also, updating the index to consider data from last and previous ECH versions, to study the index evolution along time.

References

1. Anderson, B., Lin, S., Newing, A., Bahaj, A.B., James, P.: Electricity consumption and household characteristics: Implications for census-taking in a smart metered future. Comput. Environ. Urban Syst. **63**, 58–67 (2017)
2. Chavat, J., Graneri, J., Alvez, G., Nesmachnow, S.: ECD-UY: Detailed household electricity consumption dataset of uruguay. Scientific Data (2020, submitted)
3. Chavat, J., Nesmachnow, S., Graneri, J.: Non-intrusive energy disaggregation by detecting similarities in consumption patterns. Revista Facultad de Ingeniería Universidad de Antioquia (2020)
4. Chévez, P., Barbero, D., Martini, I., Discoli, C.: Application of the k-means clustering method for the detection and analysis of areas of homogeneous residential electricity consumption at the Great La Plata region, Buenos Aires. Argent. Sustain. Cities Soc. **32**, 115–129 (2017)
5. Ford, R.: Reducing domestic energy consumption through behaviour modification. Ph.D. thesis, Oxford University (2009)
6. International Energy Agency: World Energy Outlook 2015. White paper (2015)
7. Larcher, D., Tarascon, J.: Towards greener and more sustainable batteries for electrical energy storage. Nat. Chem. **7**(1), 19–29 (2015)
8. Laureiro, P.: Determinantes del consumo de energía elíctrica del sector residencial en Uruguay. Serie Documentos de investigación estudiantil, DIE 05/18 FCS, Udela (2018)
9. Luján, E., Otero, A., Valenzuela, S., Mocskos, E., Steffenel, L., Nesmachnow, S.: An integrated platform for smart energy management: the CC-SEM project. Revista Facultad de Ingeniería Universidad de Antioquia (2019)
10. Massobrio, R., Nesmachnow, S., Tchernykh, A., Avetisyan, A., Radchenko, G.: Towards a cloud computing paradigm for big data analysis in smart cities. Program. Comput. Softw. **44**(3), 181–189 (2018)
11. McLoughlin, F., Duffy, A., Conlon, M.: Characterising domestic electricity consumption patterns by dwelling and occupant socio-economic variables: an Irish case study. Energy Build. **48**, 240–248 (2012). (July 2009)
12. Orsi, E., Nesmachnow, S.: Smart home energy planning using IoT and the cloud. In: IEEE URUCON (2017)
13. Villareal, M., Moreira, J.: Household consumption of electricity in Brazil between 1985 and 2013. Energy Policy **96**, 251–259 (2016)

Computational Intelligence
for Characterization and Disaggregation
of Residential Electricity Consumption

Mathías Esteban[(⊠)], Ignacio Fiori, Mateo Mujica, and Sergio Nesmachnow

Universidad de la República, Montevideo, Uruguay
{mathias.esteban,ignacio.fiori,mateo.mujica,sergion}@fing.edu.uy

Abstract. This article presents the application of computational intelligence techniques for the characterization of electricity consumption in
households. A specific variant of the residential energy disaggregation
problem is solved, which proposes identifying the state changes in a electrical network, using a time series of aggregate household power consumption data. This article introduces and compares three classifiers
to solve the problem: a Naive Bayes classifier, a K Nearest Neighbors
algorithm, and a Long Short Term Memory neural network. The implemented classifiers are evaluated using the UK-DALE data repository.
Experimental results show that the Long Short Term Memory network
is the most accurate to deal with the characterization problem, achieving
a successful rate of state changes up to 75% and values of *F1-score* close
to 1.0 on certain appliances.

Keywords: Computational intelligence · Energy efficiency ·
Disaggregation

1 Introduction

Residential electricity consumption represents an important share of the energy
demand worldwide. Some appliances contribute the most to electricity consumption (air conditioning ∼30%, electronic and kitchen appliances ∼20%, water
heaters ∼20%, and cooling ∼10%) [12]. Thus, energy management is a crucial
issue in nowadays smart cities. Many strategies have been proposed to guarantee
an increased access to the energy resources at affordable costs for citizens, while
ensuring the preservation of natural resources and the protection of the environment [11]. In the search of a better use of energy resources, having accurate
information about household electricity consumption is very useful to conceive
energy plans and tariffs adapted to different sectors of the population and provide personalized advice towards achieving a better use of energy resources.

Installing individual meters to get the electricity consumption of each appliance in every house of a city is not a viable option nowadays. Thus, it is necessary to develop and apply techniques capable to offer this information using

S. Nesmachnow and L. Hernández Callejo (Eds.): ICSC-CITIES 2020, CCIS 1359, pp. 58–73, 2021.
https://doi.org/10.1007/978-3-030-69136-3_5

the aggregate power consumption data that energy providers collect via global smart meters. This kind of techniques rely on the analysis of aggregate power signal to disaggregate the individual appliances loads [2].

In this line of work, this article presents the application of computational intelligence methods for solving the disaggregation problem by recognizing on/off appliances states and state changes using the aggregate consumption signal, and determine energy consumption patterns. Three methods are compared to solve the problem: a Naive Bayes classifier, a K Nearest Neighbors algorithm, and a Long Short Term Memory (LSTM) neural network. The experimental evaluation of the proposed algorithm is performed over synthetic datasets, specifically built using real energy consumption data from the well-known UK-DALE repository [6]. The main results demonstrate that the proposed LSTM neural network is able to compute accurate solution to the problem, achieving a successful rate of state changes up to 75% and values close to 1 of the of *F1-score* learning metric on certain appliances.

The research is developed within the project "Computational intelligence to characterize the use of electric energy in residential customers", funded by the National the Uruguayan government-owned power company (UTE) and Universidad de la República, Uruguay. The project proposes the application of computational intelligence techniques for processing household electricity consumption data to characterize energy consumption, determine the use of appliances that have more impact on total consumption, and identify consumption patterns in residential customers.

The main contributions of this article include the design and implementation of three classifiers to solve the stated variant of the energy consumption disaggregation problem in residential households, and their experimental evaluation over a set of problem instances.

The article is structured as follows. Section 2 presents the main concepts related to energy disaggregation. A review of the main related work is presented in Sect. 3. The studied computational intelligence methods for energy consumption disaggregation are described in Sect. 4. The experimental evaluation of the proposed methods is reported in Sect. 5. Finally, Sect. 6 presents the conclusions and the main lines of future work.

2 Energy Disaggregation in Households

This section presents the main details about the energy disaggregation problem.

2.1 Overall Description

The energy disaggregation problem consists of disaggregating the overall energy consumption of a house into the individual consumption of a number of appliances. Energy disaggregation is a special case of a classification problem.

The problem was defined by Hart [5]. The goal of the problem is to identify which appliances are switched on and off in an electrical grid over a period of time by analyzing the aggregate power measures. The main idea is that appliances operate at certain power levels during specific periods of time and change the aggregate signal in a specific way, therefore produce a characteristic signature. Other variables related to appliance usage may be taken into consideration, such as day of the week, temperature and weather information. This kind of techniques are called non-intrusive because do not require physical intervention on the grid components.

In this article, the binary variant of the problem is addressed, where appliances could be either on or off. The distinction between one state and the other is computed according to a set of threshold values called *standby consumption*, specific for each appliance. A more complex variant of the problem consists of accounting for different consumption states in the considered appliances. This is a significantly harder approach compared to the binary variant.

2.2 Mathematical Model

Consider a set of appliances available in a house $E = \{e_1, e_2, e_3...e_n\}$ and let X_t be the aggregate power consumption of the house at a given time step t. x_t can be expressed as the sum of the individual power consumption X_t^i of each appliance in use in that time step, according to Eq. 1, where y_i is the power demand of appliance e_i, $a_i(t)$ is a Boolean function returning weather or not appliance i is on at time t, and $o(t)$ represents the noise in the grid.

$$X_t = \sum_{i=1}^{n} a_i(t)y_i + o(t) \tag{1}$$

The simplest (binary) variant of the problem assumes just two possible values for the power consumption of each appliance, i.e., $x_t^i = c_i \times a_i(t)$, that is to say that the power consumption of appliance i is constant and does not depend on the activity being performed by the appliance.

Under the aforementioned conditions, the disaggregation problem consists in finding values $a_i(t)$ associated to every appliance e_i.

3 Related Work

Several articles in the related literature have proposed methods for energy consumption disaggregation. The main related works are reviewed next.

One of the first publications on monitoring of energy consumption of household appliances was developed by Hart [5], who presented the concept of Non-Intrusive Load Monitoring (NILM), defined the energy disaggregation problem, and introduced a theoretical framework to standardize studies to solve it using software products. Instead of relegating the software to the task of data collection, Hart proposed an approach based on using a simple hardware and complex software for the analysis, thus eliminating permanent intrusion in homes.

The model proposed by Hart involves a combinatorial optimization (CO) problem to determine the vector $a(t)$ from X_t and y_i^t, in order to minimize the error (Eq. 2).

$$\hat{a}(t) = \arg\min_a \left| X_t - \sum_{i=1}^{n} a_i(t).y_i^t \right| \tag{2}$$

Given that the proposed combinatorial optimization problem is NP-hard, heuristic algorithms and other soft computing methods have been applied to efficiently solve it. Even though heuristics allow computing reasonable solutions, their applicability is limited in practice due to the uncertainty on the data and the high sensitiveness of the problem. Another approach consists in treating NILM as a learning problem, to be solved with computational intelligence methods, either applying supervised or unsupervised learning.

The survey by Bonfigli et al. [2] described the main techniques used for the unsupervised NILM problem and the available datasets. One of the most popular unsupervised learning techniques is Hidden Markov Models (HMM), based on defining hidden states for the problem model, representing the operating state of each appliance (on, off, other intermediate states), and the observable result that accounts for the real state, according to the consumption data.

Kelly and Knottenbelt [6] studied Artificial Neural Networks (ANN) for disaggregation in the NILM problem. One ANN was trained for each appliance, to predict the power demanded by it. Three ANN architectures were studied: recurrent LSTM, denoising autoencoder (dAE), and a rectangle network. The ANN were trained using synthetic and real data from the UK-DALE dataset. dAE and the rectangle network outperformed baseline CO and FHMM methods in F1-score, precision, and mean absolute error. LSTM outperformed CO and FHMM in on/off appliances but had poor results in multi-state appliances.

Batra et al. [1] developed the `nilmtk` tool for handling energy consumption datasets and implementing algorithms for processing and disaggregation, and metrics. The REDD dataset for energy disaggregation was collected and introduced by Kolter and Johnson [7], who also studied HMM model for disaggregation. Prediction in the training set was 64.5%, while prediction in the evaluation set was just 47.7%.

Our recent articles [3,4] presented a pattern detection algorithm to solve the energy disaggregation problem using aggregate consumption data. The experimental evaluation was performed over scenarios with different complexity. Results of the proposed pattern similarity method outperformed two built-in algorithms in the `nilmtk` framework, based on CO and a FHMM model.

4   Computational Intelligence Methods for Disaggregation

This section presents the proposed computational intelligence methods applied to solve the energy disaggregation problem.

4.1 Naive Bayes

Naive Bayes is a supervised classifier that makes predictions based on Bayes theorem. Naive Bayes assumes conditional independence between every pair of features, hence the "naive" term. If C is a set of possible classes for a vector of features $X = (x_1, x_2, ...x_n)$, the prediction c' is given by Eq. 3.

$$c' = argmax_{c \in C} \quad P(c) \prod P(x_i|c) \tag{3}$$

In this article, the Naive Bayes Gaussian implementation for $P(x_i|c)$ in scikit-learn (scikit-learn.org) is used.

4.2 K Nearest Neighbors

The K Nearest Neighbors (KNN) algorithm classifies a vector $X = (x_1, x_2, ...x_n)$ to the most repeated class in the k nearest neighbors of X, being k a highly sensitive parameter. In this article, the Euclidean distance between data points is used and neighbors relevance is weighted, so the closest to the sample have higher influence in the prediction.

4.3 Long Short Term Memory

LSTM neural networks are special kind of Recurrent Neural Networks (RNN). Recurrent networks differ from traditional feedforward ANN by accepting backwards connections and loops between neurons. This feature makes RNN specially good for time series analysis. However, because of backward connections, RNN are prone to suffer from the vanishing gradient problem. LSTM avoid this problem by replacing traditional neurons with more complex elements called cells, capable of remembering and forgetting pieces of information over iterations.

In this article, a five layer LSTM was implemented using the Keras library (keras.io). The implemented LSTM has the following architecture, selected after preliminary experiments that studied different configurations:

- An input layer, whose number of neurons is determined by the number of considered features of the problem.
- One LSTM bidirectional layer with 128 cell, TanH activation.
- One LSTM bidirectional layer with 256 cell, TanH activation.
- One LSTM simple layer with 256 cell, TanH activation.
- An output layer with one neuron fully connected with sigmoid activation.

The LSTM network is trained using Adam optimizer during 15 epochs with binary cross entrompy as loss function. Different windows sizes were used for each application in the experimental evaluation.

5 Experimental Evaluation

This section reports the experimental evaluation of the proposed computational intelligence methods for energy disaggregation.

5.1 Evaluation Methodology

Main Goals. The are two main goals concerning experimental evaluation. The first one is to find the most suitable method for the energy disaggregation problem by comparing the achieved results. The second one aims to identify the features that best describe appliances behavior.

Evaluated Features. The main features in the considered variant of the NILM problem are the aggregate power and the difference of aggregate power between consecutive measurements. The main goal is to learn unique fluctuations in the signal that could be associated with a certain appliance being switched on or off. However, is also interesting to evaluate if including other features to learn from lead to an improvement on the classification results. In this regard, the proposed approach complements raw aggregate power data with appliance-oriented features and human-oriented features. Appliance oriented features try to capture information about the appliances specific work cycle, for example, features like previously on, off-time and on-time. In turn, human-oriented features (e.g., hour, type of day, etc.) seek to capture the routine behavior of users.

In this article, the following features are considered:

- *Aggregate power:* The aggregate power consumption of the household.
- *Previously on:* A boolean value that indicates if the appliance was on on the previous time step.
- *On time:* The time in seconds that the appliance has been ON.
- *Off time:* The time in seconds that the appliance has been OFF.
- *Weekend:* A boolean value that indicates if the sample is from a weekend day or not.
- *Hour:* An integer value that represents the hour the sample has been taken.
- *Delta power:* The aggregate power difference between samples in consecutive timesteps.

Evaluation Scenarios. The studied computational intelligence methods are evaluated in five different scenarios that consider different features. Labeled data is required for supervised learning. Thus, each input vector should be assigned to either ON class or OFF class. Since UK-DALE is a timestamp-based dataset with different channels for appliances and total power, a mechanism must be established to label data. This article explores two labeling approaches. The first one only take into account aggregate samples that have matching measurements in the appliance data. This is a precise method, but tend to discard too many samples. On the other hand, as neural networks require as much data as possible to improve learning, a discrete time approach is also explored in order to avoid data loss. In this approach, the dataset is iterated over a time window, and each aggregate power window is labeled based on the majority of individual measurements in the appliance time windows.

Table 1 summarize the details of the five scenarios designed for the experimental evaluation, each of them using a different subset of the input features or a different approach to label data (continuous/discrete). Scenarios 1, 2, and 3

Table 1. Description of scenarios for the experimental evaluation.

Feature	Scenario 1	Scenario 2	Scenario 3	Scenario 4	Scenario 5
Aggregate power	✓	✓	✓	✓	-
Previously on	✓	-	✓	✓	✓
OFF time	✓	-	✓	✓	✓
ON time	-	-	-	-	✓
Weekend	✓	✓	✓	✓	✓
Hour	-	-	✓	✓	✓
Delta power	-	-	-	-	✓
Discrete time	-	-	-	✓	✓

only take into account matching samples between individual data and aggregate data from the dataset, and continuous time is considered. On the other hand, scenarios 4 and 5 are based on discrete time steps, considering an appliance is ON at certain step if the majority of its samples surpass the standby value.

Metrics. Well-known metrics for classification are used: accuracy, recall, precision and f1-score [10]. In the considered problem variant, in addition to the general classification results, it is also interesting to evaluate the capability of the studied models to detect the state changes, i.e., when appliances are turned ON or OFF. Thus, the percentage of correctly predicted state changes ($\%cpsc$) is also reported.

Data Instances. The data samples used in this work were gathered from the UK-DALE dataset, which includes records of the aggregated and individual power demand from five houses of the United Kingdom, sampled at 1/6 Hz between 2012 and 2017.

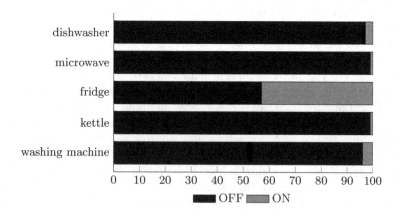

Fig. 1. Data distribution in ON/OFF classes.

In the considered instances, the five appliances that contributes the most to the overall electricity consumption are selected for the experimental evaluation: dishwasher, microwave, fridge, kettle and Washing machine. Figure 1 shows the data distribution among classes ON and OFF for each appliance.

Development and Execution Platform. The studied classifiers were implemented in Python 3.6 using Keras and scikit-learn libraries. The experimental analysis was performed on high-end servers with two Xeon Gold 6138 processors (40 cores each), Nvidia Tesla P100 GPUs (12 GB memory), 128 GB RAM memory, and 10 GbE from National Supercomputing Center (Cluster-UY), Uruguay [9].

Training. Input data was divided into three data sets for training (80%), validation (10%), and testing (10%). Scenarios 1–3 include 2702444 energy consumption records for dishwasher, 2466515 for microwave, 2343539 for fridge, 2665720 for kettle samples, and 2583668 for washing machine. On the other hand, scenarios 4 and 5 include 4531129 energy consumption records for dishwasher, 4467068 for microwave, 4464742 for fridge, 4394752 for kettle samples, and 4494437 for washing machine. Experiments to find the best parameter configuration of the learning methods were performed on a validation instance. In KNN, parameters *neighbors_number* and *weights* (whether or not neighbor relevance is pondered by distance) were tuned. In LSTM networks, the timestamp (number of past

Table 2. Parameter configuration.

Appliance	Scenario	Neighbor_number	Weigths	LSTM timesteps
Dishwasher	1	5	Uniform	-
	2	7	Distance	-
	3	7	Uniform	-
	4	-	-	5
	5	3	Uniform	3
Microwave	1	5	Uniform	-
	2	5	Uniform	-
	3	7	Uniform	-
	4	-	-	5
	5	3	Uniform	5
Fridge	1	5	Uniform	-
	2	7	Uniform	-
	3	5	Uniform	-
	4	-	-	3
	5	5	Uniform	3
Kettle	1	7	Uniform	-
	2	5	Uniform	-
	3	7	Uniform	-
	4	-	-	3
	5	7	Uniform	3
Washing machine	1	5	Uniform	-
	2	3	Uniform	-
	3	7	Uniform	-
	4	-	-	3
	5	3	Uniform	10

samples in memory) value was tuned. Table 2 reports the final values for each appliance and scenario.

5.2   Numerical Results

Tables 3, 4 and 5 reports the evaluation results for the studied classification methods over representative scenarios. The analysis focuses on the f1-score and %cpsc metrics, which provide quantitative information to assess the efficacy of the proposed methods. The best results for these metrics in each appliance are marked in bold face.

Table 3 reports the results of the Naive Bayes method in scenarios 1, 2, 3 and 5. These scenarios were considered in the evaluation in order to evaluate features impact on results (scenarios 1–3) and to compare against LSTM (scenario 5).

Table 3. Results of the Naive Bayes approach.

Appliance	Scenario	Accuracy	Precision	Recall	f1-score	% *cpsc*
Dishwasher	1	0.97	0.45	0.37	0.41	11
	2	0.97	0.43	0.37	0.40	11
	3	0.97	0.53	0.49	0.50	7
	5	0.99	0.80	0.88	0.84	5
Microwave	1	0.97	0.05	0.78	0.10	48
	2	0.96	0.03	0.60	0.06	**50**
	3	0.97	0.10	0.67	0.10	28
	5	0.99	0.18	0.79	0.29	29
Fridge	1	0.97	0.96	0.96	0.96	0
	2	0.58	0.60	0.04	0.08	2
	3	0.99	0.98	0.98	0.98	0
	5	0.98	0.98	0.98	0.98	0
Kettle	1	0.99	0.17	0.91	0.28	75
	2	0.99	0.17	0.91	0.28	75
	3	0.97	0.17	0.88	0.29	67
	5	0.99	0.35	0.69	0.47	41
Washing machine	1	0.96	0.31	0.36	0.33	4
	2	0.95	0.25	0.36	0.29	4
	3	0.96	0.37	0.35	0.36	3
	5	0.98	0.69	0.60	0.64	2

Results in Table 3 indicate that the Naive Bayes method just computed accurate values of the f1-score metric for the fridge in three out of four scenarios, while acceptable results were obtained for the dishwasher and the washing machine in just one scenario. Regarding the state changes, Naive Bayes only computed accurate results for kettle in three scenarios and for microwave in a single scenario. Results for other metrics (in particular, precision and recall) and other appliances were not accurate, suggesting that a simple Bayesian approach is not enough to solve the problem.

Table 4 reports the K Nearest Neighbors results for scenarios 1, 2, 3 and 5.

Table 4. Results of the K Nearest Neighbors method.

Appliance	Scenario	Accuracy	Precision	Recall	f1-score	% cpsc
Dishwasher	1	0.99	0.95	0.97	0.96	**41**
	2	0.97	0.61	0.17	0.26	6
	3	0.99	0.96	0.97	0.97	19
	5	0.99	0.97	0.98	0.97	31
Microwave	1	0.99	0.78	0.69	0.73	41
	2	0.99	0.37	0.25	0.30	19
	3	0.99	0.88	0.74	0.81	24
	5	0.99	0.68	0.65	0.67	22
Fridge	1	0.97	0.97	0.96	0.97	55
	2	0.64	0.57	0.62	0.60	37
	3	0.98	0.97	0.98	0.98	15
	5	0.99	0.98	0.98	0.98	49
Kettle	1	0.99	0.77	0.61	0.68	47
	2	0.99	0.35	0.19	0.25	20
	3	0.99	0.85	0.73	0.79	38
	5	0.99	0.86	0.82	0.84	53
Washing machine	1	0.99	0.75	0.82	0.78	23
	2	0.95	0.21	0.18	0.19	9
	3	0.99	0.83	0.87	0.85	11
	5	0.99	0.86	0.90	0.88	21

Results in Table 4 indicate that the K Nearest Neighbors method computed accurate results for the dishwasher and the fridge (for both appliances, in three out of four scenarios). Acceptable results were computed for microwave, kettle, and washing machine (three out of four scenarios for each appliance). Results in scenario 2 were significantly lower than for other scenarios. The efficacy on scenario 5 was significantly better than the Naive Bayes method, except for the fridge (where both methods computed accurate results). Regarding state changes, K Nearest Neighbors improved over Naive Bayes, but just managed to achieve the better result in one scenario for the dishwasher. Correctly predicted state changes for fridge were significantly better than using Naive Bayes. These results indicate that, overall, K Nearest Neighbors is a better method to solve the problem when compared with Naive Bayes.

Table 5 reports LSTM results for scenarios 4 and 5. The experimental evaluation of LSTM focused on discrete time scenarios, because continue time scenarios (1–3) have a significantly lower number of training samples and LSTM performs poorly when few data is available due to the lack of a proper training.

Table 5. Results of the Long Short Term Memory neural network.

Appliance	Scenario	Accuracy	Precision	Recall	f1-score	% cpsc
Dishwasher	4	0.99	0.97	0.97	0.97	35
	5	0.99	0.99	0.97	**0.98**	35
Microwave	4	0.99	0.92	0.72	**0.81**	28
	5	0.99	0.80	0.77	0.78	40
Fridge	4	0.99	0.99	0.99	0.99	63
	5	0.99	0.99	0.99	**0.99**	**71**
Kettle	4	0.99	0.95	0.87	0.91	69
	5	0.99	0.94	0.90	**0.92**	**75**
Washing machine	4	0.99	0.88	0.92	0.90	24
	5	0.99	0.90	0.93	**0.91**	**31**

Results in Table 5 indicate that the LSTM neural network was able to compute accurate results for both studied scenarios, for four of the five studied appliances. Results of the f1-score metric were over 0.97 for dishwasher, 0.99 for fridge, over 0.91 for kettle, and over 0.90 for washing machine. The lowest f1-score values were computed for the microwave (0.81 and 0.78), which turns to be the home appliance with the highest variability of duration and utilization period. Similar results were computed for the other learning metrics, in which LSTM consistently outperformed both Naive Bayes and K Nearest Neighbors methods. The number of correctly predicted state changes significantly improved over the other reference learning methods too, achieving maximum of 75 for kettle and 71 for fridge.

Overall Results. Overall, results reported in Tables 3, 4 and 5 indicate that the studied methods computed different f1-score values and %cpsc for each studied appliance. For the dishwasher, the highest f1-score was 0.98, achieved by the LSTM neural network in scenario 5, whereas the highest percentage of state change detection was 41%, reached by KNN in scenario 1. In microwave, both KNN and LSTM computed the maximum value of f1-score (0.81) in scenarios 3 and 4, respectively. In turn, the highest state change percentage was achieved by

Naive Bayes in scenario 1. The LSTM neural network in scenario 5 achieved the highest values of f1-score and state change detection percentage for the fridge (0.99 and 71%, respectively), the kettle (0.92 and 75%, respectively), and the washing machine (0.91 and 31%, respectively). Overall, LSTM computed the best results for discrete time scenarios and KNN was the best method for continuous time scenarios. These results suggest that if only small data sets are available for training, LSTM neural networks are not able to learn properly the utilization patterns. In these cases, KNN should be used as a promising alternative, as it provides accurate results.

The graph bars in Figs. 2, 3, 4, 5 and 6 presents the comparison of the f1-score and %cpsc metrics for each appliance, for the methods and scenarios considered in the experimental evaluation (labels of the x axis correspond to [method]-s[scenario]).

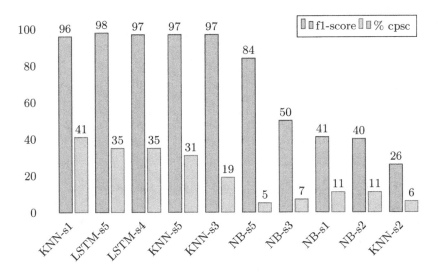

Fig. 2. Comparison of f1-score and %cpsc for the dishwasher.

5.3 Summary

Several relevant conclusion from the analysis are summarized next.

From the Appliance Perspective: Target appliances have different properties (utilization time, utilization period, power demand, etc.) that impact on the classification task. A single pair of one classifier and one feature set may not be the

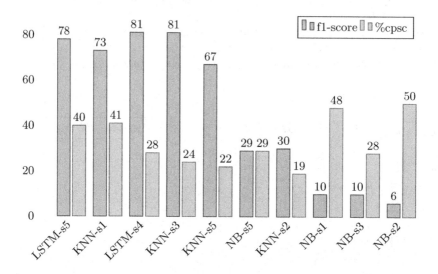

Fig. 3. Comparison of f1-score and %cpsc for the microwave.

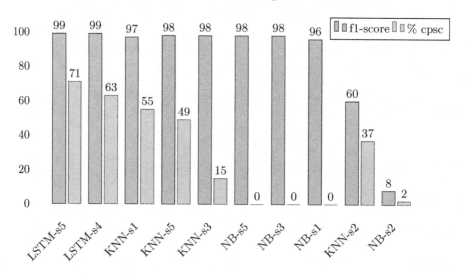

Fig. 4. Comparison of f1-score and %cpsc for the fridge.

best option to solve the problem for every appliance, so it is relevant to study results for each appliance separately.

Washing machine and dishwasher are human-activated appliances that have similar proportion of ON and OFF classes in the considered dataset. Both have multiple consumption levels over a single work cycle that could lead to miss-clasify power fluctuations as activations of other appliances in the house. On the other hand, once these appliances are switched on, they tend to operate during a fixed time. Results show that classification metrics were high for both KNN and LSTM. However, the percentage of correctly predicted state changes was poor compared to other appliances like fridge or kettle. Fridge activations are not human dependent. This appliance also has a well defined consumption pattern, with a balanced distribution between OFF and ON classes. This behavior explains high values of f1-score and correct state change predictions in LSTM networks. The kettle is a high power demand appliance that once is switched on, works over a short period of time. High values in both f1-scores and state change predictions could be associated with the impact this appliance has in aggregate signal. In turn, poor results achieved at microwave classification could be explained as it has the most variable working pattern of all appliances.

From the Method Perspective: In general, results show that the best performance among appliances is achieved by LSTM neural networks. This fact confirms the LSTM pattern recognition potential, especially considering that, in general, the next state of an appliance is determined by previous behaviour.

From the Feature Perspective: Poor results in scenario 2 confirmed that including features about previous states of appliances as input allows improving the

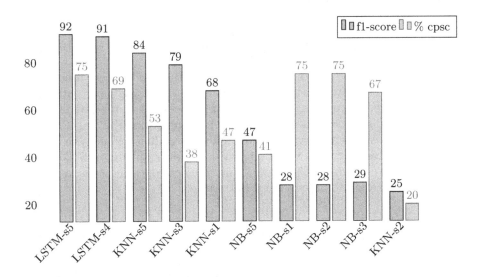

Fig. 5. Comparison of f1-score and %cpsc for the kettle.

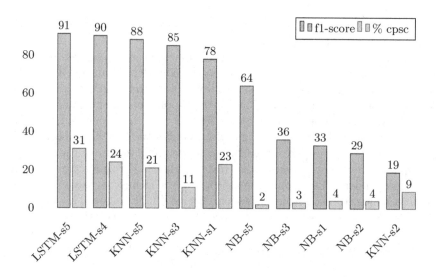

Fig. 6. Comparison of f1-score and %cpsc for the washing machine.

classification results. The LSTM improvement between scenarios 4 and 5 in every appliance allows concluding that *on time* and *delta power* features are helpful to detect on and off transitions.

6   Conclusions and Future Work

This article studied the application of computational intelligence techniques to solve the binary variant of the energy disaggregation problem. A Naive Bayes classifier, a K nearest neighbor classifier, and a LSTM neural network were evaluated on five different appliances considering real data from the UK-DALE dataset. Five different sets of input features were used.

Results of the experimental evaluation showed that LSTM neural networks are suitable for classification task and are able to reach high percentages of correctly predicted state changes for some appliances. The proposed methods can be integrated on smart energy management frameworks [8].

The main lines for future work are related to extending the analysis of relevant input features that improve classification, exploring different LSTM architectures, integrate the `nilmtk` framework into the developed methods, and analyze the generalization to unseen usage patterns.

References

1. Batra, N., et al.: NILMTK: an open source toolkit for non-intrusive load monitoring. In: 5th International Conference on Future Energy Systems, pp. 265–276 (2014)

2. Bonfigli, R., Squartini, S., Fagiani, M., Piazza, F.: Unsupervised algorithms for non-intrusive load monitoring: an up-to-date overview. In: 15th International Conference on Environment and Electrical Engineering (2015)
3. Chavat, J., Graneri, J., Nesmachnow, S.: Household energy disaggregation based on pattern consumption similarities. In: Nesmachnow, S., Hernández Callejo, L. (eds.) ICSC-CITIES 2019. CCIS, vol. 1152, pp. 54–69. Springer, Cham (2020). https://doi.org/10.1007/978-3-030-38889-8_5
4. Chavat, J., Nesmachnow, S., Graneri, J.: Non-intrusive energy disaggregation by detecting similarities in consumption patterns. Revista Facultad de Ingeniería Universidad de Antioquia (2020)
5. Hart, G.: Nonintrusive appliance load monitoring. Proc. IEEE **80**(12), 1870–1891 (1992)
6. Kelly, J., Knottenbelt, W.: The UK-DALE dataset, domestic appliance-level electricity demand and whole-house demand from five UK homes. Sci. Data **2**(150007), 1–14 (2015)
7. Kolter, J., Johnson, M.: Redd: a public data set for energy disaggregation research. In: Workshop on Data Mining Applications in Sustainability, pp. 59–62 (2011)
8. Luján, E., Otero, A., Valenzuela, S., Mocskos, E.E., Steffenel, L.A., Nesmachnow, S.: An integrated platform for smart energy management: the CC-SEM project. Revista Facultad de Ingeniería Universidad de Antioquia (2019)
9. Nesmachnow, S., Iturriaga, S.: Cluster-UY: collaborative scientific high performance computing in Uruguay. In: Torres, M., Klapp, J. (eds.) ISUM 2019. CCIS, vol. 1151, pp. 188–202. Springer, Cham (2019). https://doi.org/10.1007/978-3-030-38043-4_16
10. Sokolova, M., Japkowicz, N., Szpakowicz, S.: Beyond accuracy, F-score and ROC: a family of discriminant measures for performance evaluation. In: Sattar, A., Kang, B. (eds.) AI 2006. LNCS (LNAI), vol. 4304, pp. 1015–1021. Springer, Heidelberg (2006). https://doi.org/10.1007/11941439_114
11. Turner, W., Doty, S.: Energy management handbook. The Fairmont Press, Lilburn (2007)
12. U.S. Energy Information Administration (EIA): Energy use in homes, June 2020. https://www.eia.gov/

Demand Response Control in Electric Water Heaters: Evaluation of Impact on Thermal Comfort

Rodrigo Porteiro[1]([✉])(iD), Juan Chavat[2](iD), Sergio Nesmachnow[2](iD), and Luis Hernández-Callejo[3](iD)

[1] Administración Nacional de Usinas y Transmisiones Eléctricas, Montevideo, Uruguay
rporteiro@ute.com.uy
[2] Universidad de la República, Montevideo, Uruguay
{juan.pablo.chavat,sergion}@fing.edu.uy
[3] Universidad de Valladolid, Valladolid, Spain
luis.hernandez.callejo@uva.es

Abstract. Energy demand management is an important technique for smart grids, under the paradigm of smart cities. Direct control of devices is useful for demand management, but it has the disadvantage of affecting user comfort. This article presents an approach for defining an index to estimate the discomfort associated with an active demand management consisting of the interruption of domestic electric water heaters to perform a load shifting. The index is defined based on estimations of water utilization and water temperature using continuous power consumption measurements of water heaters. A stochastic forecasting model is applied, including an Extra Trees Regressor and a linear model for water temperature. Monte Carlo simulations are performed to calculate the defined index. The evaluation of the proposed approach is performed using real data for both the forecasting model and the temperature model. The real effect of interruptions on the water temperature of two water heaters is compared to validate that the thermal discomfort index correctly models the impact on temperature. This result allows ordering devices by their thermal discomfort index and having a fair criterion to decide which ones should be interrupted.

1 Introduction

The concept of energy demand management is very relevant in nowadays smart cities, especially considering the smart grid paradigm [12]. Energy demand management refers to administering the energy consumption of end consumers of an electric grid, in order to promote better energy utilization. The most widely applied actions for demand management are load management (aimed at modifying/reducing/shifting the demand) and energy conservation (aimed at reducing the demand via technological improvements). Other actions applied for demand management include fuel substitution and load building [2]. Among load management techniques, the most used are peak reduction (reducing consumption

© Springer Nature Switzerland AG 2021
S. Nesmachnow and L. Hernández Callejo (Eds.): ICSC-CITIES 2020, CCIS 1359, pp. 74–89, 2021.
https://doi.org/10.1007/978-3-030-69136-3_6

in periods of maximum demand), valley filling (promoting energy utilization in off-peak periods), and load shifting (from peak to off-peak periods).

In daily operation, electricity generation and transmission systems may not always meet peak demand requirements. In these situations, various demand response and demand management tools can be used in order to mitigate overloads in the electrical system. One of the simplest methods for direct load control is allowing the electrical company to remotely control those devices with thermostat, especially those that have important thermal inertia. Remote control is a very effective technique to achieve peak reduction and load shifting at critical moments. However, the benefits of the reduction in the operating cost of the electrical system must be weighted against the loss of comfort that the users of the controlled devices may have. Assigning an economic value to the loss of comfort associated with an intervention requires quantifying such comfort in advance.

In the main Uruguayan cities, more than 90% of households have a thermostat-controlled electric water heater (according to the 2019 continuous household survey by National Statistics Institute, Uruguay [6]) Furthermore, electric water heater is one of the most energy-intensive household appliances (it represents 34% of residential energy consumption, in average). Thus, it is an ideal candidate to be considered for remote load control as demand management technique.

In this line of work, this article proposes a methodology to calculate a Thermal Discomfort Index (TDI), associated with a remote intervention for load management. The computed index evaluates the discomfort for users generated by the intervention of an electric water heater. TDI is computed from real data, a linear temperature model, and a forecasting model for water utilization applying artificial neural networks (ANN). The obtained TDI makes it possible to decide in which order the electric water heaters should be interrupted to minimize total discomfort. The key aspect of the proposed methodology is to know in advance the value of the TDI, in order to decide if it is economically profitable to carry out an intervention.

The experimental analysis is performed using data from real electric water heaters in Uruguay, gathered in the ECD-UY dataset [3]. ECD-UY includes power consumption utilization of water heaters installed with remote control and power measurement device in representative households in the main Uruguayan cities. Results reported for the considered case study demonstrate that the proposed index managed to capture the impact of thermal discomfort, fulfilling the objective of sorting electric water heaters to be properly managed by applying a direct control strategy.

The article is organized as follows. Section 2 presents the formulation of the demand management problem through direct control of devices and reviews related works. Section 3 describes the proposed approach to define a TDI. Details of the developed implementation are provided in Sect. 4. Section 5 reports the experimental validation of the water utilization forecasting, the temperature model, and the proposed index for a case study. Finally, Sect. 6 formulates the main conclusions and lines for future work.

2   Demand Management and Direct Control of Electric Water Heaters

This section describes demand management strategies, direct load control applied to load shifting, and the problem of affecting comfort of the end user.

2.1   Demand Management

The traditional model of an electric system feeds electricity to the end consumers through a unidirectional power flow. This flow is supplied by centrally controlled generators. With the development of energy markets and distributed energy resources, the concept of energy demand management has emerged. This concept includes a set of techniques oriented to modify the energy demand of consumers of an electric grid to fulfill specific goals [4]. The subset of these techniques that try to reduce the energy demand of consumers in the short term is known as demand response.

This article focuses on direct load control, a technique that is considered as an effective way to achieve immediate power reduction in a very short time. To handle this technique, the electricity utility must have permission to switch off the devices of end-users, which is usually obtained via specific agreements that grant users a monetary incentive. Among the main reasons for power reduction are implementing peak reduction [5], which allows obtaining a more stable grid, and providing frequency regulation services [22], which allows maintaining the system frequency very close 60 Hz, preventing deviations that affect generators and also make the grid unstable. This article addresses some aspects related to the direct load control of electric water heaters, mainly focusing on the impact of using this tool in the thermal comfort of end-users.

2.2   Load Shifting with Direct Control of Electric Water Heaters

In most countries of the world, the profile of total electricity demand consumption shows a pronounced peak two hours after the return of workers to their homes. Usually, the power consumption of electric water heaters also presents a peak that coincides with the total consumption peak as shown in Fig. 1, which is explained by the showers that people take when they return from work. In addition, electric water heaters have the ability to accumulate energy in the form of heat inside the water tank. Thus, it is possible to switch off the device in a smart way, so that users thermal comfort is not affected.

According to the aforementioned correlation, in the presence of a demand peak, there is an amount of energy associated with the electric water heaters that can be deferred by turning off the devices in a moment, and turning them on in the future. Using this strategy, a load shifting on the demand curve is implemented, because the total amount of energy remains equal but the load profile is modified. Several studies have addressed the load shifting problem using direct control of devices, but few of them have focused on quantifying the thermal discomfort generated by the application of this technique.

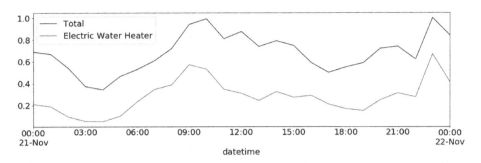

Fig. 1. (Normalized) total power and electric water heater demand in a weekday

2.3   Problem Formulation and Related Works

Problem Formulation. The problem proposes determining a *TDI* to evaluate quantitatively, the discomfort generated by the application of load shifting using a direct control of electric water heaters.

To address the problem, the first step consists in analyzing which variables are involved. In the case of electric water heaters, the variable that affects comfort is the temperature of the water in the tank. Installing a remote device to the water heater that allows measuring its power and switching it on/off is reasonable since it can be achieved without modifying its structure [15,16]. However, installing a remote thermometer to measure the temperature of the tank requires modifying structure of the water heater, which implies a large monetary investment.

The most important issue when analyzing comfort is comparing the same controlling action between several electric water heaters, in order to decide which of them can be affected while minimizing the probability of generating discomfort. Therefore, it is not crucial to determine the temperature exactly; computing a good approximation is enough to analyzing differences. Another aspect that seems trivial but worth to consider is that users perceives thermal discomfort only when they use water and its temperature is below a threshold. At any other time, users does not give relevance to the water temperature.

According to the considered aspects, to define an index of discomfort in the event of an intervention, the water utilization and the temperature of the water in the tank must be estimated. The proposed approach addresses these two lines of work and defines a discomfort index based on the corresponding findings.

Related Works. Several works in the literature refer to peak load reduction strategies implemented in smart grids [5,25]. A special type of devices to perform load shifting are thermostatically-controlled appliances (TCA), due to the flexibility to select the thermostat set point [8,18]. Some TCA can store energy, providing a great advantage when performing load shifting strategies. This is the case of domestic electric water heaters, which are the focus of this article. Nehrir [13] analyzed an interactive demand side management strategy for electric water heaters, but without elaborating on specific aspects of thermal discomfort. Xiang [23] studied a complex strategy to minimize thermal discomfort related with electric water heater control. The proposed strategy required a large amount of information. Thus, the approach is difficult to apply in practice.

TCA demand response control strategies can be effectively implemented provided that thermal comfort is not compromised. This crucial issue has been the focus of several works. Kampelis [7] evaluated thermal discomfort in demand response control of heating, ventilation, and air conditioning, but the strategy used requires knowing the real temperature. Regarding electric water heaters, the study of the user hot water utilization profile is a key aspect for estimating discomfort. Seyed [21] studied whether a smart heating system can benefit from good predictions of the user behaviour. In turn, Pirow [19] proposed an algorithm for the estimation of domestic hot water utilization, but the technique requires the installation of temperature and vibration sensors.

The main factor that defines comfort is the water temperature. Thus, a model to estimate water temperature is crucial for the effectiveness of the comfort evaluation. Paull [17] proposed a water heater model to estimate the temperature of the water in the tank as a function of time and the related variables. The study by Lutz [10] provided a comprehensive empirical analysis of a simplified energy consumption model for water heaters considering the variation of the temperature of the water in the tank. Finally, comfort evaluation must be considered in the problem of controlling a subset of electric water heaters using a ranking that sorts the devices according to an appropriate criteria. Yin [24] proposed a scheduling strategy based on a temperature state priority list. In turn, Al-Jabery [1] analyzed a scheduling strategy for electric water heaters based on approximate dynamic programming techniques and q-learning.

The analysis of related works indicates that few articles have studied the thermal comfort effect when applying direct load control of electric water heaters. This article contributes in this line of work, by proposing an approach to evaluate the thermal discomfort of an intervention on electric water heaters, without requiring installing a thermometer to measure the water temperature.

3   The Proposed Approach for Defining a Discomfort Index

This section describes the proposed approach for defining a discomfort index applying ideas described in the previous section and following a data analysis approach [9,11] over a group of 140 remotely controlled electric water heaters located in Uruguay.

3.1   Data Preparation

The data used in this article was provided by the Uruguayan National Electricity Company (UTE). It corresponds to "Electric water heater consumption", one of the three subsets included in the EDC-UY dataset [3], which gathers data from 521 households located in the main Uruguayan cities.

Electric water heater consumption records has a sample period of one minute and cover a date range from 12th July 2017 to 26th June 2019. Customer records were filtered by the recording length, keeping only those that have more than 5 months of recording (i.e., at least 216.000 records).

The disaggregated electric water heater data have several gaps caused by different problems during the data collection process (e.g., misworking of the data transmission network, power failures, etc.). The gaps were fixed using two techniques: resampling and refilling.

The resampling technique normalizes the sample period to an exact minute. First, the records are grouped by customers to build one-minute record containers. Then, records whose datetime match with the date range of the container, are assigned to it. In case one or more records match the same container, the minimum consumption value is set, otherwise, a null value is set. The resulting data is taken as the input of the refilling technique. First, data gaps (i.e., consecutive missed records) are detected and refilled according to the following criteria. Starting from both extremes of the gap up to seven minutes forward/backwards, the missing data is recreated by a linear interpolation method. Finally, if missing values are still present at the gap (i.e., gaps is larger than 14 min), zero values are assigned. The described process results in normalized time series of consumption values without gaps.

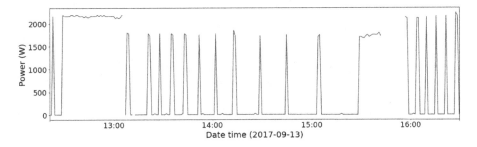

Fig. 2. A fragment of the electricity consumption of an electric water heater (meter id. 466147) before refilling the data gaps.

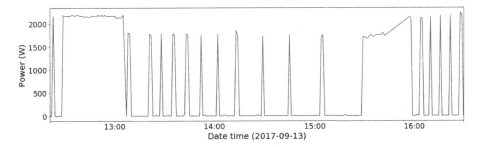

Fig. 3. A fragment of the electricity consumption of an electric water heater (meter id. 466147) after refilling the data gaps.

A Jupyter notebook was implemented for data preparation, based on scripts provided by ECD-UY, using Python (version 3) programming language, and libraries Pandas and Numpy. The resulting notebook is available to download from https://bit.ly/2RNO8SW. The effects of refilling on electric water heater activation is observed in Fig. 2 (missing records) and Fig. 3 (after processing).

3.2 Water Utilization Forecasting Model

Description. A particularity of electric water heaters is that when they are on, their power consumption has just slight variations, and it can be considered as constant. Therefore, the load curve can be represented in a binary format (0 when off and C when on). Lets consider a time interval in which the electric water heater is switched on continuously (defined as an *on block*). From the analysis of the power consumption time series, some of these blocks are associated with water utilization and other blocks correspond to thermal recoveries to maintain the target temperature of the water.

The proposed forecasting model is based on identifying the *on blocks* associated with water utilization and discarding those corresponding to thermal recoveries. In this regard, a threshold duration is defined, and any *on block* shorter than the threshold duration is considered to be a thermal recovery block and discarded. This is a robust approach, since discarding short blocks is not relevant for the main goal of identifying long-term utilization blocks, which are generally associated with showers. The analysis considers as a baseline an electric water heater with a capacity of 60 l and an average water outlet flow rate, for which the duration of the *on block* is approximately eight times the duration of the utilization period. Applying this approximation, the information about *on blocks* can be converted into water utilization. Figure 4 presents an example of *on blocks* and water utilization obtained with the aforementioned procedure.

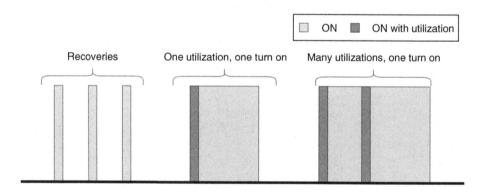

Fig. 4. Example of *on blocks* and water utilization patterns observed in the electric water heater consumption.

Features Considered for Training. An ExtraTrees Regressor model [20] was applied to train the forecasting model, considering the following input features:

- *Use* (120 Boolean values), indicating whether a water utilization occurs in the past 120 min.
- *Month* (integer), indicating the month of the horizon to forecast.
- *Day* (integer), indicating the day of the horizon to forecast.
- *Hour* (integer), indicating the hour of the horizon to forecast.
- *Dayofweek* (integer), indicating the day of the horizon to forecast.
- *Workingday* (boolean), indicating whether the horizon to forecast is a working day or not.

The output of the model is a vector of 120 Boolean values, indicating the forecast of water utilization for the next two hours.

Evaluation. The standard mean absolute percentage error (*MAPE*) metric is applied for evaluating the proposed model. *MAPE* is defined in Eq. 1, where $actual_i$ represents the measured value for $t = i$, $pred_i$ represents the predicted value, and n is the predicted horizon length.

$$MAPE = 100 \times \frac{1}{n} \sum_{i=1}^{n} \left| \frac{actual_i - pred_i}{actual_i} \right| \tag{1}$$

3.3   Water Temperature Model

The equations for water heating and cooling in a water tank have exponential components and depend on several variables, including the insulation factor, the ambient temperature, the flow of water used, the time of use, the tank volume, among other factors [10]. However, the proposed model applying the *on blocks* and the estimation of water utilization makes it possible to define a linear temperature model, which provides a good approximation in order to estimate the *TDI*.

Five parameters are defined to build the temperature model from the data of *on blocks* and water utilization:

1. T_{min}: temperature at which the electric water heater is turned on by the action of the thermostat when the water is cooling.
2. T_{max} : temperature at which the electric water heater is turned off by the action of the thermostat when the water is heating.
3. c_{heat}: slope of the line when the electric water heater is turned on.
4. c_{cool}: slope of the line when the electric water heater is turned off and no water is being used.
5. c_{use}: slope of the line when using water, whether or not water is being used.

The considered parameters depend on several factors. This article proposes a specific approach to approximate their values, to assure that if a temperature approximation error occurs, it is always underestimated. This way, the proposed model is conservative about comfort estimation. It is assumed that the user sets the thermostat at a temperature value of 60°, with $T_{min} = 55°$ and $T_{max} = 65°$. The approximation model can be improved by considering more accurate values for T_{min} and T_{max}, which could be requested to the users, e.g., via a survey or web/mobile application. Figure 5 presents a schema of the proposed model definition from *on blocks* and water utilization. Grey *on blocks* represents thermal recoveries, and *on blocks* caused by water utilization are marked in red.

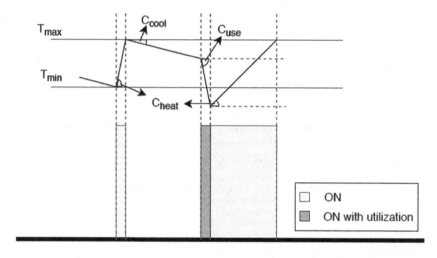

Fig. 5. Linear temperature model (Color figure online)

The analysis of the temperature curve in Fig. 5 indicates that the water cools with a slope c_{cool} until it reaches T_{min}, and at that moment the electric water heater turns on. Heating phase starts with a slope c_{heat} until the temperature reaches T_{max}. Then, another cooling phase occurs until a water utilization causes a much faster cooling with a slope c_{use}. During the water utilization, the electric water heater turns on almost immediately after opening the water stream. After the utilization ends, the electric water heater remains on because the water temperature is below T_{min}, so it heats the water with a slope c_{heat} until T_{max} temperature is reached, where the gray *on block* ends. Assuming the described behaviour, the three slopes can be computed applying simple algebra.

The described procedure allows computing an approximation of the water temperature in a given interval from a set of *on blocks* and water utilization data in that interval. Therefore, a temperature forecast can be obtained from a set of *on blocks* predicted for a future time interval.

3.4   Defining the *TDI*

The proposed *TDI* aims at capturing the thermal impact that a user suffers due to an intervention by the electrical utility in the electric water heater, using the defined water utilization forecasting and the temperature model. Since every forecast has uncertainty, *TDI* is defined in terms of the expected value of the difference of the aforementioned temperatures, as expressed by Eqs. 2 and 3.

$$TDI(I) = E_w \left[\sum_{u \in U(w)} TDI(I, u, w) \right] \tag{2}$$

$$TDI(I, u, w) = \int_{t_{ini}(u)}^{t_{end}(u)} (T_n(t, w) - T_{int}(t, w))dt + \rho \int_{t \in \tau} (T_{comf} - T_{int}(t, w))dt \tag{3}$$

In Eq. 2, I refers to the interruption of the electric water heater by the electric company, E_w represents the expected value of the indicator, considering all the forecasting realizations. $U(w)$ is the set of water utilization intervals in the analyzed time horizon (several of them can occur in the studied period).

In Eq. 3, $TDI(I, u, w)$ represents the discomfort index of an interruption, a water utilization, and a realization w that defines a single scenario of temperature evolution. $t_{ini}(u)$ and $t_{end}(u)$ are the starting and finishing time of utilization u. For realization w, $T_n(t, w)$ is the temperature curve without interruption and $T_{int}(t, w)$ is the temperature curve with interruption. Finally, T_{comf} is the water temperature below which the user feels discomfort, and τ represents the time interval in which $T_{int}(t, w) \leq T_{comf}$. The value ρ is a penalty attributed to the area below the comfort temperature.

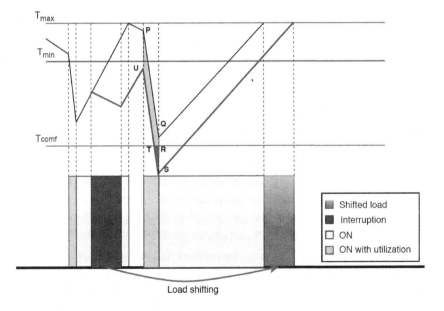

Fig. 6. Graphical representation of *TDI* (Color figure online)

Figure 6 presents a visual representation of $TDI(I, u, w)$. The green area between the curve of temperature without interruption and the curve of temperature with interruption (defined by points PQRTU) is obtained from the integral $\int_{t_{ini}(u)}^{t_{end}(u)} (T_n(t, w) - T_{int}(t, w))dt$, representing the loss of heat due to the interruption. Additionally, the area below the comfort temperature (defined by points RST and represented in red) is computed as $\int_{t \in \tau}(T_{comf} - T_{int}(t, w))dt$, and weighted by the penalty ρ.

4   Implementation

This section describes the implementation of the proposed approach for defining *TDI*.

4.1   Development and Execution Platforms

The proposed models were implemented on Python. Several scientific libraries and packages were used to handle data, train models and visualize results, including Pandas, Numpy, and Tensorflow. The experimental analysis was performed on National Supercomputing Center (Cluster-UY), Uruguay [14].

4.2   Implementation Details

Water Utilization Forecasting Model. An Extratrees regression model was trained using input features and output described in Subsect. 3.2. Parameter search techniques were applied using a grid search implemented with Grid-SearchCV, the standard tool from `scikit-learn`. GridSearchCV uses it with an estimator using cross-validation and a predetermined metric to evaluate the models.

Linear Temperature Model. The implementation of the temperature model requires knowing values T_{min} and T_{max}. Then, using the information of *on blocks* and water utilization data, coefficients c_{cool}, c_{heat} and c_{use} are determined.

4.3   *TDI* Calculation

A Monte Carlo simulation method is applied to compute the expected value of *TDI*, defined by Eq. 2. 100 realizations of w with distribution $N(0, 1)$ are sampled. Then, for each value of w, the following procedure is applied:

– The next 12 h are forecasted using the model described in Sect. 3.2.
– Using the temperature model described in Sect. 3.3 and the water utilization forecast for the next 12 h, the water temperature is obtained for that period.
– An interruption of k minutes is simulated and the temperature for the next 12 h is obtained using the proposed temperature model.

- Since T_{max}, T_{min}, T_{comf} are known, Eq. 3 is applied to compute $TDI(I, u, w)$ for all uses.
- An auxiliary variable $S_{uses}(w) = \sum_{u \in U(w)} TDI(I, u, w)$ is computed.

Finally, after computing $S_{uses}(w)$ for each realization, TDI is computed as the empirical expected value: $TDI(I) = \sum_{w=1}^{w=100} S_{uses}(w)/100$.

5   Experimental Validation

This section presents the experimental validation of the proposed approach for defining a TDI.

5.1   Water Utilization Forecasting

Metrics defined in Sect. 3.2 were applied to evaluate the implementation of the proposed two hours water utilization forecasting model. A subset of data in ECD-UY was used, consisting of ten electric water heaters with more than five consecutive months of measurements. The grid search procedure was performed on a two-dimensional grid to determine the best values for the number of trees in the forest and the maximum depth of the tree. The best parameter setting found by the grid search was $n\_estimators = 50$, $max\_depth = 200$.

Using the best parameter configuration, the ExtraTrees regressor achieved a $MAPE$ value of 11.79 in just 4.09 s of execution time. This accuracy is adequate for the estimation purposes to compute TDI, considering the high variance in the water utilization of an individual electric water heater. The method provides a useful tool for generating scenarios to apply the Monte Carlo simulation approach, to estimate the empirical probability distribution of water utilization.

5.2   Water Temperature Model

The linear model described in Sect. 3.3 was determined for a real electric water heater having a thermometer to measure the temperature of the water in the tank. Values of $T_{min} = 55\,°C$ and $T_{max} = 65\,°C$ are known for this water heater, due to the setting of the thermostat. Parameters of the model are calculated as described in Sect. 5.1. Then, data of twelve hours *on blocks* of the electric water heater were used to estimate the temperature, and compared with the real temperature measured. Table 1 reports the comparison of the real and the estimated temperature, and the largest difference in the three long utilizations in the twelve hours analyzed.

Table 1. Accuracy of the water temperature model

	1st utilization	2st utilization	3st utilization
Measured temperature	59.09 °C	53.03 °C	58.34 °C
Linear temperature	59.88 °C	55.12 °C	59.41 °C
Difference	0.79 °C	2.09 °C	1.07 °C

The second utilization had the largest temperature difference (2.7 °C, marked in light blue in Table 1), which represents a percentage error of 4.5% in the worst case. The other utilizations had a significantly lower error. The accuracy of the temperature model is adequate for the purpose of estimating *TDI*.

5.3 *TDI* Calculation

One of the main challenges related to the definition of *TDI* is modeling the differences of temperature (ΔT, quantitative factor) between performing an interruption in different moments. A relevant case is analyzing the ΔT values situations in the interruption affects the most to comfort.

As a relevant sample study, the comparison of the *TDI* for two different values of ρ and two particular electric water heaters (EWH_1 and EWH_2) is presented. The considered electric water heaters model two different utilization patterns from two different users. On weekdays, EWH_1 has two consecutive utilizations, and EWH_2 is only used once. The *TDI* associated with a 20-minute interruption between 20:10 and 20:30. Figure 7 presents the empirical distribution of uses ($P(u)$) from 19:00 to 22:00 for EWH_1 (left) and EWH_2 (right). For each case, the interruption period is represented by the orange band.

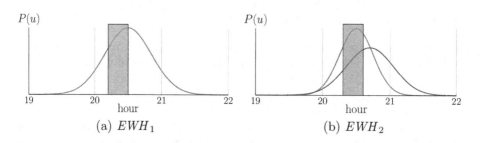

(a) EWH_1 (b) EWH_2

Fig. 7. Probability distribution for water utilization of two electric water heaters.

For the presented example, it is expected for the *TDI* value to be higher for EWH_2 than for EWH_1, because in the hours immediately after the interruption analyzed, the average historical utilization is higher for EWH_2. On the other hand, as the value of ρ increases, it is expected that the gap between the *TDI* of both electric water heaters became larger. Table 2 reports the *TDI* values computed for each electric water heater and ρ values.

Table 2. *TDI* applied for the interruption for EWH_1 and EWH_2.

Appliance	$\rho = 1$	$\rho = 2$
EWH_1	3362.3 °C s	4108.2 °C s
EWH_2	8109.6 °C s	11041.7 °C s

Results in Table 2 confirms that the proposed index correctly models discomfort. The *TDI* value is higher for EWH_2. Furthermore, the difference widens when considering larger penalty values (ρ). These results show that *TDI* properly models the differences of temperature between a scenario with an interruption and a scenario without interruption, as expected.

6   Conclusions and Future Work

This article presented an approach to evaluate the impact on the thermal comfort of direct demand response control using electric water heaters.

An index associated with the thermal discomfort is defined according to the following procedure. A water utilization forecasting model was built from real power data from a set of electric water heaters, using machine learning techniques. Then, applying the water utilization model, a linear model was developed to estimate the temperature of the water in the electric water heater tank. Finally, the *TDI* associated with an intervention on the electric water heater was defined stochastically, via Monte Carlo simulation.

The proposed models and the reliability of the proposed index were evaluated in a real case study considering two electric water heaters from different users, with different average historical utilization. The *TDI* values was analyzed for both electric water heaters for different penalization factors ρ. Results confirmed confirms that the proposed index correctly models discomfort, since higher *TDI* values were computed for the electric water heater with the higher average historical utilization. The difference on *TDI* values increased when considering larger penalty values.

The main lines for future work are related to study the applicability of the proposed approach to perform load shifting when several electric water heaters are available, by properly adjusting the value of parameter ρ. In this scenario, the ranking of *TDI* values (from lowest to highest) provides useful information for decision-making when determining which electric water heaters should be interrupted. Another line of future work is to estimate an economic value of the *TDI* index. The economic value (in USD/MWh) would be useful to characterize the profit of reducing the energy demanded by a set of electric water heaters by applying the interruption action, in order to compare this strategy with other demand response techniques (e.g., using fuel generators).

Acknowledgements. This work was partly supported by CYTED Thematic Network "Fully Integral, Efficient And Sustainable Smart Cities (CITIES)".

References

1. Al-Jabery, K., Xu, Z., Yu, W., Wunsch, D.C., Xiong, J., Shi, Y.: Demand-side management of domestic electric water heaters using approximate dynamic programming. IEEE Trans. Comput. Aided Des. Integr. Circ. Syst. **36**(5), 775–788 (2016)
2. Bhattacharyya, S.: Energy demand management. In: Energy Economics, pp. 135–160. Springer, London (2011) https://doi.org/10.1007/978-0-85729-268-1_6
3. Chavat, J., Graneri, J., Alvez, G., Nesmachnow, S.: ECD-UY: Detailed household electricity consumption dataset of Uruguay. Scientific Data (2020), (submitted)
4. Deng, R., Yang, Z., Chow, M., Chen, J.: A survey on demand response in smart grids: mathematical models and approaches. IEEE Trans. Industr. Inf. **11**(3), 570–582 (2015)
5. Hassan, N.U., Khalid, Y.I., Yuen, C., Tushar, W.: Customer engagement plans for peak load reduction in residential smart grids. IEEE Trans. Smart Grid **6**(6), 3029–3041 (2015)
6. Instituto Nacional de Estadística, Uruguay: Microdatos de la encuesta continua de hogares (2019), http://www.ine.gub.uy/microdatos. August 2020
7. Kampelis, N., Ferrante, A., Kolokotsa, D., Gobakis, K., Standardi, L., Cristalli, C.: Thermal comfort evaluation in HVAC demand response control. Energy Procedia **134**, 675–682 (2017)
8. Lu, N., Katipamula, S.: Control strategies of thermostatically controlled appliances in a competitive electricity market. In: IEEE Power Engineering Society General Meeting, pp. 202–207. IEEE (2005)
9. Luján, E., Otero, A., Valenzuela, S., Mocskos, E.E., Steffenel, L.A., Nesmachnow, S.: An integrated platform for smart energy management: the CC-SEM project. Revista Facultad de Ingeniería Universidad de Antioquia (2019)
10. Lutz, J., Whitehead, C., Lekov, A., Winiarski, D., Rosenquist, G.: WHAM: a simplified energy consumption equation for water heaters. In: ACEEE Summer Study on Energy Efficiency in Buildings (1998)
11. Massobrio, R., Nesmachnow, S., Tchernykh, A., Avetisyan, A., Radchenko, G.: Towards a cloud computing paradigm for big data analysis in smart cities. Prog. Comput. Softw. **44**(3), 181–189 (2018)
12. Momoh, J.: Smart Grid: Fundamentals of Design and Analysis. Wiley, Hoboken (2012)
13. Nehrir, M., LaMeres, B., Gerez, V.: A customer-interactive electric water heater demand-side management strategy using fuzzy logic. Winter Meet. IEEE Power Eng. Soc. **1**, 433–436 (1999)
14. Nesmachnow, S., Iturriaga, S.: Cluster-UY: collaborative scientific high performance computing in Uruguay. In: Torres, M., Klapp, J. (eds.) ISUM 2019. CCIS, vol. 1151, pp. 188–202. Springer, Cham (2019). https://doi.org/10.1007/978-3-030-38043-4_16
15. Orsi, E., Nesmachnow, S.: IoT for smart home energy planning. In: XXIII Congreso Argentino de Ciencias de la Computación, pp. 1091–1100 (2017)
16. Orsi, E., Nesmachnow, S.: Smart home energy planning using IoT and the cloud. In: IEEE URUCON, IEEE (2017)

17. Paul, L., MacKay, D., Li, H., Liuchen, C.: A water heater model for increased power system efficiency (2009)
18. Perfumo, C., Braslavsky, J.H., Ward, J.: Model-based estimation of energy savings in load control events for thermostatically controlled loads. IEEE Trans. Smart Grid **5**(3), 1410–1420 (2014)
19. Pirow, N., Louw, T., Booysen, M.: Non-invasive estimation of domestic hot water usage with temperature and vibration sensors. Flow Meas. Instrum. **63**, 1–7 (2018)
20. Porteiro, R., Nesmachnow, S., Hernández-Callejo, L.: Electricity demand forecasting in industrial and residential facilities using ensemble machine learning. Universidad de Antioquía, Revista Facultad de Ingeniería (2020)
21. Tabatabaei, S.A., Klein, M.: The role of knowledge about user behaviour in demand response management of domestic hot water usage. Energ. Effi. **11**(7), 1797–1809 (2018). https://doi.org/10.1007/s12053-017-9605-5
22. Tang, R., Wang, S., Yan, C.: A direct load control strategy of centralized air-conditioning systems for building fast demand response to urgent requests of smart grids. Autom. Constr. **87**, 74–83 (2018)
23. Xiang, S., Chang, L., Cao, B., He, Y., Zhang, C.: A novel domestic electric water heater control method. IEEE Trans. Smart Grid **11**(4), 3246–3256 (2019)
24. Yin, Z., Che, Y., Li, D., Liu, H., Yu, D.: Optimal scheduling strategy for domestic electric water heaters based on the temperature state priority list. Energies **10**(9), 1425 (2017)
25. Yoon, A., Kang, H., Moon, S.: Optimal price based demand response of HVAC systems in commercial buildings considering peak load reduction. Energies **13**(4), 862 (2020)

Conditional Generative Adversarial Networks to Model Urban Outdoor Air Pollution

Jamal Toutouh[(✉)] [iD]

Massachusetts Institute of Technology, CSAIL, Cambridge, MA, USA
toutouh@mit.edu

Abstract. Modeling, predicting, and forecasting ambient air pollution is an important way to deal with the degradation of the air quality in our cities because it would be helpful for decision-makers and urban city planners to understand the phenomena and to take solutions. In general, data-driven modeling, predicting, and forecasting outdoor pollution methods require an important amount of data, which may limit their accuracy. To deal with such a lack of data, we propose to train generative models, specifically conditional generative adversarial networks, to create synthetic nitrogen dioxide daily time series that will allow an unlimited generation of realistic data. The experimental results indicate that the proposed approach is able to generate accurate and diverse pollution daily time series, while requiring reduced computational time.

Keywords: Urban outdoor pollution modeling · Machine learning · Generative adversarial networks · Data augmentation

1 Introduction

Artificial intelligence, computational intelligence, and automated learning are already coping with different areas in our daily life due to their success in a wide range of applications [5]. In this study, we focus on generative models, which have shown success on tasks related to learning and gaining knowledge about data, data distributions, and other valuable information [24].

In particular, generative adversarial networks (GANs) is a powerful method to train generative models [6]. GANs take a training set drawn from a specific distribution and learn to represent an estimate of that distribution by using unsupervised learning. The output of this method is a generative model that produces new information units that approximate the original training set.

In general, GANs consist of two artificial neural networks (ANN), a generator and a discriminator, that apply adversarial learning to optimize their parameters (weights). The discriminator learns how to distinguish between the "natural/real" data samples coming from the training dataset and the "artificial/fake" data samples produced by the generator. The generator is trained to deceive the discriminator by transforming its inputs from a random latent space into "artificial/fake" data samples. GAN training is formulated as a minimax optimization problem by the definitions of generator and discriminator loss [6].

S. Nesmachnow and L. Hernández Callejo (Eds.): ICSC-CITIES 2020, CCIS 1359, pp. 90–105, 2021.
https://doi.org/10.1007/978-3-030-69136-3_7

GANs have been successfully applied to generate realistic, complex, and multivariate distributions. This has motivated a growing body of applications, especially those concerning multimedia information (e.g., images, sound, and video), in science, design, art, games, and other areas [14,20].

Urban design has traditionally prioritized motorized mobility (the use of the individual or collective vehicles), with the growth of the cities this is having an undesired negative effect over safety and reducing the quality of life of the inhabitants. A major concern derived from the rapid development of car-oriented cities is the high generation of air pollutants and their impacts on the citizens' health [17]. Thus, air pollution is the top health hazard in the European Union because it reduces life expectancy and diminishes the quality of health [9,18].

In the urban areas, one of the major sources of pollutants, such as nitrogen dioxide (NO_2), is road traffic [18]. Thus, reducing it would be an effective strategy to improve urban livability and their inhabitants' health. However, it is not easy to understand the different phenomena that may have implications for the production or dissipation of pollutants. For this reason, there have been different approaches to evaluate the real impact of mobility policies in the air quality [8,10,23].

The interest in modeling, predicting, and forecasting ambient air pollution has also been growing during the last years. Getting in advance accurate quality air values would allow policy-makers and urban city planners to provide rapid solutions to prevent human risk situations [13].

Traditionally, physics-based and deterministic approaches have been applied to address air pollution modeling [3,4]. These approaches are sensitive to several factors, including the scale and quality of the parameters involved, computationally expensive, and dependent on large databases of several input parameters, of which some may not be available [3].

With the rapid development of ANNs and their successful application to many different short-term and long-term forecasting applications, several researchers have proposed the use of such a data-driven methodology to deal with air outdoor pollution modeling, prediction, and forecasting [3]. On the one hand, the main advantage of this approach is that the use of ANNs does not require an in-depth understanding of the physics and dynamics between air pollution concentration levels and other explanatory variables [3,11,15]. On the other hand, it is an open question the selection of the appropriate ANN model, the interpretation of the results of that kind of black-box methods, and the results are problem specific. Besides, as the deterministic models, this kind of machine learning and deep learning methods require a vast amount of data to be trained.

In this research, we want to propose the use of a specific type of GANs, conditional GANs (CGANs) [12], to train generators able to create synthesized data, as a data augmentation approach, to feed data-driven methodologies for modeling, forecasting, and predicting outdoor pollution. The data samples generated are the daily time series of a given pollutant from a given area of a city according to a given condition (class). As a use case, we deal with the generation of daily NO_2 concentration time series at the *Plaza the España* in Madrid (Spain). The real dataset provided used to train the CGAN is build by collecting the levels of NO_2 gathered by a sensor located there. It is important to remark that we are not trying to create a pollution forecasting method, but a modeling one from training the generative models.

The main contributions of this research are: a) proposing a new approach based on CGANs to create pollution time series, and b) generating new data samples to be used by data-driven pollution modeling approaches. Thus, we want to answer the following research question: **RQ**: Is it possible to apply generative modeling to produce new daily time series to improve our understanding of the phenomena related to the pollution in our cities?

The paper is organized as follows: The next section introduces the main concepts to understand CGANs and how they are applied to generate air pollution data. Section 3 introduces the research methodology applied in this research. The experimental analysis is presented in Sect. 4. Finally, Sect. 5 draws the conclusions and the main lines of future work.

2   CGANs for Pollution Data Augmentation

The CGANs are an extension of a GAN for conditional settings (labeled data). This section introduces the main concepts in GANs and CGANs training and presents how CGANs are applied to generate pollution daily series to address pollution data augmentation.

2.1   Conditional Generative Adversarial Networks Training

GANs are unsupervised learning methods that learn the specific distribution of a given (real) training dataset, to produce samples using the estimated distribution. Generally, GANs consist of a generator and a discriminator that apply adversarial learning to optimize their parameters.

During the training process, the discriminator updates its parameters to learn how to differentiate between the natural/real samples from the training data set and the artificial/fake samples synthesized by the generator.

The GAN training problem is formulated as a minimax optimization problem by the definitions of generator and discriminator. Let $\mathcal{G} = \{G_g, \ g \in \mathbb{G}\}$ and $\mathcal{D} = \{D_d, \ d \in \mathbb{D}\}$ denote the class of generators and discriminators, where G_g and D_d are functions parameterized by g and d. $\mathbb{G}, \mathbb{D} \subseteq \mathbb{R}^p$ represent the respective parameters space of the generators and discriminators. The generators G_g map a noise variable from a latent space $z \sim P_z(z)$ to data space $x = G_g(z)$. The discriminators D_d assign a probability $p = D_d(x) \in [0,1]$ to represent the likelihood that x belongs to the real training data set. In order to do so, $\phi : [0,1] \rightarrow \mathbb{R}$, which is concave *measuring function*, is used. The $P_z(z)$ is a prior on z (a uniform $[-1,1]$ distribution is typically chosen). The goal of GAN training is to find d and g parameters to optimize the objective function $\mathcal{L}(g,d)$.

$$\min_{g \in \mathbb{G}} \max_{d \in \mathbb{D}} \mathcal{L}(g,d), \text{ where}$$

$$\mathcal{L}(g,d) = \mathbb{E}_{x \sim P_{data}(x)}[\phi(D_d(x))] + \mathbb{E}_{z \sim P_z(z)}[\phi(1 - D_d(G_g(z)))] , \tag{1}$$

This provokes that D_d becomes into a binary classifier providing the best possible discrimination between real and fake data. Simultaneously, it encourages G_g to fit the real data distribution. In general, both ANN are trained by applying backpropagation.

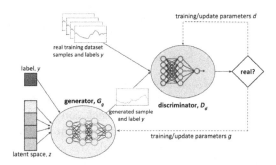

Fig. 1. Most commonly used CGANs training setups.

CGANs are an extension of GANs to deal with labeled training datasets (structured in classes). The idea is to train generative models able to create samples of a given class given according to a given label. Thus G_g and D_d receive an additional variable y as input, which represents the label of the class (see Fig. 1). The CGANs objective function can be rewritten it is shown in Eq. 2.

$$\min_{g \in G} \max_{d \in \mathbb{D}} \mathcal{L}(g, d), \text{ where}$$
$$\mathcal{L}(g, d) = \mathbb{E}_{x, y \sim P_{data}(x, y)}[\phi(D_d(x, y))] + \mathbb{E}_{z \sim P_z(z), y \sim P_y(y)}[\phi(1 - D_d(G_g(z, y), y))] , \tag{2}$$

2.2 GANs Applied to Urban Sciences

There is a consistent body of evidence that GANs excel at implicitly sampling from highly complex, analytically-unknown distributions in a great number of contexts [24]. Thus, nowadays, researchers are using such a machine learning approach to generate data across a variety of disciplines.

However, there is a lack of studies on applying GANs to problems related to our cities. Some examples of this type of research are: a generative model trained by an unconditional GAN was trained to create realistic built land use maps, i.e., the model was able to generate cities (maps of built land use). These maps showed a high degree of realism and they provided realistic values on several statistics used in the urban modeling literature with real cities [2]. Later, the same authors proposed the use of CGANs to add new levels of realism to the generated maps and the ability to predict land use maps from underlying socio-economic factors. These new maps take into account, for example, physical constraints such as water areas [1]. Physics-informed GAN (PIGAN) was proposed to enhance the performance of GANs by incorporating both constraints of covariance structure and physical laws. The idea es to improve the robustness of GANs when dealing with problems related to remote sensing [25]. This is important for applications that require the use of satellite data and could suffer from phenomena like the appearance of clouds. In turn, we could include in this class of urban sciences research by applying GANs, the study of applying GANs to create synthetic data about building energy consumption in order to be used together with real data to train a data-driven forecasting model to predict energy consumption [19]. The idea was to overcome the issues of having a lack of data to train the model to predict with enough accuracy.

2.3 Pollution Daily Time Series Generation

Dealing with the problem of not having enough data to analyze pollution in our cities, we proposed an approach for data augmentation to create synthetic daily time series of given pollutant. The approach consists in sampling from an existing dataset of real daily time series of given pollutant labeled according to different classes to train the discriminator, while the generator reads a vector z (from the latent space) and a label y to generate a fake daily time series (see Fig. 1). The generator and discriminator are trained against each other. Figure 2 illustrates samples of the real training dataset.

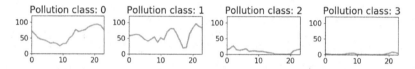

Fig. 2. Some samples of the real dataset, i.e., NO_2 pollution daily series.

3   Materials and Methods

This section presents the applied methodology for training generative models by using GANs to create synthetic pollution data.

3.1 Training Dataset Description

The training dataset studied here is provided by the Open Data Portal (ODP) offered by the Madrid City Council[1]. Specifically, the training dataset is the NO_2 concentration gathered by a sensor located at *Plaza de España*, which is in the downtown of the city. The dataset is built considering a temporal frame of five years, from January 2015 to December 2019. A given data sample is a time series that represents the NO_2 concentration of a given day which is averaged every hour. (Fig. 2). Therefore, it could be seen as a vector of 24 continuous values.

Following previous research about the pollution in Madrid, the daily NO_2 concentration is classified into eight classes according to the season (winter, spring, summer, and autumn) and the type of day (i.e., working days, from Mondays to Fridays, and weekends, Saturdays and Sundays) [9,10]. This classification follows the idea that warmer seasons have lower NO_2 concentration due

---

[1] Madird Open data Portal web - https://datos.madrid.es/.

Table 1. NO$_2$ pollution classification and number of samples per class.

Season	Type of day	Class	Number of samples
Winter	Weekend	0	439
Winter	Working day	1	1082
Spring	Weekend	2	439
Spring	Working day	3	1119
Summer	Weekend	4	445
Summer	Working day	5	1116
Autumn	Weekend	6	420
Autumn	Working day	7	1045

to meteorological reasons and weekends have better air quality because the road traffic is lower than in working days. Table 1 presents this pollution classification and the number of samples per class.

The classes are highly unbalanced (see Table 1), i.e., autumn-weekend (class 6) has 420 samples (the minimum) and spring-working day (3) has 1119 (the maximum). For our experiments, we randomly sampled over the classes to select 420 samples of each class to balance the dataset to avoid training biases. Thus, the training dataset size is 3360 (420 × 8).

Fig 3 illustrates the training dataset. The green line shows the mean value, i.e., it contains the mean pollution values for the whole data of the class (we named it as the representative time series of a given class c, i.e., rep_c). The dark green area represents the values between the border defined by the mean minus the standard deviation and the mean plus the standard deviation (mean ± the standard deviation). Finally, the lighter green area represents the values between the minimum and maximum pollution measured in a given time.

3.2   CGAN Design Details

In our research, both ANNs, the generator and the discriminator, are implemented as multilayer perceptrons (MLP) [7]. MLP are comprised of perceptrons or neurons, organized on layers. The minimum setup is formed by an input layer, which receives the problem data as input, and an output layer, which produces the results. In between, one or more hidden layers can be included to provide different levels of abstraction to help with the learning goal. The main difference between linear perceptrons and MLP is that all the neurons on the hidden and output layer apply a nonlinear activation function. MLP have shown competitive results when dealing with different kinds of machine learning, such as classification/prediction problems with labeled inputs, regression problems, etc.

Our approach explores the use of a four-layer MLP to build the generator and the discriminator. The input of the generator has a size of 64 (size of z) plus eight (size of y) to specify the label of the class of the data sample to be generated, i.e., the total input size is 72. The output of the generator has the same input of the discriminator, which in this case is 24 (the size of the generated sample)

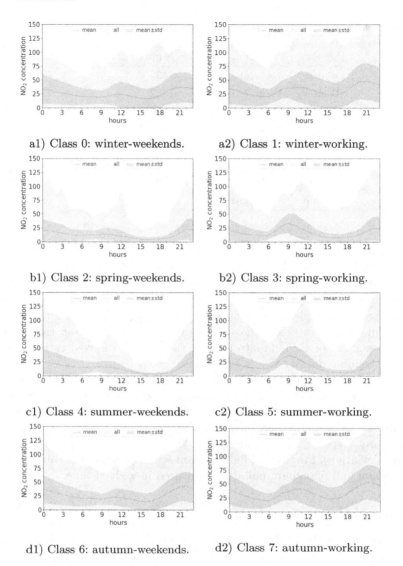

a1) Class 0: winter-weekends.   a2) Class 1: winter-working.

b1) Class 2: spring-weekends.   b2) Class 3: spring-working.

c1) Class 4: summer-weekends.   c2) Class 5: summer-working.

d1) Class 6: autumn-weekends.   d2) Class 7: autumn-working.

Fig. 3. NO$_2$ hourly values for the seven classes defined in our study (real data). (Color figure online)

plus eight (size of y) to identify the label of the sample, i.e., the total size is 32. Both types of MLP use linear layers. Hidden layers apply the leaky version of a rectified linear unit (LeakyRelu) as activation function, and the discriminator output layer the sigmoid function. The output of the generator applies a linear function since the output is in the range of real values, $\mathbb{R}$. The two hidden layers have 256 units for both trained ANN models.

3.3   Metrics Evaluated

As we are dealing with GAN training, we evaluate the loss values computed for the generator and the discriminator during the training process. The function applied to compute the loss is the binary cross-entropy (BCE) [6] ($\mathcal{L}_d$ and $\mathcal{L}_g$).

$$\mathcal{L}_d = \frac{1}{2}\mathbb{E}_{x,y \sim P_{data}(x,y)}[log(D_d(x,y))] - \frac{1}{2}\mathbb{E}_{z \sim P_z(z),y \sim P_y(y)}[log(1 - D_d(G_g(z,y),y))] \, , \tag{3}$$

$$\mathcal{L}_g = \mathbb{E}_{z \sim P_z(z),y \sim P_y(y)}[log(1 - D_d(G_g(z,y),y))] \tag{4}$$

When working with GANs it is important to assess the quality of the generated samples. In our problem, the aim is to generate accurate daily time series of pollution that follow the same distribution as the real pollution in *Plaza de España*. We propose the use of the root mean squared error (RMSE) between the fake samples produced and the time series that represents the mean (rep_c). Thus, given a fake sample of a given class c, i.e., f_c, the quality of the sample is given by the RMSE(rep_c,f_c) shown in Eq. 5, where $rep_c(t)$ and $f_c(t)$ represent the pollution level at a given time t of the representative time series c and the fake sample f_c, respectivelly. Thus, lower values indicate better sample quality.

$$RMSE(rep_c, f_c) = \sqrt{\frac{1}{24} \sum_{t \in [0,23]} (rep_c(t) - f_c(t))^2} \tag{5}$$

Finally, we also take into account the computational time in order to evaluate the cost of the proposed generative method.

4   Experimental Analysis

This section presents the numerical analysis of the proposed approach.

4.1   Development, Training Configuration, and Execution Platform

The proposed generative approach is implemented in Python3 using Pytorch as the main library to deal with ANNs (pytorch.org). The GAN training has configured with a learning rate of 0.0002, batch size of 16 samples (210 batches per training epoch), and 2000 iterations (training epochs).

The experiments have been performed on a workstation equipped with an Intel Core i7-7850H processor, 32 GB of RAM memory, 100 GB of SSD storage for temporary files, and a Nvidia Tesla P100 GPUs with 12 GB of memory.

4.2   Experimental Results

This subsection reports the experimental results. The training process has been performed 10 times. Thus this section studies: *a)* the accuracy of the generators is analyze, *b)* the evolution of the loss during the training process, *c)* the samples sythesized by the generators, and *d)* the computational time.

Accuracy of the Trained Generators. The accuracy of the generators is evaluated according to the RMSE between the created samples of a given class c and the daily time series that represents the mean of that c class. Thus, after training each generator, we create 40,000 samples (5,000 samples of each class) as fake datasets. Table 2 shows the minimum, mean, standard deviation (stdev), and maximum of the calculated RMSE. The first row includes the same values obtained when computed the RMSE taking into account real samples. The fake datasets in the table are ranked according to their mean RMSE, thus *fake-1* dataset contains the samples with the best quality (lowest RMSE) and fake-10 the samples with the highest RMSE.

Table 2. RMSE results for each dataset.

Dataset	Minimum	Mean ± stdev	Maximum
real	3.6	17.3 ± 8.5	67.0
fake-1	4.0	15.3 ± 7.8	75.8
fake-2	4.2	15.4 ± 8.1	82.1
fake-3	3.7	15.4 ± 7.7	71.0
fake-4	3.5	15.5 ± 8.3	91.7
fake-5	3.8	15.5 ± 7.9	75.6
fake-6	3.3	15.5 ± 8.2	77.3
fake-7	4.3	15.6 ± 7.9	68.3
fake-8	3.8	15.7 ± 8.3	81.4
fake-9	3.3	15.7 ± 8.4	80.2
fake-10	4.0	15.7 ± 8.2	83.7

All the fake datasets present lower mean RMSE than the samples of the real dataset. This is mainly due that the training process converges to a generator that creates samples with limited diversity (real data shows the highest standard deviation). Even the results shown by our approach are competitive, it would be desirable to add diversity to the produced samples. This is still an open question that some authors are facing by providing generative models as a mixture of several generators [22].

Table 3 shows the mean and standard deviation (stdev) of the computed RMSE taking into account the classes. Real data samples show the highest differences for the eight classes. Besides, it can be seen that the classes that represent working days (classes represented by odd numbers) show the highest differences, for both real and fake datasets. This mainly indicates that there is not a general behavior that defines all the working days and therefore, we should take into account different kinds of classification to deal with working days (maybe taking into account the day itself).

Training Process. In this section, we evaluate the behavior of the training process by showing the losses of the generator and the discriminator. In turn, we show the mean RMSE of the generated data at the end of each training

Table 3. RMSE per class for each dataset.

Dataset	0	1	2	3	4	5	6	7
Real	20.2 ± 7.1	23.8 ± 8.3	10.7 ± 5.6	13.2 ± 5.9	11.5 ± 6.3	13.4 ± 6.6	18.3 ± 6.4	22.4 ± 7.6
fake-1	17.6 ± 9.1	20.1 ± 9.0	10.5 ± 5.4	11.2 ± 5.1	10.1 ± 4.1	11.1 ± 3.9	15.3 ± 6.5	19.3 ± 7.2
fake-2	17.6 ± 9.8	19.8 ± 8.8	10.1 ± 4.7	10.7 ± 4.3	9.5 ± 3.3	11.1 ± 4.2	15.9 ± 7.6	19.5 ± 7.7
fake-3	17.7 ± 8.7	20.7 ± 9.0	9.7 ± 4.5	10.7 ± 4.0	9.7 ± 3.4	10.8 ± 3.4	15.7 ± 6.1	19.9 ± 6.9
fake-4	18.6 ± 9.3	20.6 ± 9.5	9.9 ± 5.1	10.6 ± 3.9	9.4 ± 3.8	10.7 ± 3.6	15.6 ± 7.3	20.1 ± 7.9
fake-5	17.9 ± 8.6	20.2 ± 9.1	9.8 ± 4.2	11.0 ± 4.4	10.0 ± 3.7	11.2 ± 4.1	15.3 ± 6.6	19.9 ± 7.3
fake-6	18.6 ± 9.9	20.5 ± 8.7	9.3 ± 5.1	10.9 ± 5.0	9.1 ± 3.0	11.0 ± 3.8	15.4 ± 6.6	20.1 ± 7.8
fake-7	18.1 ± 9.7	20.3 ± 8.2	10.4 ± 4.7	11.4 ± 5.6	10.0 ± 3.7	11.8 ± 4.5	15.5 ± 6.4	19.4 ± 7.3
fake-8	18.4 ± 10.0	20.9 ± 9.5	10.2 ± 5.2	11.5 ± 5.6	10.0 ± 3.9	11.4 ± 4.2	15.9 ± 6.6	19.6 ± 8.0
fake-9	18.5 ± 10.7	20.0 ± 9.0	9.7 ± 5.1	11.3 ± 4.8	9.6 ± 3.6	11.1 ± 4.4	15.6 ± 6.8	19.3 ± 7.7
kake-10	18.0 ± 8.9	20.8 ± 9.6	10.7 ± 5.1	11.3 ± 4.9	9.8 ± 4.1	11.4 ± 4.3	15.7 ± 6.5	19.7 ± 8.0

epoch. The mean RMSE score is computed by creating 10,000 samples. Figure 4 illustrates these metrics for the best, median, and worst run, i.e., *fake-1*, *fake-5*, and *fake-10*, respectivelly.

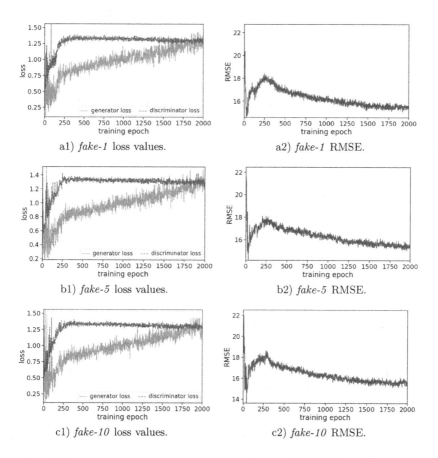

a1) *fake-1* loss values.   a2) *fake-1* RMSE.

b1) *fake-5* loss values.   b2) *fake-5* RMSE.

c1) *fake-10* loss values.   c2) *fake-10* RMSE.

Fig. 4. Discriminator and generator loss values and RMSE for three runs.

Focusing on the evolution of the losses in Fig. 4 a1, b1, and c1, we observe that the general behavior is very similar for the three evaluated runs. At the beginning (about the first 200–300 training epochs) the discriminator and the generator losses oscillate without showing a clear trend. This is mainly due to the discriminator has not been trained enough yet, and it is not able to discriminate anyhow between fake and real samples and it randomly assigns a loss value (i.e., it basically flips a coin). Thus, the generator can easily get low losses values that do not give the feedback required to learn (to update its parameters) property. For this reason, the samples produced provide increasing and oscillating RMSE (Fig. 4 a2, b2, and c2).

After that, the discriminator starts becoming stronger and reduces the loss values. Thus, it is harder for the generator to deceive the discriminator. For this reason, the generator starts increasing the computed loss values, allowing the generator to learn how to create more accurate samples. Therefore, the RMSE values start being reduced in an almost monotonically decreasing way.

After the 2,000 iterations, the generator and the discriminator seem to be in an equilibrium in which both loss values are similar. However, long runs will be able to give more insights into this concern.

It is important to remark that none of the runs shows typical GAN training pathologies, such as mode collapse, vanishing gradient, and oscillation; which would require to use more advanced GAN training methods, e.g., Lipizzaner [16] or Mustangs [21].

Synthetic Daily Pollution Time Series Generated. The robustness shown by the GAN training when addressing the problem studied here allows the generation of realistic synthetic daily pollution time series. Here, we illustrate the 40,000 samples generated that belong to *fake-1* and *fake-10* datasets, the fake datasets with the best and the worst RMSE. Figures 5 and 7 summarizes the samples by showing the mean values (the orange line), the values between the mean ± the standard deviation (the dark orange area), and all other values, i.e., between the minimum and maximum (the lighter orange area). In turn, the dotted black line presents the mean value of the real training data set (see Fig. 3).

As can be seen in both figures, the mean values of the fake data and the mean values of the real data are very close. However, the distance between the orange line and the dark line increases for *fake-10*.

The shape of the dark orange areas are different depending on the class, but similar among the different datasets, i.e., the three generators studied produce samples with similar general trends. However, the shapes are less wide for the *fake-1* dataset (it shows the lowest standard deviation in Table 2). This is mainly because it tends to generate less diverse samples than the other evaluated generators. Notice, that the fake datasets are ranked taking into account the RMSE against the mean curves of the real data set.

Thus, according to the insights got from the datasets illustrated in Figs. 5 and 7 and the results in Tables 2 and 3, we can see the effectiveness of the methodology proposed to augment the pollution daily time series; and therefore

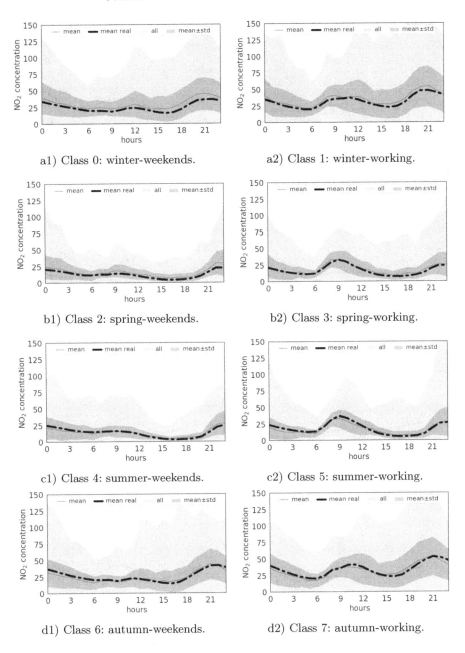

a1) Class 0: winter-weekends.

a2) Class 1: winter-working.

b1) Class 2: spring-weekends.

b2) Class 3: spring-working.

c1) Class 4: summer-weekends.

c2) Class 5: summer-working.

d1) Class 6: autumn-weekends.

d2) Class 7: autumn-working.

Fig. 5. Synthesized data samples created by *fake-1*.

the answer to **RQ**: Is it possible to apply generative modeling to produce new daily time series to improve our understanding of the phenomena related to the pollution in our cities? is yes.

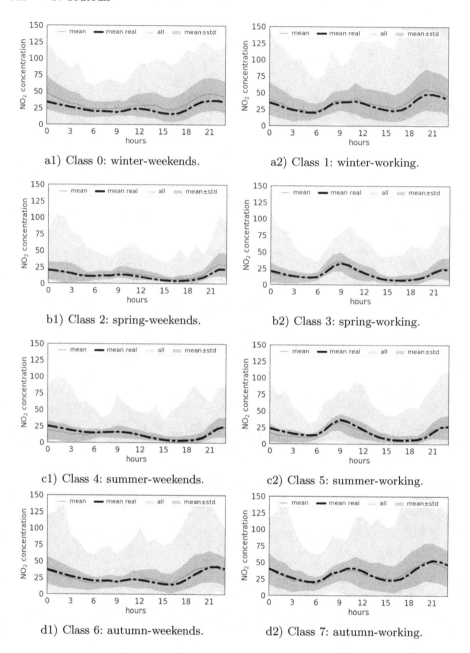

a1) Class 0: winter-weekends.

a2) Class 1: winter-working.

b1) Class 2: spring-weekends.

b2) Class 3: spring-working.

c1) Class 4: summer-weekends.

c2) Class 5: summer-working.

d1) Class 6: autumn-weekends.

d2) Class 7: autumn-working.

Fig. 6. Synthesized data samples created by *fake-10*.

Computational Time. One of the main drawbacks of applying ANNs and deep learning approaches, as CGANs, is the computational effort (time and memory) required to train the models. As the size of the data samples and the ANN models used are not significant, the memory is not an issue et al. Regarding the computational times, the minimum, mean, and maximum times were 67.68, 69.64, and 72.04 min, respectively. That represents a non-very-high time-consuming investment, mainly because once the generators are trained, they create the new samples instantaneously.

5   Conclusions and Future Work

The interest in modeling, predicting, and forecasting ambient air pollution has been growing during the last years. Data-driven methods suffer from a lack of data to provide more accurate results. Thus, we propose the use of CGANs to train generative models able to create synthesized daily time series of a given pollutant from a given area of a city according to a given label. In this research, we have modeled NO_2 concentration at the downtown of Madrid as a use case.

The main results indicate that the proposed model is able to generate accurate NO_2 pollution daily time series while requiring a reduced computational time. CGANs have shown robustness on the training because all the experiments converged to accurate generators. Thus, we are optimistic that this is the first step to develop more complex generative models to produce synthetic pollution of a whole city taking into account information as the weather or the road traffic.

The main lines for future work are related to extend the proposed model to generate the pollution of the whole city of Madrid by taking into account information from different sensors, propose other classification that will allow including road traffic density and the weather (it will require the definition of more classes), and applying the generated data to feed data-driven models to prove that they are able to improve their accuracy after including fake samples.

Acknowledgements. J. Toutouh research was partially funded by European Union's Horizon 2020 research and innovation program under the Marie Skłodowska-Curie grant agreement No 799078, by the Junta de Andalucía UMA18-FEDERJA-003, European Union H2020-ICT-2019-3, and the Systems that Learn Initiative at MIT CSAIL.

References

1. Albert, A., Kaur, J., Strano, E., Gonzalez, M.: Spatial sensitivity analysis for urban land use prediction with physics-constrained conditional generative adversarial networks. arXiv preprint arXiv:1907.09543 (2019)
2. Albert, A., Strano, E., Kaur, J., González, M.: Modeling urbanization patterns with generative adversarial networks. In: IGARSS 2018–2018 IEEE International Geoscience and Remote Sensing Symposium, pp. 2095–2098. IEEE (2018)
3. Cabaneros, S.M., Calautit, J.K., Hughes, B.R.: A review of artificial neural network models for ambient air pollution prediction. Environ. Model. Softw. **119**, 285–304 (2019)
4. Chuang, M.T., Zhang, Y., Kang, D.: Application of WRF/Chem-MADRID for real-time air quality forecasting over the Southeastern United States. Atmos. Environ. **45**(34), 6241–6250 (2011)

5. Engelbrecht, A.: Computational Intelligence: An Introduction. John Wiley & Sons, Hoboken (2007)
6. Goodfellow, I., et al.: Generative adversarial nets. In: Advances in Neural Information Processing Systems, pp. 2672–2680 (2014)
7. The Elements of Statistical Learning. SSS. Springer, New York (2009). https://doi.org/10.1007/978-0-387-84858-7_9
8. Lebrusán, I., Toutouh, J.: Assessing the environmental impact of car restrictions policies: madrid central case. In: Nesmachnow, S., Hernández Callejo, L. (eds.) ICSC-CITIES 2019. CCIS, vol. 1152, pp. 9–24. Springer, Cham (2020). https://doi.org/10.1007/978-3-030-38889-8_2
9. Lebrusán, I., Toutouh, J.: Car restriction policies for better urban health: a low emission zone in Madrid, Spain. Air Qual. Atmos. Health, 1–10 (2020). https://doi.org/10.1007/s11869-020-00938-z
10. Lebrusán, I., Toutouh, J.: Using smart city tools to evaluate the effectiveness of a low emissions zone in Spain: Madrid central. Smart Cities 3(2), 456–478 (2020)
11. Liu, H., et al.: An intelligent hybrid model for air pollutant concentrations forecasting: case of Beijing in China. Sustain. Cities Soc. 47, 101471 (2019)
12. Mirza, M., Osindero, S.: Conditional generative adversarial nets. arXiv preprint arXiv:1411.1784 (2014)
13. Moustris, K.P., Ziomas, I.C., Paliatsos, A.G.: 3-Day-ahead forecasting of regional pollution index for the pollutants NO2, CO, SO2, and O3 using artificial neural networks in Athens, Greece. Water, Air Soil Pollut. 209(1–4), 29–43 (2010)
14. Pan, Z., Yu, W., Yi, X., Khan, A., Yuan, F., Zheng, Y.: Recent progress on generative adversarial networks (GANs): a survey. IEEE Access 7, 36322–36333 (2019)
15. Qi, Y., Li, Q., Karimian, H., Liu, D.: A hybrid model for spatiotemporal forecasting of PM2.5 based on graph convolutional neural network and long short-term memory. Sci. Total Environ. 664, 1–10 (2019)
16. Schmiedlechner, T., Yong, I., Al-Dujaili, A., Hemberg, E., O'Reilly, U.: Lipizzaner: a system that scales robust generative adversarial network training. In: 32nd Conference on Neural Information Processing Systems (2018)
17. Soni, N., Soni, N.: Benefits of pedestrianization and warrants to pedestrianize an area. Land Use Policy 57, 139–150 (2016)
18. Steele, C.: A critical review of some traffic noise prediction models. Appl. Acoust. 62(3), 271–287 (2001)
19. Tian, C., Li, C., Zhang, G., Lv, Y.: Data driven parallel prediction of building energy consumption using generative adversarial nets. Energy Build. 186, 230–243 (2019)
20. Toutouh, J., Esteban, M., Nesmachnow., S.: Parallel/distributed generative adversarial neural networks for data augmentation of covid-19 training images. In: Latin America High Performance Computing Conference (CARLA 2020), p. 10 (2020)
21. Toutouh, J., Hemberg, E., O'Reilly, U.: Spatial evolutionary generative adversarial networks. In: Auger, A., Stützle, T. (eds.) Proceedings of the Genetic and Evolutionary Computation Conference, GECCO 2019, pp. 472–480. ACM (2019)
22. Toutouh, J., Hemberg, E., O'Reily, U.M.: Re-purposing heterogeneous generative ensembles with evolutionary computation. In: Proceedings of the 2020 Genetic and Evolutionary Computation Conference, GECCO 2020, pp. 425–434. Association for Computing Machinery (2020)
23. Toutouh, J., Lebrusán, I., Nesmachnow, S.: Computational intelligence for evaluating the air quality in the center of Madrid, Spain. In: Dorronsoro, B., Ruiz, P., de la Torre, J.C., Urda, D., Talbi, E.-G. (eds.) OLA 2020. CCIS, vol. 1173, pp. 115–127. Springer, Cham (2020). https://doi.org/10.1007/978-3-030-41913-4_10

24. Wang, Z., She, Q., Ward, T.: Generative adversarial networks: A survey and taxonomy. preprint arXiv:1906.01529 (2019)
25. Wu, J., Kashinanth, K., Albert, A., Chirila, D.B., Xiao, H.: Generative learning to emulate pde-governed systems by preserving high-order statistics. In: Workshop on Climate Informatics, pp. 1–2 (2018)

Performance Assessment of the Transport Sustainability in the European Union

Sarah B. Gruetzmacher[1,2](✉) ⓘ, Clara B. Vaz[2,3]ⓘ, and Ângela P. Ferreira[2]ⓘ

[1] Universidade Tecnológica Federal do Paraná,
Av. Sete de Setembro, 3165 - 80230-901 Curitiba, Brazil
sarah.gruetz@gmail.com

[2] Research Center in Digitalization and Intelligent Robotics (CeDRI), Instituto Politécnico de Bragança, Campus de Santa Apolónia, 5300-253 Bragança, Portugal
{clvaz,apf}@ipb.pt

[3] Center for Management and Industrial Engineering (CEGI/INESC TEC),
Porto, Portugal

Abstract. Based in the current growth rate of metropolitan areas, providing infrastructures and services to allow the safe, quick and sustainable mobility of people and goods, is increasingly challenging. The European Union has been promoting diverse initiatives towards sustainable transport development and environment protection by setting targets for changes in the sector, as those proposed in the 2011 White Paper on transport. Under this context, this study aims at evaluating the environmental performance of the transport sector in the 28 European Union countries, from 2015 to 2017, towards the policy agenda established in strategic documents. The assessment of the transport environmental performance was made through the aggregation of seven sub-indicators into a composite indicator using a Data Envelopment Analysis approach. The model used to determine the weights to aggregate the sub-indicators is based on a variant of the Benefit of the Doubt model with virtual proportional weights restrictions. The results indicate that, overall, the European Union countries had almost no variation on its transport environmental performance during the time span under analysis. The inefficient countries can improve the transport sustainability mainly by drastically reducing the greenhouse gas emissions from fossil fuels combustion, increasing the share of freight transport that uses rail and waterways and also the share of transport energy from renewable sources.

Keywords: Transport environmental performance · Data Envelopment Analysis · Sustainable development

1 Introduction

The interest in sustainability and sustainable development has been increasing in the past decades [1]. The rapidly growing population of the cities, their aging infrastructure and the environmental concerns continue to challenge and pressure

S. Nesmachnow and L. Hernández Callejo (Eds.): ICSC-CITIES 2020, CCIS 1359, pp. 106–119, 2021.
https://doi.org/10.1007/978-3-030-69136-3_8

policymakers. Providing the infrastructure and services to allow safe, quick and sustainable mobility of people and goods is increasingly challenging [2]. Investing in improving the quality and sustainability of the transport system will improve the productivity, attractiveness and quality of life of the cities. Therefore, the transport sector has become one of the main subjects with regards to sustainable development.

In the European Union (EU), the transport sector employs more than 11 million people and accounts for about 5% of Europe's Gross Domestic Product (GDP). Between 2010 and 2050, passenger transport activity is expected to grow by 42% and freight transport activity by 60% [3]. An effective transportation system should contribute positively to the economic growth, to social development through the fair use of the natural resources and to environmental protection [4].

Under this scenario, the European Commission's, 2011, White Paper on transport - Roadmap to a Single European Transport Area – Towards a competitive and resource efficient transport system [5] proposed strategies for deep changes in the European transport sector aiming at a more sustainable and efficient system.

The adoption of the United Nations' Sustainable Development Goals (SDG) also provided new targets to address the transport sustainability. These goals address global challenges in several areas such as poverty, inequality and climate change, in a total of 17 goals to be achieved in 2030 [6]. Some SDG targets are related directly to transport sustainability and others to areas where transport has an important impact, such as energy consumption and pollutant emissions.

The sustainable development of the transport sector has been put on the agenda of EU countries, making it clear the necessity of measuring and assessing the current transport performance towards achieving these targets. It is also evident the importance of analysing sustainable transport planning, as transport policy and planning decisions can have diverse and long-term impacts on sustainable development. A critical component of transport planning is the development of a comprehensive evaluation program that assesses the transport performance based on an appropriate set of sub-indicators.

In order to fulfill this objective, this study aimed at developing a composite indicator (CI) to measure the environmental performance of the transport sector in the EU countries, from 2015 until 2017, towards a more sustainable mobility. The CI is a practical approach that allows to summarize, compare and track the performance of the countries. It allows the measurement of complex and multi-faceted issues that cannot be captured completely by analysing individual sub-indicators [7]. To aggregate the different sub-indicators into the CI, a variant of the Benefit of the Doubt model, as proposed by Färe et al. in [8], was used.

This paper is organized as follows: the second section presents a literature review on the construction of composite indicator and the variant of Benefit of the Doubt model proposed by Fare et al. [8]. Section 3 describes the sub-indicators selected to compose the CI. Section 4 analyses the data used and the results obtained. Finally, the conclusions from this work are presented in Sect. 5.

2   Literature Review

2.1   Composite Indicators

Composite indicators have been proven to be a useful method to synthesize masses of data, benchmark countries performance in relation to desirable states, demonstrate progress towards goals and to communicate current status to stakeholders leading to effective management decisions towards the established targets [9]. It is also a recognized tool for public communication, since they provide a big picture of a subject and often make it easier for the general public to interpret its results rather than having to identify common trends across many sub-indicators [10].

The essential purposes of the CI is to summarize a complex, multi-faceted phenomenons in wide-ranging fields, e.g. environment, economy, society or technological development, enabling the performance comparison of several countries or the evolution of a country over time [11]. The CI comprises of several individual sub-indicators that measures different aspects with usually no unit of measurement in common. The sub-indicators are compiled into a single index on the basis of an underlying model [10].

The subjective judgment about the relative worth of each sub-indicator is modelled through the weight assigned to it [11]. The weight reflects the significance of the sub-indicator and assigns a value to it in relation to the others, and it has, usually, a great impact on the aggregation results [12]. The weights attributed to the sub-indicators can be derived through different methods. They can be based on opinions, such as expert judgment or public opinion poll results. When these information are unavailable, the easiest and most common approach is to use equal weights [13]. However, not all evaluated units will agree to be evaluated with equal weights, since each of them has different characteristics and preferences. Finally, to avoid the subjectivity in determination of the sub-indicators' weights, the preferred tools are the statistical methods that derive the weights endogenously, such as the Principal Component Analysis/Factor Analysis and the Data Envelopment Analysis [14].

2.2   Data Envelopment Analysis

The DEA is a linear programming method, proposed by Charnes et al. [15], that assesses the relative efficiency of several decision making units (DMU) that use multiple inputs to produce multiple outputs. Therefore, DEA measures the efficiency of each DMU, given observations on input and output values in a set of similar entities, without knowledge of the production or cost function [11]. By comparison with the best practices frontier, the DEA model enables the selection of weights that are the most advantageous for the DMU under assessment [7].

This means that the weights are derived from the data itself, avoiding *a priori* assumptions and computations involved in fixed weight choices [16]. Thus, DEA is a popular method in the CI literature as it can solve the problem of subjectivity in the weighting procedure. Another well-known property of the original DEA model is its unit invariance. This is very interesting for the construction of CI as its final value is independent of the measurement units of the sub-indicators which in turn makes the normalization stage redundant and unnecessary [17].

The application of DEA to the construction of CI, referred to as the Benefit of the Doubt model (BoD), was originally proposed by Melyn and Moesen in 1991 [18]. The BoD is equivalent to the original DEA input oriented model, with all sub-indicators considered as outputs and a single dummy input equal to one for all countries. The dummy input can be understood intuitively by regarding the model as a tool for aggregating several sub-indicators of performance, without referencing the inputs that are used to obtain this performance [19]. Since the BoD model only includes outputs it measures the country's performance rather than its efficiency.

In fact, the conventional BoD model derives the composite indicator, aggregating forward sub-indicators, which capture the positive aspect of a performance, where their increasing values are desirable. Frequently, the performance assessment has to manipulate anti-isotonic sub-indicators, which capture the negative aspect of a performance, where their increasing values are undesirable. There are many sub-indicators that fall in this category, for example, emission of a pollutant, traffic accidents, crime rate, etc. The data of these sub-indicator needs to be transformed, to allow them to be incorporated in the conventional BoD model and treated as the forward sub-indicators [8]. Previous approaches used to deal with these anti-isotonic sub-indicators were the use of data transformation techniques and of directional distance function models. One of the most common data transformation technique is the inversion of the value of the reverse sub-indicator [20]. The subtraction of the sub-indicator from a sufficiently large constant and the rescaling normalization using the maximum-minimum method are also approaches that can be found in the literature. Some of these techniques are presented and compared in [21] and [22]. Even though these transformation are simple, they can be problematic. Since the BoD model is derived from an input-oriented DEA model with constant returns to scale, it is not translation invariant for the output values. This means that, the use of translated or rescaled data will affect the CI results and, consequently, the ranking of the DMUs [8].

Färe et al. [8] proposed a new BoD model (FKHM), which directly incorporates the anti-isotonic sub-indicators without using any transformation. The model treats the anti-isotonic sub-indicators as reverse rather than as undesirable. This means that the model assumes that the reverse sub-indicators values can decrease or increase independently from the values of forward sub-indicators.

Given a cross-section of M sub-indicators and S countries, y_{ij} is the value of sub-indicator i for the country j, and w_i is the weight attributed to the i-th sub-indicator. The formulation for the FKHM model is presented in Eq. (1), where y_{ij} $(j = 1, ..., m)$ are the forward sub-indicators (i.e., capturing positive aspect) and y_{ij} $(j = m + 1, ..., M)$ are the reverse sub-indicators (i.e., capturing negative aspect).

$$\text{CI}_{j_0} = max \sum_{i=1}^{m} w_i y_{ij_0} - \sum_{i=m+1}^{M} w_i y_{ij_0}$$

$$\textbf{\textit{s.t.}} \quad \sum_{i=1}^{m} w_i y_{ij} - \sum_{i=m+1}^{M} w_i y_{ij} \leq 1 \qquad \forall j = 1, ..., S$$

$$w_i \geq 0 \qquad \forall i = 1, ..., M$$

$$\frac{w_i y_{ij_0}}{\sum_{i=1}^{m} w_i y_{ij_0} + \sum_{i=m+1}^{M} w_i y_{ij_0}} \geq 0.05 \qquad \forall i = 1, ..., M$$

(1)

The main difference from the FKHM model to the conventional BoD model is that Eq. (1) maximizes the difference between the weighted average of forward sub-indicators and the weighted average of reverse sub-indicators. Additionally, the presence of forward sub-indicators does not imply the presence of reverse ones and, when there are no anti-isotonic indicators, model FKHM can be reduced to the formulation of the conventional BoD model [8].

The formulation given by Eq. (1) has three kinds of restrictions. The first restriction imposes that no country can have a CI value greater than one, to ensure an intuitive interpretation of the indicator. The second restriction imposes that each weight attributed to the sub-indicators should be non-negative, which implies that the CI is a non-decreasing function of the sub-indicators. The third restriction prevents the model from assigning zero weights to some sub-indicators, since zero weight means that the sub-indicator associated has no influence in the global performance. By adding a virtual proportional weight restrictions, as proposed by [23], each sub-indicator is required to have a minimum percentage of contribution in the assessed composite indicator. The value of 0.05 (or 5%) was chosen as it is sufficient to prevent the attribution of zero weights to any sub-indicator, thus, guaranteeing the contribution of all sub-indicators in the final composite indicator and have a higher countries' discrimination in the performance assessment. Consequently, the CI value obtained varies between zero and one for each assessed country j_o, where higher values indicate a better relative performance [17].

3   Methodology

This paper intends to assess the transport environmental performance of EU countries through the aggregation of sub-indicators into a CI using the Fare et al. [8] (FKHM) model. Therefore, the selection of these sub-indicators is of crucial importance to compute the countries overall performance while encompassing all the important subjects.

3.1   Data and Variables

The selection of the sub-indicators was based on a literature review of CI with similar conceptual framework, the goals of transport sustainability mentioned in the Roadmap (EU's White Paper [5]) and the SDG [6], while also taking into consideration the data that was available for all the EU countries in the time span under analysis. Besides, each sub-indicator must be of easy interpretation and should measure a specific area of the performance, ensuring a minimal number of sub-indicators that assures that all dimensions are reflected in the calculation of the CI. All the data used in this work were gathered from the Eurostat database [24].

To assess the transport environmental performance of EU countries, the CI was constructed based in three forward sub-indicators (i.e., capturing positive aspect) and four reverse sub-indicators (i.e., capturing negative aspect). The forward sub-indicators are the share of buses and trains in total passengers transport, the share of energy from renewable sources in transport and the share of rail and inland waterways in total freight transport. The reverse sub-indicators are people dead in road accidents, GHG emissions by fuel combustion in transport, the average CO_2 emissions per kilometer from new passengers cars and the energy dependency on oil and petroleum products. These sub-indicators are described hereinafter.

The share of collective transport in total passengers transport (*public transport*) is expressed in percentage and measures the share of passenger's transport made by collective transport in the total inland transport. Collective transport refers to buses (including coaches and trolleybuses) and trains, while the total inland transport includes these facilities and also passenger cars. Trams and metros are not included due to the lack of harmonised data. The public transport sub-indicator is related to two Sustainable Development Goals, in which it is highlighted the importance of building resilient and sustainable infrastructure and the necessity to renew and plan cities so they offer access to basic services for all. This sub-indicator also relates to the necessity of improving the transport quality, accessibility and reliability, as discussed in the Roadmap.

The share of energy from renewable sources in transport (*renewable fuels*) is expressed as the percentage of renewable fuels in the total transport fuels. Energy by renewable sources consumed in transport is given by the sum of sustainable biofuels, renewable electricity, hydrogen and synthetic fuels of renewable origin and other reported forms of renewable energy [25]. With this sub-indicator it is possible to understand how extensive is the use of renewable energy in the transport sector and how much it has been replacing fossil fuels. The Renewable Energy Directive promotes policies for the production and promotion of energy from renewable sources in the EU, which states, in the revised version from 2018, the target of 32% share of renewable energy in the transport sector for 2030 [26]. The Roadmap also suggests a regular phase out of conventionally-fuelled vehicles from urban environments by halving their number in 2030 and phasing them out of the cities by 2050.

The share of rail and inland waterways in total freight transport (*freight transport*) is expressed in percentage. The total inland transport in the denominator of the sub-indicator includes freight on national territory made by road, rail and inland waterways transport. Sea and air freight transport are not represented in the sub-indicator. The freight transport sub-indicator was not applicable for Cyprus and Malta since these countries did not present values for railways or inland waterways. As an effort to have a complete database without excluding these countries from the evaluation in this work the lowest values observed on the dataset were used for Cyprus and Malta for every year. This method avoid that these countries become unintended benchmarks, and therefore, it will not affect the location of the best practice frontier. This method has been suggested by Morais et al. [27]. The Roadmap mentions the objective of shifting 30% of the road freight to other modes, such as rail and waterways, by 2030 and more than 50% by 2050. This sub-indicator also reflects the progress toward the Sustainable Development Goals focused on innovation and on building resilient and sustainable infrastructure.

The people dead in road accidents (*road deaths*) sub-indicator measures the number of fatalities in road accidents per hundred thousand inhabitants. This sub-indicator includes passengers and drivers of motorized vehicles and pedal cycles, as well as pedestrians, that have died up to 30 days after the accident. This sub-indicator is aligned with two Sustainable Development Goals aiming at safer cities, health and well-being status. As highlighted in the Roadmap, EU aims to reduce fatalities close to zero by 2050 with initiatives in the areas of technology, enforcement and education.

The GHG emissions by fuel combustion in transport (*GHG emissions*) measures the transport's fuel combustion contribution in the total greenhouse gas emissions inventory. The values are originally expressed in thousand tonnes and were normalized using the countries' population on 1st January of each year, to take into consideration their dimension. Therefore, the sub-indicator's data is expressed in thousand tonnes per hundred thousand inhabitants for each country. The GHG emissions from the transport by road and inland waterways accounted for 22% of the total European Union emissions in 2017 and reached 27% when including international aviation and maritime emissions [28]. The Roadmap sets out a target of 60% reduction in the GHG emissions by 2050 compared to 1990 levels.

The average carbon dioxide (CO_2) emissions per kilometer from new passengers cars (*new car emissions*) is defined as the average CO_2 emissions per kilometer in a given year for new passenger cars and expressed in grams of CO_2 per kilometer. This is a target for the average of the manufacturer's overall fleet, meaning that cars above the limit are allowed in the market as long as they are offset by the production of lighter cars. The Regulation (EU) 2019/631 sets a mandatory target for emission reduction for new cars of 95 g of CO_2 per kilometer by 2021 [29]. This sub-indicator reflects three Sustainable Development Goals related to ensuring environmentally aware consumption, to innovation in search of lasting solutions to environmental challenges and the call for climate action. The Roadmap also highlights the importance of the research and innovation on vehicle propulsion technologies and the improvement of energy efficiency performance of vehicles across all modes.

The energy dependency on oil and petroleum products (*energy dependency*) sub-indicator monitors to which extent the countries economy relies on imports of oil and petroleum products to meet its energy needs. It is calculated by dividing the net imports by the gross available energy and it is used in a percentage basis. The net imports are the difference between the total imports and the total exports. The gross available energy is the sum of primary products, recovered and recycled products and imports, minus the sum of exports and stock changes. Regarding its metrics, energy dependency may be higher than 100% with regard to countries creating a stock in a given year or it can be negative, for oil exporter countries. A negative value occurred only once in the dataset, and the value was close to zero (−4.701%) for the exporter country. To achieve the best relative position of that energy exporter country regarding the other countries, the best score of 1% for this forward sub-indicator was assigned to the exporter country, to avoid handling negative data in the model. This sub-indicator shows how the EU countries progress toward more resource efficient policies. As oil becomes scarcer each year, the necessity of reducing EU dependency on oil imports, without reducing the transport system efficiency, is one of the objectives mentioned in the Roadmap. Imports exposes the economy to volatile world market prices and the risk of supply shortages.

These seven sub-indicators are used to assess the transport environmental performance of EU countries, as presented in the next section.

4   Results and Discussion

4.1   Descriptive Analysis of the Variables

The transport environmental performance was assessed for the 28 EU countries, from 2015 to 2017. It was chosen to use the United Kingdom data, since during the time span of the assessment the country still integrated the European Union. Table 1 shows two descriptive statistics for the sub-indicators under analysis across countries for each year. The mean of the sub-indicators was calculated for each year, as well as the dispersion coefficient (DC). The DC measures the dispersion of the data around the mean and is given by the ratio between the standard deviation and the mean. It was calculated in order to facilitate the analysis among sub-indicators, since it allows the comparison of the degree of variation between different data sets even if they have different measurement units.

Analysing the forward sub-indicators in Table 1, it can be seen that the share of public transport in total passenger transport has constantly decreased in the time span under study, by 2017 it was more than 2% lower compared to 2015 levels. The share of renewable energy in transport decreased in 2016 but by 2017 its average had increased more than 5% above 2015 value. And the share

Table 1. Mean and DC of the indicators data used in the construction of the CI.

	2015		2016		2017	
Sub-indicator	Mean	DC	Mean	DC	Mean	DC
Public transport	18.175	0.241	18.011	0.238	17.768	0.246
Freight transport	27.979	0.731	26.982	0.728	26.936	0.724
Renewable energy	6.544	0.795	6.191	0.746	6.884	0.733
Road deaths	5.800	0.366	5.625	0.325	5.325	0.358
GHG emissions	208.670	0.771	211.493	0.714	213.696	0.696
New car emissions	120.946	0.078	118.757	0.066	119.168	0.064
Energy dependency	92.605	0.245	90.736	0.248	89.935	0.250

of freight transport decreased between 2015 and 2017 staying 3.7% lower than 2015 levels.

Regarding the reverse sub-indicators, the average of road deaths for all countries has decreased more than 8% from 2015 to 2017. The average of GHG emissions for all countries has increased more than 2.4% during the time span studied. The mean of CO_2 emissions from new passengers cars has increased from 2016 to 2017 but still remained 1.5% below 2015 levels. And the average energy dependency of the EU countries decreased almost 3% between the years under analyse.

The highest data dispersion relative to the mean was observed in the share of renewable energy, which translates the difference among countries in available renewable energy. Another high DC value was obtained by the GHG emissions sub-indicator, reflecting the different policies of EU countries for reducing emissions. The share of freight transport also had a high DC, since some countries have geographical locations and environmental conditions that facilitate the utilization of rail and inland waterways. The DC for these three sub-indicators, however, have been constantly decreasing during the time span of the data, reflecting a tendency to increase the homogeneity among EU countries.

The lowest variability relative to the mean was observed for the CO_2 emissions from new passengers cars. This can be reflecting a higher homogeneity in the energy efficiency performance of vehicles engines among car manufacturers.

4.2   Performance Assessment of the EU Countries

The transport environmental performance for each country in a given year was computed by aggregating the seven chosen sub-indicators using the FKHM model, presented in Eq. (1).

The CI of the transport environmental performance was calculated using the data from the time span of three years, from 2015 to 2017 and it is assessed by comparison to the best practices observed during this time period. The results are summarized in Table 2. The countries are ranked based on their 2017 CI results from the highest to the lowest.

Table 2. Transport environmental performance results.

Country	2015	2016	2017
Denmark	0.972	0.937	1.000
Hungary	1.000	1.000	1.000
Netherlands	1.000	0.906	1.000
Sweden	0.878	0.960	1.000
Romania	1.000	0.977	0.948
Slovakia	0.886	0.927	0.895
Latvia	1.000	0.918	0.856
Austria	0.826	0.821	0.803
Czechia	0.761	0.773	0.800
Lithuania	0.790	0.763	0.784
Finland	0.842	0.620	0.759
Bulgaria	0.700	0.693	0.662
Poland	0.633	0.600	0.594
Belgium	0.548	0.570	0.583
France	0.540	0.522	0.542
Germany	0.531	0.550	0.538
Italy	0.539	0.550	0.525
Slovenia	0.488	0.416	0.494
Luxembourg	0.491	0.469	0.489
UK	0.420	0.410	0.416
Portugal	0.378	0.395	0.395
Spain	0.312	0.442	0.381
Croatia	0.463	0.348	0.341
Greece	0.189	0.162	0.216
Estonia	0.161	0.165	0.164
Ireland	0.141	0.125	0.131
Malta	0.139	0.126	0.130
Cyprus	0.131	0.120	0.120
Mean	0.599	0.581	0.592
St. Dev.	0.290	0.283	0.286

The average of the CI results in the three years analysed was around 0.591 and had only slight variations through the years. The average decreased by almost 3% in 2016 when compared to 2015, increased again in 2017 but still kept slightly bellow 2015 levels, by 1.17%. The standard deviation of the CI results was similar in the three year, showing that the results variability was kept the same during this period.

This assessment identifies nine efficient units: Denmark (in 2017), Latvia (in 2015), Hungary (in 2015, 2016 and 2017), Netherlands (in 2015 and 2017), Romania (in 2015) and Sweden (in 2017). From 2015 to 2017, half of the countries followed a small improvement and half of the country had a slight decrease in their overall performance. The highest improvement in the CI score between 2015 and 2017 were observed in Greece, Spain and Sweden, which increased in 2017 by 14%, 22% and 13% above 2015 levels, respectively.

The highest decrease during this time frame were observed for Croatia (26.4%) and Latvia (14.4%). The highest improvement in the time-span of one year was observed in Greece, that had a large decrease in its CI score between 2015 and 2016, but between 2016 and 2017 its CI value increased more than 33%. Estonia, Ireland, Cyprus and Malta were the most inefficient countries in this analysis with almost no improvement in the considered years. Besides Estonia, all these countries also had a decrease in their CI value in 2017 when compared to 2015.

This study also compares the forward and reverse sub-indicators of the benchmark countries, which obtained a CI score of 1, with the inefficient ones. The mean for each sub-indicator is calculated for both groups (benchmarks and inefficient countries). Figure 1 shows a comparison for each sub-indicator between the benchmark countries and the inefficient ones.

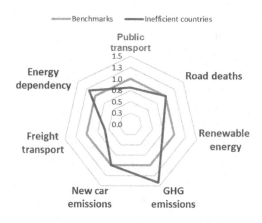

Fig. 1. Comparison between benchmarks and inefficient countries.

Analysing Fig. 1, it is possible to notice the areas where the inefficient countries need improvement, for instance, by setting out policies and/or redefine output standards. Except for the number of road deaths and the new car emissions indicators, in which both groups had a very similar performance, the inefficient countries were always outperformed by the benchmarks. The inefficient countries have 80% of the share of public transport presented by the benchmarks and almost 75% of the renewable energy share presented by the benchmark group. In the freight transports sub-indicator, the inefficient countries have less than 60% of the value presented for the benchmarks. Considering the reverse sub-indicators, with regard to the GHG emissions, the inefficient countries had a value more than 40% higher than the benchmarks. The average of energy dependency sub-indicator of the inefficient countries was almost 20% higher than the average for the benchmarks.

Most of the work to improve transport sustainability should be done in reducing the GHG emissions from fossil fuel, improving the infrastructure and promote policies to increase the share of freight transport that uses rail and waterways and also increasing the share of transport energy from renewable sources. The public transport of the inefficient countries also needs improvements in its accessibility and quality to allow a larger share of passenger to benefit from it. There is still also margin to reduce the oil and petroleum dependency through changes in the transport energy consumption.

5   Conclusions

The assessment of the transport environmental performance was made through the aggregation of seven transport sub-indicators. The model used to obtain the CI values was derived from a variant BoD model with virtual proportional weights restrictions. Based on the results achieved, it is possible to conclude that, in general, the EU countries had almost no variation on their transport environmental performance and by 2017 were, on average, 1.17% lower than 2015 values. This result points out that EU countries should make efforts to enable them to develop and strengthen their ability towards sustainability.

The performance assessment identified that only nine units were efficient: Denmark (in 2017), Latvia (in 2015), Hungary (in 2015, 2016 and 2017), Netherlands (in 2015 and 2017), Romania (in 2015) and Sweden (in 2017). By using these units as benchmarks and comparing their performance in each sub-indicator with the remaining units (the inefficient ones), it was possible to identify the areas that need improvement. Most of the work to improve transport sustainability should be done by drastically reducing the GHG from fossil fuel, increasing the share of freight transport that uses rail and waterways and also the share of transport energy from renewable sources.

Future works should explore other models for treating anti-isotonic sub-indicators in order to allow results comparison among those different models. Furthermore, some other sub-indicators can be taken into account, to calculate the composite indicator for each country.

Sub-indicator	Mean	DC	Variation 2015–17
Public transport	17.985	0.242	**−2.24%**
Renewable energy	6.540	0.756	*+5.20%*
Freight transport	27.979	0.731	**−3.73%**
Road deaths	5.583	0.350	*−8.20%*
GHG emissions	211.286	0.727	**+2.41%**
New car emissions	119.624	0.069	*−1.47%*
Energy dependency	91.092	0.247	*−2.88%*

Acknowledgements. This work has been supported by FCT – Fundação para a Ciência e Tecnologia within the Project Scope: UIDB/05757/2020.

References

1. Litman, T.: Well Measured. Victoria Transport Policy Institute, Victoria (2016)
2. Sustainable Mobility Project 2.0. Integrated sustainable mobility in cities - a practical guide. World Business Council for Sustainable Development (2016)
3. European Commission: EU mobility package: Europe on the move briefing note. http://nws.eurocities.eu/MediaShell/media/EuropeonthemoveBriefingnote.pdf. Accessed 10 Mar 2020
4. Dobranskyte-Niskota, A., Perujo, A., Pregl, M.: Indicators to assess sustainability of transport activities. European Comission, Joint Research Centre (2007)
5. European Commission: White Paper on Transport: Roadmap to a Single European Transport Area: Towards a Competitive and Resource-efficient Transport System. Publications Office of the European Union (2011)
6. About the sustainable development goals. https://www.un.org/sustainabledevelopment/sustainable-development-goals/. Accessed 13 Mar 2020
7. Reisi, M., Aye, L., Rajabifard, A., Ngo, T.: Transport sustainability index: Melbourne case study. Ecol. Ind. **43**, 288–296 (2014)
8. Färe, R., Karagiannis, G., Hasannasab, M., Margaritis, D.: A benefit-of-the-doubt model with reverse indicators. Eur. J. Oper. Res. **278**(2), 394–400 (2019)
9. Mitchell, G., May, A., McDonald, A.: PICABUE: a methodological framework for the development of indicators of sustainable development. Int. J. Sustain. Dev. World Ecol. **2**(2), 104–123 (1995)
10. Joint Research Centre-European Commission: Handbook on constructing composite indicators: methodology and user guide. OECD Publishing, Paris (2008)
11. Cherchye, L., Moesen, W., Rogge, N., Van Puyenbroeck, T.: An introduction to 'benefit of the doubt'composite indicators. Soc. Indic. Res. **82**(1), 111–145 (2007)
12. Kunicina, N., et al.: Indicators of environmental sustainability in transport. An interdisciplinary approach to methods (2010)
13. Gudmundsson, H., Regmi, M.B.: Developing the sustainable urban transport index. Transp. Sustain. Dev. Goals, 35 (2017)
14. Zhou, P., Ang, B.W., Poh, K.L.: A mathematical programming approach to constructing composite indicators. Ecol. Econ. **62**(2), 291–297 (2007)
15. Charnes, A., Cooper, W.W., Rhodes, E.: Measuring the efficiency of decision making units. Eur. J. Oper. Res. **2**(6), 429–444 (1978)

16. Cooper, W.W., Seiford, L.M., Tone, K.: Data envelopment analysis: a comprehensive text with models, applications, references and DEA-solver software. J. Oper. Res. Soc. **52**(12), 1408–1409 (2001)

17. Cherchye, L., et al.: Creating composite indicators with DEA and robustness analysis: the case of the technology achievement index. J. Oper. Res. Soc. **59**(2), 239–251 (2008). https://doi.org/10.1057/palgrave.jors.2602445

18. Melyn, W., Moesen, W.: Towards a synthetic indicator of macroeconomic performance: unequal weighting when limited information is available. Public economics research papers, pp. 1–24 (1991)

19. Chung, W.: Using DEA model without input and with negative input to develop composite indicators. In: International Conference on Industrial Engineering and Engineering Management (IEEM), pp. 2010–2013. IEEE (2017)

20. Lovell, C.K., Pastor, J.T., Turner, J.A.: Measuring macroeconomic performance in the OECD: a comparison of European and non-European countries. Eur. J. Oper. Res. **87**(3), 507–518 (1995)

21. Dyson, R.G., et al.: Pitfalls and protocols in DEA. Eur. J. Oper. Res. **132**(2), 245–259 (2001)

22. Scheel, H.: Undesirable outputs in efficiency valuations. Eur. J. Oper. Res. **132**(2), 400–410 (2001)

23. Wong, Y.H., Beasley, J.E.: Restricting weight flexibility in data envelopment analysis. J. Oper. Res. Soc. **41**(9), 829–835 (1990). https://doi.org/10.1057/jors.1990.120

24. Eurostat Database. https://ec.europa.eu/eurostat/data/database. Accessed 20 Mar 2020

25. European Commission: SHARES Tool Manual. Directorate E: Sectoral and regional statistics. Unit E.5: Energy (2018)

26. European Commission: DIRECTIVE 2018/2001 of the European parliament and of the council. Official Journal of the European Union (2018)

27. Morais, P., Camanho, A.S.: Evaluation of performance of European cities with the aim to promote quality of life improvements. Omega **39**(4), 398–409 (2011)

28. European Commission: Proposal for a Regulation of the European Parliament and of the Council setting CO2 emission performance standards for new heavy duty vehicles (2011)

29. European Commission: Regulation (EU) 2019/631 of the European parliament and of the council. Official Journal of the European Union (2019)

Mobility and IoT

Public Transportation and Accessibility to Education Centers in Maldonado, Uruguay

Renzo Massobrio$^{(\boxtimes)}$ ⓘ, Sergio Nesmachnow ⓘ, Emiliano Gómez,
Facundo Sosa ⓘ, and Silvina Hipogrosso ⓘ

Universidad de la República, Montevideo, Uruguay
`renzom@fing.edu.uy`

Abstract. This article presents a study of public transportation and accessibility to public services in Maldonado, Uruguay. Accessibility is a crucial concept in nowadays smart cities, to guarantee a proper mobility, citizen participation in social, economic, and cultural activities, and an overall good quality of life. Several data sources are studied and processed to characterize the accessibility provided by the public transportation system of Maldonado to public services, specifically to education centers. A matrix of travel times by public transportation is computed and used to define a flexible accessibility indicator to reach destinations of interest. Finally, an interactive visualization tool is developed to graphically display the computed information. The accessibility indicator constitutes an input for the decision-making of the transportation authorities of the studied area, as well as it allows identifying potential inequity situations.

Keywords: Smart cities · Mobility · Public transportation · Accessibility · Public services

1 Introduction

The characterization of urban accessibility is an important tool to determine the quality of transportation systems and their impact on the daily activities of citizens [5]. Several recent researches have studied different aspects of accessibility, e.g., regarding urban public facility spaces [13], urban planning [3], neighborhood retail [15], and other relevant issues.

Evaluating accessibility is a challenging task, even considering a simple definition of accessibility, related to the capability of reaching certain relevant destinations in the city. The challenges are consequence of the plethora of theoretical concepts to be considered (including land utilization, universal access, transportation modes, etc.), and also the lack of sound methodologies for empirical evaluation. Thus, accessibility is often considered as a poorly understood concept, which is not correctly evaluated, and rarely taken into account for elaborating polices for urban development, transportation design and operation,

ⓒ Springer Nature Switzerland AG 2021
S. Nesmachnow and L. Hernández Callejo (Eds.): ICSC-CITIES 2020, CCIS 1359, pp. 123–138, 2021.
https://doi.org/10.1007/978-3-030-69136-3_9

infrastructure investments, and other relevant actions for improving quality of life. Overall, knowledge about accessibility is very useful for assisting policy-makers and planners to evaluate different approaches to develop transportation with a special focus on inequities and phenomena with high social impact.

This article presents a characterization of public transportation and accessibility to education centers in the metropolitan area of Maldonado, Uruguay. The case study is an important urban conglomeration in the Southeast of Uruguay, with more than 135.000 inhabitants. The proposed research focuses on public transportation, as it is understood to be the most efficient, sustainable, and socially fair transportation mode [4]. The distances and total travel times between different zones by using public transportation are studied via a data analysis approach [17] to identify areas with poor mobility provision that imply high travel times, and therefore impose restrictions on territorial accessibility.

In order to quantify the provision of the transportation system in the Maldonado metropolitan area, a matrix of travel times between different areas of the city is computed. Trips in different modes (walking, with a direct bus line, and trips involving transfers) are considered. Then, geolocated data about public services is used to compute the accessibility offered by the public transportation system. As a case study, the accessibility to education centers is computed, as it is a relevant public service for the Municipality of Maldonado. By incorporating the scope of different mobility options, the proposed methodology advances on a factor for the definition of indicators of inequity in intra-urban accessibility and their subsequent use for support and decision-making on urban planning.

The main contributions of the reported research include: i) a matrix of travel times on public transportation in the Maldonado metropolitan area, at the census segment level; ii) an accessibility indicator by public transportation to education centers located in the studied area; and iii) a web visualization tool that allows graphically displaying the accessibility indicator. The reported results are useful for transit and transportation authorities of the Municipality of Maldonado, since they constitute an important input when defining public policies, designing new transportation lines, or redesigning current ones in order to serve identified areas as of poor accessibility.

The article is organized as follows. Section 2 reviews relevant concepts and related works about accessibility and related initiatives in Uruguay. The proposed data analysis approach and the case study are described in Sect. 3. The implementation details are presented in Sect. 4, including the calculation of the matrix of travel times for public transportation and the accessibility indicator to education centers. The results of the analysis are shown and discussed in Sect. 5 along with a brief description of the web visualization tool. Finally, Sect. 6 presents the main conclusions and lines for future work.

2   Accessibility and Related Works

Citizen participation in social, economic, and cultural activities requires people to travel, sometimes long distances and involving long periods of time [8].

The ability of individuals to overcome limitations imposed by distances and other mobility-related difficulties is critical when actively participating in city life [2]. This measure of the ability of transportation systems to allow individuals to overcome distances is known under the concept of accessibility.

The term accessibility has been extensively studied in the literature, with the first definitions emerging from the area of geographical studies more than 60 years ago [6]. Although the term is widely disseminated, there are multiple (and complementary) definitions, which vary according to the area of study and the point of view from which its quantification is proposed. Generally speaking, accessibility can be defined as a measure of the effort (or ease) of overcoming spatial separation. Specifically, accessibility seeks to measure the spatial distribution of opportunities (e.g., jobs, study sites, hospitals) adjusted for people's ability or desire to overcome separation (e.g., distance, time, cost) to such opportunities. Within the classification established by Ingram [14], this project focuses on comprehensive accessibility, which contemplates the degree of interconnection of a point or area with all the others on the same surface.

Several indicators have been proposed to measure the separation between points/areas when evaluating accessibility, among them, travel time is one of the most intuitive, as it is strongly related to the perception of users of a transportation system. Lei and Church [16] presented a review on the use of travel time when quantifying the accessibility offered by public transportation systems. The authors show that various works in the literature focus on the physical characteristics offered by transportation systems (e.g., distance to the bus stop) rather than focusing on travel time. Furthermore, within the works that do focus on travel time, there are a number of assumptions that significantly affect the final measure, including considering fixed waiting and transfer times or a constant speed for vehicles. Salonen and Toivone [19] presented a comparison of different techniques for estimating travel times, both for private and public transport. The authors evaluated different travel time estimation models on a case study in the capital region of Finland. The results achieved show that those models that incorporate a greater amount of information regarding the transportation system are able to estimate travel times with greater precision, although the differences between models were less in the downtown areas.

In Uruguay, some studies have addressed the issue of accessibility, particularly using public transportation. Hansz [7] studied the disparity between public transportation supply and transportation needs in Montevideo. The author defined a public transportation provision index that combines the frequency of buses and the number of stops in a given area. The provision offered by the Montevideo public transportation system, measured according to this index, is strongly biased towards the city center. Hernández [9] studied inequities in access to employment and educational opportunities between different social classes as a consequence of the offer of public transport. This work used the travel time to compute accessibility, which was obtained through How to Go, a web application offered by the Municipality of Montevideo to estimate travel times by public transport. The study showed that there is an unequal distribution of mobility opportunities, particularly for access to job opportunities and access to higher level education. Later, Hernández et al. [10] built a matrix of travel times using theoretical timetables of buses in Montevideo, which was used as input to generate an index of accessibility to job opportunities in the city.

Other research efforts developed within our research group include the socio-economic analysis of the transportation system in Montevideo using big data and distributed computing [18], the analysis of sustainable transportation initiatives in Montevideo [12] evaluating the accessibility index proposed by the World Business Council for Sustainable Development [20], and the empirical study performed in Parque Rodó neighborhood using face-to-face surveys [11].

3   Case Study and Data Analysis Approach

This section describes the studied area and the methodology applied for data analysis to characterize accessibility.

3.1   Maldonado Metropolitan Area

The metropolitan area of Maldonado includes the conurbation of the cities of Maldonado and Punta del Este, which progressively joined, including transportation routes. Maldonado is the administrative capital of the department and Punta del Este is considered the tourist capital at national level. The city of San Carlos is considered as part of this conurbation, although Maldonado and San Carlos are separated by a suburban space. These three cities are the arteries of an urban network that extends even west to Portezuelo and east to José Ignacio. The suburban area has specific mobility needs and the demand for public transportation, and currently has problems with traffic congestion and accessibility to important points. In addition, the cities of Piriápolis and Pan de

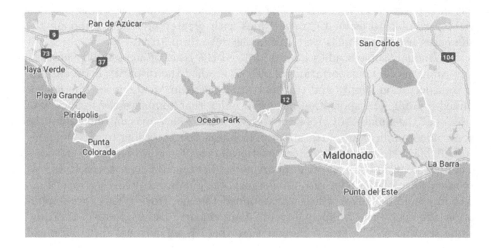

Fig. 1. Metropolitan area of Maldonado

Azúcar are less than 30 km from Maldonado and public transportation lines connect them frequently. More than 150.000 people live in the studied area, while about 20.000 live in Piriápolis and Pan de Azúcar.

3.2 Data Analysis Approach

The Municipality of Maldonado granted access to a set of public transportation data, including lines, stops, and timetables of the different routes. Each dataset has specific features, which are described in the following paragraphs.

Bus Lines and Stops. This dataset includes the layout of routes lines and the location of the bus stops of the public transportation system. From a geographical point of view, the main difficulty with these data lies in the fact that the dataset of lines and stops are independent. Figure 2 shows the set of stops and lines of the public transportation system, according to the provided data.

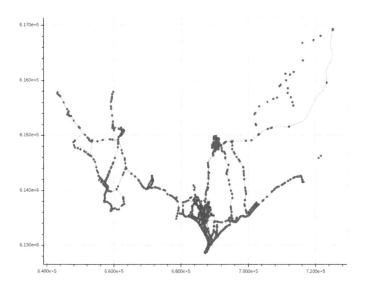

Fig. 2. Bus lines and stops of the public transportation system in Maldonado

Certain problems and particularities of the studied datasets pose challenges for building a matrix of travel times for public transportation to compute the accessibility indicator. Three main problems were identified: stops located in places without defined bus lines; stops located very close to each other (which clearly correspond to the same physical stop); and stops that do not coincide with the layout of the bus lines. This last point is the most challenging, since there is no direct association that indicates to which line(s) a certain stop corresponds.

An automated process was implemented to solve the aforementioned problems applying geospatial operations to associate lines and stops. The algorithm

works as follows: i) for each bus line a *buffer* operation is performed to convert
the line to a 10 m wide polygon; ii) the polygon is intersected with the stop layer
to obtain stops that are less than 10 m from the line; and iii) the set of stops is
traversed according to the direction of the line and consecutive stops that are
less than 50 m from each other are eliminated, on the understanding that it is the
same physical stop. Figure 3 shows the implemented correction process (stops in
the original set are marked in red and the stops after applying the correction
procedure are marked in green).

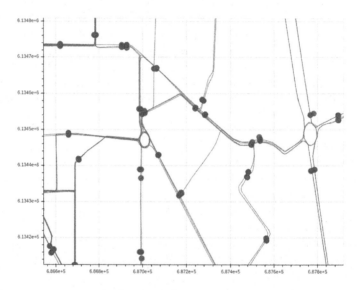

Fig. 3. Bus stop correction (red–original bus stops; green–corrected bus stops) (Color
figure online)

Timetables and Trip Times. The other provided dataset corresponds to the
timetables of the different lines of the public transportation system. The data
are separated according to the transportation company that operates the service.
The provided dataset consist of Excel files that do not follow a standardized
format, which makes its automated processing extremely difficult. Since it does
not account for a large volume of data, the processing was carried out manually.
For each line, departure times and passing times for some notable points along
the route are reported. These notable points are identified by a name that does
not necessarily match the name defined in the transportation system. Therefore,
the procedure involved associating these points with their corresponding stops
and associating the average travel time from the start of the route to that stop,
based on the published timetables. Finally, for the rest of the stops on the line,
travel times are interpolated from the known travel times.

Since the information of lines and stops is separated from the data of the
timetables, there are differences between both datasets. In particular, timetable

information is not available for a few lines (line 32 from Pan de Azúcar to Nueva Carrara, line 62 from/to Punta del Este, line 25 from San Carlos to José Ignacio, line 26 from Garzón to San Carlos, line 27 of Guscapar company, and direct line Punta del Este–San Carlos). In these cases, it is not possible to know the travel times between the stops on the route and, therefore, they were not considered within the model. Other lines were partially included in the model, according to the available data: e.g., line 34 from Las Flores (and not from Pan de Azúcar) to Piriápolis, line 55 from Manatiales (and not Buenos Aires) to Maldonado, and line 62 between Maldonado and La Capuera (and not from/to Punta del Este).

Overall, a total number of 66 lines/variants operated by six companies were included in the developed model.

4   Accessibility to Education Centers

This section describes the methodology for computing the proposed accessibility indicator to education centers, describing the studied area and the two needed inputs: the matrix of travel times and the location of education centers.

4.1   Definition of the Studied Area

The basic unit of the analysis is the census segment, defined by the National Institute of Statistics (INE). The file published by INE was corrected, since it had some invalid geometries that prevented the correct data processing.

The process used to define the studied area is graphically described in Fig. 4 and commented next. Initially, all census segments that have at least one stop of the transportation system within the polygon that defines them are considered (Figs. 4a–4b). Then, neighboring towns that do not have stops are considered to avoid gaps in the studied area, computing the convex hull of the set of census segments (Fig. 4c) and intersecting with the total of census segments (Fig. 4d) to obtain all census segments to consider. The centroid of each census segment in the resulting set is computed, assuming that all trips from/to a certain segment begin (or end) at the centroid of that segment (Fig. 4e).

4.2   Matrix of Travel Times

The matrix of travel times for public transportation was built considering trips with up two legs (one transfer). Travel times include: i) the walking time from the centroid of the origin segment to the first bus stop; ii) the walking time from the descent stop of the last bus of the trip to the centroid of the destination segment; iii) the walking time between stops on those trips that involve transfers; and iv) the time traveling on each bus involved in the trip. Also, direct walks (up to 30 mins) are considered between nearby centroids, since walking can be a more

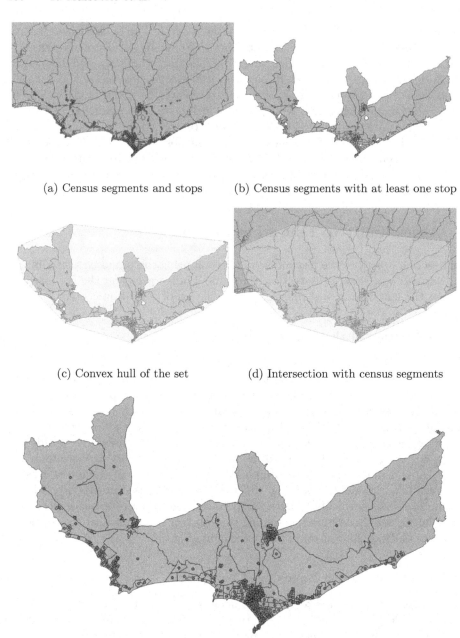

(a) Census segments and stops   (b) Census segments with at least one stop

(c) Convex hull of the set   (d) Intersection with census segments

(e) Final set: census segments and their centroids

Fig. 4. Process for defining the studied area

attractive option than public transportation. Walks from the origin centroids to the first bus stop and from the last bus stop to the destination centroids are limited to 30 mins. Walks between transfer stops are limited to 20 mins. The fastest travel connecting a pair of centroids is considered, assuming that people make optimal decisions to move within the city, within the rules imposed in the model regarding maximum walks and number of transfers allowed.

A directed and weighted multigraph is constructed to build the matrix. Nodes of the graph represent the centroids of census segments and the bus stops. Nodes can be connected by more than one edge. The weight of each edge represents the travel time between nodes (walking or by bus). A shorter path algorithm is applied to compute the fastest travel time between each pair of centroids.

Walking times between centroids, between centroids and stops, and between stops, are computed on the road network of the city. Each centroid/stop is moved to the nearest road and times are computed using Open Source Routing Machine, an engine implemented in C++ that combines routing algorithms with Open-StreetMap road network data to efficiently compute shorter paths. The `table` method was used to compute the travel times between pairs in a list of geographic coordinates, using the average speed for each type of road and traffic rules imposes in the `foot.lua` profile. Routes for a small subset of 41 nodes cannot be computed using this approach, as they were located in areas far from the road network. The travel times to/from these nodes was computed using the geographical distance and a walking speed of 5 km/h.

Bus travel edges are weighted according to the average travel time between the nodes they connect. To ensure that the shortest path does not have more than one transfer, two different nodes are used to represent each centroid (one when the centroid acts as the origin and the other when it acts as the destination) and four to represent each physical stop (which represent the stop when it is the origin or destination of the first or second trip within the total route). Origin centroids have only outgoing edges, while destination centroids have only inward edges. This allows routes to be modeled with a direct trip and even with a transfer, considering the walk between stops in the eventual transfer. A penalty of 15 mins (added to the weight of the walking edges that connect stops) is considered on those roads that involve a transfer.

The NetworkX library of Python was used to represent the graph and compute the shortest paths. The generated graph includes a total number of 6382 nodes (253×2 centroids $+ 1469 \times 4$ stops) and 642 775 edges.

4.3   Location of Education Centers

The geographical location of education centers (initial, primary, secondary, and technical-professional education) are obtained from the Open Data Catalog [1]. Figure 5 shows the location of these centers in the studied area.

Fig. 5. Education centers in the metropolitan area of MaldonadoEducation centers in the metropolitan area of Maldonado

4.4 Accessibility Indicator

The matrix of travel times and the location of the education centers are used as input to compute the accessibility indicator to education centers by public transportation, using census segments as unit. The proposed indicator is based on the notion of accumulated opportunities, originally proposed by Hansen [6]. The method consists of characterizing the accessibility of every census segment by adding all education centers that are reachable from it, traveling for up to m mins by public transportation. The threshold m is parameterizable, allowing to perform the accessibility study under different conditions. The proposed indicator is flexible, since it allows varying the travel time threshold, and can even be used to evaluate accessibility to other opportunities, provided that geolocated information of their location is available. An improved version of the proposed indicator could consider the opening hours of each education center computing the value for each hour of the day. However, opening hours is not included in the open dataset used in this study. The proposed indicator can be extended to contemplate the time dimension, if this information is published in the future.

5   Results and Discussion

This section reports the main results achieved and presents the web tool developed to display the accessibility indicator.

5.1   Travel Time Matrix

The computed matrix of travel times for Maldonado metropolitan area is publicly available in CSV format at www.fing.edu.uy/~renzom/TTM.csv, The corresponding entry for or each pair of census segments reports the travel time using public transportation, in minutes. The matrix is a relevant result in itself, since it is an important input to address various types of design and optimization problems related to public transportation in the studied area.

The matrix has dimension 253×253. According to the implemented model, the travel time reflected in the matrix is the fastest option that connects each pair of census segments, considering direct walks, direct bus trips or even a transfer. Transfer trips add 15 mins to walk between stops, transfer walks are limited to 20 mins, and direct walks between centroids and entrance/exit to the transportation network are limited to 30 mins. For this reason, some segments are disconnected, either due to the absence of lines connecting it with up to a transfer or because the stops are at a distance from the centroid that exceeds the limit allowed for walks. The results show that 13 021 origin-destination pairs (out of 64 009) are disconnected.

The average travel time between all pairs of connected census segments is 52.5 mins. Figure 6 shows a histogram with the frequency of each travel time value (in minutes), considering the total number of connected census segments. Regarding travel modes, 58.1% of the trips correspond to direct trips involving a single bus, 40.5% correspond to trips with a transfer, and 1.4% correspond to direct walks, without using the public transportation system.

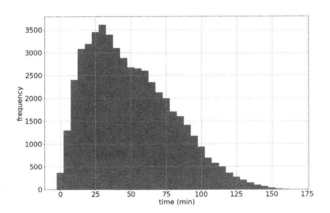

Fig. 6. Histogram with the frequency of travel times between census segments

5.2   Accessibility Indicator

The accessibility indicator combines the matrix of travel times and the location of education centers. By definition, each census segment accesses all education centers in it and in census segments that can be accessed by public transportation on trips of up to m minutes. By varying the parameter m it is possible to study different situations, based on different assumptions. Using $m = 0$, each census segment only accesses the education centers that are located within the polygon that defines them. In the choropleth map in Fig. 7, the color of each segment indicates the percentage of education centers it contains, with respect to the total number of centers available. The figure shows that the rural census segments (those with the largest area) are mostly covered by at least one education center.

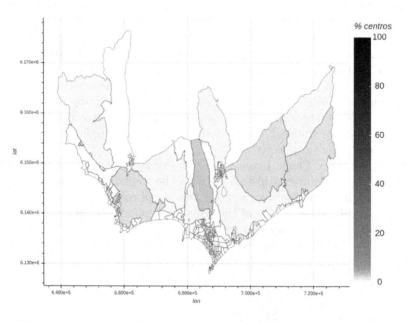

Fig. 7. Percentage of education centers located in each census segment

The accessibility of different scenarios can be studied varying the threshold m. Figure 8 shows the accessibility indicator for $m = 10$ mins. Results indicate that a small change in the threshold m implies a significant change on the spatial distribution of the accessibility indicator. The census segments located in the central areas of Maldonado and San Carlos show higher accessibility values than the large census segments of the rural periphery. This effect occurs because census segments without an education center can access one in a neighboring segment through public transportation trips or short walks.

The coastal areas of Punta Ballena, Pinares, and Punta del Este still have low accessibility with low time thresholds. This phenomenon change when a slightly higher threshold is set. Figure 9 shows the accessibility indicator with up to 20 mins of travel ($m = 20$). In addition, accessibility continues improving both from the center of Maldonado and from San Carlos. In turn, it is observed that the coastal areas to the east (e.g., San Rafael, La Barra) present low accessibility indices when considering trips of up to 20 mins.

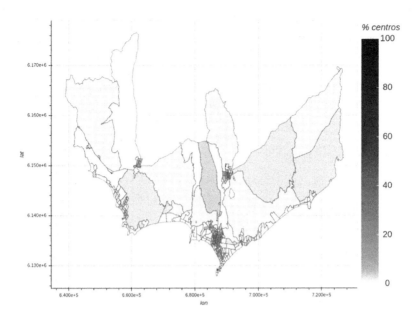

Fig. 8. Percentage of accessible education centers traveling up to 10 mins

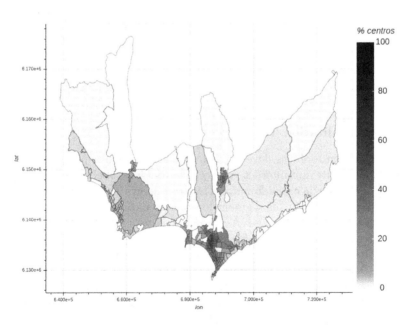

Fig. 9. Percentage of accessible education centers traveling up to 20 mins

Finally, Fig. 10 shows the accessibility indicator using a 40-min threshold. In this case, good accessibility exists in most urban census segments. However, there is a clear stagnation in terms of accessibility in most rural segments, which only access to centers located in them and fail to access to centers in other areas. Likewise, an inequality phenomenon is observed in the coastal census segments, where the segments to the west of Punta del Este have better accessibility values than those located to the east of the peninsula.

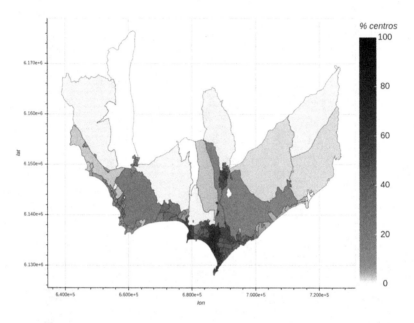

Fig. 10. Percentage of accessible education centers traveling up to 40 mins

5.3   Web Visualization Tool

A web visualization tool was developed to present the results of the accessibility indicator in a friendly and interactive way. The tool is publicly available at www.fing.edu.uy/~renzom/acc_maldonado. The tool shows the studied area on an interactive map, at the census segment level. The map has tools to zoom, scroll, and download the current image. A slider bar is provided to allow configuring the time threshold m considered for computing the accessibility index.

Once a threshold is set, the map is updated to report the accessibility indicator to education centers. The result is shown through a choropleth map where each census segment is assigned a color based on its accessibility indicator value. Positioning the cursor on a specific census segment displays the code that identifies the census segment, the name of the city, the number of education centers reached, and the percentage of the total that they represent.

6   Conclusions and Future Work

This article presented a study of the accessibility to public services in Maldonado, Uruguay, when using the public transportation system. In order to compute an accessibility index a travel time matrix for the public transportation was built using open datasets and data provided by the local authorities, including bus lines, bus stops, and timetable information. With these data the public transportation was modeled as a graph, accounting for every alternative to connect origin and destination pairs in the studied scenario. A shortest-path algorithm was executed over this graph to compute the fastest travel time between each origin and destination. Computed travel times include walking times to/from the bus stop and in-vehicle time of both direct trips and multi-leg trips involving up to one bus transfer. The computed travel time matrix is publicly available and is a highly useful resource for authorities and researchers alike.

Then, the accessibility to education was studied combining the computed travel time matrix with the location of education centers in the studied area. Following the usual methodology in the field, accessibility was measured accumulating the opportunities (i.e., centers) that can be reached from a given origin when traveling up to a certain threshold of time via public transportation. An interactive web application was developed that outlines the accessibility measures of the studied zone when varying the travel time threshold. The application shows a map of the area and colors different zones according to their accessibility to education centers.

According to our review of the related works, this research is one of the first steps of studying the public transportation system of Maldonado, Uruguay. The results of this research (i.e., the travel time matrix, accessibility indicator, and web application) are valuable to transport and urban planning authorities and research interested in improving the public transport accessibility in the area.

The main lines of future work involve feeding the model with richer information including: up-to-date GPS bus location data, ticket-sale data from on-board smartcard readers present in the buses of the system, as well as historic passenger information to improve the travel time estimations and make recommendations to improve the quality of service of neglected areas with significant inequalities.

References

1. Administración Nacional de Educación Pública: Centros anep. https://catalogo-datos.gub.uy/dataset/anep-centros-anep [12/2019] (2019)
2. Cardozo, O., Rey, C.: La vulnerabilidad en la movilidad urbana: aportes teóricos y metodológicos. In: Aportes conceptuales y empíricos de la vulnerabilidad global, pp. 398–423. Resistencia, Chaco: EUDENE (2007)
3. Duranton, G., Guerra, E.: Developing a common narrative on urban accessibility: An urban planning perspective. Technical reports, Brookings, Moving to Access (2016)
4. Grava, S.: Urban Transportation Systems. McGraw-Hill Education (2002)

5. Sten Hansen, H.: Analysing the role of accessibility in contemporary urban development. In: Gervasi, O., Taniar, D., Murgante, B., Laganà, A., Mun, Y., Gavrilova, M.L. (eds.) ICCSA 2009. LNCS, vol. 5592, pp. 385–396. Springer, Heidelberg (2009). https://doi.org/10.1007/978-3-642-02454-2_27

6. Hansen, W.: How accessibility shapes land use. J. Am. Inst. Planners **25**(2), 73–76 (1959)

7. Hansz, M.: Analysis of the spatial disparity in transport social needs and public transport provision in Montevideo. Master's thesis, University of Leeds (2016)

8. Harvey, D.: Social justice, postmodernism and the city. Int. J. Urban Regional Res. **16**(4), 588–601 (1992)

9. Hernandez, D.: Uneven mobilities, uneven opportunities: social distribution of public transport accessibility to jobs and education in montevideo. J. Transport Geography **67**, 119–125 (2018)

10. Hernández, D., Hansz, M., Massobrio, R., Davyt, J.: Transporte público urbano y la accesibilidad a las oportunidades laborales. https://ucu.edu.uy/es/node/47195, December 2019 (2019)

11. Hipogrosso, S., Nesmachnow, S.: Analysis of sustainable public transportation and mobility recommendations for montevideo and parque rodó neighborhood. Smart Cities **3**(2), 479–510 (2020)

12. Hipogrosso, S., Nesmachnow, S.: Sustainable mobility in the public transportation of Montevideo, Uruguay. In: Nesmachnow, S., Hernández Callejo, L. (eds.) ICSC-CITIES 2019. CCIS, vol. 1152, pp. 93–108. Springer, Cham (2020). https://doi.org/10.1007/978-3-030-38889-8_8

13. Huang, B., Chiou, S., Li, W.: Accessibility and street network characteristics of urban public facility spaces: Equity research on parks in fuzhou city based on GIS and space syntax model. Sustainability **12**(9), 3618 (2020)

14. Ingram, D.: The concept of accessibility: a search for an operational form. Regional Stud. **5**(2), 101–107 (1971)

15. Krizek, K., Horning, J., El-Geneidy, A.: Perceptions of accessibility to neighbourhood retail and other public services. In: Accessibility Analysis and Transport Planning, pp. 96–117. Edward Elgar Publishing (2012)

16. Lei, T., Church, R.: Mapping transit-based access: integrating gis, routes and schedules. Int. J. Geogr. Inf. Sci. **24**(2), 283–304 (2010)

17. Massobrio, R., Nesmachnow, S.: Urban data analysis for the public transportation system of montevideo, uruguay. In: Smart Cities, pp. 199–214 (2020)

18. Nesmachnow, S., Baña, S., Massobrio, R.: A distributed platform for big data analysis in smart cities: combining intelligent transportation systems and socioeconomic data for montevideo, uruguay. EAI Endorsed Transactions on Smart Cities **2**(5) (2017)

19. Salonen, M., Toivonen, T.: Modelling travel time in urban networks: comparable measures for private car and public transport. J. Transport Geography **31**, 143–153 (2013)

20. World Business Council for Sustainable Development: Methodology and indicator calculation method for sustainable urban mobility. Technical report 978-2-940521-26-5 (2015)

Crowdsourcing and IoT Towards More Resilient Flooding Prone Cities

Ponciano J. Escamilla-Ambrosio[(⊠)] [iD], Maria G. Pulido-Navarro,
Isabel V. Hernández-Gutiérrez, Abraham Rodríguez-Mota,
and Marco A. Moreno-Ibarra

Centro de Investigación en Computación,
Instituto Politécnico Nacional, Mexico City, Mexico
pescamilla@cic.ipn.mx

Abstract. Crowdsourcing is a phenomenon where groups of persons some-times from different backgrounds participate to accomplish a task by making use of technology. Internet of Things (IoT) is able to incorporate a large number of heterogeneous devices such as sensors, surveillance cameras, smartphones, home appliances, etc., all data generated by these devices is processed and analysed to incorporate applications that will make life easier for the end users. This article proposes that community members of a specific urban zone, prone to flooding, collaborate in sharing information about weather conditions using IoT techniques. The gathered information is sent to a cloudlet to be analysed together with information from weather forecast and a network of sensors and surveillance cameras installed in specific areas inside and surrounding the studied zone. Having members of the very community studied involved in the process will exploit the available IoT technologies and the use of crowdsourcing at a lower cost leading to the development of what is called Smart City. This paper revises the available technology and proposes a system that will help in collecting and evaluating information for prediction purposes as to whether the community involved is at risk of being flooded. It is being noted that this risk is getting higher every year due to overpopulation, bad urbanisation, and climate change. Results show that the use of this technology will improve weather forecast so the community could react in time in case of flooding threats.

Keywords: Crowdsourcing · Internet of things · Smart cities · Flooding risk · Resiliency

1 Introduction

Flooding risks in densely populated urban zones is becoming a big threat for its inhabitants; these cities are at danger not only for the material loses but for health hazards and even loss of lives. The problem arises principally from the lack of urban planning; it is possible that the urban services were initially designed for a number of houses and little by little were overpopulated leading to a disaster when the pluvial rain couldn't get its course through the normal planned way. Another situation that worsens this condition is the waste thrown at the drainage that clots it. Anyway, this circumstance

© Springer Nature Switzerland AG 2021
S. Nesmachnow and L. Hernández Callejo (Eds.): ICSC-CITIES 2020, CCIS 1359, pp. 139–153, 2021.
https://doi.org/10.1007/978-3-030-69136-3_10

requires a preventive plan to give its residents enough time to react in case that flooding might occur. Thus, this paper reviews some already proposed systems and how they have helped distinct communities, in some cases information regarding flooding problems has been obtained through interviewing members of the affected communities. These investigations helped to identify communities' needs, concerns, and experiences about past flooding events, to finally propose a technology solution system to help attend these requirements. IoT and Crowdsourcing are techniques that support multiple data sources and are equipped with the latest technologies offering broader range of capabilities for enhanced connectivity, storage, real-time analytics, and cost-effective applications [1]. The system we are proposing consists in developing applications like flooding prediction and early warning system (EWS) with the help of incoming data from residents and data from surveillance cameras and sensors especially installed in specific points at the studied zone. These data will be helpful to predict the flooding phenomena. This is achieved by acquiring data in real time and being able to process it and present it in an easy way in order to support the residents in decision making in a fast manner.

Crowdsourcing is a concept where masses of the public get together to work in a specific task that otherwise would be done by employees or specialised persons. In our specific case the persons are members of the studied community that will help in reporting situations that they consider contribute to the flooding problem; reporting what they observe in their community and weather changes that will be of help to predict a possible flood event. This information is intended to be directed to the local authorities and, accordingly, they would have to attend the needs of the community. In this sense, utilising IoT leads to what is known as Smart City which constitutes a concentrated use of information and communications technologies (ICT) [2].

There are many projects that have integrated IoT with smart city environments such as the work of Zanella et al. [3], where a complete review of the architectures, protocols and technologies for a web-centred service based IoT structure for a smart city project is presented. In [4] a framework for the development of a smart city by implementing IoT is proposed. Here the authors emphasise the need for intelligent cities as it mentions that by 2050, 70% of the world's population will live in cities and surrounding areas. In their work Mitton et al. [5] combine Cloud and sensors to develop a smart city and define the concept Cloud of Things (CoT) as more than just interconnecting things. It provides services by abstracting, virtualising, and managing things according to the specified needs of the end users. Hence, new and heterogeneous things can be aggregated and abstracted enabling things as a service known as CoT.

2 Crowdsourcing and IoT

Crowdsourcing [6] is the process by which streams of data are collected by a large number of people. These data are sent to a server to be analysed using different types of models. This data analysis task turns out to be high time consuming, so big-data techniques need to be included resulting in a more robust modelling approach. According to [3] IoT is nowadays present in all ways of life where global connection and big data applications are enabling innovation all around the world. It is seen as a possible solution for many problems such as air pollution, transportation, weather changes, health monitoring, etc. There is also the fact that many people are living now in big cities, which means that the demand on services will increase exhibiting the reality that urban infrastructure is not meeting the needs of its citizens due to bad planning and overcrowding. Such needs can be and should be met using IoT technologies. Flooding prone cities would benefit from crowdsource flood reports combined with IoT and traditional detection data from forecast environmental monitoring stations as well as on site installed sensors. All these data could be of help in deciding whether a given community is at risk. According to Fenner et al. [7] crowdsourcing by itself has around 80% accuracy but combined with other techniques like weather forecast and in site sensing could reach an accuracy of 96%. From here, it is seen the importance of combining IoT and crowdsourcing; together will lead to an efficient preventive and warning method. In addition, as stated in [8, 9], smart cities depend on ICT solutions to improve our quality of life.

Today, daily used objects equipped with computing, storage and sensing abilities, enabled to communicate with other similar objects, can become part of an IoT system. In this case, citizens equipped with intelligent phones can generate data about environmental changes that both sensors in their smartphones and they themselves are seeing in their communities in real time. They can upload photos and text or voice messages to a collector. All this information together with the local weather forecast system could be analysed for mitigation and prediction purposes. A local network of surveillance cameras and sensors planned for a project like this is justified because the forecast environmental monitoring stations present high spatial and temporal variability inside urban areas. When sensors and cameras identify changes in the ambience, they could be compared to the other sources to identify if flooding is prone to occur. Sensors may be able, via an application, to request users nearby for more information such as description of ambience, images, videos, etc. This information together with weather forecast could help in evaluating and assessing if whether flooding is about to occur so citizens could decide what actions to take.

3   Technical Background

The applications required for this project will have to handle an enormous variety of data for the IoT system. Therefore, the need is for a communication infrastructure capable of unifying the heterogeneous technologies available to develop a smart city. This article presents a general reference background for the design of an urban IoT. IoT is the convergence of both sensing environments and the Cloud. The Cloud provides services by abstracting, virtualising, and managing things, its purpose is to implement services to provide indexing and querying methods applied to things such as sensors, actuators, computing, storage, and energy sources [10]. The huge amount of data and services that the Cloud must manage gives way to another concept: Edge Computing. Edge Computing attends the requirements of shorter response time, processing, bandwidth cost saving and data safety and privacy. Within Edge Computing there are basically three types: Fog computing, Mobile Edge Computing and Cloudlet computing.

Fog computing is an intermediate layer between edge and cloud that provides distributed computing, storage and networking services between end devices and cloud computing data centres [11]. Mobile Edge Computing (MEC) focuses on mobile clients within the radio access network (RAN), works with edge servers at the RAN base stations [12]. Cloudlet Computing [5] is an evolution of Mobile Cloud Computing (MCC) which are small resource rich data centres that can be positioned strategically in close proximity to end users, it mimics the cloud allowing for intense computing closer to the data source. The proposal is the development of a system that analyses data coming from multiple sources in real time that will assist in the inquiry on whether the urban zone in question is at risk of flooding.

In crowdsourcing, participation from the very own inhabitants is crucial as the users share information from IoT mobile devices [13]. Under this scheme, it is inevitable to congest the actual computing service called the Cloud, getting a drop in the quality of service (QoS) that in this case is of critical importance when flooding might occur. The solution for this matter is the use of Edge Computing where resources are positioned at the Edge of the Network, so these resources can handle computational demanding tasks, reducing latency. This information is sent to a collector by a gateway where it is examined together with information from official weather forecast, surveillance cameras, and a network of sensors installed in specific areas surrounding the studied zone. As this information must be accurate and in real time, it cannot rely on cloud systems, there is the need for a private system (cloudlet). Efforts to concrete edge computing have been significant in recent years giving birth to Fog computing [14], where a virtualised platform for networking ad computing services are distributed within the cloud to things continuum. Satya et al. [15] first defined cloudlet computing: a network of small data centres in a box (cloudlets) to act as an intermediate layer between user and cloud, this is a local processing unit used for temporary storage and processing.

The cloudlet evaluates the data coming from smartphones identifying spatiotemporal patterns; users can report weather changes such as temperature, humidity, and wind [16]. This information can be used by applications to infer to a certain degree of accuracy the severity of a possible rainfall. In this scenario, when there are enough data taken trough time it is possible to observe patterns that as well will be useful in flooding prediction. Once patterns are available, it is probable to model how weather changes lead to strong rainfall flooding and then direct alerts to citizens. In this case, social media plays a big role when there is the need of exploring people's experiences such as how they describe their impressions about weather changes [17]. Considerations like different types of characterisation of land use such as buildings, green areas, areas that used to be unoccupied and now have been paved for private use, commercialisation, both fixed and itinerant, use of land with bad disposal of material residues, etc., have to be taken into account for design purposes.

4 Architecture

Architecture has been defined [18] as a set of functions, states, and objects together with their structure, composition and spatial-temporal distribution. The development of a smart city is usually based around a centralised architecture, where it must have the ability to work with a heterogeneous type of devices which generate different types of data. These data are sent via ICT to a control centre where will be stored, processed, and retrieved according to the needs of the end user. Hence, the integration of different technologies is the main feature enabling this architecture to evolve if required, to allow for other devices to be connected to support new applications and services. In the development of this project the actual technology of the urban zone in question needs to be addressed, to make possible the monitoring and control for the weather prediction. Therefore, new IoT technology needs to be installed. Setting up this technology represents a huge challenge due to the considerable number of heterogeneous devices. Correspondingly, to be considered in this project is the IoT infrastructure maintenance to keep up with Smart Cities. Citizen participation sums up to IoT infrastructures by applications on their smartphones generating vast amounts of data. For these records, data models need to be created considering semantic descriptions of the urban atmosphere. This project proposes a platform to facilitate the services to the community members. In smart cities is important to adjust citizen's data streams to a data model that would facilitate its usage. The logic used will depend on the background of each community, as the model must take into consideration social, economic and idiosyncrasy to create new rules to integrate the community organisation into a decision model. Also, these data would be accessible to local authorities, making them aware of the situation in real time. Using these information/data the authorities could implement or improve the appropriate actions to control/prevent the flooding risk in the community.

Lots of issues need to be attended during the system designing, such as: how citizens can have easy access to the generated data, coming from heterogeneous sources? Is the proposed infrastructure robust enough for the collection of data from community members? How to use information coming from installed sensors and surveillance cameras? The proposed platform implements a directory that contains all data sources generated within the IoT infrastructures, from crowdsourcing data streams, data generated from the network of sensors and surveillance cameras. These data in time could also be of help when needed for statistical purposes as to detect whether climate change is worsening the flooding problem. To construct a model for weather prediction as in our case, variables such as temperature, wind, air pressure etc., must be established from theory like physical equations and from the empirical experience. These models are based on everyday language concepts. The relationship between different concepts should be automatically detected by a machine learning algorithm. This paper proposes the following architecture to show how an application would perform in analysing weather conditions for flooding prediction. The order is as follows: crowdsourcing and sensors, data transmission, data collection, data processing, and application.

Crowdsourcing and Sensors. This layer consists of three types of data sources: smartphones, sensors and surveillance cameras. The users also can send voice or text messages as well as photos. The members of the community can send information daily or whenever they detect the environment is changing like air, wind, humidity etc. Additionally, they can co-operate giving information when they see situations like for example when they see that litter is clotting the drainage, or any other situation they consider might worsen flooding.

Transmission of Data. All data coming from members of the community, sensors and surveillance cameras should be sent to a server for processing and analysing. At this point, forwarding and routing protocols must be well defined in advance as the nature of the heterogeneous data calls for enhanced nodes able to perform fine.

Data Collection. Data is collected from selected nodes that can preserve privacy for all data contributors. This layer depends on both computing and human interaction, so its function has more weight over the other three layers.

Data Processing. At this point what really is important is the fact that it is possible to singularise frequent data patterns that will be useful when it comes to compare how climate change is affecting or not the studied community. To solve this problem, a method is developed to transform the raw data that would allow clearly identifying patterns and measuring them.

Application. The function of this layer is multiple, such as data management, user interface, etc. It generates services for the crowd, so they can see results in a manner easily understood for them. A user interface is generated to enable communication between machines and humans. There should be an application that combines human interaction and electronic mechanisms. This layer has the task of integrating data streams with other events from lower layers to be stored in a common data storehouse.

5 Technological Requirements for the Community

People need to have access to an early warning system (EWS) in order to mitigate flood risk within communities including an evacuation or emergency plan. This EWS will help in taking measures of adaptation, preventive and reactive procedures by collaborating with neighbours and local authorities to build resilience. For the preventive plan, the community participation in detecting possible situations that worsens floods is of importance as well as acting upon it for alleviation purposes. Nowadays, many people are familiarised with the use of technology (being social media or web pages) to report or receive information they consider important about the issues that affect their community. Therefore, it would be interesting and important to take advantage of this matter by implementing a web page with an easy access and understanding of the information. This might be quite substantial to present it in a graphical way, so people that is not very technical can be informed in time when an event has a high probability to happen giving them as much time as possible to act appropriately. According to Alexander et al. [19], resilience includes the capacity to resist, to absorb and recover, and to adapt. Based on the work of Mees et al. [20] where the authors present an analysis on flooding in 5 different European countries, each country present different levels of flooding risk, and for all of them most of the responsibility in finding solutions depend on the state. Thus, being aware of this, in their work they start to consider the participation of citizens together with the authorities for a better understanding of the problem and ways of solving it. To accomplish this goal, they present an analysis of coproducing flood risk management through citizen involvement. They gathered information mainly from citizens, although analyse government documents as well. By analysing both kind of information, enhancement of the whole data was attained.

From the conclusions presented in [20], on every country studied there were stated that coproduction was an important issue about flood risk and for a suitable management of the problem. They developed coproduced practices on Flood Mitigation and Flood Preparation. As for mitigation in England, they analysed flood highs on the floodplain, took measures for property level protection (PLP) across the country. As for Belgium they developed a project on flood-resilient building and PLP only in exceptional cases. In France there were limited PLP and implemented local programs for some buildings. Netherlands increased water retention in neighbourhoods, also had plot projects on flood-proof houses. Finally, Poland rarely have flood protection at property level. For the same countries, in respect to coproduction in flood preparation, England generates community flood action groups with voluntary schemes, as well as national and local awareness raising campaigns. Belgium presents only in very few cities voluntary emergency teams. In France local authorities are obliged to give information about risk and how to behave on an event by volunteers and civil servants. As for the Netherlands they have campaigns of awareness through volunteers and professional fire services. Finally, Poland works through local citizen initiatives with voluntary fire brigades along with professional fire services.

It is increasingly argued that a diversification, coordination and alignment of Flood Risk Management Strategies (FRMSs), including flood risk prevention through proactive spatial planning, flood defence, flood risk mitigation, flood preparation and flood recovery, will make urban agglomerations more resilient to flood risks [22].

In their paper, Mees et al. [20] conclude that co-participation of citizens in resolving the problem of flooding is important for resilient purposes. Also, they state that it really does not matter what country is under study and the differences in which they tackle flooding, the problematic is much alike and the main stages to deal with it are quite similar such as: mitigation, preparedness before and during the event, and continued work after the event. Therefore, for the project proposed in this article it is possible to adapt these data to some areas of Mexico, particularly in Mexico City where there are many communities prone to flooding. Accordingly, we have proposed in the following table the different stages and possible technology aids to the cocreation of smart cities. Later on, it is expected to corroborate this study in a small community within Mexico City, where it is expected to research the perception and adaptation of the communities to climate change-related risks, and in particular to understand people's perceptions and experiences on flooding events towards determining specific needs to mitigate such events. From the literature review and in order to adapt the technology to the community needs, it is observed that some of these needs are solved only with information supply, others with the combination of sensors, processing and communication technologies. Regarding to the use of technology, for a better management of a flood event, four stages have been identified: Mitigation, Before, During, and After flood. Hence, we propose technology requirements to attend each identified need in each stage of flood management. An example of these is described in Table 1.

An EWS needs data analysis, prediction models, and sensor fusion to forecast possible flood events based on data supplied by sensors and people. From the analysis in the literature of flooding events the technological aids requirements can be divided into three levels (see Fig. 1):

First Level Technology Aids (Informative). This consists of storage and communications technology to concentrate and supply information, about local reaction plans in a flood event, for example, to the community inhabitants, namely, a platform like a web page and/or a mobile application.

Table 1. Matching of needs and technology requirements for flood events management.

Stage	Aspect	Need	Possible technology aids
Mitigation	Infrastructure maintenance and adaptation	Insufficient drainage	Sensor Technology for monitoring the amount of rain Processing Technology to analyse the data in a rainy season to evaluate the current drainage system Communications Technology to report the results
Before	Information for risk management for inhabitants	Reduce damage to homes	Communications Technology to send information to inhabitants about what they must do before, during and after suffering a flood
During		Vehicular mobility problems to get to their houses	Sensor Technology for monitoring avenues and/or streets Processing Technology to analyse the sensors information Communications Technology to present safe streets in a map
After	Health risks	To know about the health problems that the community faces after a flood and the stagnation of water. (Moreover, if they are sewage)	Communications Technology to issue prevention recommendations for health (cleaning, etc.)

Second Level Technology Aids (Monitoring). Monitoring and situational awareness information on flood events in real-time. This can include the installation of sensors and crowdsourcing data from community inhabitants by means of text messages, social networks or from mobile apps; dashboard integrated with maps for real-time visualisation of information and registry of historical data and trends.

Third Level Technology Aids (Analytics). Analytics of the captured data, prediction models, and sensor fusion algorithms to forecast future flood events, generate automated alerts, notifications, and data sharing.

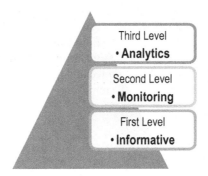

Fig. 1. Levels of technology aids for flood management.

The overall smart technology intervention will allow to go from a reactive to a proactive response to flooding events and ultimately to a predictive flood management. Furthermore, the overall aim of any technology aid is to increase community's resilience to flooding. IoT based smart cities depend on ICT, so the study of the main communication protocols is a must. IoT uses many short and wide range communication protocols with the purpose of transporting data between devices and servers. ZigBee, Bluetooth, Wi-Fi, WiMAX and IEEE 802.11p are the most used short-range wireless technologies. Within wide range technologies are Global System for Mobile Communication (GSM), General Packet Radio Service (GPRS), Long Term Evolution (LTE), Third Generation Partnership Project (3GPP). There is also Low Power Wide Area Network (LPWAN) technology which is a promising solution for long range and low power IoT and machine to machine (M2M) communication applications. The major proprietary and standards-based LPWAN technology solutions available in the market include Sigfox, LoRaWAN, Narrowband IoT (NB-IoT), and long-term evolution (LTE)-M, among others. For the development of this project the LoRaWAN, Wi-Fi and GPRS communications protocols are proposed to be explored for the monitoring of flooding prone areas.

6 Related Issues

Another big problem is the fact that people need to have an incentive to participate, be economical or social. In this case a social benefit is the key. Community members need to know that they are part of the solution, highlighting this is the biggest incentive in overpopulated urban zones attracting and encouraging more involvement. An additional challenge is how to send data from members of the community to the server/cloud because these data can be text messages, voice or images. Accordingly, for example, in the case of text or voice messages, there is the need for analysis that depends a lot on language, culture or semantics. Also, characteristics of the server's devices must be considered, such as bandwidth, wireless communications, frequency of data sending from users, etc., all these problems should be addressed with data management and data processing. Data redundancy is another important issue as most of the time there are data coming from multiple sources such as sensors systems, or multiple members of the community which causes what is called data redundancy. In this case, it is of importance to have a selection data system able to estimate the best approach. Especially when there is also the semantics problem involved, this represents a more intricate issue. Therefore, detection technology must be developed to guaranty the quality of the data. The proposed IoT architecture is the simplified three layers IoT model presented in Fig. 2.

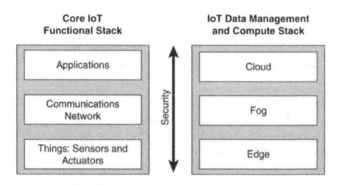

Fig. 2. Simplified three layers IoT architecture (adapted from [21]).

At the bottom layer are the sensors (and, if needed, actuators) nodes, which are proposed to be located at points in the studied zone where certain amount of rain flow comes into the zone, as for example, communities located at valleys which are surrounded by hills where it has been detected that in a matter of seconds huge amount of water may come into de urban zone. Therefore, a set of sensors could be used to measure rainfall, e.g. rain gauge sensors and/or water level measurement sensor (radar or ultrasonic sensors) are proposed to be installed at specific locations at these points at street level. Another set of sensors could be installed at street lights in the surrounding area of study with the purpose of sensing the level of rain fall on such streets so the locals could know if it is safe to walk or drive through theses streets. Finally, and most importantly are the sensors that could be installed at street level in the actual community to detect the amount of rainfall that will lead to the decision on whether the community is at risk of flooding. Also, considering at this layer is the information gathered through smartphones and surveillance cameras.

The communications and network layer will collect measurements from sensors nodes, send these data together with the information from smartphones and cameras to gateways which then will send all collected data to the cloud (or to a private server) via Internet where these can be analysed, or alternatively edge computing technology can be used to perform data analytics closer to where the data are collected. The cloud has three basic types of services to offer: as infrastructure for storage of data, as platform for computing and as software for delivering IoT services.

At the application layer services can be provided such as data processing for analysing the data fetched from the devices (sensors, social networks, cameras, etc.) and transforming these into usable information, for example prediction of flooding, alarm activation if thresholds are surpassed or statistical analysis and trending. Also, graphical user interfaces (GUI) can be provided for users, for example to use smartphones to provide users access to data or to other IoT applications. In addition, clouds can be used to analyse, sort out and store the data, and websites can be used as interfaces.

For the processing and management of data, a pre-processing and event detection must be performed in advance to convert it into knowledge. For this task it is essential to implement algorithms such as genetic algorithm or neural networks. As for data interpretation it is important to present to the end users' information that is easily understood. In this case visualisation is important for the residents so they can take decisions on whether flood is prone to occur. Visualisation for this project is expected to be through a web page where residents will have easy access by their phones or computers. It is proposed that data is going to be visualised using geo-spatial maps for a more friendly presentation for the end user being keyword based, semantic based and quality based.

7 Proposed Technologies

At the first level a website is proposed and/or a mobile application to concentrate and make available diverse flood management relevant information. This information should be shown in a friendly form, especially for those citizens that have little knowledge of digital technologies. The proposed informative webpage could present sections as Memory Reinforcement to show past events, actions taken and which of them worked and/or failed; Risk Management to inhabitants; Days of waste collection information, Vulnerable areas map, Institutions information and a Health Risk consequences guideline. In Fig. 3 a proposed web page for informative needs about flooding events is shown.

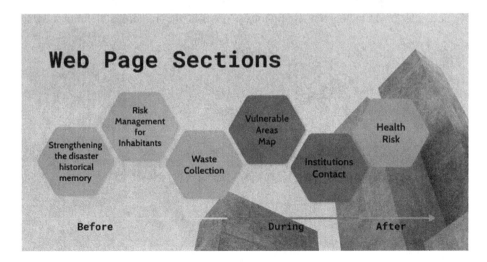

Fig. 3. Informative web page.

The second level considers monitoring and visualisation for situational awareness of flood events in real-time, which includes the installation of sensors and the use of communications technology using the three layers IoT architecture and crowdsourcing technology. Therefore, the first proposal to attend this need level is to integrate a minimum sensors kit by a block (street) to be monitored, which is scalable and modular; hence, can be scaled up to a suburb, town or even a city. Also, at this level a dashboard will be integrated with maps for real-time visualisation of information and registry of historical data and trends. This technology proposal is described as follows:

By Block:

- HD (High Definition) outdoor camera (powered with solar panel).

A camera designed to withstand rain, snow, and extreme temperatures, typically connected to a Wi-Fi network, which allow to view live video of the activities occurring outside. HD is defined by specific resolutions at specific frame rates with a specific aspect ratio. HD refers to cameras with a standardised resolution of 720p or 1080p (horizontal). This sensor could help in monitoring the streets and strainers.

- Water level sensor (radar or ultrasonic) for level monitoring in regulating streets. A water level sensor is a device that is designed to monitor, maintain, and measure liquid (and sometimes solid) levels. Once the liquid level is detected, the sensor converts the perceived data into an electric signal. This sensor could help to monitor the water level on the streets.
- Smartphones for data collection. This device could help to send images and/or videos, texts and even voice messages.

By Suburb:

- Disdrometer and / or weather station with rain gauge (powered with solar panel).

A disdrometer or rain spectrometer is a laser instrument that measures the drop size distribution falling hydrometeors. Based on the principle of optical laser active detection, the disdrometer can continuously observe the raindrops definition size,

Fig. 4. OTT Persival2 laser disdrometer (https://www.ott.com/products/meteorological-sensors-26/ott-parsivel2-laser-weather-sensor-2392/).

velocity, and quantity of raindrops. This device could help to monitoring the amount of precipitation and help to predict the trends in rain fall. Figure 4 shows an OTT Persival[2] laser disdrometer.

A weather station is a facility with instruments and equipment for measuring atmospheric conditions to provide information for weather forecasts and to study the weather and climate. The measurements taken include temperature, atmospheric pressure, humidity, wind speed, wind direction, and the amount of liquid precipitation (rainfall).

Finally, the third level oversees the analytics. The data signals will be processed, therefore depend on the results, to send messages to inhabitants and/or institutions (using ICT). Besides, warning or announcements can be sent through a website and/or mobile applications. The processing could be done on the edge or in the cloud. Also, a deeper analysis could include neural networks to predict a hazard.

8   Conclusion

Building smart cities calls for the participation of its citizens defining strategies that involves them, getting their participation in discussions and proposals for the development of technologies that help them with the actual issues that affect the whole community. Implementation of IoT technologies in urban zones will enable the development of the concept of smart city, giving rise to a system able to help in dealing with the problematic that overpopulated urban zones generate by applying multidisciplinary strategies. By involving the residents in the problem-solving leads to the co-creation of a more resilient community implementing state of the art technological tools to communicate, monitor and mitigate flooding risk in vulnerable population. We have presented a system able to analyse heterogeneous data coming from crowdsourcing, surveillance cameras and a local network of sensors for an overpopulated urban zone. Many urban zones in Mexico suffer from severe flooding every year; this flooding may be the result of bad urban planning and climate change. The resulting information gather from these three sources is going to be used for statistical analysis to determine the probabilities of flooding in the studied zone. In this work a text analysis is proposed to be used to obtain information on ambience changes. Reported events will be computed by sampling different text messages which have been organised on type of event by determining a set of keywords indicating the weather state. The system we propose can be adapted for several applications to enhance community life (such as air pollution monitoring, health care, transport systems, etc.) as well as been adapted for other similar communities. Additionally, the development of this project highlights several challenges areas and research opportunities within communities. Investigation should be addressed on models and design patterns for crowdsensing systems using multidisciplinary sources of knowledge which should include social science, computing, sensor systems, community members etc.

9 Future Work

This project will enable the implementation in the short time of a crowdsourcing and IoT system to collect, communicate, store, process and visualise data and information that is going to mitigate flooding risk, towards creating resilient communities facing these events. At the time of writing this paper, we already have identified some communities that present flooding problems in Mexico City and for mitigation purposes the project is in the stage of technology identification, purchase, and integration of the overall system. This will enable future research and experimentation with smart city solutions as cities will, in time, depend more on technology to provide facilities to support solution to other worrying issues such as transportation, energy usage, waste management, health care, mobility, etc., in ever increasing overpopulated urban zones.

Acknowledgment. The authors would like to thank the Consejo Nacional de Ciencia y Tecnología (CONACYT) for its support in this research, under grant CONACYT-296528. We also acknowledge support from the UK Newton Fund and ESRC, under grant ES/S006761/1.

References

1. Shah, S., Seker, D., Hameed, S., Draheim, D.: The rising role of big data analytics and IoT in disaster management: recent advances, taxonomy and prospects. IEEE Access **7**, 54595–54614 (2019)
2. Mehmood, Y., Ahmad, F., Yaqoob, I., Adnane, A., Imran, M., Guizani, S.: Internet-of-Things-based smart cities: recent advances and challenges. IEEE Commun. Mag. **55**(9), 15–24 (2017)
3. Zanella, A., Bui, N., Castellani, A., Vangelista, L., Zorzi, M.: Internet of Things for smart cities. IEEE Internet Things J. **1**(1), 22–32 (2014)
4. Jin, J., Gubbi, J., Marusic, S., Palaniswami, M.: An Information framework of creating a smart city through Internet of Things. IEEE J. **1**(2), 112–121 (2013)
5. Mitton, N., Papavassiliou, S., Puliafito, A., Trivedi, K.: Combining Cloud and sensors in a smart city environment. J. Wireless Commun. Networking **1**, 1–10 (2012)
6. Caragliu, A., Del Bo, C., Nijkamp, P.: Smart cities in Europe. Urban Technol **18**(2), 65–82 (2011)
7. Knüsel, B., et al.: Applying big data beyond small problems in climate research. Nature Climate Change **9**, 196–202 (2018)
8. Gutiérrez, V., Amaxilatis, D., Mylonas, G., Muñoz, L.: Empowering citizens toward the co-creation of sustainable cities. IEEE Internet Things J. **5**(2), 668–676 (2018)
9. Fenner, D., Meier, F., Bechtel, B., Otto, M., Scherer, D.: Intra and inter 'local climate zone' variability of air temperature as observed by crowdsourced citizen weather stations in Berlin. Germany. Meterologishe Zeitschift **26**(5), 525–547 (2017)
10. Bonomi, F., Milito, R., Zhu, J., Addepalli, S.: Fog computing and its role in the internet of things. In: Proceedings of the MCC Workshop on Mobile Cloud Computing, vol. 1, pp. 13-16 (2012)
11. Sabella, D., Vaillant, A., Kuure, P., Rauschenbach, U., Giust, F.: Mobile-edge computing architecture: the role of mec in the internet of things. IEEE Consum. Electr. Mag. **5**(4), 84–91 (2016)

12. Satyanarayanan, M., Bahl, P., Caceres, R., Davies, N.: The case for vm-based cloudlets in mobile computing. IEEE Pervasive Comput. **8**, 14–23 (2009)
13. Fiandrino, C., Anjomshoa, F., Kantarci, B., Kliazovich, D., Bouvry, P., Matthews, J.: Sociability-driven framework for data acquisition in mobile crowdsensing over fog computing platforms for smart cities. IEEE Trans. Sustain. Comput. **2**(4), 345–358 (2017)
14. Bonomi, F., Milito, R., Natarajan, P., Zhu, J.: Fog computing: a platform for internet of things and analytics, in Big data and internet of things: a roadmap for smart environments. Studies in Computational Intelligence, vol 546, pp. 169–186. Springer, Cham (2014). https://doi.org/10.1007/978-3-319-05029-4_7.
15. Satyanarayanan, M.: The emergence of edge computing. Computer **50**(1), 30–39 (2017)
16. Ganti, R., Ye, F., Lei, H.: Mobile crowdsensing: current state and future challenges. IEEE Commun. Mag. **49**(11), 32–39 (2011)
17. Ghermandi, A., Sinclair, M.: Passive crowdsourcing of social media in environmental research: a systematic map. Global Environ. Change **55**, 36–47 (2019)
18. Zahariadis, T., et al.: Towards a Future Internet Architecture. In: Domingue, J., et al. (eds.) FIA 2011. LNCS, vol. 6656, pp. 7–18. Springer, Heidelberg (2011). https://doi.org/10.1007/978-3-642-20898-0_1
19. Alexander, M.: Constructions of flood vulnerability across an etic-emic spectrum. Middlesex University, Flood Hazard Research Centre, London UK (2014)
20. Mees, H., Crabbé, A., Alexander, M., Kaufmann, M., Bruzzone, S., Lévy, L., Lewandowski, J.: Coproducing flood risk management through citizen involvement: insights from cross-country comparison in Europe. Ecol. Soc. **21**(3), 1–4 (2016)
21. Hanes, D., Salgueiro, G., Grossetete, P., Barton, R., Henry, J.: IoT fundamentals: networking technologies, protocols, and use cases for the Internet of Things. Cisco Press (2017).
22. Hegger, D.L.T., et al.: A view on more resilient flood risk governance: key conclusions of the STAR-FLOOD project. STAR-FLOOD Consortium (2016).

Smart Mobility in Cities: GIS Analysis of Solar PV Potential for Lighting in Bus Shelters in the City of Ávila

M. Sánchez-Aparicio[⊠] [iD], S. Lagüela[iD], J. Martín-Jiménez[iD],
S. Del Pozo[iD], E. González-González[iD], and P. Andrés-Anaya[iD]

University of Salamanca, 05003 Ávila, Spain
mar_sanchez1410@usal.es

Abstract. The reduction of CO_2 emissions in cities implies the generation of clean energy for the supply of the municipal energy demand. In the conversion to Smart Cities, the consumption sources and the generation possibilities should be considered as a whole, in such a way that all the urban elements can be integrated in the energy mix. In this study, bus shelters are evaluated as potential energy generators. The installation of PV panels with the optimal configuration can contribute to the supply of the energy needed in the bus shelter, but also to the generation of surplus energy. The analysis of the possibilities and the definition of the recommendable configuration of PV installations in bus shelters are performed using the city of Ávila (Spain) as case study. In this city, the PV generation reached with the optimal configuration (3500 kWh/year) can cover the energy demand of the bus shelters, including their role as lighting points in the city, and being able to contribute to other energy demands. For this study, geospatial information and a solar radiation model are incorporated in a Geospatial Information System (GIS) tool, specially developed to replicate this study in other cities.

Keywords: Solar energy · Bus shelters · Municipal self-consumption

1 Introduction

The Sustainable Development Goals (SDG) [1], and the goals established by the European Union [2] at urban level regarding the reduction of CO_2 emissions in the automotive sector focus on electrical mobility, mainly applied to cars and buses. In addition, the conversion to a more sustainable society in terms of mobility includes promoting the use of alternative individual transport, such as bicycles and scooters, also electrical, which allow a more agile mobility and a better management to be within the reach of most users [3, 4].

The integration of electrical transport, both public and private, incorporates a new component to the municipal energy demand, which is spatially distributed throughout the city [5]. This transport energy demand is added to others with the same characteristics, such as public lighting demand [6]. Thus, in the context of decarbonization of the municipal energy consumption through its electrification, the reduction of CO_2

© Springer Nature Switzerland AG 2021
S. Nesmachnow and L. Hernández Callejo (Eds.): ICSC-CITIES 2020, CCIS 1359, pp. 154–166, 2021.
https://doi.org/10.1007/978-3-030-69136-3_11

emissions needs the inclusion of clean energies for the energy supply [7]. Among the existing clean energies, solar energy is the energy source more evenly distributed in space and with the more versatile technology to be used at different scales and from different locations [8].

The implementation of self-consumption strategies associated to the use of natural resources implies a reduction in municipal spending on services such as public lighting and transport [9]. This reduction could affect the economy of the citizens through a reduction in public taxes and could expand the supply of public transport [10], more adapted to the real needs and economic resources of the users. Consequently, the gap caused by energy poverty can be minimized thanks to the fact that the facilitation of transport can imply the removal of barriers to employment [11]. In addition, the supply of energy from renewable energy sources, together with the improvement in the public transport service, would lead to an improvement in the habitability of municipalities facing problems of depopulation [12, 13]. In this way, renewable energy for the energy supply of public services would be a solution to the depopulation of rural areas, acting as an incentive for the incorporation of new inhabitants and for the return of the original ones [14].

For a proper planning, distribution and design of solar installations to supply the municipal energy consumption, a prior knowledge of the characteristics of each individual consumption, as well as the possibilities of combined consumption among several components is required.

An example of a combined service is the incorporation of the bus shelters as part of the public lighting, with the dual purpose of increasing the level of lighting with street furniture already in use and the consequent increase in the sense of security for citizens. It has been proved that higher levels of lighting provide a higher sense of security and, consequently, a higher willingness towards mobility [15]. Another example is the equipment of bus shelters as connectivity points, with WiFi stations, USB chargers and Air Control Quality stations, also supplied with solar energy for their contribution to smart cities [16].

For these reasons, the main objective of this work is to analyze the viability of incorporating PV solar installations in bus shelters that serve for the energy supply of municipal services towards their decarbonization. The work is aligned with many SDGs, such as SDG 1 (end of poverty), 7 (clean and affordable energy) and 11 (sustainable cities and communities) [1]. Similar works have been published for the incorporation of the bus shelters as energy providers of an electric system of public transport with PV panels [17], as well as for the combined installation of solar and wind energy systems in the bus shelters in order to maximize their contribution to the supply of municipal services [18].

The analysis of municipal energy demand and the availability of solar energy has an important geospatial component. In addition, the three dimensions of space should be analyzed, provided that the height component is key regarding the intensity of the incoming solar radiation and the shadow projection [19]. Thus, the study is based on the development of a 3D-GIS that, together with numerical analysis of energy needs of the municipal services in terms of public lighting and transport, will be the basis for the design of solar installations in bus shelters.

2 GIS of Bus Shelters in the City of Ávila

Spain is one of the European countries with highest number of solar hours along the year [20], due to its climate conditions and geographic situation. This results in a greater potential of PV solar energy. Within the territory of the Iberian Peninsula, Ávila is the city that receives the second higher solar insolation (2700 h/year) as the highest city (1132 m above sea level) of the Iberian Peninsula [21]. For these reasons, Ávila has been chosen as pilot case study.

The first step for the analysis of the spatial distribution of street furniture and for the incorporation of bus shelters as a solar energy resource is to perform an inventory of the existing urban furniture related to public transport. This inventory includes the geospatial location of each element and information about its connection to the elec-trical grid. The connection to the electrical grid allows the possibility to exchange energy from the solar installation to the grid in those hours when production is higher than consumption, and vice versa.

The inventory of urban furniture related to public transport resulted in 64 bus shelters and 131 bus stops, respectively (Fig. 1). Among bus shelters, 41 of them are 4 m long, and 23 are 5 m long.

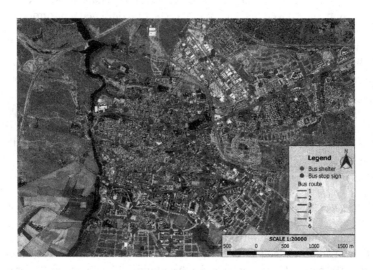

Fig. 1. GIS of the bus shelters (in red) and the bus stops (in blue) of the city of Ávila (plan view). Color lines represent the different bus routes in the city. (Color figure online)

Thus, the GIS for street furniture related to public transport includes the geospatial distribution of the bus shelters and bus stops. This can be associated with the different bus routes to manage the number of passengers in each stretch of the tour and for each tour schedule to size the lighting requirements and the possible energy demand regarding some services of the bus shelters such as the use of interactive screens.

In addition, the environment of the bus shelters is modelled in 3D, so that the tool can provide information on the shadow cast on each bus shelter throughout the year.

The modelling is performed using as a basis the LiDAR data of the city freely offered by the Spanish Geographic Institute (IGN), as in [22]. The 3D modelling includes the buildings that can cast shadows over the bus shelters (those located East, South or West with respect to the bus shelter), as well as the trees that are taller than the shelters in those orientations.

2.1   Energy Demand in Shelters

In order to assess whether the solar potential of bus shelters meets their supply needs, it is key to determine the main consumption sources in bus shelters.

In the context of digitalization and Smart Cities, the objective of giving a double use to bus shelters as furniture for public transport and as public lighting elements determines the sources of energy in bus shelters. Regarding the first condition of Smart Cities, the bus shelter should be equipped with: (i) a LED panel that offers information on the incoming buses and their estimated arrival times, (ii) an interactive screen for the user to obtain information about the city and the public transport, and (iii) a digital advertising panel that minimizes the consumption of paper billboards. These elements should work 24 h a day in order to cover the public transport service hours (mainly during the day) and to reinforce the lighting in the bus shelters during non-service hours, at night. With respect to the integration of the bus shelters as part of the public lighting system, LED lighting would be included with operating hours that match with that of the street lamps, which are adapted to the duration of the night along the year (Table 1). To estimate the total energy demand for lighting, an average operation of 11.8 h has been considered (Table 2).

Table 1. Summary of possible sources of energy consumption in bus shelters.

Element	Power (W)	Average daily usage time (h)	Daily demand (W)
LED panel	18	24	432
Interactive screen	7	24	168
Digital advertising panel	350	24	8400
Lighting	40	11.8	473

According to the average value of hours of sun per month, the total energy demand required per bus shelter in the City of Ávila would be that detailed in Table 2. This table distinguishes between the energy demand required if the complete equipment is installed and if only the basic equipment (information LED panel, interactive screen and lighting) is installed. This distinction is made because the high consumption of the digital advertising panels can limit the efficiency of the PV solar installation, and also because of the commercial value of the panels, which makes their energy supply with municipal services arguable.

The main source of variability on consumption shelters is lighting. Therefore, the energy demand decreases in summer, when the length of the day is longer, and increases gradually until winter, when there is a greater need for lighting.

Table 2. Daily energy demand on the bus shelters.

Month	Street lighting daily usage time (h)	Demand with a complete equipment (W)	Demand without digital advertising panels (W)
Jan.	14.21	9568	1168
Feb.	13.41	9536	1136
Mar.	12.02	9481	1081
Apr.	10.65	9426	1026
May	9.54	9382	982
June	8.98	9359	959
July	9.39	9376	976
Aug.	10.22	9409	1009
Sep.	11.55	9462	1062
Oct.	12.93	9517	1117
Nov.	14.11	9564	1164
Dec.	14.77	9591	1191

3 Analysis of PV Solar Potential in Bus Shelters

3.1 Shadow Analysis

The analysis of shadows cast on the bus shelters has been performed using the NOAA Solar Calculator [23] and the 3D modelling and geospatial information from the GIS created for the street furniture related to public transport (and presented in Sect. 2).

The NOAA Solar Calculator determines the azimuth and altitude coordinates of the Sun for specific times, considering the position under study. With these azimuth and altitude values, the NOAA Solar Calculator determines the Sun position for each hour, and consequently the sunrise, sunset, and solar noon through the year. The calculations of solar position and incoming solar radiation are based on [24], including the computation of the refraction effect on the incoming solar radiation, increasing the precision of the results.

The shadow analysis is based on the tracing of rays from the Sun to the position of the bus shelter, and the determination of an obstacle (building, tree) within the path of the rays. If an obstacle is present, it would cast a shadow on the bus shelter, consequently reducing the generation of energy of the solar installation on the shelter. The size of the obstacle determines the size of the shadow projected on the bus shelter.

In order to include the loss of energy generation caused by the shadows cast on each bus shelter, the hourly position of the Sun was calculated for one representative day of each month. In this pilot case study, the day 15th of each month was considered.

In addition to the visual analysis shown in Fig. 2, which shows the results of the presence of obstacles (shadow projectors) within the rays between the Sun position and the bus shelter, a summary table has been created for each bus shelter (Fig. 3). The summary table shows in which hours the bus shelter is covered by shadows, and therefore for what times the total PV solar production initially calculated is minimized. As a criterion established for this pilot case study, a bus shelter is considered as "overshadowed" if more than 50% of its surface is covered by shade. In the GIS tool developed, this percentage can be adapted to the characteristics of each case also, the reduction in production can be proportional to the percentage of surface in the shade.

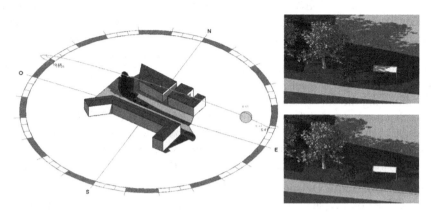

Fig. 2. Example of the simulation of shadow projection on a bus shelter, 4 m long. Left: Sun path; right: detail of shadow projected at two different times.

Hour	Months											
	January	February	March	April	May	June	July	August	September	October	November	December
6.00					YES	YES	YES					
7.00				YES	YES	YES	YES	YES	YES			
8.00		YES	NO	NO	NO	NO	NO	NO	NO	YES	YES	
9.00	YES	YES	NO	NO	NO	NO	NO	NO	NO	NO	YES	YES
10.00	YES	NO	NO	NO	NO	NO	NO	NO	NO	NO	YES	YES
11.00	YES	NO	NO	NO	NO	NO	NO	NO	NO	NO	YES	YES
12.00	YES	NO	NO	NO	NO	NO	NO	NO	NO	NO	YES	YES
13.00	YES	NO	NO	NO	NO	NO	NO	NO	NO	NO	YES	YES
14.00	YES	NO	NO	NO	NO	NO	NO	NO	NO	NO	YES	YES
15.00	YES	YES	NO	NO	NO	NO	NO	NO	NO	NO	YES	YES
16.00	YES	YES	NO	NO	NO	NO	NO	NO	NO	YES	YES	YES
17.00	YES	NO	NO	NO	NO	NO	NO	NO	NO	NO	NO	YES
18.00	NO	NO	NO	YES	YES	YES	YES	YES	NO	YES		
19.00				YES	YES	YES	YES	YES	YES			
20.00					YES	YES	YES	YES				

NO — The bus shelter is **NOT** overshadowed   YES — The bus shelter **IS** overshadowed

Fig. 3. Summary of the presence of shadows in the bus shelter of Fig. 2, for each month and with hourly resolution.

3.2 Optimal PV Panels Design

The bus shelters are structures that can be open to different designs for PV solar installations. The key to an optimal design is to analyze the different options available, calculate the total energy production for each option and decide which production regime is best suited to each case. In turn, there is a criterion of generating the maximum amount of energy or generating energy for the longest possible time each day.

In the case of Spain, the energy production in bus shelters can benefit from the possibility of discharging the surplus of energy to the electricity grid and proportionally reduce the cost of the energy consumed from the grid when there is no generation. In other countries, where discharging the surplus of energy to the electricity grid is not possible, there is the possibility of installing batteries to store the surplus of energy and make it available in non-generation hours.

Among the design possibilities contemplated in the study, the following are included: (i) maximum annual production, consisting on panels oriented to the south (northern hemisphere) and optimal inclination (35° for the city of Ávila); (ii) energy production for the longest period per day, which consists on the horizontal position of the panels that guarantees that the panels receive solar radiation from the sunrise to the sunset; and (iii) highest level of geometrical integration of the panels, with flexible panels following the curved shape of the shelter.

For the three possibilities, the computation of energy production includes the subtraction of the energy that is not generated due to the presence of shadows cast over the shelter. For this reason, in the case study of Ávila, the months with zero energy production are those in which the bus shelter is in the shade during the entire day.

PV Panels with South Orientation and Optimal Inclination

The installation of PV panels on orientable supports is a common strategy in order to adapt the position of the panels to the desired design of the PV installation. In the case of cities located in the northern hemisphere, the panels must be oriented towards the south in order to receive the incoming solar radiation from the most perpendicular angle. The opposite orientation (north) is recommended in the south hemisphere. In the case of Ávila, the optimal inclination of the panels is 35°. This is the inclination that guarantees the capture of Sun rays as perpendicular as possible throughout the year, allowing the generation of the maximum energy possible.

Table 3 shows the estimated energy production of the bus shelter of Fig. 2 with PV panels facing south and inclined 35°. As shown in Fig. 3, there is only one hour in which the shelter is not covered by shadows for the months of January and November, while the solar radiation never reaches the bus shelter in December. This is the reason why low or no energy generation is obtained during those months.

Table 3. Daily maximum power production per month, in watts, for the bus shelter of Fig. 2 with a PV installation facing south and inclined 35°.

Jan.	Feb.	Mar.	Apr.	May.	Jun.	Jul.	Aug.	Sep.	Oct.	Nov.	Dec.
60	3038	5264	5462	6021	6493	7077	6966	6366	4436	199	0

By analyzing the energy demands, the percentages of self-consumption and the possible energy surplus can be computed. Table 4 shows an example of the self-consumption level achieved for the example shown in Fig. 2.

In addition to the energy production, another criterion to be considered is the structural and visual integration of the panels on the bus shelter. In the case of establishing a design with south orientation and 35° inclination, the panels would require the installation of an additional support to facilitate the installation in this position. This support would imply: (i) an additional weight for the shelter, which may have not been designed to support such load and that caused by the resistance offered against the wind; and (ii) an over-height that would not favor either the visual integration nor the conservation of the panels (possibility of vandalism).

Table 4. Daily percentage of self-consumption and energy surplus for solar panels facing south and with an inclination of 35° on bus shelters in Ávila.

	Self-consumption (%) with all sources of consumption (Table 1)	Self-consumption (%) with no digital advertising panels	Energy discharged to the electricity grid with no digital advertising panels (Wh/day)
Jan.	1	5	0
Feb.	32	267	1902
Mar.	56	487	4183
Apr.	58	532	4436
May	64	613	5040
June	69	677	5534
July	75	725	6102
Aug.	74	691	5958
Sep.	67	599	5304
Oct.	47	397	3322
Nov.	2	17	0
Dec.	0	0	0

Horizontal PV Panels

The PV panels can be installed horizontally directly on the top of the bus shelters or using a support in case the shelter has a pronounced curvy design. Table 5 shows an example of the energy production of horizontal panels for the bus shelter of Fig. 2.

Table 5. Daily maximum production per month, in watts, for the bus shelter of Fig. 2 when installing PV panels horizontally.

Jan.	Feb.	Mar.	Apr.	May	Jun.	Jul.	Aug.	Sep.	Oct.	Nov.	Dec.
30	2126	4217	5037	6064	6813	6813	6529	4592	3165	107	0

As in the case of south orientation and 35° inclination panels, the percentages of self-consumption and the generation of surplus energy can be computed in the case of horizontal panels. Table 6 shows an example of the self-consumption level achieved for the example of Fig. 2.

Regarding the analysis of integration of horizontal panels and the need of supports for the panels, both depend on the specific design of the bus shelters. In the case of the bus shelters of the city of Ávila, these have a curved shape of 30° (angle formed by the horizontal plane and the shelter), in such a way that supports would be necessary to stabilize the panels in a horizontal position. This position, closer to the shelter, implies a reduction of the wind loads regarding the load caused by the 35° panels. A higher level of integration also decreases the risk of damage caused by vandalism. On the other hand, horizontal panels are easily damaged by natural causes such as snow or hail, which are typical in Ávila in winter and summer. In addition, the panels are more susceptible to accumulating dust, reducing their performance.

Table 6. Daily percentage of self-consumption and energy surplus for bus shelters with a horizontal PV panel configuration.

	Self-consumption (%) with all sources of consumption (Table 1)	Self-consumption (%) with no digital advertising panels	Energy discharged to the electricity grid with no digital advertising panels (Wh/day)
Jan.	0.3	3	0
Feb.	22	187	989
Mar.	44	390	3136
Apr.	53	491	4011
May	65	618	5082
June	73	710	5854
July	73	698	5838
Aug.	69	647	5520
Sep.	49	432	3529
Oct.	33	283	2048
Nov.	1	9	0
Dec.	0	0	0

Flexible PV Panels Integrated on the Shelter
The latest advances in adaptable materials have allowed the generation of flexible PV panels. The position of these panels can be adjusted to the geometry of the bus shelters, which mostly present curved shelters. The main limitation of flexible panels is that their curvature must not exceed 30°.

The average curvature value of the shelters in Ávila is 30°, which is exceeded in some parts of the shelters. Therefore, and in order to satisfy the curvature requirement, the proposal was to install flexible panels in the middle of the shelter, in such a way that each panel had half of its surface facing towards one orientation and half towards the opposite orientation.

For the bus shelter in Fig. 2, 50% of the panel faces south and 50% of the panel faces north. With this configuration, the average degree of curvature is 25°, which is within the technical requirements of the flexible panels. The maximum monthly production obtained with this PV solar design is shown in Table 7.

Table 7. Daily maximum production per month, in watts, for the bus shelter of Fig. 2 when installing flexible PV panels.

Jan.	Feb.	Mar.	Apr.	May	Jun.	Jul.	Aug.	Sep.	Oct.	Nov.	Dec.
14	715	1526	1825	2190	2453	2601	2341	1901	1142	45	0

Again, the percentages of self-consumption and the generation of surplus energy were computed as shown in Table 8.

Table 8. Daily percentage of self-consumption and energy surplus for bus shelters with flexible PV panels.

	Self-consumption (%) with all sources of consumption (Table 1)	Self-consumption (%) with no digital advertising panels	Energy discharged to the electricity grid with no digital advertising panels (Wh/day)
Jan.	0.2	1	0
Feb.	7	63	0
Mar.	16	141	445
Apr.	19	178	799
May	23	223	1208
Jun.	26	256	1493
Jul.	28	267	1625
Aug.	25	232	1333
Sep.	20	179	839
Oct.	12	102	25
Nov.	0.5	4	0
Dec.	0	0	0

In terms of structural and visual integration, flexible PV panels are the best configuration. On the one hand, their position, parallel to the bus shelter, eliminates the need for additional support and reduces the visual impact. On the other hand, the lightness of the flexible material reduces the additional weight on the shelter, also reducing the structural demand and possibility of being damaged by the wind or other meteorological phenomena. In addition to minimizing the visual impact, the integrated panels reduce the possibility of vandalism due to the unawareness of their presence.

4 Discussion

Applying the methodology proposed in Sect. 3 and making use of the GIS of bus shelters, it is possible to know the PV solar potential in all the bus shelters of the city of Ávila. The average annual production for the different PV designs considering all the bus shelters in Avila (and their different dimensions) is shown in Table 9.

Table 9. Annual average production, in gigawatts-hour, for the city of Ávila and the different configurations of the panels.

	Conventional PV panels		Flexible PV panels
Inclination	0°	35°	25°
Annual average production for the bus shelters in Ávila (GWh)	122	132	52

For all the configurations, the highest production was obtained for PV panels with the optimal inclination (35°), followed by the configuration with a 0° inclination.

Although the flexible panels have an inclination (25°) closer to the optimal in this pilot case study, the energy production was reduced by half for two reasons:

- Maximum power. Conventional solar panels can reach high production power (330 W has been used for computation of this work) while flexible solar panels are currently limited to 200 W (for the computations of this work, 170 W panels have been considered).
- Available radiation. Although the incident radiation on solar panels with an inclination of 25° is greater than on a horizontal surface, the available radiation is practically the same. This is due to the limitation of the curvature of the flexible panels on the shelter, which means that the entire panel cannot be oriented optimally.

Table 10 sums up the percentage of self-consumption considering (i) all consumption sources considered in Table 1, and (ii) without considering the digital advertising panels. For the first case, with conventional PV panels, the self-consumption percentages were between 55% and 59% while for flexible panels the self-consumption did not reach 25%. For the second case, without the digital advertising panels, the percentage of self-consumption was always more than 100%. Specifically, for conventional panels with 35° inclination, self-consumption reaches 527%, while 487% of the demand was covered with the energy generated with horizontal panels (0° inclination). For flexible panels, the percentage was reduced in a half (208%). As a result, the energy discharged to the electricity grid was 107 GWh/year, 97 GWh/year and 27 kWh/year when using a 35°, 0° and 25° inclination, respectively. With the current average price of the energy in Spain (0.09 €/kWh), savings will be around 9630 €, 8730 € and 2430 €, respectively.

Table 10. Annual percentage of self-consumption and energy surplus for bus shelters depending on the inclination of the solar PV panels.

	Self-consumption (%) with all sources of consumption (Table 1)	Self-consumption (%) with no digital advertising panels	Energy discharged to the electricity grid with no digital advertising panels (GW)
0°	55	487	97
25°	24	208	27
35°	60	527	107

5 Conclusions

This work presents the development of a tool based on geospatial data with the aim of analyzing the PV potential of bus shelters. With this tool, bus shelters could play a dual role: (i) serve as street furniture, and (ii) contribute to the energy supply of the municipal demand with clean resources. In addition, the analysis of energy capabilities of bus shelters has been performed seeking the integration of the bus shelters in the street lighting, and in the public transport system.

Taking this into account, an analysis of the solar PV potential in bus shelters has been performed with two combined approaches: the presence of shadows, and the configuration of the panels.

The presence of shadows in the bus shelters reduces energy production during certain months and depend on the location of the bus shelters. Due to the greater intensity of solar radiation in summer, if shadows cannot be avoided, it is possible to reduce their influence in the annual energy production if their presence occurs mainly in winter.

The results of the analysis of the configuration of the panels have shown that the maximum production occurred when the panels are installed on the shelters with their optimal inclination (determined by the location of the city under study, 35° in the city of Ávila). A 7% reduction of the production was obtained when the panels are horizontally installed, while the installation of flexible panels resulted in a 60% loss of energy production. Thus, considering other criteria such as the visual and structural integration level as well as the safety of the panels, the most recommended configuration for the panels would be that with horizontal position.

References

1. United Nations: Transforming our world: the 2030 Agenda for Sustainable Development A/RES/70/1. United Nations (2020)
2. European Commission: The European Green Deal. COM 2019, Brussels (2019)
3. Bortoli, A., Christoforou, Z.: Consequential LCA for territorial and multimodal transportation policies: method and application to the free-floating e-scooter disruption in Paris. J. Clean. Prod. **273**, 122898 (2020)
4. Maas, S., Attard, M., Caruana, M.A.: Assessing spatial and social dimensions of shared bicycle use in a Southern European island context: the case of Las Palmas de Gran Canaria. Transp. Res. Part A Policy Pract. **140**, 81–97 (2020)
5. Sierpinski, G., Staniek, M., Klos, M.J.: Decision making support for local authorities choosing the method for siting of in-city ev charging stations. Energies **13**(18), 4682 (2020)
6. Yao, J., Zhang, Y., Yan, Z., Li, L.: A group approach of smart hybrid poles with renewable energy, street lighting and EV charging based on DC micro-grid. Energies **11**(12), 3445 (2018)
7. Dong, K., Dong, X., Jiang, Q.: How renewable energy consumption lower global CO2 emissions? Evidence from countries with different income levels. World Econ. **43**(6), 1665–1698 (2020)

8. Guangul, F.M., Chala, G.T.: Solar energy as renewable energy source: SWOT analysis. In: 4th MEC International Conference on Big Data and Smart City. IEEE, Muscat (Oman) (2019)

9. Arcos-Vargas, A., Núñez, F., Román-Collado, R.: Short-term effects of PV integration of global welfare and CO2 emissions; An application to the Iberian electricity market. Energy **200**, 117504 (2020)

10. Pestana, C., Prieto-Rodríguez, J.: A revenue-neutral tax reform to increase demand for public transport services. Transp. Res. Part A Policy Pract. **42**(4), 659–672 (2008)

11. Mohammadi, A., Elsaid, F., Amador-Jiménez, L., Nasiri, F.: Optimizing public transport for reducing employment barriers and fighting poverty. Int. J. Sustain. Dev. Plan. **13**(69), 861–871 (2018)

12. Heras, J., Martín, M.: Social issues in the energy transition: effect on the design of the new power system. Appl. Energy **278**, 115654 (2020)

13. Stastná, M., Vaishar, A.: The relationship between public transport and the progressive development of rural areas. Land Use Policy **67**, 107–114 (2017)

14. García, A.V., Muñiz, V.L.: Actions from public administration to avoid depopulation of rural areas. What can be done by provincial government and local councils? Revista Galega de Economía **29**(2), 1–14 (2020)

15. Markvica, K., Richter, G., Lenz, G.: Impact of urban street lighting on road users' perception of public space and mobility behavior. Build. Environ. **154**, 32–43 (2019)

16. Mutani, G., Vodano, A., Pastorelli, M.: Photovoltaic solar systems for smart bus shelters in the urban environment of Turin (Italy). In: INTELEC 2017, pp. 20–25, October 2017

17. Santos, T., Lobato, K., Rocha, J., Tenedório, J.A.: Modeling photovoltaic potential for bus shelters on a city-scale: a case study in Lisbon. Appl. Sci. **10**(14), 4801 (2020)

18. Ashwin, M., Mounika, V., Kommineni, M., Swetha, K.: Secure design for smart bus shelter using renewable energy. J. Critical Rev. **7**(1), 387–394 (2020)

19. Sánchez-Aparicio, M., Martín-Jiménez, J., Del Pozo, S., González-González, E., Lagüela, S.: Ener3DMap-SolarWeb roofs: a geospatial web-based platform to compute photovoltaic potential. Renew. Sustain. Energy Rev. **135**, 110203 (2021)

20. Suri, M., Huld, T.A., Dunlop, E.D., Ossenbrink, H.A.: Potential of solar electricity generation in the European Union member states and candidate countries. Sol. Energy **81**(10), 1295–1305 (2007)

21. Sancho, J.M., Riesco, J., Jiménez, C., Sánchez, M.C., Montero, J., López, M.: Atlas de Radiación Solar en España utilizando datos del SAF de Clima de EUMETSAT. AEMET, Madrid (Spain) (2012)

22. Martín-Jiménez, J.A., Del Pozo, S., Sánchez-Aparicio, M., Lagüela, S.: Multi-scale roof characterization from LiDAR data and aerial orthoimagery: automatic computation of building photovoltaic capacity. Autom. Constr. **109**, 102965 (2020)

23. NOAA Solar Calculator – Global Monitoring Laboratory, Earth System Research Laboratories. https://www.esrl.noaa.gov/gmd/grad/solcalc/. Accessed 10 Sept 2020

24. Meeus, J.: Astronomical Algorithms, 2nd edn. Atlantic Books, London (1998)

Computational Intelligence for Analysis of Traffic Data

Hernán Winter[1][✉] [iD], Juan Serra[1][✉] [iD], Sergio Nesmachnow[1][✉] [iD],
Andrei Tchernykh[2,3] [iD], and Vladimir Shepelev[3]

[1] Universidad de la República, Montevideo, Uruguay
{hernan.winter,juan.serra,sergion}@fing.edu.uy
[2] CICESE, Ensenada, Mexico
chernykh@cicese.mx
[3] South Ural State University, Chelyabinsk, Russia
shepelevvd@susu.ru

Abstract. This article presents a system developed for the collection and analysis of traffic data obtained from traffic camera videos using computational intelligence. The proposed system is developed using the modern object detection library Detectron2. A pipeline-type architecture is used for frame processing, where each step is an independent, configurable functional module, loosely coupled to the others. The validation of the proposed system is performed on real scenarios in Montevideo, Uruguay, under different conditions (daylight, nightlight, and different video qualities). Results demonstrate the effectiveness of the system in the considered scenarios.

Keywords: Computational intelligence · Neural networks · Traffic data · Smart cities

1 Introduction

The growth of cities and traffic density have led to an increased demand for surveillance systems capable of automating traffic monitoring and analysis. The main goal of these automatic systems is to aid or even remove the human labor for vision based tasks that can be performed by a computer, providing regulators and authorities the ability to respond quickly to diverse traffic issues and situations.

Tasks such as vehicle counting and infraction detection are of great importance for Intelligent Transportation Systems [23]. Recently, computer vision based detection and counting algorithms [22] have shown to be more effective and outperform traditional traffic surveillance methods, such as methods using different kinds of sensors [12]. However, there are still many challenges and open issues in computer vision based vehicle detection and counting processes, caused by illumination variation, shadows, occlusion, and other phenomena.

In this line of work, this article presents a system applying computational intelligence (based on Artificial Neural Networks, ANN) to solve traffic analysis

© Springer Nature Switzerland AG 2021
S. Nesmachnow and L. Hernández Callejo (Eds.): ICSC-CITIES 2020, CCIS 1359, pp. 167–182, 2021.
https://doi.org/10.1007/978-3-030-69136-3_12

problems using video recordings provided by surveillance cameras. The problems solved include vehicle detection, counting, classification, tracking, and detection of different types of traffic offenses, such as red light intersection crossing and parking vehicles in not allowed zones. The validation of the proposed system is developed using real traffic videos from the city of Montevideo, Uruguay.

The main contributions of the reserch reported in this article include: i) a methodology for the design of traffic analysis software systems using videos; ii) specific implementations of vehicle detection, counting, classification and tracking methods, and iii) the validation of the proposed methods on real scenarios.

The article is structured as follows. Section 2 presents a background on computational intelligence for image analysis. A review of the main related work is presented in Sect. 3. The technical aspects of the solution, including the proposed architecture, modules, and supporting libraries are described in Sect. 4. The experimental validation is reported and results are discussed in Sect. 5. Finally, Sect. 6 presents the conclusions and the main lines of future work.

2 Computational Intelligence for Image Analysis

This section describes the main concepts about the analysis of traffic data using computational intelligence.

2.1 Detection

One of the fundamental problems in computer vision is the task of assigning a label from a fixed set of categories to an input image. This task is known as image classification and is divided into tree subtasks: segmentation, location, and detection.

The goal of semantic segmentation is to obtain a category for each pixel given an input image. It does not differentiate instances of the same object because each pixel in the image is classified independently. The classification and location task consists of classifying an image with a label that describes an object and drawing the box within the image around the object. The output in this task are a label that identifies an object and a box that indicates where that object is located. Object detection takes as input a set of categories of interest and an image. The goal of this task is to draw a box around each one of these categories, each time they appear in the image, and also predict the category. This problem is different from classification and localization since there can be a variable number of outputs for each input image.

Another task to consider is instance segmentation. Given an input image, this task seeks to predict the locations and identities of the objects in that image. Additionally, instead of simply predicting a region for each of those objects, this task seeks to predict a segmentation mask for each of those objects and to predict which pixels in the image correspond to each object instance.

In the last few years, computational intelligence and deep learning have led to successful results on a variety of problems, including image classification.

Among different types of deep ANNs, Convolutional neural networks (CNN) have been extensively studied [8]. CNNs assume that the input to be classified is an image. This assumption allows the network to be more efficient and to design architectures that greatly reduce the number of network parameters.

Solving the object detection problem involves determining all the regions where objects to be classified can be located. Given an input image, a Region Proposal Network (RPN) uses signal processing techniques to create a list of proposed regions in which an object can exist. This architecture class is named R-CNN. Given an input image, an RPN is executed to obtain the proposals, also called Regions of Interest (RoI). The main drawback of this approach is its very high computational demands. In practice, the network training is slow and needs significant memory. Fast R-CNN was proposed to mitigate these problems, working in a similar way to R-CNN. In terms of speed, Fast R-CNN has proven to be nine times faster than CNN in training time [7]. However, the computation time is dominated by the calculation of the RoI, which turns out to be a bottleneck. This last problem is solved in Faster R-CNN [17].

Finally, one of the most recent methods to solve the instance segmentation task is the Mask R-CNN architecture. Similarly to Faster R-CNN, this method follows a multi-stage processing approach. It receives the complete image, which is executed through a convolutional network and a learned RPN. Once the RoIs are learned, they are projected onto the convolutional vector. Then, instead of simply performing the classification and the regression of the regions of each RoI, the method additionally predicts a segmentation mask for each region, solving a semantic segmentation problem within each of the regions proposed by the RPN. The RoI is finally wrapped to the proper shape.

2.2   Tracking

Object tracking consists in the process of accurately estimating the state of an object -position,identity,configuration- over time from observations [14], thus generating a trajectory given by the position of the object in each frame. When several objects are located at the same time, the problem is called Multiple Object Tracking. In this scenario, the difficulty of the task increases considerably due to the occlusion generated by the interaction of the objects, which in turn may have similar appearances. On the other hand, conditions such as the speed at which the objects move, the lighting or that these change their appearance depending on the position, require that the tracking system must be robust, maintaining the object identifier in such situations.

In classical tracking methods, object features are extracted in each frame and used to search for the same object in subsequent frames [25]. This causes errors to accumulate in the process and if occlusion or frame skipping occurs, tracking fails because of the rapid change of appearance features in local windows. Thus, modern tracking methods apply two steps: object detection and data association. First, objects are detected in each frame of the sequence and then, detected objects are matched across frames. This paradigm is called tracking by detection [10] and it relies on the performance of the detection algorithm. Detected objects are matched across frames using different approaches, including optical flow with mean shift of color signature, Earth mover's distance to compare color distributions, fragment-based features, and computational intelligence.

Another simple but effective method based on the tracking by detection approach is Intersection Over Union (IOU) [2]. This method requires a detection algorithm with a high rate of true positive results, as a detection is expected in each frame for each object to be tracked. It is also assumed that the detection of the same object in two consecutive frames present a great overlap of the intersection over the union (defined in Eq. 1), which is common for videos that present a high refresh rate.

$$IOU(a,b) = \frac{Area(a) \cap Area(b)}{Area(a) \cup Area(b)} \tag{1}$$

The advantage of the IoU method, in addition to its simplicity, is that it has lower computational cost than other methods. IoU can be integrated on other methods to achieve a more robust and accurate monitoring

3   Related Work

Several articles have proposed automated systems for the analysis of traffic data applying image processing and computational intelligence techniques. The most related to the research reported in this article are reviewed next.

Zhou et al. [28] studied the vehicle detection and classification problem applying deep neural networks. The You Only Look Once (YOLO) architecture was used for vehicles detection and post-processing was performed to eliminate invalid results. The Alexnet architecture was applied for classification, feature extraction, and fine-tuning. The YOLO network obtained similar precision than a Deformable Parts Model, while the Alexnet network using Support Vector Machines (SVM) outperformed other methods such as Principal Component Analysis and Absolute Difference in a public dataset.

Uy et al. [20] studied methods for identifying traffic offenses using genetic algorithms (GA) and the recognition of offenders through ANN. GA were applied to detect vehicles obstructing pedestrian crossings and to identify the location of license plates in images, while a ANN is used to recognize the license plate number. The license plates recognition accuracy was high (91.6% on 47 test images), but some license plates were not properly located due to the vehicle position respect to the camera. Zhang et al. [26] applied a Fully CNN with Long Short Term Memory for the vehicles counting problem. Compared to the state of the art, the proposed ANN architecture reduced the mean absolute error (MAE) from 2.74 to 1.53 on the WebCamT annotated dataset and from 5.31 to 4.21 on the TRANCOS dataset. In addition, the training time was accelerated by up to 5 times. However, the proposed ANN was not capable of handling long periods of information due to the large amount of memory required.

Dey et al. [5] applied CNN in a System-On-a-Programmable-Chip to analyze and categorize traffic, including the quality-of-experience variable to improve predictions. A combination of transfer learning with re-training CNN models, allowed improving the prediction accuracy. Arinaldi et al. [1] applied computer vision techniques to automatically collect traffic statistics using Mixture of Gaussian (MoG) and Faster Recurrent CNN. Training and validation were developed on Indonesian road videos and a public dataset from MIT. Faster Recurrent CNN was best suited for detecting and classifying moving vehicles in a dynamic traffic scene, since MoG was weak for separating overlapping vehicles.

Chauhan et al. [3] studied CNN or real-time traffic analysis on Delhi, India. A YOLO network was used, pre-trained on the MS-COCO dataset and fitted with annotated datasets. The best trained model achieved a performance of 65–75% mean average precision, depending on the camera position and the vehicle class. This article provides the expected performance of YOLO models optimized using annotated data. The recent article by Zheng et al. [27] proposed TASP-CNN for predictinig the severity of traffic accidents, considering relationships between accident features. The proposed method was successfully adapted to the representation of traffic accident severity features and deeper correlations of accident data. The performance of TASP-CNN was better than previous models when evaluated using data from an eight years period.

Our research group has developed research on detection on pedestrian movement patterns applying computational intelligence [4]. A flexible system was developed to process multiple image and video sources in real time applying a pipes and filters architecture to address different subproblems. The proposed system has two main stages: extracting relevant features of the input images, by applying image processing and object tracking, and patterns detection. The experimental analysis of the system was performed over more than 1450 problem instances, using PETS09-S2L1 videos and the results were compared with part of the MOTChallenge benchmark results. Results indicate that the proposed system is competitive, yet simpler, than other similar software methods.

4   The Proposed System for Traffic Data Analysis

This section presents the implemented system for traffic data analysis, describing the function of each module and the input and output parameters.

4.1   Overall Description

The proposed approach is based on a modular architecture that implements an image processing pipeline [6]. The pipeline executes a set of tasks over input images (e.g., translation/rotation, resizing, etc.) to extract useful features. The modular architecture allowed for a progressive development process, starting from a few general modules and incorporating specific modules for relevant data.

Figure 1 shows the final architecture of the pipeline for traffic video analysis, consisting of twelve modules. The pipeline has 40 parameters that allow controlling different aspects of the processing in each module.

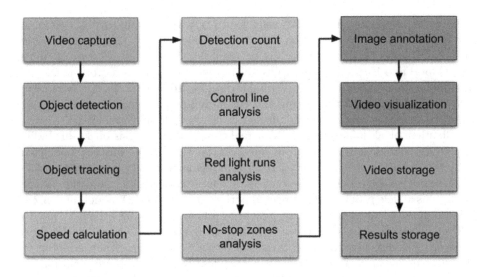

Fig. 1. The proposed pipeline for traffic video análisis (Color figure online)

Four main stages are identified: i) video capture, object detection and tracking (in green in Fig. 1), detection data analysis (in orange), results visualization (in blue), results storage (in red). They are described in the following subsections.

4.2 Video Capture and Object Detection

The goal of video capture is producing the frames used in the pipeline. A video stream (e.g., a local file or a webcam) is captured by a fast method using multithreading parallel computing to read the video frames, using OpenCV utilities. Video capture initialize the cumulative data transfer object (DTO), used by all modules to read and write data, and stores several fields in the DTO, including *frame number*, *image* object, and *annotations*.

Then, the object detection process each frame to produce a bounding box, mask, score and class of the detected objects. This module is based on Detectron2 framework by Facebook [21], whose modular design allows using different state-of-the-art detection algorithms, such as Faster R-CNN, Mask R-CNN, or RetinaNet. The implemented module uses both synchronous and asynchronous detection, and adds different functionalities on top of the detection framework such as the possibility of defining regions of interest for the detection or filtering the classes of the detected objects. The output of the detection module is converted to the standard format used by the rest of the pipeline, so it might be replaced by other detection module without affecting the other modules in the pipeline. The output can contain bounding boxes or instance segmentation. The rest of the pipeline is compatible with both type of outputs and can take advantage of instance segmentation when available to compute more precise results when analyzing patterns.

4.3   Detection Data Analysis

Detection analysis includes five modules to extract information from data generated by previous modules in the pipeline.

The *speed calculation* module computes an estimation of the average speed of each detected object in recent frames, in pixels per frame (PPF) or pixels per second (PPS). The system stores the position of the center of each detected object in the last n frames (n is a parameter) and so the speed is given by the Euclidean norm of the first and last stored positions.

Detection count requires defining one or more counting lines on the video image. Based on a structure that keeps each detected vehicle as an object with several identifying properties, the counting module analyzes the vehicles that overlap with the counting lines. This analysis considers the intersection of the polygon of the mask or box with respect to the defined lines as an input parameter. If an overlapping is found, the vehicle information is updated with the lines it overlapped and the frame number in which it did so.

With *control lines analysis* it is possible to define a relationship between two lines, meaning that a vehicle should not cross both as doing so would be consider an infraction. This allows detecting different types of infractions that involves a vehicle circulating in a no-driving zone, e.g., a wrong turn or lane change near a corner. This module uses detected bounding boxes or masks to recognize if a vehicle overlaps with both lines in the relationship through the video.

The *red light runs analysis* module detect driving offenses of failing to comply with red light signal. The region where each semaphore is located is defined as an input parameter and each traffic light is associated with a line. The defined traffic lights are analyzed to determine their color frame by frame, applying an algorithm that transforms the cropped frame of the traffic light to Hue, Saturation, Value (HSV) color model.

The *no-stop zones analysis* considers zones, represented by polygons, in which vehicles should not stop (or park). The module analyzes the bounding box or mask of those vehicles that intersects with the defined non-stop zone. If an intersection greater than a certain value is detected, then the average speed of the vehicle in the last n frames (n is a parameter) is considered. When the average speed reaches a value lower than one, the vehicle is considered in infraction and labeled as stopped.

4.4   Annotation and Results Visualization

The *annotation* module is responsible of modifying frames to show information generated by the previous modules. The modified frames will be part of the output video. Additionally, this module is in charge of drawing the detected objects, boxes, or masks as appropriate. Figure 2 presents an example of an annotated frame in one of the scenarios studied in this article.

The *video visualization* module is in charge of displaying the output frames as they are produced, using OpenCV to create a window and display the frames.

Fig. 2. Frame annotated with object masks, labels, text, lines, and polygons

4.5 Storage

The *video storage* module saves the frames in a file in a given path, considering the output format and FPS rate specified an parameters. Finally, the *results storage* module shows the information generated in each frame and the cumulative one, using a JSON-based logging system.

5 Validation Experiments

This section reports the validation experiments of the proposed system.

5.1 Case Studies in Montevideo, Uruguay

The experimental evaluation considered two case studies in Montevideo, Uruguay. The first case study correspond to the intersection of 8 de Octubre and Garibaldi avenues, representing a classic intersection between two avenues in Montevideo. The second case study correspond to the intersection between Rambla Wilson and Sarmiento Avenue. This case is relevant because it involves the avenue considered as the main traffic lane during rush hour.

The test dataset used consists of four videos taken by video surveillance cameras from the two studied locations. The cameras model is AXIS P1365 Mk II and record up to 60 frames per second. Recordings were taken at two different times of the day, in the morning (8:00 AM) and in the evening (7:00 PM) to analyze the efficacy of the proposed system under different lighting conditions. Figure 3 presents sample images of the considered scenarios. In turn, Table 1 summarizes the main properties of the analyzed videos.

(a) G8

(b) G19

(c) R8

(d) R19

Fig. 3. Testing video scenarios

Table 1. Properties of the test videos

Reference	Format	Resolution	# Frames	Rate	Duration
G8	MP4	1280 × 720 pixels	2393	8 FPS	5 min
G19	MP4	1280 × 720 pixels	2398	8 FPS	5 min
R8	MP4	1280 × 720 pixels	5998	20 FPS	5 min
R19	MP4	1280 × 720 pixels	5997	20 FPS	5 min

5.2 Development and Execution Platform

The proposed system was developed using Python and Anaconda for project environment management allowing to install and maintain the required libraries easily. For the implementation, training, and execution of the presented ANN models, the Detectron2 framework [21], based on pytorch, was used. The tracking service was provided by a Node.js server [19] running an implementation of the Node Moving Things Tracker [15] library. OpenCV [13] was used for image and video manipulation and processing.

The experimental evaluation was performed on a virtual environment defined on a high-end server with Xeon Gold 6138 processors (40 cores and 80 threads per core), 8 GB RAM, a NVIDIA P100 GPU and a 300 GB SSD, from National Supercomputing Center (ClusterUY) [16]. Using this high performance computing platform, it was possible to dynamically reserve the resources needed for the batch jobs for the system execution and validation.

5.3   Metrics for Evaluation

Statistical measures were considered for the evaluation of the developed system. To account for the performance of stages that involve a binary classification, the standard metrics were applied: True Positive (TP), which indicates the number of occurrences where the model correctly predicts the positive class; True Negative (TN) is the number of occurrences where the model correctly predicts the negative class; False Positive (FP) the number of occurrences where the model incorrectly predicts the positive class; and False Negative (FN) indicates the number of occurrences where the model incorrectly predicts the negative class.

Metrics proposed by Sokolova and Lapalme [18] were applied to evaluate the performance of detection and classification algorithms, including:

- *Avarage Accuracy*: indicates the overall effectiveness of a classifier (Eq. 2).
- *Error Rate*: indicates the average per-class classification error (Eq. 3).
- *Precision*: reflects the percentage of the results which are relevant (Eq. 4).
- *Recall*: refers to the percentage of total relevant results correctly classified (Eq. 5).

$$\frac{\frac{TP+TN}{TP+TN+FP+FN}}{n} \tag{2}$$

$$\frac{FP+FN}{TP+TN+FP+FN} \tag{3}$$

$$\frac{TP}{TP+FP} \tag{4}$$

$$\frac{TP}{TP+FN} \tag{5}$$

Metrics proposed by MOTChallenge [11] were used to evaluate the tracking method. Special metrics are required for evaluating multiple object tracking:

- Identity Switches ($IDSW$): indicates the number of occurrences where an already identified object is assigned a new identificator.
- Multiple Object Tracking Accuracy ($MOTA$): is a global performance indicator of the tracker combining three sources of error. (Eq. 6, where t represents the frame and G_t the number of objects in frame t).

$$MOTA = 1 - \frac{\sum_t (FN_t + FP_t + ID_{Sw})}{\sum_t G_t} \tag{6}$$

5.4   Results: Object Detection

For the evaluation of the object detection module, the configuration baseline of Detectron2 and the detection confidence threshold were taken into consideration.

The Detectron2 configuration baseline is a set of parameters which determines the type of ANN to be executed and the weight model. These baselines are part of the Model Zoo in Detectron2 [21]. The main properties of the selected baselines are presented in Table 2.

Table 2. Details of the configuration baselines of Detectron2 used in the experimental evaluation of object detection

	R101-box	*X101-box*	*R101-mask*	*X101-mask*
Backbone	R101-FPN	X101-FPN	R101-FPN	X101-FPN
Weights model	R101	X-101-32x8d	R101	X-101-32x8d
Using masks	No	No	Yes	Yes

The selected backbones used are ResNet-101+FPN (R101-FPN) which is a Faster R-CNN and ResNeXt-101+FPN (X101-FPN) which is a Mask R-CNN. The weight model R101 is an adaptation of the original ResNet-101 model [9] and X-101-32x8d is a ResNeXt-101-32x8d model trained with Caffe2 [24]. In turn, the detection confidence threshold allows discarding detected objects which classification score value is lower than a given value.

Tables 3 and 4 reports the results of the considered detection metrics for the G8 and G19 videos, respectively. These videos were selected as they account for a representative traffic flow of the city in rush hours in the morning (G8) and

Table 3. Classification metrics obtained with different settings in video G8

Configuration	*Average accuracy*	*Error rate*	*Precision*	*Recall*
R101-box-t03	0.93	0.07	0.91	0.73
R101-box-t05	0.87	0.13	1.00	0.48
R101-box-t07	0.78	0.22	0.93	0.23
X101-box-t03	0.93	0.07	0.89	0.75
X101-box-t05	0.88	0.12	1.00	0.49
X101-box-t07	0.79	0.21	1.00	0.24
R101-mask-t03	0.94	0.06	0.90	0.80
R101-mask-t05	0.93	0.07	0.97	0.72
R101-mask-t07	0.90	0.10	0.96	0.58
X101-mask-t03	0.93	0.07	0.89	0.79
X101-mask-t05	0.91	0.09	0.96	0.66
X101-mask-t07	0.91	0.09	1.00	0.61

in the night (G19). In these videos the camera angle is such that the North to South flow of vehicles occasionally occludes the vehicles in the West to East flow. Additionally, this scenario has a crossing with multiple traffic lights which makes the vehicles stop and accumulate producing interesting detection situations.

Table 4. Classification metrics obtained with the different settings in video G19

Configuration	Average accuracy	Error rate	Precision	Recall
R101-box-03	0.89	0.11	0.78	0.67
R101-box-05	0.82	0.18	0.89	0.40
R101-box-07	0.75	0.25	1.00	0.23
X101-box-03	0.84	0.16	0.70	0.53
X101-box-05	0.83	0.17	0.90	0.42
X101-box-07	0.73	0.27	1.00	0.21
R101-mask-03	0.87	0.13	0.67	0.67
R101-mask-05	0.85	0.15	0.67	0.60
R101-mask-07	0.86	0.14	1.00	0.49
X101-mask-03	0.89	0.11	0.77	0.70
X101-mask-05	0.87	0.13	0.92	0.56
X101-mask-07	0.87	0.13	0.96	0.53

Results in Tables 3 and 4 indicate that the proposed system had an overall average accuracy of 85% and indicate that the mask configurations computed better results than the box configurations in most cases (10 out of 12 instances). No significant performance differences between R101 and X101 models on box nor segmentation mask prediction were detected, but X101 had slightly better results in the night cases for segmentation.

5.5   Object Tracking

The main parameter to consider is the *tolerance*, i.e. the number of frames before the algorithm concludes that a tracked object is no longer in the sequence. The tolerance value depends on the frame rate of the recording. Values corresponding to half, one, and two seconds were considered in the study, as they represent time windows in which the probability of a identity switch among detections is low. That is, 4, 8, and 16 frames for G8 and G19 videos, and 10, 20, and 40 frames for R8 and R19. The performance of the object tracking module depends on the detection module. The X101-mask-05 detection setting was defined as basis for all tracking tests as it was the best performing detection configuration.

Table 5. Tracking tests results

Configuration	MOTA	Configuration	MOTA
G8-t04	0.81	R8-t10	0.86
G8-t08	0.83	R8-t20	0.87
G8-t16	0.82	R8-t40	0.89
G19-t04	0.47	R19-t10	0.10
G19-t08	0.49	R19-t20	0.14
G19-t16	0.46	R19-t40	0.13

Results in Table 5 show average MOTA scores of 85% for the daylight cases and significantly lower (30%) for the cases in the night. This indicate that the module performs significantly better in daytime scenarios. In 3 out of 4 cases, the configurations with one second of tolerance (8 frames in G8 and G19, and 20 frames in R8 and R19) had slightly better results than for nighttime scenarios. MOTA was mainly affected by FN values. In the tracking evaluation this occurs when an existing vehicle is not detected in a given number of frames, therefore it is not tracked. Based on this observation, improving the detection module in bad lighting conditions would also improve the tracker performance.

5.6   Pattern Analysis

For the evaluation of the counting module, the vehicle count resulting from the pipeline execution was compared to the number of vehicles obtained using manual counting. The performance of the method to count vehicles was measured using the detection and classification metrics presented above. To perform the evaluation, 30-second video segments were extracted from the four videos in the original test dataset. Four segments were considered for each video, thus having a total dataset of 16 segments from the two studied scenarios, eight taking place during the day and eight during the night.

Table 6 reports the results of the counting module evaluation, using the following configuration: the R101-mask-05 configuration was established for detection; the tracking module uses an IoU of 0.05, and a loss tolerance of eight frames for G8/G19 videos and 20 frames for R8/R19 videos.

Table 6. Counting test results

Reference	Average accuracy	Error rate	Precision	Recall
G8	0.92	0.08	0.92	1.00
G19	0.52	0.48	0.62	0.76
R8	0.87	0.13	0.91	0.95
R19	0.19	0.81	0.27	0.33

Results in Table 6 show an average accuracy of 89% for the daylight cases and 36% for the cases in the night. This indicate that the counting module performs better under good lighting conditions. In this case there is still room to improve the classification of the counted vehicles as the comparison of *precision* and *recall* shows that the main source of error are the *FP*, This means that the counting algorithm correctly counts a vehicle, but classifies it in the wrong class. Under bad lighting conditions the performance is poor, this is also caused by the large number of *FP*, which in this case happens because the counting algorithm counts not existing vehicles. The performance of this module can be mainly improved by using a more precise classification model in the detection module, while a better detection under bad lighting conditions would also improve the performance of the counting module. Improving the classification under poor lightning conditions is one of the main lines for ongoing and future work.

6   Conclusions and Future Work

This article presented the design and implementation of a system for the analysis of traffic data using computational intelligence techniques.

The proposed system was developed following a flexible pipeline-type architecture built over the modern object detection library Detectron2. The proposed design provides an efficient frame processing, by using independent, configurable functional modules, loosely coupled between them. This feature allows including new methods, modifying existing ones, and evaluate different alternatives and configurations.

The problems of object detection and tracking are solved using the Detectron2 framework and the Node Moving Things Tracker library, respectively. The information generated by these modules from the traffic videos allowed implementing a set of modules for the collection and analysis of traffic data.

The validation of the proposed system is carried out using real videos from two scenarios that include important streets of Montevideo, Uruguay, under different conditions (daylight, nightlight, and different video qualities). These recordings were taken in rush hours and show an interesting flow of vehicles.

Results demonstrate the effectiveness of the system in scenarios with proper lightning conditions. The detection results shown a overall average accuracy of 85%, and better performance using the mask models. In object tracking, the average MOTA scores were 85% in daylight. Results dropped to 30% in nighttime, indicating that improvements are required to deal with bad lightning conditions. Similarly, the counting module performed an average accuracy of 89% in daylight and 36% in nighttime.

The main lines for future work are related to improve the object detection module training the models with bad lightning conditions or bad weather annotated examples. In turn, the experimental evaluation of the proposed system can be extended to consider the analysis of red light runs and no-stop zones modules. Another interesting line of work is related to developing more sophisticated pattern detection methods to capture relevant events such as abrupt lane change or even traffic accidents. We are working on these topics right now.

References

1. Arinaldi, A., Pradana, J., Gurusinga, A.: Detection and classification of vehicles for traffic video analytics. Procedia Comput. Sci. **144**, 259–268 (2018)
2. Bochinski, E., Eiselein, V., Sikora, T.: High-speed tracking-by-detection without using image information. In: 14th IEEE International Conference on Advanced Video and Signal Based Surveillance, pp. 1–6 (2017)
3. Chauhan, M., Singh, A., Khemka, M., Prateek, A., Sen, R.: Embedded CNN based vehicle classification and counting in non-laned road traffic. In: 10th International Conference on Information and Communication Technologies and Development (2019)
4. Chavat, J.P., Nesmachnow, S.: Computational intelligence for detecting pedestrian movement patterns. In: Nesmachnow, S., Hernández Callejo, L. (eds.) ICSC-CITIES 2018. CCIS, vol. 978, pp. 148–163. Springer, Cham (2019). https://doi.org/10.1007/978-3-030-12804-3_12
5. Dey, S., Kalliatakis, G., Saha, S., Kumar Singh, A., Ehsan, S., McDonald, K.: MAT-CNN-SOPC: Motionless analysis of traffic using convolutional neural networks on system-on-a-programmable-chip. In: NASA/ESA Conference on Adaptive Hardware and Systems (2018)
6. Gilewski, J.: detectron2-pipeline: Modular image processing pipeline using OpenCV and Python generators powered by Detectron2. https://github.com/jagin/detectron2-pipeline (2019) 15 March 2020
7. Girshick, R.: Fast R-CNN. In: Proceedings of the IEEE International Conference on Computer Vision (December 2015)
8. Gu, J., et al.: Recent advances in convolutional neural networks. Pattern Recogn. **77**, 354–377 (2018)
9. He, K., Zhang, X., Ren, S., Sun, J.: Deep residual learning for image recognition. arXiv preprint arXiv:1512.03385 (2015)
10. Leal-Taixé, L.: Multiple object tracking with context awareness. CoRR abs/1411.7935 (2014)
11. Leal-Taixé, L., Milan, A., Reid, I., Roth, S., Schindler, K.: MOTChallenge 2015: Towards a benchmark for multi-target tracking. arXiv:1504.01942 [cs] (2015)
12. Lou, L., Zhang, J., Jin, Y., Xiong, Y.: A novel vehicle detectionmethod based on the fusion of radio received signal strength andgeomagnetism. Sensors **19**(1), 58 (2019)
13. Mahamkali, N., Vadivel, A.: OpenCV for computer vision applications (2015)
14. Moussy, E., Mekonnen, A.A., Marion, G., Lerasle, F.: A comparative view on exemplar 'tracking-by-detection' approaches. In: 2015 12th IEEE International Conference on Advanced Video and Signal Based Surveillance (AVSS), pp. 1–6 (2015)
15. Move-lab: Tracking things in object dectection videos. https://www.move-lab.com/blog/tracking-things-in-object-detection-videos (2018) 15 Mar 2020
16. Nesmachnow, S., Iturriaga, S.: Cluster-UY: collaborative scientific high performance computing in Uruguay. In: Torres, M., Klapp, J. (eds.) ISUM 2019. CCIS, vol. 1151, pp. 188–202. Springer, Cham (2019). https://doi.org/10.1007/978-3-030-38043-4_16
17. Ren, S., He, K., Girshick, R., Sun, J.: Faster R-CNN: towards real-time object detection with region proposal networks. In: Cortes, C., Lawrence, N.D., Lee, D.D., Sugiyama, M., Garnett, R. (eds.) Advances in Neural Information Processing Systems 28, pp. 91–99 (2015)

18. Sokolova, M., Lapalme, G.: A systematic analysis of performance measures for classification tasks. Inf. Process. Manage. **45**(4), 427–437 (2009)
19. Tilkov, S., Vinoski, S.: Node.js: Using javascript to build high-performance network programs. IEEE Internet Comput. **14**(6), 80–83 (2010)
20. Uy, A., et al.: Automated traffic violation apprehension system using genetic algorithm and artificial neural network. In: IEEE Region 10 Technical Conference, pp. 2094–2099 (2016)
21. Wu, Y., Kirillov, A., Massa, F., Lo, W., Girshick, R.: Detectron2. https://github.com/facebookresearch/detectron2 (2019)
22. Yang, H., Qu, S.: Real-time vehicle detection and counting in complex traffic scenes using background subtraction model with low-rank decomposition. IET Intel. Transport Syst. **12**, 75–85 (2018)
23. Yang, Z., Pun-Cheng, L.: Vehicle detection in intelligent transportation systems and its applications under varying environments: A review. Image Vis. Comput. **69**, 143–154 (2018)
24. Yangqing, J., et al.: Caffe: Convolutional architecture for fast feature embedding (2014)
25. Zhang, K., Zhang, L., Yang, M.-H.: Real-time compressive tracking. In: Fitzgibbon, A., Lazebnik, S., Perona, P., Sato, Y., Schmid, C. (eds.) ECCV 2012. LNCS, vol. 7574, pp. 864–877. Springer, Heidelberg (2012). https://doi.org/10.1007/978-3-642-33712-3_62
26. Zhang, S., Wu, G., Costeira, J., Moura, J.: Fcn-rlstm: Deep spatio-temporal neural networks for vehicle counting in city cameras. In: International Conference on Computer Vision, pp. 3687–3696 (10 2017)
27. Zheng, M., et al.: Traffic accident's severity prediction: a deep-learning approach-based CNN network. IEEE Access **7**, 39897–39910 (2019)
28. Zhou, Y., Nejati, H., Do, T., Cheung, N., Cheah, L.: Image-based vehicle analysis using deep neural network: a systematic study. In: IEEE International Conference on Digital Signal Processing, pp. 276–280 (2016)

Exact and Metaheuristic Approach for Bus Timetable Synchronization to Maximize Transfers

Sergio Nesmachnow⬤, Jonathan Muraña$^{(\boxtimes)}$⬤, and Claudio Risso⬤

Universidad de la República, Montevideo, Uruguay
jmurana@fing.edu.uy

Abstract. This article presents the application of mathematical programming and evolutionary algorithms to solve a variant of the Bus Timetabling Synchronization Problem. A new problem model is proposed to include extended synchronization points, accounting for every pair of bus stops in a city, the transfer demands for each pair of lines, and the offset for lines in the considered scenario. Mixed Integer Programming and evolutionary algorithm are proposed to efficiently solve the problem. A relevant real case study is solved, for the public transportation system of Montevideo, Uruguay. Several scenarios are solved and results are compared with the no-synchronization solution and the current planning of such transportation system too. Experimental results indicate that the proposed approaches are able to significantly improve the current plannings. The Mixed Integer Programming algorithm computed the optimum solution for all scenarios, accounting for an improvement of up to 95% in successful synchronizations when compared with the actual timetable in Montevideo. The evolutionary algorithm is efficient too, improving up to 68% the synchronizations with respect to the current planning and systematically outperforming the baseline solutions. Waiting times for users are significantly improved too, up to 33% in tight problem instances.

Keywords: Smart cities · Mobility · Public transportation · Timetabling · Synchronization

1 Introduction

Transportation systems are a crucial component of modern society, and they are one of the most important services to improve efficiency of activities in nowadays smart cities [6,10]. Transportation systems include a wide range of logistic activities related to transporting passengers and goods. One of the main goals of transportation systems is coordinating the movement of people, providing efficient mobility at reasonable fares. In this regard, public transportation is the most efficient and environmental friendly mean for mobility of citizens. However, the efficacy of public transportation systems in large cities requires

© Springer Nature Switzerland AG 2021
S. Nesmachnow and L. Hernández Callejo (Eds.): ICSC-CITIES 2020, CCIS 1359, pp. 183–198, 2021.
https://doi.org/10.1007/978-3-030-69136-3_13

a proper planning of several issues that affect the quality of service, including routes design and management, timetabling, drivers assignment, and others [3].

A transportation system usually includes timetables accounting for reporting the expected location of vehicles during a day. Timetables are closely related to the transportation network design, and they are usually built to account for specific origin-destination demands. Synchronization of multi-leg trips or *transfers* is usually a secondary goal of the timetabling problem, although it is important for providing an adequate quality-of-service, allowing passengers to wait reasonable times for transfers from one route to another.

The proposed problem is very relevant for the case study proposed: the transportation system of Montevideo, Uruguay [13]. Montevideo has a rather uniform public transportation system, operated by buses with similar capacities and service provision. Many users of the system manage to complete their end-to-end journey using only one line, but several other users rely on connections between different lines to make their trips, using transfers. Transfers can be made between different (geographically separated) bus stops. They are allowed without additional charge and are controlled by the intelligent Metropolitan Transportation System (STM), which identifies users using personal smart cards.

The STM also maintains historical records of the mobility of users. From these data, time periods in the day are identified during which the use of the system is regular, that is, where the utilization numbers have little dispersion and their average values are known. These numbers include: number of passengers boarding or alighting, number of transfers between lines and combinations of stops, bus circulation times at stops on their routes, and transfer times between stops for passengers seeking to transfer. These data are the main inputs used by the local administration to plan the frequency of each line within the uniform periods. Even knowing the frequency of each line, that is, the number of buses to use in the service period to satisfy the demand of the system (including direct and transfer trips), and knowing the circulation times between stops, there is room to adjust the departure time of each bus, which in turn determines the arrival time of that bus at each stop on its route.

Considering the case study described above, the main goal of this article is to optimize the number of successful transfers allowed by a timetable realization. The types of transfer are identified, and for each one a maximum threshold is established for the time that a passenger waits for their connection. If the passenger manages to transfer within a waiting time below that threshold, the transfer is successfully timed. The variant of the transfer synchronization problem elaborated here studies how to coordinate the departure schedule of buses–and therefore of arrivals at stops on their routes–, in order to maximize the number of successful transfers during a uniform time period, for which all previous data are known and fixed.

The article is organized as follows. Section 2 introduces the bus synchronization problem and the variant solved in this article. Section 3 reviews related works. The proposed approaches for bus synchronization are described in Sect. 4. The experimental evaluation of the proposed methods over realistic instances in Montevideo is reported in Sect. 5. Finally, the conclusions and the main lines for future work are formulated in Sect. 6.

2   Bus Timetable Synchronization to Maximize Transfers

This section describes the bus timetable synchronization problem to maximize transfers.

2.1   Problem Model

The problem accounts for the main goals of a modern transportation system: providing a fast and reliable way for the movement of citizens, while maintaining reasonable fares. The problem model mainly focuses on the quality of service provided to the users, i.e., a better traveling experience with reduced waiting times when using more than one bus for consecutive trips.

In the proposed model, the events of favoring passenger transfers with limited waiting times are called *synchronization* events. The study is aimed at solving real scenarios, based on real data from urban transit systems that accounts for the number of passengers that perform transfers between lines on each bus stop.

The main idea of the problem model is to divide any day into several planning periods on the basis of demand and travel time behavior of passengers. This way, the analysis of historical data allows obtaining similar accurate and almost deterministic information to build the problem scenarios.

2.2   Problem Formulation

The mathematical formulation of the bus timetable synchronization problem to maximize transfers is presented next.

Problem Data. The set of data that defines an instance of the bus synchronization problem includes the following elements:

- A planning period $[0, T]$.
- A set of lines of the bus network $I = \{i_1, i_2, \ldots, i_n\}$, with predefined routes, and the number of trips f_i needed to fulfill the demand for each line i within the planning period $[0, T]$, accounting for both directs trips and transfers.

- A set of *synchronization nodes*, or *transfer zones*, $B = \{b_1, b_2, \ldots, b_m\}$. Each synchronization node $b \in B$ is a triplet $<i, j, d_b^{ij}>$ indicating that lines i and j may synchronize in b, and that the bus stops for lines i and j are separated by a distance d_b^{ij}. Each synchronization node represents a pair of bus stops for which regular transfers between lines i and j are registered. The value of d_b^{ij} defines the time needed for a passenger that transfers from line i to line j to walk from one stop to another in the transfer zone (see next item).
- A *traveling time function* $TT : I \times B \rightarrow \mathbf{Z}$. $TT_b^i = TT(i, b)$ indicates the time needed to reach the synchronization node b for buses in line i (from the origin of the line). Generally, this value depends on several features, including the bus type, bus velocity, traffic in roads, passengers' demand, etc.
- A *demand function* $P : I \times I \times B \rightarrow \mathbf{Z}$. $P_b^{ij} = P(i, j, b)$ indicates the number of passengers that transfer from line i to line j in synchronization node b, in the planning period. Assuming a uniform demand hypothesis in the planning period, the number of passengers that transfer from a given trip of line i to a given trip of line j is P_b^{ij}/f_i. This is a realistic assumption for planning periods where demand does not vary significantly, such as in the case study presented in this article.
- A maximum waiting time W_b^{ij} for each transfer zone, indicating the maximum time that passengers are willing to wait for line j, after alighting from line i and walking to the stop of line j, in a synchronization node b. Trips of line i and j are considered synchronized for transfers if and only if the waiting time of passengers that transfers is lower or equal to W_b^{ij}.
- The departing time of the first trip of each line i (the *offset* of the line) must be lower than a maximum headway time H_i, which is defined by the bus system operator. Subsequent trips depart at a fixed frequency ΔX^i. All trips of each line must start within the planning period $[0, T]$.

Mathematical Model. The bus synchronization problem proposes finding appropriate values for the departure time of the first trip of each line to guarantee the maximum number of synchronizations for all lines with transfer demands in the planning period T.

The control variables of the problem are the offset of each line (X_1^i), which define the whole set of departing times for all trips of each line. Auxiliary variables are needed to capture the synchronization events in each transfer zone. Binary variables Z_{rsb}^{ij} takes value 1 when trip r of line i and trip s of line j are synchronized in node b (i.e., trip r of line i arrives before trip s of line j and allows passengers to complete the transfer, i.e., walk between the corresponding bus stops and wait less than the waiting threshold for that transfer, W_b^{ij}).

The mathematical model of the bus synchronization problem as Mixed Integer Programming (MIP) problem is formulated in Eq. 1.

$$\text{maximize} \quad \sum_{b \in B} \left(\sum_{r=1}^{f_i} \sum_{s=1}^{f_j} Z_{rsb}^{ij} \right) \cdot \frac{P_b^{ij}}{f_i} \tag{1a}$$

$$\text{subject to} \quad Z_{rsb}^{ij} \leq 1 + \frac{(A_{rb}^i + d_b^{ij} + W_b^{ij}) - A_{sb}^j}{M} \quad \forall b \in B \tag{1b}$$

$$Z_{rsb}^{ij} \leq 1 + \frac{A_{sb}^j - (A_{rb}^i + d_b^{ij})}{M} \quad \forall b \in B \tag{1c}$$

$$\text{with} \quad A_{sb}^j = X_1^j + (s-1)\Delta X^j + TT_b^j$$

$$A_{rb}^i = X_1^i + (r-1)\Delta X^i + TT_b^i$$

$$Z_{rsb}^{ij} \in \{0,1\}, 0 \leq X_1^i \leq H_i, \ \forall i \in I \tag{1d}$$

The objective function of the optimization problem (Eq. 1a) proposes maximizing the number of passengers that successfully complete a transfer in the planning period in every synchronization point. The value $\sum_{r=1}^{f_i} \sum_{s=1}^{f_j} Z_{rsb}^{ij}$ is the total number of successful connections between trips of each pair of lines i and j involved in each synchronization point b, while P_b^{ij}/f_i is the demand for each transfer.

Equations 1b–1d specify the constraints of the problem. According to Eq. 1a, the optimization will seek to activate as many variables Z_{rsb}^{ij} as possible. Constraints for variables Z_{rsb}^{ij} prevent them from taking the value 1 if the corresponding transfer is not synchronized. In both, Eqs. 1b and 1c, A_{rb}^i denotes the arrival time of trip r of line i to transfer zone b and A_{sb}^j denotes the arrival time of trip s of line j to transfer zone b. For an interpretation of constraint 1b, consider the maximum time passengers from trip r of line i are willing to wait for a transfer with trip s of line j at transfer zone b. This value defines the limit time $A_r^i + d_b^{ij} + W_b^{ij}$. Whenever the arrival time of trip s of line j does not surpass that limit, the right-hand side of Eq. 1b is greater or equal to 1, so the synchronization variable Z_{rsb}^{ij} is allowed to be 1. In addition, it is also necessary for passengers alighting from trip r of line i to walk to the transfer point (arriving at time $A_{rb}^i + d_b^{ij}$) before the arrival time of the corresponding trip s of line j (A_{sb}^j). Otherwise, those passengers would lose the connection. Whenever this second condition is met, the right-hand side of constraints Eq. 1c also allow Z_{rsb}^{ij} to take the value 1. So far, there is a potential issue when non-synchronized trips lead to values lower than 0 on the right-hand side of Eq. 1c, which derives into unfeasible constraints sets. The proposed model only needs that either $(A_{rb}^i + d_b^{ij} + W_b^{ij}) - A_{sb}^j$ or $A_{sb}^j - (A_{rb}^i + d_b^{ij})$ to be negative to deactivate synchronization variables Z_{rsb}^{ij}. Hence, suffices to get a constant value M, large enough to guarantee that both Eqs. 1b and 1c are always feasible. However, using extremely large values for M might cause numerical stability problems when the model is implemented in a solver. The procedure applied in this article to find compliant and relatively low values for M consisted in computing the maximum value within the union of sets $\{(H_i(j) + (f_i(j) - 1) \times \varDelta X^j + TT_b^j) - (TT_b^i + d_b^{ij} + W_b^{ij})\}$ and $\{(H_i(i) + (f_i(i) - 1) \times \varDelta X^i + TT_b^i + d_b^{ij}) - TT_b^j\}$, for all synchronization points $b \; in B$. These values of M can be easily calculated during the process of crafting the MIP formulation before using a specific solver, so the problem of finding M is of polynomial complexity. Finally, Eq. 1d defines the domain for decision variables Z_{rsb}^{ij} (binary variables).

The problem formulation assumes, without loss of generality, that $\varDelta X^j > W_b^{ij}$, $\forall j \in I$, i.e., headways of bus lines are larger than the waiting time thresholds for users. The case where $\varDelta X^j \leq W_b^{ij}$ correspond to a scenario in which the headway of line j is lower than the time users are willing to wait, thus all transfer with line j would be synchronized and they would not be part of the problem to solve.

3   Related Work

The bus timetable synchronization problem was recognized as a relevant issue for modern public transportation systems in early works by Ceder [3]. One of the first approaches for schedule synchronization on bus network systems was presented by Daduna and Voß [4], studying several objective functions (e.g., weighted sum considering transfers and the maximum waiting time at a transfer zone). Metaheuristic algorithms were evaluated for simple versions of the problem with uniform frequencies, using data from the Berlin Underground network and other German cities. Tabu Search computed better solutions than Simulated Annealing over randomly generated examples, and a trade-off between operational costs and user efficiency was concluded.

Ceder et al. [2] studied the Transit Network Timetabling problem to optimize the number of synchronization events between bus lines at shared stops, by maximizing the number of simultaneous arrivals. A greedy algorithm was proposed to solve the problem, based on selecting specific nodes from the bus network to define custom timetables. The article focused on simultaneous bus arrivals, and just some examples to illustrate synchronizations on small instances with few nodes and few lines were reported.

Fleurent et al. [5] proposed a subjective metric to evaluate synchronizations, using weights defined by experts and public transport authorities. The authors solved an optimization problem to minimize variable (vehicle) operation costs. A heuristic method was proposed for optimization, using the defined synchronization metric. Several timetables were computed for small scenarios from Montréal, Canada, using different weights for costs.

Ibarra and Ríos [8] studied a flexible variant of the synchronization problem, considering time windows between travel times. A Multi-start Iterated Local Search (MILS) algorithm was applied to solve eight instances modeling the bus network in Monterrey, Mexico with between three and 40 synchronization points. MILS was able to compute efficient solutions for medium-size instances in less than one minute, when compared with a simple upper bound and a Branch &

Bound exact method. Later, Ibarra et al. [7] applied MILS to solve the multi-period bus synchronization problem, to optimize multiple trips of a given set of lines. MILS was able to compute similar results than a Variable Neighborhood Search and a simple population-based algorithm on synthetic instances with few synchronization points. Results for a sample case study using data for a single line of Monterrey demonstrated that maximizing synchronizations for a specific node usually reduces the number of synchronizations for other nodes.

Our previous article [12] proposed an evolutionary approach for a specific variant of the bus synchronization problem. Results for realistic case studies in Montevideo demonstrated that the evolutionary approach outperformed real timetables by the city administrator and other heuristic methods. This article extends our previous research, accounting for a different variant of the bus synchronization problem aimed at determining the optimal offset values while keeping the headways and number of trips as indicated by the real timetable, in order to not impact in the quality of service offered to direct passengers.

4   Proposed Resolution Approaches

This section describes the exact and metaheuristic approaches developed to solve the bustimetable synchronization problem to maximize transfers.

4.1   Exact Mathematical Programming

The exact resolution of the proposed MIP model was developed using AMPL.

IBM ILOG CPLEX was used as the optimization tool, over the environment defined by ptimization Studio 12.8. Optimal solutions are computed applying a branch-and-cut heuristic, considering the following stop conditions for the execution:

- The time limit for the execution (parameter CPX_PARAM_TILIM) was set to ... (explicar: not relevant)
- The GAP tolerance in CPLEX (parameter CPX_PARAM_EPGAP) was set to the default value of 0.01% (0.0001). It is considered the default value since, the main goal is to compare with previous solutions obtained with that specific limit. The GAP represents, in percentage terms, the distance between the solution found and the best achievable solution. It is defined as $(f(x) - bestBound)/f(x)$, where x is the solution found and $bestBound$ is the best value achievable by the objective function.

4.2   Evolutionary Algorithm

The proposed EA was implemented in C++, using the Malva library (github.com/themalvaproject).

Solution Encoding. Candidate solutions to the problem are represented using integer vectors. In a solution representation, each integer value represents the offset (in minutes) of each bus line, i.e., the time between the start of the planning period and the depart of the first trip of each line. Formally, a candidate solution to the problem is represented by $X = X_0^1, X_0^2, \ldots X_0^n$, where n is the number of bus lines in the problem instance, $X_0^i \in \mathbf{Z}^+$, and $0 \leq X_0^i \leq H^i$.

Evolution Model. The $(\mu + \lambda)$ evolution model [1] is applied in the proposed EA: μ parents generate λ offsprings, which compete between them and with their parents, to determine the individuals that will be part of the new population on the next generation. Preliminary experiments demonstrated that $(\mu + \lambda)$ evolution was able to provide better solutions and more diversity than a traditional generational model.

Initialization Operator. A random initialization operator is applied. Randomly generated solutions are included in the initial population, accounting for the constraints defined for the offset of each line. This initialization procedure intends to provide diversity to the evolutionary search.

Selection Operator. A tournament selection is applied. The tournament size is three individuals, and one individual survives. Tournament selection computed better results than proportional selection in preliminary calibration experiments, mainly due to the appropriate level of selection pressure for the evolution.

Recombination Operator. The recombination operator is a specific variant of two-point crossover. It defines two crossover points randomly in $[1, n-1]$ and exchanges the information encoded in both parents between the crossover points. This operator was conceived to preserve specific features of lines already synchronized in parent solutions, trying to keep useful information in the offspring generation process. The recombination operator is applied to individuals returned by the selection operator, with a probability p_R.

Mutation Operator. The mutation operator applied is a specific variant of Gaussian mutation. Specific position(s) in a solution are modified according to a Gaussian distribution, and taking into account the thresholds defined by the minimum and maximum frequencies for each line. The mutation operator is applied to every gene in the proposed representation with a probability p_M.

5 Experimental Evaluation

This section reports the experimental evaluation of the proposed methods for the bus synchronization problem.

5.1   Methodology

Problem Instances. The experimental evaluation of the proposed methods for bus synchronization is performed in problem instances built using real data from the Metropolitan Transportation System in Montevideo, Uruguay.

Several sources of data from the National Open Catalog were considered to gather information about bus lines description, routes, timetables, and bus stops location in the city. The information about transfers was provided by Intendencia de Montevideo and processed applying a urban data analysis approach [9].

The key elements of the scenario and problem instances are described next: the period is the interval of hours considered for the schedule; the demand function is computed from transfers information registered by smart cards used to sell tickets; the synchronization points are chosen according to their demand, i.e., the pairs of bus stops with the largest number of registered transfers for the period are selected; the bus lines correspond to the lines passing by the synchronization points; the time traveling function TT for each line is computed empirically by using GPS data; the walking time function is the estimated walking speed of a person (assumed constant at $ws = 6\,\text{km/h}$) multiplied by the distance between bus stops in each transfer zone computed using geospatial information about stops. The maximum waiting time is equal to λH, with $\lambda \in [0.3, 0.5, 0.7, 0.9]$, to allow configuring instances with different levels of tolerance/quality of service.

Sixty problem instances were defined, accounting for three different dimensions (including 30, 70, and 110 synchronization points), using real information about bus operating in Montevideo, Uruguay. The synchronization points of each instance were chosen randomly from the most demanded transfer zones for the considered period in the city (a total number of 170 zones).

Each defined problem instance is identified by the following name convention: [NP].[NL].[λ].[id], where $NP = n$ is the number of synchronization points, $NL = m$ is the of bus lines, λ is the coefficient applied to W_b (percentage) and id is a relative identifier for instances with the same values of NL, NP, and λ. Scenarios are available at https://www.fing.edu.uy/inco/grupos/cecal/hpc/bus-sync/.

Execution Platform. The experimental evaluation was performed on a Quad-core Xeon E5430 at 2.66 GHz, 8 GB RAM, from National Supercomputing Center (Cluster-UY), Uruguay [11].

Baseline Solutions for the Comparison. Two main baseline solutions were considered for the comparison of the solutions computed by the proposed methods. A relevant baseline for comparison is the current timetable applied in the transportation system of Montevideo (the *real* timetable), which provides the actual level of service regarding direct travels and transfers. In turn, another relevant baseline for comparison is the solution without applying any explicit approach for synchronization of transfers, i.e., a solution where the first trip of each line departs at the beginning of the planning period (time 0, the *zeros* timetable). This solution provides a number of synchronized transfers according to the predefined headways for each line.

Metrics. The metrics applied for the evaluation include: i) the number of synchronized trips for passengers, as proposed in the summatory that defines the objective function of the problem; ii) the improvements over the baseline solutions, iii) the average waiting time each passenger wait for the connection (bus of line j) in a synchronization point.

Parameter Setting. EAs are stochastic methods, thus parameter setting analysis are needed to determine the parameter configuration that allows computing the best results. The values of stopping criterion ($\#gen$), population size (ps), recombination probability (p_R), and mutation probability (p_M) were studied for the proposed EA on three instances, different from the ones used in validation experiments, in order to avoid bias. The best results were obtained with the configuration $\#gen = 10000$, $ps = 20$, $p_R = 0.9$ and $p_M = 0.01$.

5.2   Numerical Results

Table 1 reports the objective function values computed by EA and the exact resolution approach for the considered problem instances. In turn, the relative improvements over the baseline solutions are reported: Δ_r is the relative improvement over the real timetable and Δ_z is the relative improvement over the zeros solution.

Table 1. Objective function results of exact and EA

scenario	real	zeros	EA			exact		
			obj	Δ_r	Δ_z	obj	Δ_r	Δ_z
30.37.90.0	276.08	286.89	302.09	0.09	0.05	302.09	0.09	0.05
30.37.70.0	224.62	232.79	271.75	0.21	0.17	271.75	0.21	0.17
30.37.50.0	162.41	151.99	208.65	0.28	0.37	208.99	0.29	0.38
30.37.30.0	111.58	107.85	154.49	0.38	0.43	154.62	0.39	0.43
30.40.90.0	218.61	229.78	237.05	0.08	0.03	243.02	0.11	0.06
30.40.70.0	163.64	175.85	199.40	0.22	0.13	219.97	0.34	0.25
30.40.50.0	126.11	127.07	146.39	0.16	0.15	173.24	0.37	0.36
30.40.30.0	92.28	90.97	101.18	0.10	0.11	127.08	0.38	0.40
30.40.90.1	227.36	248.57	252.45	0.11	0.02	262.36	0.15	0.06
30.40.70.1	178.07	193.32	219.92	0.24	0.14	238.19	0.34	0.23
30.40.50.1	129.80	140.22	163.30	0.26	0.16	190.16	0.47	0.36
30.40.30.1	80.24	108.97	117.42	0.46	0.08	156.44	0.95	0.44
30.41.90.0	246.99	260.32	279.49	0.13	0.07	279.49	0.13	0.07
30.41.70.0	197.16	201.00	248.29	0.26	0.24	248.42	0.26	0.24
30.41.50.0	141.93	136.07	186.27	0.31	0.37	186.36	0.31	0.37
30.41.30.0	93.79	98.26	141.87	0.51	0.44	142.63	0.52	0.45
30.42.90.0	241.44	241.45	255.78	0.06	0.06	255.78	0.06	0.06
30.42.70.0	195.96	191.28	228.08	0.16	0.19	228.08	0.16	0.19
30.42.50.0	145.01	140.28	172.52	0.19	0.23	172.52	0.19	0.23
30.42.30.0	95.81	93.08	124.88	0.30	0.34	125.74	0.31	0.35
70.60.90.0	568.51	579.73	609.29	0.07	0.05	609.68	0.07	0.05
70.60.70.0	463.02	454.24	545.02	0.18	0.20	546.03	0.18	0.20
70.60.50.0	339.70	296.11	414.29	0.22	0.40	415.80	0.22	0.40

(continued)

Table 1. (*continued*)

scenario	real	zeros	EA obj	Δ_r	Δ_z	exact obj	Δ_r	Δ_z
70.60.30.0	218.71	213.86	301.34	0.38	0.41	304.07	0.39	0.42
70.62.90.0	543.67	560.98	590.80	0.09	0.05	591.17	0.09	0.05
70.62.70.0	443.22	443.89	524.86	0.18	0.18	525.81	0.19	0.18
70.62.50.0	325.70	317.75	393.66	0.21	0.24	394.13	0.21	0.24
70.62.30.0	212.04	215.66	295.31	0.39	0.37	298.68	0.41	0.38
70.63.90.0	550.17	575.71	609.44	0.11	0.06	609.68	0.11	0.06
70.63.70.0	441.71	455.92	546.46	0.24	0.20	547.61	0.24	0.20
70.63.50.0	316.46	300.67	427.58	0.35	0.42	429.74	0.36	0.43
70.63.30.0	208.82	202.82	324.20	0.55	0.60	328.02	0.57	0.62
70.67.90.0	510.16	535.04	567.09	0.11	0.06	567.43	0.11	0.06
70.67.70.0	409.57	418.35	512.30	0.25	0.22	513.00	0.25	0.23
70.67.50.0	302.15	299.78	400.06	0.32	0.33	402.49	0.33	0.34
70.67.30.0	194.05	201.63	298.87	0.54	0.48	302.55	0.56	0.50
70.69.90.0	522.36	550.33	583.61	0.12	0.06	583.85	0.12	0.06
70.69.70.0	406.63	435.12	529.19	0.30	0.22	531.05	0.31	0.22
70.69.50.0	298.53	292.98	416.07	0.39	0.42	418.24	0.40	0.43
70.69.30.0	193.05	205.18	324.08	0.68	0.58	328.15	0.70	0.60
110.76.90.0	815.78	843.26	894.86	0.10	0.06	895.72	0.10	0.06
110.76.70.0	656.63	669.18	798.41	0.22	0.19	799.61	0.22	0.19
110.76.50.0	479.29	451.85	622.49	0.30	0.38	627.71	0.31	0.39
110.76.30.0	333.66	294.90	467.28	0.40	0.58	474.09	0.42	0.61
110.78.90.0	847.33	879.90	900.09	0.06	0.02	931.35	0.10	0.06
110.78.70.0	699.49	667.77	763.71	0.09	0.14	835.26	0.19	0.25
110.78.50.0	507.05	453.87	551.42	0.09	0.21	644.97	0.27	0.42
110.78.30.0	324.79	317.42	379.43	0.17	0.20	477.47	0.47	0.50
110.78.90.1	867.23	895.99	910.82	0.05	0.02	941.85	0.09	0.05
110.78.70.1	708.89	689.30	780.93	0.10	0.13	845.71	0.19	0.23
110.78.50.1	525.85	460.71	567.71	0.08	0.23	654.75	0.25	0.42
110.78.30.1	338.42	319.33	390.82	0.15	0.22	489.02	0.45	0.53
110.78.90.2	848.47	872.66	894.37	0.05	0.02	932.92	0.10	0.07
110.78.70.2	681.46	676.82	765.56	0.12	0.13	836.45	0.23	0.24
110.78.50.2	494.80	449.03	571.35	0.15	0.27	654.02	0.32	0.46
110.78.30.2	333.19	309.13	397.57	0.19	0.29	492.76	0.48	0.59
110.83.90.0	810.76	850.69	897.02	0.11	0.05	897.65	0.11	0.06
110.83.70.0	624.94	674.88	803.28	0.29	0.19	806.25	0.29	0.19
110.83.50.0	463.61	460.48	634.77	0.37	0.38	639.36	0.38	0.39
110.83.30.0	299.88	300.96	490.14	0.63	0.63	498.28	0.66	0.66

Results reported in Table 1 indicate that exact and EA methods significantly outperform the baseline solutions in all studied scenarios. The improvements of EA over the real solution were up to 68% in instance 70.69.30.0 and the improvements of the exact method over the real solution were up to 95% in instance 30.40.30.1. Regarding the comparison with the zeros solution, the improvements of EA were up to 63% and the improvements of the exact method were up to 66%, both in instance 110.83.30.0. Average improvements over the real timetable were 20% for EA and 25% for the exact solution.

In turn, the proposed EA was able to compute solutions close to the exact method (i.e., the optimal value) in low dimension and high tolerance scenarios, computing the optimal solution in six scenarios.

Table 2 reports the average improvements of exact and EA over the baseline solutions, grouped by scenario size and tolerance. Improvements of the exact method are up to 52% over the real timetable (in scenarios with NP = 70 and λ = 30) and up to 52% over zeros (in scenarios with NP = 100 and λ = 30). In turn, the EA improved up to 50% over the real timetable and up to 49% over zeros, both in scenarios with NP = 70 and λ = 30. The values grouped by tolerance allow concluding that for all sizes, the improvements increase as user tolerance decreases. This result indicates that the proposed methods scale with the complexity of the problem, effectively increasing the quality of service. Improvements of the exact method also increase with the size of the scenario.

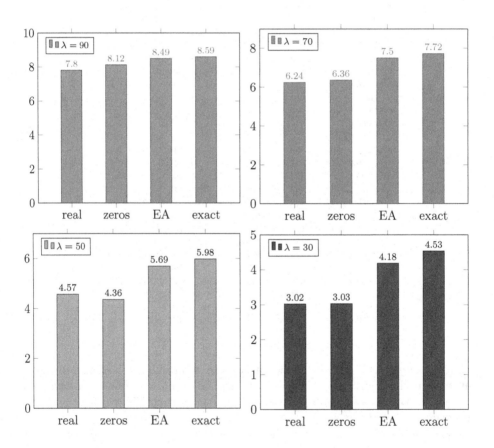

Fig. 1. Objective function comparison grouped by tolerance

Table 2. Improvements of exact and EA over baseline solutions, grouped by dimension and tolerance

NP	λ	EA		exact	
		Δ_r	Δ_z	Δ_r	Δ_z
30	90	0.10	0.05	0.11	0.06
30	70	0.22	0.17	0.26	0.21
30	50	0.24	0.26	0.32	0.34
30	30	0.35	0.28	0.49	0.42
70	90	0.10	0.06	0.10	0.06
70	70	0.23	0.20	0.23	0.21
70	50	0.30	0.36	0.30	0.37
70	30	0.50	0.49	0.52	0.50
110	90	0.07	0.04	0.10	0.06
110	70	0.16	0.16	0.22	0.22
110	50	0.19	0.30	0.30	0.42
110	30	0.30	0.38	0.49	0.58

Figure 1 shows the average objective values (normalized by NP) for all scenarios, grouped by tolerance. The largest difference in objective values is 1.51 (4.53–3.02), between the exact approach and the real timetable in scenarios with low user tolerance ($\lambda = 30$). The lowest difference is 0.37, between EA and zeros, when λ=90. As for results in Table 2, the graphic clearly shows that improvements of the proposed approaches increase for tight scenarios.

Table 3 reports three values ($r - l_s/l_n$) for the considered solutions, grouped by NP and λ. The value r is the ratio of the average waiting time results over the maximum waiting time for each synchronization point, which evaluates the number of successful synchronized trips and the relative waiting time for each synchronization point. Successful synchronization are represented by $r \leq 1.0$, and unsuccessful synchronization are represented by $r > 1.0$. In turn, l_s is the average number of lines successfully synchronized and l_n is the average number of lines not synchronized.

Table 3. Average waiting time results for the considered solutions

NP	λ	real	zeros	EA	exact
30	90	0.47–22/0	0.48–22/0	0.46–22/0	0.47–22/0
30	70	0.59–22/0	0.61–21/1	0.54–22/0	0.53–22/0
30	50	0.85–16/6	0.87–16/6	0.76–19/3	0.75–19/3

(continued)

Table 3. (*continued*)

NP	λ	real	zeros	EA	exact
30	30	1.33–3/19	1.37–3/19	1.19–5/16	1.12–7/15
70	90	0.47–39/0	0.49–39/0	0.46–39/0	0.47–39/0
70	70	0.59–38/1	0.62–38/1	0.54–39/0	0.52–39/0
70	50	0.85–28/10	0.88–28/10	0.74–35/3	0.73–35/4
70	30	1.35–5/33	1.40–4/35	1.14–11/28	1.13–12/27
110	90	0.49–49/0	0.50–49/0	0.48–49/0	0.46–49/0
110	70	0.61–46/2	0.64–47/2	0.57–48/1	0.53–49/0
110	50	0.87–34/14	0.91–34/15	0.79–41/8	0.72–44/5
110	30	1.38–7/42	1.43–4/45	1.24–11/38	1.10–17/32

Results in Table 3 indicate that the proposed approaches significantly improve the quality of service with respect to the baseline solutions, accounting for lower values of the waiting time metric for all scenarios. Largest improvement of EA over baseline solutions occur where NP = 70 and λ = 30 (0.26 over zeros solution and 0.21 over real solution). Largest improvements of the exact method occur where NP = 110 and λ = 30 (0.33 over zeros solution and 0.28 over real solution). The proposed approaches achieve better waiting time values in lower tolerance scenarios, with respect to baseline solutions.

Figure 2 presents a histogram comparison of the waiting times (normalized by W_b) for bus lines of a sample scenario (70.63.30.2) for a baseline solution (left) and the exact solution (right). The graphic shows that the exact solution manages to reduce the waiting time in a significant percentage of lines in the scenario. The exact solution has more bus lines with a waiting time less than or equal to 1 (16 vs. 6). Also, the exact solution has two lines with wait less than 0.5 while the baseline solution has none. Regarding higher waiting times, in the exact solution only 6 lines are higher than 1.5 of the expected value, while the baseline solution has 13 bus lines where users wait more than 1.5 of the expected value. The histogram comparison clearly indicates that the proposed solution improves the QoS, by synchronizing a larger number of lines of the system.

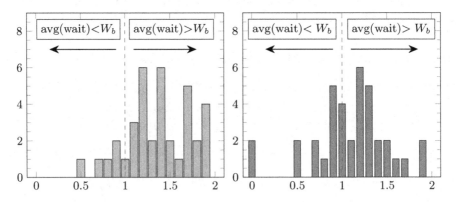

Fig. 2. Histogram comparison of the waiting time metric for baseline (left) and exact solutions (right) in scenario 70.63.30.2

6   Conclusions and Future Work

This article presented exact and evolutionary approaches to solve a variant of the Bus Timetabling Synchronization Problem considering extended synchronization points for every pair of bus stops in a city, transfer demands, and the line offsets.

A Mixed Integer Programming approach and an evolutionary algorithm were proposed to efficiently solve the problem. Results were compared with the no-synchronization solution and also with real timetables for a real case study in Montevideo, Uruguay.

Experimental results indicate that the proposed approaches significantly improve over current timetable. The exact method computed the optimum solution for all scenarios, improving successful synchronizations up to 95% (25% in average) over the real timetable in Montevideo. The EA is efficient too, improving up to 68% the synchronizations (20% in average) over the current timetable and systematically outperforming other baseline solutions. The proposed EA can be useful for addressing larger scenarios of the considered problem. Waiting times for users are significantly improved too, up to 33% in tight problem instances.

The main lines of future work include solving different variants of the bus timetable synchronization problem, accounting for different headways in the planning period, and modeling the real demand for direct trips too. Multiobjective version of the problem must be included too, by considering other relevant functions: cost and quality of service.

References

1. Bäck, T., Fogel, D., Michalewicz, Z. (eds.): Handbook of Evolutionary Computation. Oxford University Press, New York (1997)
2. Ceder, A., Golany, B., Tal, O.: Creating bus timetables with maximal synchronization. Transp. Res. Part A: Policy Pract. **35**(10), 913–928 (2001)
3. Ceder, A., Wilson, N.: Bus network design. Transp. Res. Part B Methodol. **20**(4), 331–344 (1986)
4. Daduna, J., Voß, S.: Practical experiences in schedule synchronization. In: Daduna, J.R., Branco, I., Paixão, J.M.P., (eds.) Computer-Aided Transit Scheduling. Lecture Notes in Economics and Mathematical Systems, vol. 430, pp. 39–55. Springer, Berlin (1995) https://doi.org/10.1007/978-3-642-57762-8_4
5. Fleurent, C., Lessard, R., Séguin, L.: Transit timetable synchronization: Evaluation and optimization. In: 9th International Conference on Computer-aided Scheduling of Public Transport (2004)
6. Grava, S.: Urban Transportation Systems. McGraw-Hill, New York (2002)
7. Ibarra-Rojas, O., López-Irarragorri, F., Rios-Solis, Y.: Multiperiod bus timetabling. Transp. Sci. **50**(3), 805–822 (2016)
8. Ibarra-Rojas, O., Rios-Solis, Y.: Synchronization of bus timetabling. Transp. Res. Part B Methodol. **46**(5), 599–614 (2012)
9. Massobrio, R., Nesmachnow, S.: Urban mobility data analysis for public transportation systems: a case study in Montevideo. Uruguay Appl. Sci. **10**(16), 5400 (2020)

10. Nesmachnow, S., Baña, S., Massobrio, R.: A distributed platform for big data analysis in smart cities: combining intelligent transportation systems and socioeconomic data for Montevideo, Uruguay. EAI Endorsed Trans. Smart Cities **2**(5), 1–18 (2017)
11. Nesmachnow, S., Iturriaga, S.: Cluster-UY: collaborative scientific high performance computing in Uruguay. In: Torres, M., Klapp, J. (eds.) ISUM 2019. CCIS, vol. 1151, pp. 188–202. Springer, Cham (2019). https://doi.org/10.1007/978-3-030-38043-4_16
12. Nesmachnow, S., Muraña, J., Goñi, G., Massobrio, R., Tchernykh, A.: Evolutionary approach for bus synchronization. In: Crespo-Mariño, J.L., Meneses-Rojas, E. (eds.) CARLA 2019. CCIS, vol. 1087, pp. 320–336. Springer, Cham (2020). https://doi.org/10.1007/978-3-030-41005-6_22
13. Risso, C., Nesmachnow, S.: Designing a backbone trunk for the public transportation network in Montevideo, Uruguay. In: Nesmachnow, S., Hernández Callejo, L. (eds.) ICSC-CITIES 2019. CCIS, vol. 1152, pp. 228–243. Springer, Cham (2020). https://doi.org/10.1007/978-3-030-38889-8_18

Towards a Sustainable Mobility Plan for Engineering Faculty, Universidad de la República, Uruguay

Silvina Hipogrosso[✉][iD] and Sergio Nesmachnow[✉][iD]

Universidad de la República, Montevideo, Uruguay
{silvina.hipogrosso,sergion}@fing.edu.uy

Abstract. This article presents an analysis of the current situation regarding sustainable mobility in Engineering Faculty, Universidad de la República, Montevideo, Uruguay. Sustainable mobility is a relevant issue in transportation within the novel paradigm of smart cities. The presented analysis is oriented to provide specific recommendations towards developing a sustainable mobility plan for Engineering Faculty and the surrounding neighborhood. The case study is analyzed considering the main concepts from related works and well-known quantitative and qualitative indicators. An empirical study based on questionnaires performed in the zone is introduced, providing interesting information for the study. The main results are discussed, including the motivations and issues that prevent users to move towards sustainable transportation modes. Specific suggestions are formulated to develop and improve sustainable mobility in the studied zone.

Keywords: Sustainable mobility · Public transportation · Smart cities

1 Introduction

Mobility is a crucial component of modern smart cities, which allows people to efficiently perform daily activities on urban areas [17]. Mobility is also part of the great environmental challenges existing nowadays. Related to this last issue, the main concepts of sustainability and sustainable development have been applied to conceive new models to guarantee the movement of people with minimal environmental impact, in order to not compromising the ability of future developments in this regard.

Sustainable cities in the twenty-first century are expected to prioritize people by integrating transport and urban development, in order to create vibrant, low-carbon cities where people want to live and work. Sustainable mobility is one of the big challenges of this twenty-first century. Sustainable mobility is defined as the ability to "meet the needs of society to move freely, gain access, communicate, trade and establish relationships without sacrificing other essential human or ecological values, today or in the future" [21].

© Springer Nature Switzerland AG 2021
S. Nesmachnow and L. Hernández Callejo (Eds.): ICSC-CITIES 2020, CCIS 1359, pp. 199–215, 2021.
https://doi.org/10.1007/978-3-030-69136-3_14

Sustainable mobility works under three interconnected pillars: environmental, social, and economic. These pillars can be applied to make mobility sustainable, accessible to more people, and integrated in multimodal ecosystems for higher overall efficiency. Sustainable mobility solutions must respect the three pillars to contribute positively to the communities they serve and also the collaboration across public and private players, along with citizens, is a necessary requirement to develop sustainable mobility by the people and for the people.

Sustainable mobility also requires a mind-shift: one where citizens, administrators, and decision-makers move from carbon-intense modes of transport to more sustainable solutions, like electric vehicles, car sharing, the expansion of bicycle and pedestrian lanes, as well as an overall shift from road to rail freight. With the rapid urbanization and increase of the environmental awareness and concerns, urban development have resulted in an urgent need and opportunity to rethink how we built and manage our cities to create climate-safe cities and ensure a better quality of life to citizens. However, governments should endeavour to move beyond simply pledging to reduce carbon emission to a specific level by a certain year it is necessary to adopt a sustainable mobility plan that could be developed for the future of our communities. There is a urgent need for re-planning the correct type and mix of transport modes to provide people efficient transport solutions to get to their activites.

In Montevideo, Uruguay, few initiatives have been proposed towards sustainable mobility. Most of the recent steps were focused in the public transportation, e.g., with the introduction of electric buses in the system. On the other hand, a few initiatives to promote sustainable private mobility have been developed in the last years (e.g., a leasing plan to acquire electric vans for last mile distribution of people and goods. However, no concrete mobility plans have been conceived for specific zones of the city.

In this line of work, this article presents a study oriented to characterize the mobility demands of a specific zone of Montevideo, namely the surroundings of Engineering Faculty in Parque Rodó neighborhood. Besides analyzing infrastructure and specific conditions of the transportation modes available in the zone, an empirical approach is followed to consider subjective opinions, based on personal questionnaires to people traveling from/to the area. The resulting data are processed and analyzed following a urban data approach, in order to extract useful information and elaborate specific suggestions towards a sustainable mobility plan in the studied zone.

The article is organized as follows. Next section introduces the main concepts regarding the sustainable mobility paradigm. A review of the main related work is presented in Sect. 3. The analysis of the current situation in the studied zone is reported in Sect. 4. The suggestions and recommendations for developing and improving sustainable mobility in Engineering Faculty are described in Sect. 6. Finally, Sect. 7 presents the conclusions and the main lines for future work.

2   Sustainable Mobility

In the last thirty years, sustainability has been a major concern of modern society. The concept of sustainable development, referring to development to fulfill important roles of nowadays, but without compromising the future, has been promoted as crucial to build more equitable, environment friendly, and inclusive model of society.

The sustainable mobility paradigm integrates many relevant concepts, including those related with their impacts on environment and society [2]. Overall, the main idea is to consider mobility as a valued activity regarding environmental, social, and economic concerns [12]. One of the most studied aspects has been the impact of mobility on the environment, with the main idea of conceiving new transportation paradigms accounting for cleaner means, accessibility, and integration of people. Other important aspects have also been analyzed, including the impact on economy, and the overall quality of life (safety, health, etc.).

Raising awareness and involving citizens are key aspects for sustainabe mobility. In turn, technology has been identified as one of the most valuable tools to help developing environmental friendly sustainable mobility. Different methods and indicators have been proposed to analyze means of transportation [6] and other important issues related to sustainable mobility.

3   Related Work

Several articles in the related literature have proposed initiatives towards sustainable mobility. Litman and Burwell [10] stated that the lack of holistic plans for transportation lead to poorly effective policies. They proposed that a sustainable transportation plan must be conceived from a broad point of view, considering several aspects (e.g., energy efficiency, health, economic and social welfare, etc.) and their and interrelated impacts. The authors formulated a paradigm shift for rethinking transportation, considering different integrated solutions for sustainable transportation systems.

The importance of developing a correct strategic plan for sustainable urban mobility was highlighted by Banister [2]. Such a plan must include several actors, and stakeholders must play a major role for the implementation of specific initiatives. Similar conclusions were extracted by Miller et al. [16], who elaborated about the role of public transportation regarding sustainability and proposed recommendations for for developing sustainable public transportation systems, based on several case studies.

The proposal by Gudmundsson at el. [6] introduced a framework for sustainability transportation evaluation and two real-world cases in Europe were studied. The importance of quantitative and qualitative assessment using indicators for decision-makers and operators was highlighted. Other relevant case studies in developed countries include the analysis of the impact of transportation in an integrated urban model of California by Johnston [9], and the empirical analysis for designing innovative sustainable innovative mobility solutions in three urban areas in Copenhagen [5].

In Latin America, Rodrigues et al. [19] studied the development of sustainable urban mobility in several Brazilian cities, regarding several dimensions of sustainability. The analysis allowed identifying key elements to be included in the proposal of public policies for improving sustainable mobility. Lyons [11] studied the actions for economic and social sustainability, and environmental protection in Bogotá, Colombia, emphasizing on the importance of the integration between transportation and social planning. The authors concluded that the main concepts of the case study regarding sustainable transportation can be replicated in other developing countries.

In Uruguay, project 'Public transportation planning in smart cities' [18] studied diverse features of sustainable public transportation in Montevideo and proposed interesting lines of works for improving bus lines in the city [4]. The analysis of sustainable mobility in the public transportation of Montevideo was addressed in our previous conference article [8] and later extened with sustainable mobility recommendations [7]. This article elaborates on the previous proposal, including a in-depth analysis of the situation and main motivations for developing a sustainable mobility plan for Engineering Faculty.

4   Sustainable Mobility Analysis for Engineering Faculty, Montevideo, Uruguay

This section describes the analysis of sustainable mobility developed for Engineering Faculty, Montevideo, Uruguay.

4.1   Motivation and Objectives of the Study

The main motivation of the study is to understand the mobility demands to Engineering Faculty and from Engineering Faculty surroundings to other zones of the city. This is a relevant case study, which includes several interesting features: is located in a residential area, but having other high education centers, a shopping center and several health centers nearby, among other relevant services.

The main objectives of the study include identifying, analyzing, and characterizing the current mobility situation in the studied zone, to extract useful information for elaborating a sustainable mobility plan for Engineering Faculty. In 2020, Engineering Faculty has more than 10 000 students, 1 000 professors, and 200 administrative employees. In addition, students and professors of other faculties also assist to lectures in Aulario Massera. All these persons have specific mobility demands to access to the institution. The study is based on a survey, and the opinions of interviewed people are taken in consideration.

The analysis of the current mobility situation provides useful information for developing a sustainable mobility plan in the studied zone. This is a relevant result considering some actions taken by Engineering Faculty to promote sustainable mobility (e.g., the creation of a program to promote the use of bicycles between students and professors, and joint works with the city administration of Montevideo to create bike lanes in a circuit connecting faculties of Universidad de la República).

4.2   Methodology

The proposed study is based on two main methodological stages: a first stage applying urban data analysis approach to characterize the current reality of mobility in the studied area, and a second stage based on a survey to capture the experiences, opinions, and feelings of people traveling from/to the studied area. This way, the proposed methodology combines quantitative and qualitative elements and analysis to provide an holistic view of mobility demands, and also perceptions and perspectives of sustainable mobility in Engineering Faculty and the surrounding neighborhood. The main details of the applied methodology are described next.

Methodology for Data Collection. Two main sources of data were considered. In the first stage, the study gathered operational data (e.g., bus lines that operates in the zone, timetables, etc.) and also information about the available infrastructure (e.g., bus stops, bicycle lanes, parking facilities, etc.) either from open data sources or by personal inspection.

In the second stage, a survey was performed in-situ in the studied area, to gather the data for the analysis. A total number of 617 persons were interviewed: 538 commuting from other zones of the city and 79 living in the area. Four relevant groups of people were identified: students of Engineering Faculty and other faculties that shares Aulario Massera, professors and employees of Engineering Faculty, people who live in the neighborhood, and people who work on the neighborhood.

The survey considered not only Engineering Faculty, but also the surrounding neighborhood to capture a more holistic view of mobility demand from/to the studied area.

The survey was focused on gather relevant mobility information of the studied groups of people, including: frequency of travel, origin/destination of trips, relevant aspects of transportation mode(s) used for commuting, willingness to switch to a more sustainable transportation mode, and issues that prevent changing to a more sustainable transportation mode.

The questionnaires were performed during 15 November–15 December 2019, from Monday to Friday, from 8:00 AM to 7:00 PM. Weekend trips were not considered in the analysis because they are significantly lower than working days trips. People who already commute in sustainable transportation modes were not asked if they would be willing to change towards a more sustainable transportation.

Indicators. The analysis considers quantitative and qualitative sustainable mobility indicators proposed by the World Business Council for Sustainable Development:

- *Coverage* (quantitative) defined as the ratio of the area covered by each sustainable mobility service (ci) and the total urbanized area studied (ta), *coverage* = ci/ta. The total urbanized area for the case study in this article is considered to extend for $0.52\,\mathrm{km}^2$.

- *Affordability* (*af*, quantitative), defined as the mobility expenses as a percentage of the income, considering the cost of each transportation mode and socio-economic data (middle income, according to values reported for 2019 by National Institute of Statistics [3]): $af = nt \times p/i$, where nt is the number of trips, p is the cost of a single trip, and i is the income per capita.
- *Access to mobility service* (*am*, quantitative), defined as the share of population with appropriate access to a sustainable mobility service $am = \sum_i PR(i)/nh = 1 - \overline{PR}/nh$, where nh is the number of citizens and $PR(i)$ is the percentage of people living within $400\,\mathrm{m}$ from a transportation stop. Service area is limited to $400\,\mathrm{m}$, as the maximum distance that a person considers to walk to use a public transportation service [1].
- *Origin and destination of trips* (quantitative), which account for the specific zones that originate trips to the studied zone and also the destination of trips that initiate in the studied zone.
- *Commuting travel time* (quantitative), defined as the average time spent by a person when traveling from/to the studied zone. The average walking speed is assumed to be $5\,\mathrm{km/h}$. For bus, the commuting travel time includes the time for a person to walk to the bus stop and the time waiting for the bus to arrive. For bicycles, the average speed is $13.5\,\mathrm{km/h}$.
- *Travel distance* (quantitative), accounting for real distances that people travel, considering origin and destination of trips to/from the studied zone.
- *Mobility preferences: transportation modes* (qualitative/quantitative), transportation modes used for commuting to/from the studied area.
- *Mobility preferences: relevant aspects for mobility* (quantitative), accounting for those features of mobility and transportation modes that are most regarded by people commuting to/from the studied area.
- *Willingness to use or change to more sustainable transportation modes* (qualitative), accounting for the opinion of people about sustainable mobility and sustainable transportation modes.

Methodology for Data Analysis. The study applies a urban data analysis approach [13,14] to evaluate global characteristics of mobility demand in the area. Well-known mobility indicators are used (e.g., coverage and commuting travel time) and other relevant aspects related to sustainable mobility are analyzed (e.g., modal-choice preferences for trips, which is linked to affordability, travel time, comfort, accessibility, and sustainability).

A specific focus of the analysis is public transportation, which is a major component of sustainable mobility. Public transportation is a rational alternative to private transportation modes with high impact in the environment (automobiles, motorcycles) due to emissions of air pollution and greenhouse gases [16].

The approach for computing affordability and access to mobility service is the same applied for Montevideo in our previous article [8]. For the case study considered in this article, we take in consideration that most of the interviewed people have middle/high income and trips from/to low income zones of the city are below 8%. The quality service of transportation modes from/to the studied zone is also analyzed, according to the preferences of users while commuting.

5   Practical Approach for Analysis and Implementation of a Sustainable Mobility Plan for Engineering Faculty

This section describes the sustainable mobility research for Engineering Faculty.

Description of the Studied Area. The studied area includes the surroundings of Engineering Faculty, Universidad de la República, Uruguay, located in Parque Rodó neighborhood (South of Montevideo).

The studied area covers $0.52\,km^2$ and includes three main avenues: Herrera y Reissig, where Engineering Faculty is located, Sarmiento, and Sosa. Nearby the Engineering Faculty is Aulario Massera, a large classroom building shared with other faculties. The main features of the studied area include:

- *Public transportation stops*: the studied zone includes ten public transportation stops. Six of them are located at less than 200 m of Engineering Faculty. Only one bus stop correspond to the electric bus service.
- *Bicycle lanes*: an exclusive lane for bicycles was projected to be built in the studied zone, continuing the one existing in Herrera y Reissig and reaching Engineering Faculty. However, this lane has not been built and the local administration has no plans to build it in the near future.
- *Parking facilities*: Engineering Faculty has two parking lots with parking capacity for about 140 vehicles. The building also has bicycle parking (open from 7:00 to 23:00 from Monday to Saturdays) with security monitoring and a parking capacity of 330 bicycles. The bicycle parking has restrooms with showers and lockers to promote students using their own bicycles for traveling. This facility is under current norms for bicycles parking in public institutions, according to the administration of Montevideo. No other parking facilities are available in the studied zone.
- *Sidewalks, illumination and urban furniture*: the studied zone is properly equipped with modern illumination and urban furniture. Sidewalks are built in all roads in the studied area, but some segments are deteriorated, making it difficult to walk for elder and impaired people. Curb cut have been recently installed at street intersections for wheelchair users, also benefiting pedestrians using canes and baby carriages.

Analysis of Results

Coverage. The studied area is fully covered by the public bus service, since all locations are within the 400 m range of a bus stop. Six bus lines operate in the zone: 117, 199, 300, and 405 (all of them have stops in both Engineering Faculty and Aulario Massera), 174 (the nearest stop is on Bulevar Artigas, 350 m from Engineering Faculty), and E14 (the nearest stop is on Sarmiento Avenue, 400 m from Engineering Faculty). However, just one line (E14) is operated by an electric bus, since July 2020. The total coverage of the public bus transportation service in the zone is 100%, while electric bus only covers 80% of the studied area. The public bicycle system does not cover the studied zone. The local administration has proposed a plan for extending the area of service to include Parque Rodó neigborhood and other areas, but it has not been implemented yet.

Affordability and Access to Mobility Service. The affordability index was computed considering a trip length of 30 min, which is close to the commuting time for trips in Montevideo [15] and also from/to the studied zone.

A medium level of income per capita in Montevideo (USD 691) is considered, according to the profile of most people commuting from/to the studied zone. Buses apply a flat rate for standard one-hour trips (0.85 USD/trip), allowing one transfer. A trip using a private bicycle is considered free, but the amortization cost of a bicycle accounts for 0.20 USD per trip.

The public bicycle service is free up to 30 min, and it costs 0.74 USD after that. A car trip is about 2 USD, considering amortization and fuel costs as for July, 2020.

According to the results, most of the interviewed people (97%) can afford a bicycle and almost all (99%) can afford a bus ticket. On the other hand, less than 15% of the people can afford a private motorized mean (car or motorcycle).

Mobility Preferences: Transportation Modes. Table 1 reports the number of trips from/to the studied zone, using each transportation mode (listed from more sustainable to less sustainable).

Table 1. Transportation modes used for commuting to/from the studied zone.

Transportation mode	#Trips	Percentage
Walking	83	13.0%
Bicycle	40	6.3%
Bus	361	56.4%
More than one	69	10.8%
Motorcycle	9	1.4%
Car	78	12.2%
Total	640	100.0%

Results reported in Table 1 indicate that less than 20% of the trips to/from the studied zone currently use sustainable transportation modes. The analysis also shows that the bus is the preferred mode for commuting, accounting for more half of the trips. In turn, other non sustainable transportation modes sum 13.6% of the trips, most than people that walk to the studied area. Most of the surveyed people agreed that they use bus because it is the most accessible and affordable transportation mode, especially for medium/large distances. Results also show that the potential of using bicycle is not properly developed, as only 6.3% of the people use this mean of transportation. These are relevant results to consider when developing a sustainable mobility plan in the zone.

Travel Distances. Table 2 reports the number of trips (using any transportation mode) according to their travel distances from/to the studied zone. The percentage and the accumulated percentage are also reported.

Table 2. Number and percentage of trips according to travel distance ranges

Distance	#Trips	Percentage	Accumulated
0–1 km	41	6%	6%
1–2 km	33	5%	11%
2–3 km	127	20%	31%
3–4 km	103	16%	47%
4–5 km	80	12%	59%
5–6 km	44	7%	66%
6–7 km	13	2%	68%
7–8 km	52	8%	76%
8–9 km	19	3%	79%
9–10 km	5	1%	80%
>10 km	125	20%	100%

The analysis of travel distances reported in Table 2 indicates that a significant number of people travel from/to near locations. One-third of them travel between 2 to 3 km, and 60% of the surveyed people commute from a maximum distance of 5 km. This is a relevant result to consider in a sustainable mobility plan, as short instances allow implementing specific strategies to promote the use of sustainable transportation modes. Of the 125 trips from/to more than 10 km, 84% of them have origin/destination from outside Montevideo, mainly in the nearby department of Canelones. Figure 1 geographically presents the accumulated percentage of trips according to the distance to Engineering Faculty.

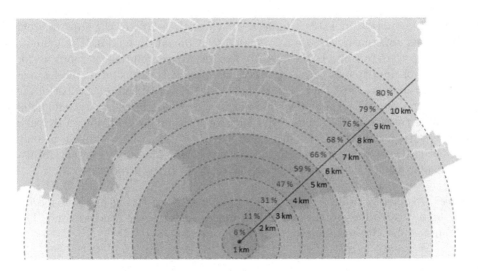

Fig. 1. Travel distances to the studied zone.

Table 3. Transportation modes by distance

Distance	Walking	Bus	Bicycle	Motorcycle	Car	Bus and other
0–1 km	24	6	2	0	1	7
1–2 km	18	2	6	0	4	2
2–3 km	26	60	17	1	8	12
3–4 km	13	49	9	0	12	11
4–5 km	2	57	4	1	9	5
5–6 km	0	32	1	1	7	2
6–7 km	0	7	0	0	3	3
7–8 km	0	39	1	1	8	3
8–9 km	0	15	0	1	3	0
9–10 km	0	4	0	0	1	0
>10 km	0	90	0	4	22	7

Another relevant result is that 95% of people make a round trip and more than 90% commute from/to the same location at least three times a week. Thus, the regularity of mobility demands in the studied zone supports the proposed data analysis approach based on patterns detection for mobility characterization.

Mobility Preferences: Transportation Modes by Distance. Table 3 reports the summary of transportation modes by distance.

The analysis of results reported in Table 3 indicate that most of the people that walk from/to the studied area travel less than 3 km. In turn, bus is preferred

Fig. 2. Origin of trips to the studied zone.

Fig. 3. Destination of trips from the studied zone.

by people that travel from 2–3 km and more, and completely dominates in the range of 4–9 km. Most of the people that use bicycle travel 2–4 km. Private vehicles are used by people that travel more than 2 km.

Table 4. Commuting travel time to Engineering Faculty from the most frequent neighborhoods as origin/destination of trips.

Neighborhood	Distance	Bus	Bicycle	Walking	Car
Parque Rodó	1.0 km	–	4.4 min	12.0 min	5.7 min
Cordón	2.5 km	18.9 min	11.0 min	30.0 min	12.0 min
Tres Cruces	3.0 km	21.2 min	13.3 min	36.0 min	15.2 min
Pocitos	3.5 km	28.4 min	15.5 min	42.0 min	17.0 min
Centro	3.7 km	24.4 min	21.4 min	44.4 min	20.8 min
Prado	8.0 km	44.4 min	35.5 min	–	28.8 min

Table 5. Sustainable transportation modes users will be willing to change to.

Transportation mode	#Trips	Percentage
Electric public transportation	298	48.3%
Bicycle	149	24.1%
Electric motorcycle	8	1.3%
Walking	7	1.1%
Scooter	6	1.1%
Use sustainable transportation	113	18.3%
Would not change	36	5.8%

Origin and Destination of Trips. Figure 2 graphically reports the origin of trips to the studied zone. The discretization level is given by the 63 neighborhoods identified by the National Statistical Institute in Montevideo. In turn, Fig. 3 graphically reports the destination of trips starting in the studied zone.

The analysis of Fig. 2 and Fig. 3 demonstrate the regular pattern followed by origin and destinations, according to the regularity of mobility demands commented in the previous paragraph. The neighborhoods that contribute the most as origin/destination of trips to Engineering Faculty are Centro and Pocitos (as origin) and Centro, Pocitos, and Cordón (as destination). Both maps also demonstrate that most of trips come from/go to central neighborhoods of the city, and neighborhoods located in the East also contributes to the demand.

Commuting Travel Time. The average travel times from/to the five most demanded origin/destination of trips to/from the studied zone are reported in Table 4.

Bicycle is the fastest transportation mode for travels up to 3.5 km, where most of the people travel from/to. For distances between 3 km and 8 km, car has similar travel time than bicycle, and always lower than bus. Walking is not a reasonable option, regarding travel times, for travels larger than 2 km.

Willingness to Change to More Sustainable Transportation Modes. Almost all people (93.2%) that use non-sustainable transportation modes stated that they would be willing to change to a more sustainable transportation mode. Table 5 reports the sustainable transportation modes users will be willing to change to.

62% of the people would be willing to change to electric public transportation, and 31% to bicycle. The main reasons for changing are the mitigation of environmental damages, energy efficiency, and avoiding health issues. 49 people that use automobile and 151 that use bus would change to electric public transportation. In turn, 149 people would change to bicycle as transportation mode. Most bus travelers would use a public bicycle system if it was operative in the area.

The survey also recognized the reasons why people do not change to electric bus and bicycle. The main reasons for not changing to bicycle included: poor safety conditions (29.6%),no bicycle parking (22.2%),cost (19.7%), poor public bicycle system (18.5%), bad climate conditions (6.2%). The main reasons for not changing to electric bus include: slow, many stops (50.5%), not direct (21.9%), uncomfortable (13.3%), inefficient (7.6%), low frequency (4.8%).

Safety and the lack of infrastructure are the main reasons that prevent users from changing to bicycle. In turn, reasons why people do not change to electric bus are related to characteristics of the bus system in Montevideo, which is perceived as slow, with many stops, and not providing direct connections.

These results are related to the most relevant aspects for mobility to the studied area.

Almost half of the people (44%) prioritize speed. Comfort is the second most regarded aspect (22%) and cost the third (17%). Sustainability is not perceived as a relevant feature for mobility (6%).

6   Recommendations for a Sustainable Mobility Plan in Engineering Faculty

The analysis of results are a useful input to conceive specific recommendations for developing a sustainable mobility plan in Engineering Faculty.

The mobility characterization is a valuable first input to elaborate suggestions. Since mobility demands follow a regular pattern, plans can have an important impact on all people commuting from/to the zone. In turn, the very large number of people (93.2%) willing to change to sustainable mobility options should encourage to take actions on this regard.

Any plan toward promoting sustainable mobility must consider the inherent features of the studied zone and the transportation system of Montevideo. In this regard, a relevant issue to address is the poor development of bicycle, which provides the cleaner and faster option for short and medium-distance trips.

Furthermore, bicycles are also the most affordable transportation mode, although interviewed people do not In this line, one of the first suggestions is to take strong actions to promote the use of bicycles for traveling from/to the studied zone. This action will effectively aim at the large universe of people that travel from/to distances up to 5–6 km, i.e., about 60% of the commuting people. Of course, such actions must be coordinated with other institutions because the survey revealed that infrastructure changes are needed, such as building the exclusive line for bicycles to Engineering Faculty, and also extending the public bicycle system to cover the studied zone. In turn, safety should be addressed too, as it is one of the main concerns of possible users of this sustainable transportation mode. It is not enough to signal bicycle lines on the street or sidewalks, but to provide a physical separation for safety of cyclist and pedestrians. Thus, introducing bicycle stations, improving parking facilities, and designing an articulated network of exclusive lanes are a must to improve sustainable mobility in the zone.

The development of electric public transportation is also another major line of work to improve sustainable mobility in the zone. The coverage of the electric bus must be expanded, by including at least one line directly connecting Engineering Faculty and the South of the studied zone with relevant origin/destinations in the city. This is a relevant issue that will require the participation of local authorities and the main bus companies. However, extending coverage is not enough. The study confirmed that people will not change to electric public transportation if the service does not improve. A throughout review of routes, bus stops, and travel times must be considered. This suggestion extends to the whole city, because the redesign of the bus network must be be performed from an holistic view. A specific suggestion is to introduce lines with fewer stops and higher frequencies than the current service, to allow commuters to travel faster. In turn, bus companies should focus on offering a better travel experience. Some suggestions related to improve travel conditions and comfort include appropriate dimensioning of vehicles according to the demand, provide air-conditioning, guaranteeing universal accessibility, providing accurate real-time information via mobile applications, and improve bus stops facilities. Another specific suggestion, in this case for the city administration, is defining preferential lanes for buses, which are currently not available in the zone. Some avenues in the zone (e.g., Herrera y Reissig and Bulevar Artigas) can take advantage of preferential lanes to avoid traffic congestion and speed up public transportation.

Another relevant result of the research is that sustainability is not regarded by people as a relevant aspect for mobility. This is a consequence of the poor development of the concept in Montevideo, where just isolated and limited sustainability mobility initiatives have been developed. Engineering Faculty and Universidad de la República should assume an active role in formation and dissemination about this topic, in joint works with local and national governments.

Improving infrastructure is not an easy task, mainly due to the lack of a proper urban planning. In this regard, specific initiatives should be conducted following the Transit-Oriented Development (TOD) [20] paradigm for urban planning and development to create a revitalized and environmentally friendly neighborhood. Initiatives oriented to reduce automobile utilization (e.g., pedestrianization or limiting private traffic) must be implemented, jointly with the promotion of sustainable mobility. Applying the TOD principles should certainly help to achieve that goal. In turn, Engineering Faculty can also contribute by limiting the access to private car parking only to shared vehicles, and improving the bicycle parking.

Another relevant suggestion is to develop/improve intermodal connectivity in the area. Combining bicycle and bus is a worth idea for people commuting from/to long distances, e.g., from outside Montevideo. This idea has been proposed to the local administration to improve the access and connection to the main large-distance bus terminal in the city using bicycle. The proposal will certainly contribute to improve quality, safety, accessibility, and cost-effectiveness of the mobility system in the studied zone and Montevideo.

The reported results, descriptive statistics, main findings of the survey, and suggestions are very valuable to design an effective sustainable mobility plan in the studied area. To conceive such a plan, the main concepts of sustainable mobility must be taken into account, to satisfy the mobility needs guaranteeing a better quality of life. These concepts include developing an integrated approach, considering strategic objectives and coordinating policies between sectors (transportation, territorial, social, environment, energy, etc.). In turn, initiatives must be carefully planned and its performance properly assessed via a systematic monitoring and long-term evaluation plan. Any of the proposed suggestions must be implemented by actively involve citizens, stakeholders, administrators, operators, and other relevant actors, accounting for their needs and opinions.

7   Conclusions and Future Work

This article presented an analysis of the current mobility reality in Engineering Faculty, Universidad de la República, Montevideo, Uruguay.

A methodology applying quantitative and qualitative indicators was applied to characterize the mobility demands, including subjective opinions from people commuting to/from the studied area. A survey was performed to gather information about origin/destination of trips to/from Engineering Faculty, mobility preferences, willingness to change to more sustainable transportation modes, the main reasons why people do not change, and other relevant aspects for mobility.

The main findings of the analysis are the universal affordability of sustainable transportation and that 93% of the people would be willing to change to a more sustainable transportation mode. According to the analysis, 60% of the people commute a maximum distance of 5 km, which suggest that implementing specific strategies to promote the use of sustainable transportation modes is viable. The high acceptance of sustainable transportation modes is highlighted and it sets a solid base for developing a sustainable mobility plan in the zone.

Based on the results of the analysis, specific recommendations are provided to develop a sustainable mobility plan for Engineering Faculty, mostly focused on improving traffic efficiency and accessibility, which is a direct contribution, as no previous similar studies have been developed in Montevideo.

The main lines for future work are related to extend the analysis including other relevant issues (e.g., private vehicles and traffic in the city, environment and pollution, etc.). The analysis of other mobility needs is also important to assess the impact of sustainable mobility in the studied zone. The proposed methodology can be applied to characterize mobility demands and sustainable mobility on other relevant neighborhoods in the city.

References

1. Atash, F.: Redesigning suburbia for walking and transit: emerging concepts. J. Urban Plann. Dev. **120**(1), 48–57 (1994)
2. Banister, D.: The sustainable mobility paradigm. Transp. Policy **15**, 73–80 (2008)
3. Carruthers, R.: Affordability of public transport. In: International Conference Series on Competition and Ownership in Land Passanger Transport, pp. 1–15 (2005)
4. Fabbiani, E., Nesmachnow, S., Toutouh, J., Tchernykh, A., Avetisyan, A., Radchenko, G.: Analysis of mobility patterns for public transportation and bus stops relocation. Program. Comput. Softw. **44**(6), 508–525 (2018)
5. Freudendal, M., Hartmann, K., Friis, F., Rudolf, M., Grindsted, T.: Sustainable mobility in the mobile risk society—designing innovative mobility solutions in copenhagen. Sustainability **12**(17), 7218 (2020)
6. Gudmundsson, H., Hall, R.P., Marsden, G., Zietsman, J.: High-speed rail in England. Sustainable Transportation. STBE, pp. 233–250. Springer, Heidelberg (2016). https://doi.org/10.1007/978-3-662-46924-8_9
7. Hipogrosso, S., Nesmachnow, S.: Analysis of sustainable public transportation and mobility recommendations for Montevideo and Parque Rodó neighborhood. Smart Cities **3**(2), 479–510 (2020)
8. Hipogrosso, S., Nesmachnow, S.: Sustainable mobility in the public transportation of Montevideo, Uruguay. In: Nesmachnow, S., Hernández Callejo, L. (eds.) ICSC-CITIES 2019. CCIS, vol. 1152, pp. 93–108. Springer, Cham (2020). https://doi.org/10.1007/978-3-030-38889-8_8
9. Johnston, R.: Indicators for sustainable transportation planning. Transp. Res. Rec. **2067**(1), 146–154 (2008)
10. Litman, T., Burwell, D.: Issues in sustainable transportation. Int. J. Glob. Environ. Issues **6**(4), 331–347 (2006)
11. Lyons, W.: Sustainable transport in the developing world: a case study of Bogota's mobility strategy. In: International Conference on Sustainable Infrastructure (2017)
12. Marshall, S.: The challenge of sustainable transport. In: Layard, A., Davoudi, S., Batty, S. (eds.) Planning for a Sustainable Future, pp. 131–147. Spon (2001)
13. Massobrio, R., Nesmachnow, S.: Urban mobility data analysis for public transportation systems: a case study in Montevideo Uruguay. Appl. Sci. **10**(16), 5400 (2020)
14. Massobrio, R., Nesmachnow, S.: Urban data analysis for the public transportation system of Montevideo, Uruguay. In: Nesmachnow, S., Hernández Callejo, L. (eds.) ICSC-CITIES 2019. CCIS, vol. 1152, pp. 199–214. Springer, Cham (2020). https://doi.org/10.1007/978-3-030-38889-8_16
15. Mauttone, A., Hernández, D.: Encuesta de movilidad del área metropolitana de Montevideo, August 2019
16. Miller, P., de Barros, A.G., Kattan, L., Wirasinghe, S.C.: Public transportation and sustainability: A review. KSCE J. Civil Eng. **20**(3), 1076–1083 (2016). https://doi.org/10.1007/s12205-016-0705-0

17. Neckermann, L.: Smart Cities, Smart Mobility: Transforming the Way We Live and Work. Troubador Publishing Ltd. (2017)
18. Nesmachnow, S., Chernykh, A., Cristóbal, A.: Planificación de transporte urbano en ciudades inteligentes. In: Iberoamerican Congress on Smart Cities, p. 204 (2018)
19. Rodrigues, A., Costa, M., Macedo, M.: Multiple views of sustainable urban mobility: the case of Brazil. Transp. Policy 15(6), 350–360 (2008)
20. Sung, H., Oh, J.: Transit-oriented development in a high-density city: identifying its association with transit ridership in seoul. Cities 28, 70–82 (2011)
21. World Business Council for Sustainable Development: The sustainable mobility project (2002)

Impact of the Covid-19 Pandemic on Traffic Congestion in Latin American Cities: An Updated Five-Month Study

Jesús Ortego[1]([⊠]) (iD), Renato Andara[2]([⊠]) (iD),
Luis Manuel Navas[1]([⊠]) (iD), Carmen Luisa Vásquez[2]([⊠]) (iD),
and Rodrigo Ramírez-Pisco[3] (iD)

[1] Universidad de Valladolid, Valladolid, Spain
jesus.ortego@uva.es
[2] Universidad Nacional Experimental Politécnica Antonio José de Sucre,
Barquisimeto, Venezuela
[3] Universidad de Barcelona y Universitat Politécnica de Catalunya,
Barcelona, Spain

Abstract. This study analyzes the impact of the COVID-19 pandemic on traffic congestion in 15 metropolitan areas of 13 Latin American countries. The database of the Traffic Congestion Intensity (TCI) of the IDB Invest Dashboard is used, it was developed from the alliance between the IDB and Waze and it is correlated with the contagions of the population published by Johns Hopkins Hospital University, for the period from March 9 to July 31, 2020, approximately five (5) months. For the analysis, the areas have been categorized into four (4) clusters, based on the Coefficient of Variation and the TCI/ WHO ratio. For each cluster, the graphs of the variation of the ΔTCI, the contagion cases, and the mobility recovery rate are analyzed. Among the conclusions include that the decrease in the number of infections and the flexibility of social distancing measures can be related to a recovery from congestion and that this can be measured as a function to the rate of recovery of mobility. In addition, the pandemic has revealed less collective and more agile forms of mobility, being this an important opportunity for the region to develop new forms of transport.

Keywords: Traffic congestion · COVID-19 infections · IDB Invest
Dashboard · Intensity of traffic congestion · Mobility recovery rate

1 Introduction

The global pandemic due to SARS-CoV-2 or COVID-19 has been public since its appearance in Wuhan, China, in 2019 [1]. Latin America comes to suffer it later, compared to other regions such as Asia and Europe. The first case of contagion officially detected in the region was on February 26, 2020 in Brazil [2] and the first death, announced in Argentina, the following March 7 [3]. This situation has led to the implementation of sanitary measures to try to understand and stop its spread, according to sociodemographic characteristics, mobility and reports on the number of infections and deaths by country and region of the world [4]. Among the sanitary measures are social distancing based on measures such as quarantine and mandatory, total or partial

© Springer Nature Switzerland AG 2021
S. Nesmachnow and L. Hernández Callejo (Eds.): ICSC-CITIES 2020, CCIS 1359, pp. 216–229, 2021.
https://doi.org/10.1007/978-3-030-69136-3_15

confinement. These measures have been heterogeneous among the countries of the region [5] and have directly impacted the mobility of people, among other effects [6–9].

The direct measures that affect mobility are the closure of regional and international borders, suspension or restrictions on the use of urban transport systems, reduction of their levels of occupation, enabling of bicycle lanes and location of medical equipment in transport stations for monitor the temperature of the users or request their identification to guarantee traceability in case of contagion, among others [7, 8, 10–12].

Currently, the conception of mobility goes beyond just the transport of people and goods, being the reflection of a social expression by interrelating in different ways, giving rise to patterns of behavior due to different social experiences, to guarantee communication to different distances, and influencing the regional and world economy [13]. This is in a constant process of change, being a basic need for people in the world. It is part of urban life and an important cultural component and of political, economic and sociocultural development, being essential for its analysis to consider the phenomenon of traffic congestion [14].

Latin America is a flourishing region, whose urban growth has accelerated dramatically in recent decades in an uncontrolled manner [15]. According to [16], it is the second region in the world with the highest urban growth and, with this, its service needs, including mobility and transportation. Traffic congestion problems are evident in the region [17] and, especially, in cities such as Bogotá [18], Cali [19], Mexico City [20], Santiago de Chile [15] and Buenos Aires [21], among others. Accelerating the need for higher levels of urban infrastructure, transportation and investment modalities, representing in expenses up to 3.5% of the region's GDP [13] and, for families, one significant cost to achieve mobilization [22].

Mostly, traffic congestion is an incident problem in capital cities, where its root is due to a complex context, in which political, economic, social, cultural and historical heritage variables are articulated [19]. In this framework, Table 1 shows the number of hours that a driver remains detained during the year due to congestion and the average speed of advance of vehicles in some of the cities of Brazil, Colombia, Ecuador and Mexico during 2019, according to the INRIX Global Traffic Scorecard [23]. In this ranking, 975 cities and 43 countries in the world regions are analyzed and positioned, based on traffic congestion.

Table 1. Congestion time and average vehicle speed for 2019 [23]

Country	City	Number of peak congestion hours	Variation of the average congestion rate with respect to the previous year (%)	Average vehicle speed (mph)
Brasil	Rio de Janeiro	190	−5	11
	Sao Paulo	152	+5	13
Colombia	Bogotá	191	+3	9
	Cali	94	-8	12
Ecuador	Quito	144	0	10
	Guayaquil	130	+4	13
México	Mexico City	158	+2	12
	Guadalajara	85	−10	13

Among other variables, congestion depends on the motorization of travel in cities, where Latin America is one of the highest in the world, along with Asia and the Middle East [24]. The number of vehicles per area (km^2) is higher in Costa Rica (21), Mexico (19) and Guatemala (17) than in European countries. This motorization is reflected in the modal share of travel in the city and in the performance of public transport. This has brought problems and impacts to the accessibility of the population to jobs and education, public health and also, to recreational and cultural activities, in addition the consumption of fuel and other resources.

Currently, as a result of the global pandemic COVID-19, congestion levels have been reduced in Latin America [4, 5]. This decrease has been significant in the first days of the implementation of various social distancing measures. Which indicates that this distancing can be analyzed through mobility patterns. Platforms of the Inter-american Development Bank (IDB) [25], Moovit [26] and Google [27], among others, have published their databases and comparisons with months prior to the pandemic, to be used for the different studies on COVID-19.

The IDB has published the IDB Invest Dashboard [25] which allows monitoring the distancing measures in the region based on its mobility, in real time, with the purpose of tracking the variables so that they serve as input for the public policy-making in the countries. The traffic data published in this Dashboard [25] comes from the alliance between the IDB and Waze [28], with these the Traffic Congestion Intensity indicator (TCI) can be estimated. According to this Index, in the first weeks of the implementation of the distancing measures, congestion in 69 metropolitan areas in Latin America fell significantly. The most extreme case being the city of Lima [29] where a decrease of up to 88% of the TCI is registered.

The purpose of this article is to analyze the TCI of 15 Latin American areas belonging to 13 countries, for the period from March 9 to July 31, 2020, approximately five (5) months. In addition to the data published in the IDB Invest Dashboard [25], the information from Johns Hopkins Hospital University [30], has been used for the COVID19 number of infections. The 15 metropolitan areas have been grouped into four (4) clusters, to serve for the analysis. As shown in the methodology, descriptive statistical measures were estimated for each area from the graphs, based on observing the recovery of traffic congestion, once the contagions decrease. From this analysis, the mobility recovery rate (MRR) is defined, which in most cases is positive and distinctive of the analyzed area. For each case, the dispersion and correlation of the data is estimated for the period of increase of the ΔTCI, after the maximum decrease.

2 Methodology

The data used in this article are obtained from the IDB Invest Dashboard [25], according to the Methodological Note [2], from the agreement of this institution with Waze [28]. This data comes from the information of the mobile phones of Waze users [28], which is aggregated and geocoded in real time every two (2) minutes. The Dashboard [25] uses as the reference or comparison period the week of March 1 to 7, 2020, because traffic patterns were not affected by regional holidays and there were still very few reported cases of contagion in the region. Additionally, governments had not yet issued restrictions or recommendations for social distancing.

It is difficult to compare different cities, with different administrative, legal and historical limits [2, 30] and that do not necessarily reflect their functional and economic reach. In this sense, using IDB's methodology to create urban centers as adjacent grid groups (with more than 1,500 inhabitants/ grid and more than 100,000 inhabitants), the IDB Invest Dashboard [25] limits its publication to urban centers with more 750,000 inhabitants. That is, it restricts the analysis to centers with sufficient activity and historical information from Waze [28], remaining in only 64 metropolitan areas in 19 countries. Using the TCI as indicator for the analysis.

According to [2], the TCI is the sum of the total times and lengths of congestion for periods of 24 h compared to those carried out on the days of March 1 to 7, 2020. With this, a ΔTCI is estimated, which It allows the percentage comparison between the same days of the week, called the ratio-20.

In [25] the information of 64 metropolitan areas is published, however for the present study are considered the cities of Buenos Aires (AR-BA), Santa Cruz de la Sierra (BO-SC), Brasilia (BR-BR), Sao Paulo (BR-SP), Rio de Janeiro (BR-RJ), Santiago de Chile (CL-ST), Bogotá (CO-BO), San José (CR-SJ), Quito (EC-QU), San Salvador (SV-SS), Tegucigalpa (HN-TE), Guatemala City (GT-GT), Mexico City (MX-MX), Panama City (PA-PA) and Lima (PE-LI). The analysis period comprises from March 9 to July 31 of this year, approximately five (5) months. Only for Bogotá, Colombia, the start date is taken from March 9, since the data from the IDB Invest Dashboard [25] started from that day. This country announces the start of its closure on March 2 [29].

The areas were grouped into four (4) clusters, based on the Coefficient of Variation (CV) (which is an indicator developed by the IDB) and the TCI/ WHO ratio, published in [2] as a methodological guide. For each cluster, the ΔTCI variation graphs are analyzed, as a function of time and, in turn, of the daily cases of contagions detected for the same day. The contagion data is taken directly from those published by the Center for Systems Engineering and Sciences (CSSE) of the Johns Hopkins Hospital University (JHU) [31].

For each area, graphic analyzes were carried out and descriptive statistical measures were estimated, based on observing the recovery of traffic congestion, once contagions decrease. These graphs show the lowest point of the ΔTCI and, from this moment, the recovery of traffic congestion in the area, as a line product of the linear regression. With these, the MRR is estimated as the slope of this line, which in most cases is positive and distinctive of the analyzed area. For each case, the dispersion and correlation of the data is estimated for the period of increase of the ΔTCI, after the maximum decrease.

3   Results and Their Analysis

Figure 1 shows the conformation of the clusters of the 15 cities under study, according to the Coefficient of Variation (CV) and the TCI/ WHO ratio, published in [2]. Additionally, Table 2 shows the description of each of these clusters. Next, the graphs of TCI [25] and daily contagions [30]. Are shown for each group of clusters. Subsequently, the cluster analysis shows the general statistical analysis of the areas in summarized in Table 3.

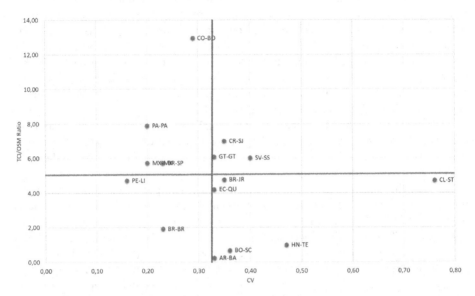

Fig. 1. Distribution of the clusters of the cities (CV, Coefficient of Variation; TCI/WHO, Traffic Congestion Intensity indicator)

Table 2. Definition of the clusters

Group	Definition [1]	Number of cities	Percentage (%)	Member Cities
A	0,33 < CV TCI/WHO < 4,93	2	13,3	Brasilia, Lima
B	0,33 < CV TCI/WHO ≥ 4,93	4	26,6	Bogotá, Mexico City, Panamá City, Sao Paulo
C	CV ≥ 0,33 TCI/WHO < 4,93	6	40,0	Buenos Aires, Quito, Santa Cruz de la Sierra, Tegucigalpa, Rio de Janeiro, Santiago de Chile
D	CV ≥ 0,33 TCI/WHO ≥ 4,93	3	20,0	Guatemala City, San José, San Salvador

(1) Definition: CV, Coefficient of Variation; TCI/WHO, Traffic Congestion Intensity indicator

3.1 Cluster A

Cluster A is made up of the cities of Brasilia and Lima. Figures 2 and 3 show their graphs of ΔTCI and number of infections for the same day, as expressed in the methodology, respectively. In these figures, it is observed that as the number of contagion decreases, there is a relaxation from the point of view that there is a recovery of the TCI. As discussed in the methodology, the MRR for both cities has a positive slope of 30.9 and 44.94%, with a dispersion of 0.1661 and 0.7261, respectively.

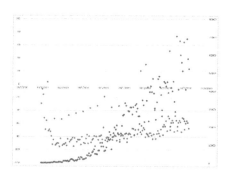

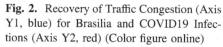

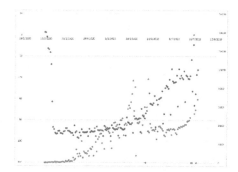

Fig. 2. Recovery of Traffic Congestion (Axis Y1, blue) for Brasilia and COVID19 Infections (Axis Y2, red) (Color figure online)

Fig. 3. Recovery of Traffic Congestion (Axis Y1, blue) for Lima and COVID19 Infections (Axis Y2, red) (Color figure online)

3.2   Cluster B

Cluster B is made up of the cities of Bogotá, Mexico City, Panama City and Sao Paulo. Figures 4, 5, 6 and 7 show their graphs of ∆TCI and number of infections for the same day, as expressed in the methodology, respectively. During 2019, Bogotá has been ranked number 1 among the cities with the highest traffic congestion, thanks to its high levels of motorization and other variables. Additionally, Mexico City and Sao Paulo are within the top ten (10). In this sense, this grouping is to be expected. The MRR of the cities is 40; 43.89; 23.2; 54.57%, respectively, with dispersions above 0.5455. This shows that the recovery from congestion is one of the fastest in the region.

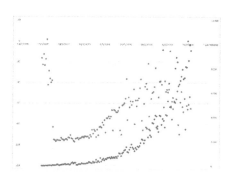

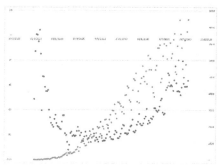

Fig. 4. Recovery of Bogota Traffic Congestion (Axis Y1, blue) and COVID19 Infections (Axis Y2, red) (Colo figure online)

Fig. 5. Recovery of Mexico City Traffic Congestion (Axis Y1, blue) and COVID19 infections (Axis Y2, red) (Color figure online)

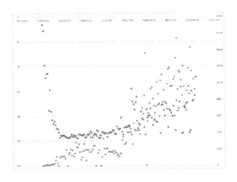

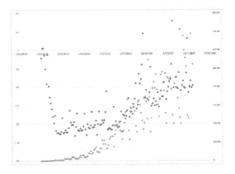

Fig. 6. Recovery of Panama City Traffic Congestion (Axis Y1, blue) and COVID19 Infections (Axis Y2, red) (Color figure online)

Fig. 7. Recovery of Sao Paulo Traffic Congestion (Axis Y1, blue) and COVID19 Infections (Axis Y2, red) (Color figure online)

3.3   Cluster C

Cluster C is made up of the cities of Buenos Aires, Quito, Santa Cruz de la Sierra, Tegucigalpa, Rio de Janeiro and Santiago de Chile. Figures 8, 9, 10, 11, 12 and 13 show their graphs of ΔTCI and number of infections for the same day, as expressed in the methodology, respectively. In this conglomerate, unlike the previous ones, it is observed that the MRR is 16.7; 29.9; 11.6; 10.4; 51.1 and 5.4%, respectively, with dispersions ranging from 0.013 to 0.8217. Of this group, Rio de Janiero stands out, for having the highest MRR in the group, comparable to conglomerate B, and Santiago de Chile. The latter, unlike all the others, stands out by a recovery in the number of infections from the week XX and in this sense, a correlation of its data close to zero (0.013).

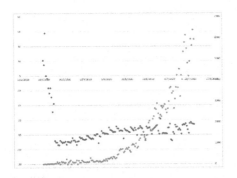

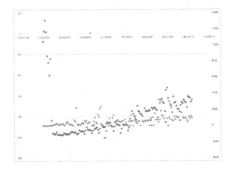

Fig. 8. Recovery of Buenos Aires Traffic Congestion (Axis Y1, blue) and COVID19 Infections (Axis Y2, red) (Color figure online)

Fig. 9. Recovery of Quito Traffic Congestion (Axis Y1, blue) and COVID19 Infections (Axis Y2, red) (Color figure online)

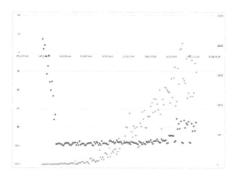

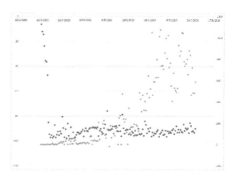

Fig. 10. Recovery of Santa Cruz de la Sierra Traffic Congestion (Axis Y1, blue) and COVID19 Infections (Axis Y2, red) (Color figure online)

Fig. 11. Recovery of Tegucigalpa Traffic Congestion (Axis Y1, blue) and COVID19 Infections (Axis Y2, red) (Color figure online)

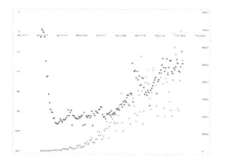

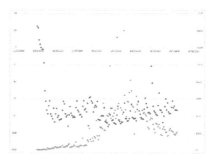

Fig. 12. Recovery of Rio de Janeiro Traffic Congestion (Axis Y1, blue) and COVID19 Infections (Axis Y2, red) (Color figure online)

Fig. 13. Recovery of Santiago de Chile Traffic Congestion (Axis Y1, blue) and COVID19 Infections (Axis Y2, red) (Color figure online)

3.4 Cluster D

El Cluster D is made up of the cities of Guatemala City, San José and San Salvador. Figures 14, 15 and 16 show their graphs of ΔTCI and number of infections for the same day, as expressed in the methodology, respectively. In this group, it is observed that the measures implemented for social distancing were aimed at restricting the use of private vehicles or public transport. Their MRR is 2.12; 14.6 and 28.87%, respectively, with dispersions from 0.0017 to 0.6413. The highest dispersion is for Guatemala City and the lowest for San Salvador.

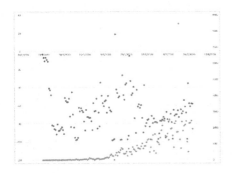

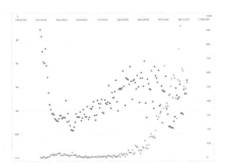

Fig. 14. Recovery of City of Guatemala Traffic Congestion (Axis Y1, blue) and COVID19 Infections (Axis Y2, red) (Color figure online)

Fig. 15. Recovery of San Jose Traffic Congestion (Axis Y1, blue) and COVID19 Infections (Axis Y2, red) (Color figure online)

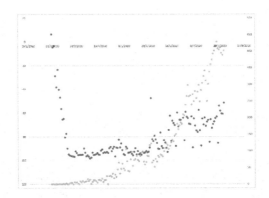

Fig. 16. Recovery of San Salvador Traffic Congestion (Axis Y1, blue) and COVID19 Infections (Axis Y2, red) (Color figure online)

Table 3. Statistical data per area

Country	Argentina	Bolivia	Bazil	Brazil	Brazil	Chile	Colombia	Costa Rica
City	Buenos Aires	Santa Cruz de la Sierra	Brasilia	Rio de Janeiro	Sao Paulo	Santiago	Bogotá	San José
Average Variation in Congestion	-72,41	-87,93	-66,79	-64,58	-59,02	-70,93	-68,04	-70,49
Maximum value	57,64	14,75	73,93	3,05	31,93	25,11	1,38	-11,28
Minimum value	-94,08	-99,74	-95,04	-94,22	-92,74	-92,52	-97,00	-96,99
Standard deviation	21,93	22,74	28,26	23,80	26,99	21,14	23,58	16,94
Median	-76,10	-96,23	-76,14	-73,90	-65,30	-75,81	-68,44	-73,65

Country	Ecuador	El Salvador	Guatemala	Honduras	Mexico	Panamá	Perú	
City	Quito	San Salvador	Guatemala City	Tegucigalpa	Mexico City	Panamá City	Lima	
Average Variation in Congestion	-79,33	-79,50	-66,35	-88,89	-64,54	-83,42	-71,85	
Maximum value	12,75	6,38	18,65	-6,28	4,44	-6,30	2,72	
Minimum value	-98,26	-98,33	-98,38	-98,06	-92,05	-97,97	-97,24	
Standard deviation	20,32	19,41	22,80	15,16	20,42	15,73	24,71	
Median	-86,26	-88,46	-69,23	-92,22	-71,86	-89,17	-84,20	

4   Analysis of Results

In order to understand how the pandemic will affect in the future and, above all, the different changes that may occur from this health emergency, it is necessary to review the transformations that occurred, especially from the 12th and 19th centuries. Fundamentally, these pandemics highlight the health problems associated with overcrowding and industrial development. According to [32] it indicates the rezoning and ordering of the city as a space for "social reproduction" in order to solve the problems derived from unhealthy conditions and overcrowding of people.

If in previous centuries, the bubonic plague in Florence in 1348, which of 1665 in London or the diseases in the city of Seville in 1786, motivated the processes of transformation of the cities. At the beginning of this 21st century, practically the same reasons plague cities globally, with inequality in said social reproduction, health and the environment being a matter of concern for the United Nations System. It is estimated that approximately 828 million people live in slums. In addition, the levels of energy consumption and pollution in urban areas are also considered worrisome, although cities occupy only 3% of the earth's surface, they represent between 60 and 80% of energy consumption and 75% of carbon emissions [33] and nine (9) out of ten (10) people suffer from health problems derived from poor air quality and 7 million people die each year from respiratory diseases of contaminated air particles [34].

The main recommendations of the WHO for the transformation of transport in cities establish lines of concrete actions for its future in cities:

"Adoption of clean electricity generation methods; prioritization of rapid urban transport, pedestrian and bicycle paths in cities, and interurban freight and passenger transport by rail; use of cleaner heavy duty diesel engine vehicles and low emission vehicles and fuels, especially low sulfur fuels" [34].

An indicator of the change in the behavior model associated with mobility in this period of restrictions is the increase in Internet data traffic BID 2020 [35]. According to an IDB report during the first months of the application of mobility restrictions, the Internet pressure index (KASPR) was affected in some cities up to 40%, as shown in Table 4. Which can be inferred as the reduction of face-to-face activities and its substitution to virtual ways of work and communications. Since the selected cities are the major cities of each country (Table 2), we assume a proportionality between the behavior of the country and the corresponding behavior of its major cities and capitals.

Table 4. Increase in data traffic on the Internet, according to data in [35]

Country	Percentage (%)
Argentina	22 y 25
Brazil	10 y 20
Ecuador	30 (fixed networks) y 8 (mobile networks)
Colombia	40 (fixed networks) y 12 (mobile networks)

Another indicator of behavior changes in the pandemic has been the impact of restrictions, this time on people's mobility behavior (5). As it can be seen in Table 5, only trips to second homes increased perhaps as a way to flee from areas with more demographic density, and it can be noted the decrease in movements associated with areas with close personal contact such as leisure and parks.

The pandemic and the different mobility restrictions have shown the need for more agile and less collective forms of transport services. Already in 2014, at the ITS Conference in Helsinki, the concept of MaaS appeared as a set of subscription mobility services [36]. This is defined as the integration of various forms of accessible transport services based on demand for individual mobility. MaaS services provide various menus of transport options, both public, bicycle, taxis, shared or rental car and combinations of both. COVID-19 represents an opportunity for the development of new public-private transport services that would contribute to sustainability, resilience, mitigation of so-called climate change and the health of the population.

For the case of Latin America and the study cities, there are several challenges that must be addressed [37]. To the low quality in time cost of public transport, are added the road insecurity for the most vulnerable (pedestrians), the high level of polluting emissions, its impact on health, as well as the high traffic congestion and a very limited management that prevents the optimization of road infrastructure, as well as the effective prioritization for buses, pedestrians and cyclists. COVID-19 highlights the importance of health when facing these challenges in the future.

Table 5. Mobility in the face of COVID-19 in Latin America [27]

Contry	Stores and Leisure (%)	Supermarkets and Drugstores (%)	Parks (%)	Transport Stations (%)	Work (%)	Second residences (%)
Argentina	-61	-21	**-83**	-54	-28	17
Bolivia	-53	-31	-42	-56	-43	23
Brazil	-40	-2	-39	-38	-22	14
Chile	-66	**-46**	-67	**-66**	-50	28
Colombia	-47	-24	-38	-48	-35	20
Costa Rica	-36	-23	-46	-46	-30	15
Ecuador	-36	-20	-38	-47	-45	23
Guatemala	-48	-32	-40	-63	-42	24
Honduras	-56	-32	-39	-65	-46	20
Mexico	-46	-18	-39	-52	-39	17
Panamá	-60	-36	-50	-61	-53	**30**
Perú	**-67**	-35	-46	-58	**-54**	28
El Salvador	-51	-28	-50	-60	-52	24
Venezuela	46	-27	41	56	-38	19

5 Conclusions

This study begins with the analysis of the impact of the COVID-19 pandemic on traffic congestion in 15 metropolitan areas of 13 Latin American countries. The database of the Intensity of traffic congestion of the IDB Invest Dashboard and the number of infections in the population published by Johns Hopkins Hospital University were used, for the period from March 9 to July 31, 2020, approximately five (5) months. From the categorization of four (4) clusters, the graphs of the variation of the ΔTCI, the cases of contagion and the rate of recovery of mobility are analyzed. It should be noted that the decrease in the number of infections brings flexibility of social distancing measures and the recovery of congestion, which is observed based on the rate of recovery of mobility.

It is observed that the mobility recovery rate for conglomerates A and B is higher than for the rest, coinciding with the areas of the cities with the greatest traffic congestion. In cluster D, this rate is lower, however, they present greater dispersion (seen from the point of view that their correlation is not very significant), coinciding with the areas where the distancing measures were related to restrictions on the use of vehicles individuals or public transport.

Similar to what happens with pandemics of the twelfth and nineteenth centuries, this brings as evidence that social inequality, health and the environment are reasons for concern. Non-negligible effects for citizens, especially in large urban centers, are evident: the rapid recovery of pollution levels and traffic congestion as the economic recovery becomes more pressing

Finally, the COVID-19 pandemic has revealed that less collective and more agile forms of mobility are needed, being an important opportunity for the region to develop new forms of transport in the face of a pandemic which has required people to have physical distance and yet they need to move from one place to another.

However, if the problems associated with the pandemic continue, a review of the World Health Organization recommendations regarding the use of public transport will be necessary. This fact raises a dilemma between maintaining state-of-the-art urban mobility policies (mitigation of climate change), versus public health and the well-being of citizens.

Acknowledgements. The authors of this article would like to thank the *Programa Iberoamericano de Ciencia y Tecnología para el Desarrollo* (CYTED), since it was carried out within the framework of the *Red Iberoamericana de Transporte y Movilidad Urbana Sostenible* (RITMUS, 718RT0566).

References

1. Chen, N., et al.: Epidemiological and clinical characteristics of 99 cases of 2019 novel coronavirus pneumonia in Wuhan, China: a descriptive study. The Lancet, **365**, 507–513 (2020)
2. Invest, I.: Coronavirus Impact Dashboard Methodological Note, IDB (2020)

3. Pierre, R., Harris, P.: COVID-19 en América Latina: Retos y oportunidades. Revista Chilena de Pediatria, **91**(2), 179–182 (2020)
4. Ribeiro-Dantas, M., Alves, G., Gomes, R., Bezerra, L., Lima, L., Silva, I.: Dataset for country profile and mobility analysis in the assessment of COVID-19 pandemic. Data in Brief, **31**, p. 4 (2020)
5. IDB: Del Confinamiento a la reapertura: Consideraciones estratégicas para el reinicio de actividades en América Latina y el Caribe en el marco del Covid-19, IDB, New York (2020)
6. Iranzo, A.: COVID-19: ¿(in)seguridad sin (in)movilidad? Acercando la política de la movilidad a los Estudios Críticos de Seguridad. Geopolítica(s) Revista de estudios sobre espacio y poder, **11**, 61–68, (2020)
7. Kraeme, M., et al.: CORONAVIRUS. The effect of human mobility and control measures on the COVID-19 epidemic in China. Science, **368**, 493–497 (2020)
8. Sirkeci y, I., Murat, M.: Coronavirus and migration: analysis of human mobility and the spread of COVID-19. Migr. Lett. **17**(2), 379–398 (2020)
9. Peñafiel-Chang, L., Camelli y G., eñafiel-Chang, P.: Pandemia COVID-19: Situación política - económica y consecuencias sanitarias en América Latina, Revista Ciencia UNEMI, **13**(33), 120–128 (2020)
10. Lasry, A., Kidder, D., Hast, M., Poovey, J., Sunshine, G., Winglee, K.: Timing of community mitigation and changes in reported COVID-19 and community mobility—Four U.S. Metropolitan Areas, February 26–April 1, 2020. Morb. Mortal. Wkly Rep. **69**, 451–457 (2020)
11. Lokhandwala y S., Gautam, P.: Indirect impact of COVID-19 on environment: a brief study in Indian context. Environ. Res. **188**, 1–10 (2020)
12. Shezen: Combating COVID-19, Shezen Bus Group (2020)
13. Alonso y R., Lugo-Morìn, D.: El estado del arte de la movilidad del transporte en la vida urbana en ciudades latinoamericanas. Revista Transporte y Territorio **19**, 133–157 (2018)
14. Alonso, G.: El estado del arte de la movilidad del transporte en la vida urbana en ciudades latinoamericanas. Revista Transporte y Territorio **19**, 133–157 (2018)
15. Jans, M.: Movilidad Urbana: En Caminos a sistemas de trasnporte Colectivos Integrados. Artículo **6**, 6–11 (2018)
16. Terraza, H., Rubio y D., Vera, F.: De ciudades emergentes a ciudades sostenibles. Comprendiendo y Proyectando las ciudades del Siglo XXI BID (2016)
17. Rivasplata, C.: Congestion pricing for Latin America: prospects and constraints. Res. Transp. Econ. **40**, 56–65 (2013)
18. Alirio, R., Escobar y R., Liberona, D.: Government and governance in intelligent cities, smart transportation study case in Bogotá Colombia. Ain Shams Eng. J. **11**, 25–34 (2020)
19. Vergara, R., Arias y J., Rodríguez, M.: Congestión urbana en Santiago de Cali, un estudio de caso de política pública. Territorios **42**, 1–29 (2020)
20. Luyando y J., Herrera, J.: Propuesta vial para atacar el problema de contaminación en la Ciudad de México. Revista de Direito da Cidade **11**(2), 316–336 (2019)
21. Mauricio y C., Pilar, M.: Planificación Multiescalar. Las desigualdades territoriales. Volumen II, CEPAL (2017)
22. Gandelman, N., Serebrisky y T., Suárez-Alemán, A.: Household spending on transport in Latin America and the Caribbean: a dimension of transport affordability in the region. J. Transp. Geogr. **79**, 1–14 (2019)
23. INRIX: INRIX Global Traffic Scorecard, INRIX (2020). https://inrix.com/scorecard/
24. Rivas, M., Suárez-Aleman y A., Serebrisky, T.: Hechos estilizados de transporte urbano en América Latina y el Caribe, BID (2019)
25. IDB: Tablero de Impacto del Coronavirus (2020). https://www.iadb.org/es/topics-effective-ness-improving-lives/coronavirus-impact-dashboard

26. Moovit: Moovit Public Transit Index (2020). https://moovitapp.com/insights/en/Moovit_ Insights_Public_Transit_Index-countries
27. GOOGLE: Informes de Movilida Local sobre el COVID-19 (2020). https://www.google. com/covid19/mobility/
28. Waze: WAZE for Cities (2020). https://www.waze.com/es/ccp
29. IADB: IDB Mejorando Vidas IDB (2020). https://blogs.iadb.org/efectividad-desarrollo/es/ tablero-de-impacto-del-coronavirus-midiendo-los-efectos-del-distanciamiento-social-en-la-movilidad-de-america-latina-y-el-caribe/
30. Dijikstra y L., Poelma, H.: Cities in Europe: The New OECD-EC Defintion. Regional Focus 1/2012, European Commission (2012). https://ec.europa.eu/regional_policy/sources/ docgener/focus/2012_01_city.pdf
31. JHU: Coranovirus Research Center, John Hopskin Hospital (2020). https://coronavirus.jhu. edu/map.html
32. Álvarez, A.: La ciudad como productor versus la ciudad como obra, o la realidad urbana entre el espacio de la renta y el espacio social. Universidad de Valladolid, Valladolid (2015)
33. ONU: 17 Objetivos que transforman el mundo. https://www.un.org/sustainabledevelopment/ es/. Último acceso 03 Apr 2020
34. OMS: Calidad del aire y salud, 2 May 2018. https://www.who.int/es/news-room/fact-sheets/ detail/ambient-(outdoor)-air-quality-and-health. Último acceso 03 Apr 2020
35. IDB: Coronavirus: generando nuevo tráfico en América Latina,1 Apr 2020. https://blogs. iadb.org/transporte/es/coronavirus-generando-nuevo-trafico-en-america-latina/.   Último acceso: 6 May 2020
36. Serafimova, T.: Covid-19: an opportunity to redesing mobility towards great suatainability and resilience? European University Institute (2020)
37. CAF: Transpote y Desarrollo en América Latina. vol. 1, no.1 (2018)

Infrastructure, Environment, Governance

Reimaging the Book ... Again! A New Framework for Smart Books Using Digital Twins Technology

H. Kolivand[1], E.C. Prakash[2], M.C. López[3], D. Hernández[3], and A.A. Navarro-Newball[3(✉)]

[1] Liverpool John Moores University, Liverpool, UK
h.kolivand@ljmu.ac.uk
[2] Cardiff Metropolitan University, Cardiff, UK
eprakash@cardiffmet.ac.uk
[3] Pontificia Universidad Javeriana Cali, Cali, Colombia
{mclopez09,davidher28,anavarro}@javerianacali.edu.co

Abstract. Technology enabled learning and communication are at the crossroads, which need flexible solutions. Flexible learning enables a learner to move seamlessly between the real and virtual world. We propose a novel flexible communication tool, "the smart book" to address these challenges. First, we review the role of the traditional book, its role in society today and the recent advances in augmented reality books. Next, we present a novel approach that integrates digital twins and mixed realities that is useful in communication, learning and for making decisions. We propose an initial vision of the architecture. Finally, we follow the Spiral of Creative Thought to create a first prototype with promising results. Our plan to further develop the architecture is to integrate this spiral with other software development methods. We need further iterations within the spiral to include final users and diverse applications.

Keywords: Book · Mixed Reality · Digital twin · Augmented reality · Virtual Reality

1 Introduction

Humanity and books have a long relationship. Smart societies living in smart cities within a smart world demand innovative ways of communication and understanding of both traditional and new communication channels. Crisis such as the Covid-19 have evidenced the need and surge of novel interaction and collaboration mechanisms. This is evident from the author's own experience lecturing and researching during the crisis. This is only one of multiple examples that could come out. As we will discuss, the book in its multiple formats is still a current and versatile communication medium. Our goal is to create a smart book, an important communication tool in smart cities within a smart world to make reading, learning and teaching amusing and more efficient. We visualise

S. Nesmachnow and L. Hernández Callejo (Eds.): ICSC-CITIES 2020, CCIS 1359, pp. 233–245, 2021.
https://doi.org/10.1007/978-3-030-69136-3_16

the smart book as a tool that would be able to enhance the current state of the book, respecting its multiple formats and allowing different usages. Even though our examples and experience are mainly related to education; while we continue in the search for a smart education, we believe the book plays an important role in different sectors currently experiencing difficulties (for example, tourism, commerce, health care, maintenance, etc.).

1.1   About the Book and Its Evolution

María Angélica Thumala Olave starts her paper questioning "why do people in the UK read and collect books when there are so many other sources of information and forms of story-telling available?" [1] (p.1). In her qualitative analysis, she [1] highlights the powerful appeal of books due to the fusion of the act of reading, book's iconic value as cultural goods and their surface material properties. In another study, James M. Donovan [2] (p.1) "provide a reasonable basis to support an expectation that readers perform better on reading comprehension tasks performed in book-rich environments," while challenging projects that remove print collections to provide space to other amenities and evidencing physical collections have a role in today's digital society. Indeed, books also play and important role in education and are subject of diverse studies [3]. Evans et al. [3] present a study comparing pre-schoolers' behaviour interacting with alphabet books in paper format and interactive alphabet books in an eBook. They [3] conclude that children spend less time on letter-related behaviour (e.g. saying object names) and more time oriented to the book. Potnis et al. [4] evidence difficulties in the adoption of e-books by millennials but highlights the potential benefit of available resources and strategies for their adoption. Learning books are diverse, for example, Reynolds [5] studies the role, limitations ad possibilities of comic books in higher education. In another example, Gaylor et al. [6] claims the potential input for mathematics learning in children using counting books and study the impact of using tactile and narrative content within these books. Whatever the case, books seem to be important. Indeed, Beimorghi, Hariri, Babalhavaeji [7] suggest that books play an important role in transforming knowledge to wisdom. Finally, a study from Bavishi, Slade and Levy [8] suggest that those who read books may acquire better survival skills. Of course, there is still a lot to study about books, however, the continuous interest in books is a strong evidence of their importance in humankind.

From the previous paragraph, it is evident that books have had an evolution too. The paragraph refers to paper books, eBooks, tactile books, and comic books, among others. Wikipedia [9], the modern version of the collection of books known as encyclopaedia, offers an effective summary of book evolution that goes from tablets and codex to eBooks and presents the type of content they can provide and multiple uses they can have. Following the evolution of the book, the pioneering work by Billinghurst, et al. [10], the Magic Book, constituted the first book to include Augmented Reality (AR) and Virtual Reality (VR). The Magic Book project [10], presented in 2001 explored the concept of "how interfaces can be developed that allow for seamless transition between Physical

Reality, Augmented Reality (AR), and immersive Virtual Reality (VR) in a collaborative setting," [10] (p.25). As such, the Magic Book [10] was a book that could be read as a traditional book, without any technology; but the book could be read using a handheld device capable of displaying 3D virtual content. The reader could view AR scenes with 3D content overlaid on the pages from any perspective or they could fly into immersive VR scenes. A communication between the readers in AR and VR world could also be stablished [10].

1.2   Previous Work

According to Do and Lee [11] as cited by Navarro-Newball et al. [12] (p.3), "AR books enhance the reading experience, visualise products, tell stories and teach. They can provide other views of complex situations, increasing understanding and are an evolution of traditional books, the main medium of teaching and learning." Then, in our previous work, Navarro-Newball et al. [12] identified some limitations in AR books. AR Books so far [12]: (1) did not mean to include contents using all major data types (e.g. 2D static, 2D dynamic, 3D content and sound); (2) apart from few cases [11], did not offer a usable authoring interface; (3) did not offer authoring tools to create pages and to introduce markers with related display elements such as virtual models, animations, videos, sounds, images and gestures in order to create any book; (4) limited reader interactions to flipping pages, and AR cards for additional content; (5) barely used natural features [13], but relied on abstract fiducial markers; (6) and, content creation possibilities from readers, although existent [14], were rare.

More recently, the work from Bischof et al. [15] overcome the problems of fiducial markers using Vuforia SDK, allowing the use of images of the book as AR markers; however, the kind of content displayed is still limited to video only and the work is focused on one book only. Leela, Chookeaw and Nilsook [16] presented a study to describe the effectiveness of mobile learning and AR books through the microlearning approach and concluded that books supported by technology increase interest and promote teamwork; however, they do not give details about the AR books. Kljun et al. [17] (p.103) state that "digital-augmentation of print-media can provide contextually relevant audio, visual, or haptic content to supplement the static text and images. The design of such augmentation - its medium, quantity, frequency, content, and access technique - can have a significant impact on the reading experience;" and provide evidence of this fact; however, their sample books only use video as the augmented media and falls short in testing other interactive possibilities. Yamamoto et al. [18] propose a method to integrate tactile sensation into an eBook using AR, reinforcing the importance of texture and physicality in a book. Mokhtar et al. [19] describe a framework which is reusable and allows the creation of new colouring content; however, the books display only 3D pop up images synthetized from the coloured pages, by visualizing them in 3D on a user's view of the real world; and, the 3D models are still drawn by a modeller but texturized with the colours used by the user. Recently [20], researchers have presented the e-mmersive Book, capable of assist readers relying on a HoloLens device. Moreover, users read in an inspectional way more than one book to find answers to questions [20].

Finally, it is important to note that Gazcón and Castro [21] claimed back in 2015 an interactive and collaborative application for traditional books augmentation which allows the incorporation of AR content to any pre-existent traditional book and collaboration among readers.

The use of AR markers has evolved to using natural features taken from book pages thanks to SDKs such as Vuforia, but tools for content creation in AR books are still scarce. However, following the spirit of Gazcón and Castro [21], which allows the inclusion of AR content and collaboration; and, aware of the important role of books, we propose to develop further the book as it will be explained in the next sections. The book is widely presented in all its formats and requires a constant evolution so that new ways to convey information to readers, authors, teachers, students, guides and followers are discovered.

1.3   Problem Statement

There is a positive impact from VR and AR in formal and informal educational environments [22]; these technologies provide novel ways to learn, communicate and teach. Indeed, AR/VR may enhance the learning process in all content areas, are now more affordable and new user-oriented interfaces allow people from all over the world to connect in unique and exciting educational experiences [20]. One of these experiences is provided by AR books. AR books enhance the reading experience and can increase understanding by providing other interactive views of complex situations while visualising products, telling stories and teaching [12]. The first AR Book, the Magic Book [10], explored transitional interfaces between physical reality, AR and VR. In The Magic Book, readers could use AR to display content, but the interaction with the displayed content was limited to observing mostly.

AR book creation have had difficulties such as requiring complex image processing or relying on software configuration or scripting. Creation of multiple books and upload of diverse content; display of representative multimedia data such as video, text, image, animation and 3D and; integration of alternative interaction techniques which use game technology have also been limited in the AR book world. In a previous research described in a chapter by Praksh and Rao [23] (co-author of this paper) we proposed an AR book and we were able to overcome some of these problems. Firstly, we offered to include all major data types such as 2D static; 2D dynamic; 3D content and sound. Secondly, we offered an authoring interface in which the author could create pages and introduce AR markers with related elements such as virtual models, animations, videos, sounds, images and gestures in order to create his/her desired book. Thirdly, we explored a novel way of interaction, integrating body gestural interaction to the book, besides projecting 3D objects and animations with synchronised rotation and translation on pages. Figure 1A shows our previous book with a fiducial marker, video content displayed and, 3D content interaction through zooming. Our book was novel because:

- We provided a kind of flexibility to include major media data types (for example video and audio), while existing books focused on a subset of them. Focusing on a subset of media types is still common.
- We were able to create any book based on standard fiducial markers provided by the AR kit we used. In contrast, many existing AR book projects focused on the development of one single book, which is still a common practice.
- We included "take", "move" or "zoom" gestures to virtual objects displayed in every page, while many books used additional AR cards for this. Also, with gestures we provided integration to basic VR scenarios.

However, our book had limitations:

- We could only create AR versions of books with no more than 48 pages, due to the limited set of fiducial markers offered by the SDK those days.
- We relied on fiducial markers and did not take advantage of natural features within the real book content to display AR content.
- We did not include mobile devices capabilities to the book.
- We did not allow the creation and sharing of content by readers.
- We did not take great advantage of gamification technologies to make reading more engaging.
- We did not implement a way to store book usage statistics; for instance, we did not know how the book was read and understood.

Therefore, we missed the chance to create more complex books, to utilise handier interaction strategies and to gather anonymous information about the reader's learning, reading, authoring and sharing processes.

In his blog at IEEE's Future Directions [24], Roberto Saracco answers to the question "what would education be like in 2050?", with two words: "Digital Twins." Saracco believes that VR Digital Twins are a new tool that will be key for education by 2050 [24]. We believe that the current Covid-19 crisis could accelerate their evolution in education. In essence, Saracco [24] explains that each person has several fragments of his/her own digital twin; these fragments can be used to represent both our skills and knowledge; and, Digital Twins offer the possibility to study in the digital representation rather than studying on the real thing. For instance, we believe we will have the chance to take advantage from the real world, the virtual world and the mixed world. As Saracco said more recently [25], Digital Twins bridge the physical space and the cyberspace. Digital Twins are a trend in the field of Mixed Reality (MR). "Digital Twin models are computerized clones of physical assets that can be used for in-depth analysis," [26]. With current technology we see a chance to take the AR book beyond. That leads us to propose the research question: how to use Digital Twins to create a smart book which overcomes limitation from previous books?

To answer this and focusing on the learning applications of books first, we need to support complex contents in educational scenarios such as museums and classrooms using tools that favour learning and user's entertainment. We expect to enhance flexibility, while staying independent of the technology used and taking care of not being disruptive with the real book. We believe the concept can be extended to any sustainable paper-based communication material such as brochures. Additionally, the content management model is fundamental to provide a flexible tool for the creation of content and narrative to entertain and educate. Finally, the digital twin approach can be useful to find out how the book is read and understood.

1.4   Objectives

Our main objective is to develop a smart book creation framework using the Digital Twins technology and taking advantage of MR. In order to achieve that we need to:

- Investigate how to integrate smart book content and interactions in a digital twin.
- Develop a digital twin architecture to support a smart books creation framework.
- Validate the resulting framework introducing a smart book.
- Validate the use of the smart book created using the framework.

2   Methodology

After a continuous study of learning with children, Professor Mitchel Resnick [27], dedicated to helping children of all ages play, think and experiment with design and technology, came up with an approach with which students would engage in project analysis, implementation, and evaluation. To achieve this, Resnick gave life to the infinite Spiral of Creative Thought (SCT) specified below (1B). Basically, the projection of the future expressed in the spiral denotes the ability that everything that is imagined can become reality, through the repetition of five key steps [27]:

- Imagine: Visualize what you want to create without limit, detaching from value judgments such as the previous knowledge that binds imaginative capacity.
- Create: Make the thought or imagined a reality through compositions, drawings, or artifacts.
- Play: Explore, enjoy, listen, touch, and use all creations with an emphasis on recognizing that everything is upgradeable and that evolutions will arise at any time.
- Share: Teach or show the project to others taking into consideration their opinions.
- Reflect: Carry out a feedback process where the appropriate changes are made.

The iterative execution of the SCT leads to the creation of artifacts that promote research and experimental thinking. Therefore, for the realization of this project we will use SCT as the main source of the methodological process, at the same time we will integrate the phases of the software engineering process into this research. Additionally we will need to realise a number of tasks to achieve our goals. To investigate how to integrate smart book content and interactions in a digital twin we need to:

- Implement the prototype of a smart book based on a real book and using MR.
- Identify potential interactions.
- Identify potential data of interest within a focus group.
- Identify requirements.

To develop a digital twin architecture to support a smart books creation framework we need to:

- Design the architecture.
- Design a data model to support the architecture.
- Design a way to measure book's usage and understanding.
- Identify the most suitable technology for development.
- Implement the architecture.
- Design and implement a user interface for smart book creation.

To validate the resulting framework introducing a smart book we need to:

- Use the architecture to create one smart book inspired on a real book.
- Validate framework's usability.

To validate the use of the smart book created using the framework we need to:

- Validate usability of the smart book within a focus group.
- Validate how the book is read and understood using statistics.

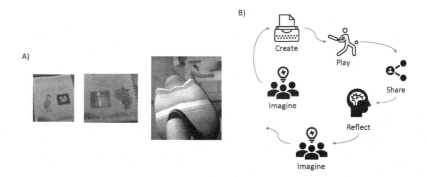

Fig. 1. Previous book and method. A) Previous AR book. B) SCT.

3   Proposed System

Figure 2 shows the proposed architecture and flow of smart book use. While in real books one author proposes content to the reads, AR, MR and VR technologies create a window that expands the book to the smart book allowing multiple readers become collaborative authors and the authors become collaborative readers. Users in both roles (readers and authors) can upload and download content that may come from different sources and media, such as text, 3D content, images and video, audio, interactions. This content is inspired in the real, imaginary, and virtual worlds. The smart book must be supported by an interconnected architecture based on the Digital Twins concept, which includes a layered model, a novel user interface, storage, and processing of data. This approach will integrate the real and virtual versions of the book allowing collaboration and allowing users to include their imaginary into the book.

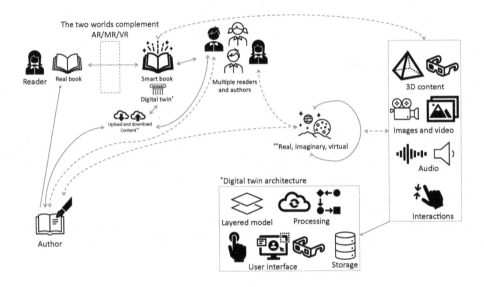

Fig. 2. Smart book's architecture.

4   Early Prototype

At the end of the year, we will have the prototype of a smart book and a list of feasible interaction oriented by the book. We chose "Journey of the Beetle" book [28] as a field test for the smart book early prototype. Following the idea of SCT, we started a creativity workshop with nine undergraduate students under the guidance of Miguel Fernando Caro, the author of the chosen book, who specialises in educational books and tales. During this workshop, the students had to: (1) write letter to their inner self (self-discovery) talking about their experiences in life and feelings; and, (2) write a short fictional story. In all cases, students were free to share their writings or not. This served to spark creativity and motivate story writing for video games and animation. Then, students had to study previous publications related to AR books and present a summary analysis of one paper to the rest of the group. These two activities were related to the "imagine phase" of the SCT. Finally, we had a brain storming session. Next, we started preparation for the "create phase" and all students participated in Unity, Unreal and Vuforia basic training and developed the first prototypes. Figure 3 shows "Journey of the Beetle." Here, one example of the proposed interactions obtained from the first iteration displays and AR interactive game the first time the beetle is shown in the book. In the game the beetle must catch as many dung balls as possible. This game was played by two students who programmed the game ("play phase") and then shared to the rest of the group ("share phase"). After the "reflect phase" we found that:

- There are many ways a the book can be used to interact. For example, you could go to the real word, photograph a beetle and upload it in new page of the book; you could expand the book by superimposing animation or videos as in previous books; or, you could write new pages in the digital twin.
- Some pages or chapters could contain video games. Particularly, the first video game implemented could be enhanced to include multiple players and collaboration mechanisms among a number of beetles.
- The book itself could be an interaction device for a narrative educational video game.
- Apart from the original game of the beetle making dung balls. Two other video game narratives for different sections of the book were proposed. The first one is about the illegal burning of fields versus the reforestation of the field to raise cattle in a sustainable way (the book explains the relationship between the beetle and the cattle). The second one is a survival game where beetles must avoid being caught by hungry birds. All proposed video game narratives can be a test field for AI (flocking and path finding for cattle), collaborative reading (reading/writing with other author-readers taking advantage of a digital twin), multiplayer interactive techniques (each reader becomes a beetle and compete to make the biggest dung ball), among others.
- Finally, different reading reward mechanisms were proposed, such as: access to books, documentaries and movies related to the book's thematic and guided field visits where the situations explained on the book can be experienced in real life.

Fig. 3. Early prototype.

5   Discussion

We believe that if we manage to implement it, the smart book will become an important communication tool within a smart city environment supporting education, tourism, maintenance, training, health, environment, culture, etc. We expect our approach will respect and give relevance to other book formats while expanding those to different ways of interactions, collaborations and applications that may be used when required. The most important thing about the Digital Twins approach is that it will allow for a book that can not only be used to expand the real world but to take decisions from the data gathered during its usage, for example, to enhance learning or other processes that could be achieved through the book.

6   Conclusion

We finished the first iteration in the SCT. The process of the SCT has sparked initial ideas and interaction mechanism that will enrich the smart book and challenge the developer to create and architecture that supports such interactions. However, a few more iterations are needed to refine the prototype before we start implementing the architecture. Despite that, we dare to envision a possible basic architecture and work usage flow. Further iterations within the SCT should include reflection of the applications of the book in fields different from education and potential users. The completion of the smart book project will require funding and time to cause the desired impact.

We are aware that during the latest book evolution (the AR book), there have been advances which allow some content creation, inclusion of different data formats, introduction of new books and, the use of natural features of the book. However, we found no evidence of a book creation framework that takes advantages of all these features altogether; neither we found a vision of the book which takes advantage of the Digital Twins concept. Our previous project has now become obsolete because the software tools we used are no longer usable. We believe our Digital Twins approach is an opportunity for reimaging the book . . . again!

Acknowledgements. Authors would like to acknowledge: – The thematic network from CYTED "CIUDADES INTELIGENTES TOTALMENTE INTEGRALES, EFI-CIENTES Y SOSTENIBLES (CITIES)" no 518RT0558. – Carolina Giraldo Echeverry, Miguel Fernando Caro Gamboa, Fernando Uribe Trujillo authors of the "Journey of the Beetle". CIPAV for freely distributing the book.

References

1. Olave, M.A.T.: Book love. a cultural sociological interpretation of the attachment to books. Poetics, p. 101440 (2020)
2. Donovan, J.M.: Keep the books on the shelves: library space as intrinsic facilitator of the reading experience. J. Acad. Librarianship **46**(2), 102104 (2020)
3. Evans, M.A., Nowak, S., Burek, B., Willoughby, D.: The effect of alphabet ebooks and paper books on preschoolers' behavior: an analysis over repeated readings. Early Childhood Research Quarterly **40**, 1–12 (2017)
4. Potnis, D., Deosthali, K., Zhu, X., McCusker, R.: Factors influencing undergraduate use of e-books: a mixed methods study. Library Inf. Sci. Res. **40**(2), 106–117 (2018)
5. Reynolds, P.J.: From Superman to Squirrel Girl: Higher Education in Comic Books, 1938–2015, pp. 33–54. Palgrave Macmillan, New York (2017)
6. Gaylord, S.M., O'Rear, C.D., Hornburg, C.B., McNeil., N.M.: Preferences for tactile and narrative counting books across parents with different education levels. Early Childhood Res. Q. **50**, 29–39 (2020). Parents supporting early mathematical thinking
7. Atarodi, A., Dr. Hariri, N., Babalhavaeji, F.: Transforming knowledge into wisdom: a grounded theory approach. Library Philosop. Pract. (e-Journal), **2955**, 1–13 (2019)
8. Bavishi, A., Slade, M., Levy, B.: The survival advantage of reading books. Innov. Aging, **1**(suppl 1), 477–477 (2017)
9. Wikipedia. Book (2020). https://en.wikipedia.org/wiki/Book. Accessed 12 Aug 2020
10. Billinghurst, M., Kato, H., Poupyrev, I.: The magicbook&#151moving seamlessly between reality and virtuality. IEEE Comput. Graph. Appl. **21**(3), 6–8 (2001)
11. Do, T.V., Lee, J.W.: Creating 3d e-books with arbookcreator. In: Proceedings of the International Conference on Advances in Computer Enterntainment Technology, ACE 2009, pp. 429–430. ACM, New York (2009)
12. Navarro-Newball, A., Moreno-Sanchez, I., Arya, A., Prakash, C., Mike-Ifeta, E., Mejia-Mena, J.: An interactive modelling architecture for education and entertainment at museums. Dyna **92**(3), 269–273 (2017)

13. Scherrer, C., Pilet, J., Fua, P., Lepetit, V.: The haunted book. In: Proceedings of the 7th IEEE/ACM International Symposium on Mixed and Augmented Reality, ISMAR 2008, pp. 163–164. IEEE Computer Society Washington, DC (2008)

14. Clark, A., Dünser, A., Grasset, R.: An interactive augmented reality coloring book. In: SIGGRAPH Asia 2011 Emerging Technologies, SA 2011, p. 25:1. ACM, New York (2011)

15. Bischof, D., Sieck, J., Fransman, J., Kassung, C., Klingner, E.: Interactive recipe book - enhance your traditional recipe book: showing cultural heritage through cooking. In: Proceedings of the Second African Conference for Human Computer Interaction: Thriving Communities, AfriCHI 2018, New York, NY, USA. Association for Computing Machinery (2018)

16. Leela, S., Chookeaw, S., Nilsook, P.: An effective microlearning approach using living book to promote vocational students' computational thinking. In: Proceedings of the 2019 The 3rd International Conference on Digital Technology in Education, ICDTE 2019, pp. 25–29, New York, NY, USA. Association for Computing Machinery (2019)

17. Kljun, M., et al.: Augmentation not duplication: considerations for the design of digitally-augmented comic books. In: Proceedings of the 2019 CHI Conference on Human Factors in Computing Systems, CHI 2019, pp. 1–12, New York, NY, USA. Association for Computing Machinery (2019)

18. Yamamoto, T., Aida, H., Yamashita, D., Honda, Y., Miki, M.: E-book browsing method by augmented reality considering paper shape. In: 2017 International Symposium on Ubiquitous Virtual Reality (ISUVR), pp. 30–33 (2017)

19. Mokhtar, M.K., Mohamed, F., Sunar, M.S., Arshad, M.A.M., Sidik, M.K.M.: Development of mobile-based augmented reality colouring for preschool learning. In: 2018 IEEE Conference on e-Learning, e-Management and e-Services (IC3e), pp. 11–16 (2018)

20. Kim, S., Park, J., Kim, J.: E-mmersive book: the ar book that assists the syntopical reading. In: Proceedings of the 9th Augmented Human International Conference, AH 2018, New York, NY, USA. Association for Computing Machinery (2018)

21. Gazcón, N., Castro, S.: ARBS: an interactive and collaborative system for augmented reality books. In: De Paolis, L.T., Mongelli, A. (eds.) AVR 2015. LNCS, vol. 9254, pp. 89–108. Springer, Cham (2015). https://doi.org/10.1007/978-3-319-22888-4_8

22. Mones, B.: Before and after ar/vr: empowering paradigm shifts in education. In: SIGGRAPH Asia 2017 Symposium on Education, SA 2017, New York, NY, USA. Association for Computing Machinery (2017)

23. Prakash, E.C., Rao, M.: Gamification in informal education environments: a case study. Transforming Learning and IT Management through Gamification. ISCEMT, pp. 73–97. Springer, Cham (2015). https://doi.org/10.1007/978-3-319-18699-3_5

24. Saracco, R.: What would education be like in 2050? Digital Twins (2018). https://cmte.ieee.org/futuredirections/2018/02/21/what-would-education-be-like-in-2050-digital-twins/. Accessed 12 Aug 2020

25. Saracco, R.: Digital twins: bridging physical space and cyberspace. Computer 52(12), 58–64 (2019)

26. Song, S.-J., Jang, Y.-G.: Construction of digital twin geotechnical resistance model for liquefaction risk evaluation. In Proceedings of the 2nd International Symposium on Computer Science and Intelligent Control, ISCSIC 2018, New York, NY, USA, 2018. Association for Computing Machinery

27. Resnick, M.: All i really need to know (about creative thinking) i learned (by studying how children learn) in kindergarten. In: Proceedings of the 6th ACM SIGCHI Conference on Creativity & Cognition, pp. 1–6, New York, NY, USA. Association for Computing Machinery (2007)
28. Giraldo, C., Caro, M.F., Uribe, F.: La travesía del escarabajo. Editorial CIPAV (2019)

A Methodology for the Conversion of a Network Section with Generation Sources, Storage and Loads into an Electrical Microgrid Based on Raspberry Pi and Home Assistant

Oscar Izquierdo-Monge[1]([⊠]), Paula Peña-Carro[1],
Luis Hernández-Callejo[2]([⊠]), Oscar Duque-Perez[3],
Angel Zorita-Lamadrid[3], and Roberto Villafafila-Robles[4]

[1] CEDER-CIEMAT,
Autovía de Navarra A15 salida 56, 422290 Lubia (Soria), España
{oscar.izquierdo,paula.pena}@ciemat.es
[2] University of Valladolid, Campus Universitario Duques de Soria,
42004 Soria, España
luis.hernandez.callejo@uva.es
[3] University of Valladolid, Paseo del cauce 59, 47011 Valladolid, España
{oscar.duque,zorita}@eii.uva.es
[4] Centre d'Innovació Tecnològica en Convertidors Estàtics i Accionaments
(CITCEA-UPC), Departament d'Enginyeria Elèctrica, Universitat Politècnica de
Catalunya, ETS d'Enginyeria Industrial de Barcelona,
Av. Diagonal 647, 08028 Barcelona, Spain
roberto.villafafila@citcea.upc.edu

Abstract. This paper presents a methodology to convert a network section with generation sources, storage, and loads into an electrical microgrid. This conversion will allow greater autonomy and efficiency in its management. Besides, after the analysis of the recorded data, a reduction in the consumption of the distribution network can be achieved, and therefore, a reduction in the costs of the electricity bill. To achieve this transformation it is necessary to provide the network with intelligence, proposing a methodology based on four steps: identification and description of the elements that form it, choice of hardware and software for monitoring and controlling the system, establishment of communication between the different elements and creation of a control network framework for visualization. As a case study, the microgrid of the Renewable Energy Development Centre (CEDER) located in the province of Soria (Spain) is shown, formed by different sources of generation, storage systems, and consumption. All the elements of this microgrid are integrated with single free software, Home Assistant, installed in a Raspberry Pi 4 to provide the network with basic intelligence, control and monitoring in real-time through different communication protocols.

Keywords: Smart electric microgrids · Home assistant · Monitoring and control system

© Springer Nature Switzerland AG 2021
S. Nesmachnow and L. Hernández Callejo (Eds.): ICSC-CITIES 2020, CCIS 1359, pp. 246–258, 2021.
https://doi.org/10.1007/978-3-030-69136-3_17

1 Introduction

The concept of a microgrid is a term that can be defined as the U.S. Department of Energy [1] proposes; "a group of interconnected loads and distributed energy resources within clearly defined electrical boundaries that act as a single controllable entity respect to the network. A microgrid can be connected and disconnected from the network to allow it to operate in grid or island mode. A remote microgrid is a variation of a microgrid operating in island conditions". Or define it more simply "Microgrids are decentralised distribution networks that integrate distributed energy resources and balance power generation and loads at the local level" [2].

This form of energy production, consumption, and management is becoming increasingly important today. It was born to reduce the different environmental problems that currently exist through a greater implementation of renewable energy sources. However, this proposal of management using microgrids is complex to implement and certain institutional changes are necessary to reach its maximum potential since at present the management of the network is monopolized by large generating companies and governments at different levels. The justification for the monopolies in the energy sector has weakened over time with the appearance of new companies, which, although smaller in size, are gaining more and more followers, betting on the purchase of clean energy from sources closer to the place of consumption.

The break-up of the monopoly will open up possibilities for intelligent local utility networks, microgrids, and automated building energy management. Their presence in the energy market, and the possibility of compensating for the surplus or deficit of power in the distribution network, makes the current energy system more resilient and efficient in terms of power quality, electricity costs and continuity of supply at critical loads in the event of prolonged outages [3].

But microgrids also have certain disadvantages, some relevant, such as temporary uncertainty, which can lead to some reluctance to implement them. This uncertainty is always associated with volatile load profiles and changes in climate conditions, which affect the uncontrollable generation and prevent the optimization of economic planning [4, 5], making it challenging to make accurate forecasts about the future state of supply and demand [6–8].

To make the system more reliable and secure in terms of generation [9], storage systems such as batteries, flywheels or supercapacitors, are established as key elements within the microgrid system in slowing down power fluctuations and counteracting the energy imbalances produced [10] by matching the generation and total load of the microgrid [3, 11].

To operate the whole microgrid more efficiently, it is necessary to have a measurement, communication, and data management system to allow the semi-autonomous or autonomous operation of the system, being able to solve the supply problems in the shortest time possible [12, 13]. There are several communication technologies within this context, such as copper conductors, fibre optics, power line communication, and wireless communication.

Regardless of the communication technology selected, all microgrids must have the following elements at the communication level: local communication structure, hierarchical monitoring, control and management system, and intelligent controllers for the loads, consumptions and storage systems.

As mentioned above, a microgrid can operate either connected to the main distribution network through a common coupling point (PCC), or disconnected from it, on the island mode [14]. A stable and economically efficient way of operating is required [15].

The microgrid is managed by a central controller that is at the head of the hierarchical control system. This central controller (MGCC) provides the setpoints to the controllers of the rest of the equipment, such as generation sources, loads, and energy storage systems. The control system will be responsible for regulating the frequency and voltage in all modes of operation, as well as for distributing the load between the various elements of distributed generation (DG) and storage, managing the flow with the main network, and optimising operating costs.

To be able to control all the generation and consumption systems that make up the microgrid, it is necessary to have Smart Meters in each of the elements to be monitored. At present, Arduino devices are being used, which consist of a board with a microcontroller hardware and free software. For this case, they are configured for a real-time data collection of all the variables [16]. As for the software used, many microgrids are monitored and controlled by LabVIEW, a payment platform that allows the design of both real and virtual environments through visual programming [17].

The variations proposed respect to the software and hardware previously mentioned are the installation of a Raspberry, a computer with a reduced board with which greater versatility, calculation power, WiFi, or Ethernet connectivity integrated into the board is achieved. As for the software installed Home Assistant, it does not require a paid license for its use and its programming is simpler and more intuitive, which facilitates its integration into the microgrid and a significant reduction in monitoring costs.

With these implementations, we achieve the objective set out in this project, which is the transformation of a production and consumption microgrid into a smart microgrid that allows us to act autonomously thanks to the software and hardware configurations installed.

The rest of the paper is as follows: Sect. 2 addresses the steps required to convert a network section into a microgrid, such as the identification and description of the passive network elements, the selection of the control hardware and software, the establishment of communication between the elements and finally the creation of a network control framework for the management of the microgrid; Sect. 3 presents a case study. Finally, the conclusions obtained are presented.

2 Methodology to Provide Intelligence to the Grid

As indicated in the introduction, this paper aims to describe a methodology that makes it possible to provide intelligence to an electricity network to which a set of generation, storage, and load elements are connected and to transform it into a smart microgrid that can operate as such, with high efficiency.

The steps to be able to convert an electrical network with independent elements of generation, storage and consumption that do not communicate with each other into a smart microgrid and that are developed in this article are shown in Fig. 1.

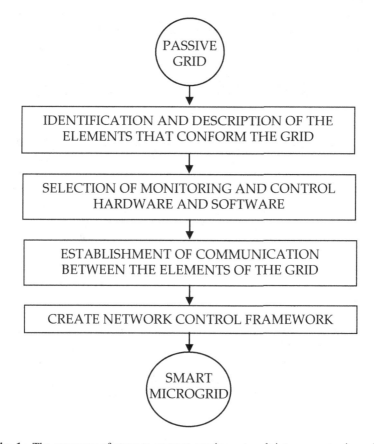

Fig. 1. The sequence of steps to convert passive network into a smart microgrid.

Step 1. Identification and description of the elements that make up the network: The first step in providing intelligence to an electricity network is to identify and describe all the connected elements of generation, storage, and consumption. It is essential to know at least the installed nominal power of each generation source, the capacity in the case of storage systems, the consumption of the most significant loads, a ranking of loads by priority and influence of load profile. It is also necessary to know for each system if they allow direct communication with some of the equipment that composes it and the communication protocols that this equipment uses.

Step 2. Selection of the monitoring and control hardware and software: The hardware and software chosen will condition the human-machine interface (HMI) to be used as a microgrid management system. In this section lies the main novelty of this methodology and its main advantages. A Raspberry Pi is used, as will be shown later, together with the free software Home Assistant.

Step 3. Establishment of communication between the elements of the network: once the components of the network have been described, the forms and protocols of communication permitted by each of them are known, and the control software has been selected, communication must be established between all of them, so that they do not function independently, but as a whole in which there can be an interaction between them. This will allow the behaviour of each of the elements of the system to be subordinated to that of the others so that the operation of the microgrid can be optimized, with the consequent cost savings in the electricity bill. Besides, Home Assistant allows to establish communication with any element through the multiple communication protocols it has integrated, in a simple way.

Step 4. Creation of a control network framework: once the communication between all the elements has been established, a control network framework or interface (HMI) must be developed to observe, in a simple and as intuitive way as possible, the operation of each of the elements of the network, and to send them operation instructions to optimize the operation of the microgrid by increasing its efficiency as much as possible. It should also allow the recording of monitored data for subsequent analysis to define management strategies, and once implemented, to validate their effectiveness.

3   Case Study

The case study to apply the proposed methodology is the network of the Centre for the Development of Renewable Energy (CEDER), which belongs to the Centre for Energy, Environmental and Technological Research (CIEMAT), a Spanish Public Research Organisation, currently dependent on the Ministry of Science and Innovation. It is located in the town of Lubia, province of Soria (Spain), and has an area of 640 ha with more than 13000 m2 built in three separate areas (see Fig. 2).

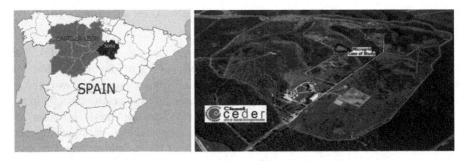

Fig. 2. Location and buildings distribution at CEDER.

CEDER's grid is connected to a 45kV distribution network and carries out a transformation at its entrance to 15kV. The grid is made up of eight transformation centres that reduce voltage to 400V. The network has multiple renewable generation systems that are not controllable (wind and photovoltaic), controllable renewables (hydraulic turbine), non-renewable (diesel generator), different mechanical (pumping system with tanks at different levels) and electrochemical (lithium-ion and Pb-acid batteries) storage systems, as well as several consumption elements connected to each transformer station which are monitored with a network analyser (PQube) installed in the low voltage part of each transformer station.

Instead of considering the entire microgrid, only the elements connected to one of the transformer stations will be considered, to simplify the control system and not to repeat cases, since all the photovoltaic inverters are practically the same, the PQubes network analysers too, etc.

3.1   Identification and Description of the Network Components

According to the previous section, the first step consists of identifying and describing all the elements connected to the network (see Fig. 3). In this case study, they are the following:

- Photovoltaic generation system of 5 kW, consisting of 24 polycrystalline silicon panels of 210 W distributed in 4 series of 6 panels. The panels are assembled on a floor structure with a variable tilt angle and connected to an Ingeteam inverter model Ingecon Sun Lite.
- To read photovoltaic generation values, it is necessary to communicate with the photovoltaic inverter, which has a network card to connect it to the CEDER data network (Ethernet) and allows communication using the Modbus TCP/IP protocol.
- Wind generation system consisting of a three-bladed wind turbine of 15 m in diameter and 50 kW power. It is a horizontal axis and works leeward.
- There was no connection to the wind turbine or its control panel, so it has been necessary to install some equipment that allows communication. In this case, a National Instruments FieldPoint compact data acquisition system [18] has been installed, which allows variables such as power, wind speed, etc. to be measured and can be connected to the CEDER data network. This equipment allows communication under the Modbus TCP/IP protocol.
- Electrochemical storage system consisting of 120 Tudor Pb-acid 7EAN100T batteries of 2 V each. The capacity is 1080 Ah at 120 h (C120). It is connected to a 50 kW inverter/charger/regulator developed by CEDER together CIRCE.
- The inverter/charger is connected via an RS485 connector to the serial port of a computer with a SCADA (Supervisory Control and Data Acquisition) for battery control. Therefore, the control system of the microgrid to be developed will communicate locally with the inverter via Modbus RTU.
- Consumption: The loads are the different laboratory and workshop buildings that make up the part of CEDER considered and its equipment, which are connected to the low voltage side of the transformation centres. To measure consumption, a power quality/network analyser (PQube) has been installed. In this case study there

are no critical loads to be powered in case of serious disturbances or microgrid failure. All of them have the same level of significant.

• The PQube can be connected to the CEDER data network through Ethernet and allows Modbus TCP/IP communication.

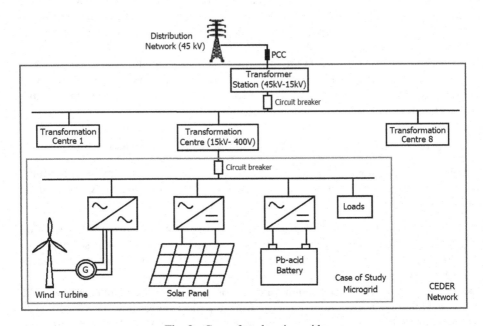

Fig. 3. Case of study microgrid.

3.2   Selection of Monitoring and Control Hardware and Software

Once all the elements of the microgrid have been described, and their characteristics and the form in which the communication with them is established, the following step is the election of the hardware and the software to carry out the control system.

There are several software packages available on the market for the analysis of energy systems, but not all of them allow the analysis and management of microgrids based on real-time data for the prediction and behaviour of the system [19], among which ETAP Real-Time 24 [20] is one of them. Another tool that allows this is Acciona's Microgrid Energy Management System – μGEMS [21]. However, as seen in the introduction, the most common way is to use software such as Labview to design a specific program for the ad-hoc monitoring and control of each microgrid.

In this case, it is proposed to use a Raspberry Pi 4 Model B [22, 23], with a tool developed specifically for the management of microgrid such as CIRCE and its Energy Box [24]. The Raspberry Pi 4 Model B was introduced in June 2019 to replace the Raspberry Pi 3 B+, with a significant improvement in its specifications, which will increase the smoothness of operation of our control system. Raspberry Pi 4 B features a

Broadcom BCM2711B0 quad-core ARM Cortex-A72 1.5 GHz processor, LPDDR4–3200 MHz SDRAM up to 4 GB, Gigabit Ethernet network connectivity (up to 1000 Mbps) and Wi-Fi 2.4 GHz/ 5 GHz wireless connectivity, IEEE 802.11 b/g/n/ac and Bluetooth 5.0, BLE. It works with a Raspbian operating system, which is the Linux (Debian) distribution prepared specifically for Raspberry.

As software, HomeAssistant is chosen [25] which is generally used for home automation applications but that is a robust solution, economically affordable (it is free software) and with great potential for monitoring and managing microgrids in real-time. This system allows communication with all the elements of generation, storage, and consumption of the network under study, through different communication protocols and their integration into a single HMI (Human Machine Interface). Home Assistant is a system developed in Python, free and open that allows to monitor all the elements connected to the microgrid, to control them from a unique interface (which allows its control from mobile devices), as well as to define advanced rules to control each one of the elements in a simple and intuitive form.

To store data collected by Home Assistant the best solution is to use MySQL [26], which is an open-source relational database management system. It can be installed on the same Raspberry, with a slight slowdown in the operation of the system, or on a different one exclusively for the database, achieving a higher system performance.

The use of MySQL is optional, although highly recommended whenever it is required to store the monitored data for later analysis, allowing to define much more efficient strategies for energy management of the microgrid.

The proposed control system of the microgrid is made up of three blocks:

- A communication block integrates the different communication protocols of the microgrid's generation, storage and consumption systems.
- A database: for information storage and subsequent analysis.
- A management block: with a user interface that allows real-time monitoring of all elements of the microgrid and programming of energy strategies to be defined.

3.3 Establishment of Communication Between the Elements that Make up the Network

Next, the communication of each of the elements of the microgrid with Home Assistant has to be established. Different communication protocols allow the transmission of information, provided that all the equipment is connected to the same data network or other equipment in local mode and that they are in turn connected to this network.

Among the most common communication protocols, Modbus [27] stands out above all others. It allows us to control a network of devices (in our case, generation, storage, and consumption elements) and to communicate them with a control system (Raspberry Pi 4 with Home Assistant). It is the standard communication protocol in the industry since it is robust, easy to use, open-source and therefore free and, above all, reliable.

All elements of the CEDER network described in Sect. 3.1 allow communication via the Modbus protocol, namely:

- RTU: It is based on master/slave architecture, to connect a control system to a Remote Terminal Unit (RTU) via a serial port. Typically, the master is a human-machine interface (HMI) or a supervisory and data acquisition (SCADA) system that sends a request and the slave is a sensor or a programmable logic controller (PLC) that returns a response. It uses a Cyclic Redundancy Checksum (CRC) to ensure the reliability of the data and as an error checking mechanism.

- TCP/IP (Transmission Control Protocol/Internet Protocol): It is based on a client/server architecture and allows communication over an Ethernet network. No CRC required.
- RTU over TCP: It is a combination of the two previous ones. It is based on client/server architecture for communications over Ethernet as Modbus TCP/IP but uses a CRC as Modbus RTU.

The microgrid scheme communications are shown in Fig. 4.

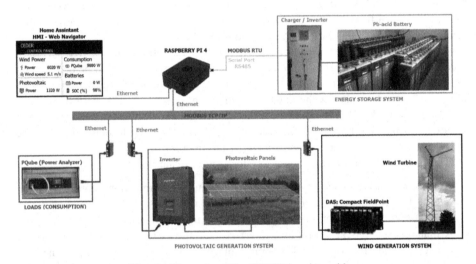

Fig. 4. Elements of the CEDER's microgrid.

To communicate each element with Home Assistant, first all the microgrid components must be defined in the configuration file, assigning them a name and indicating the type of communication, the IP, the port.

Once all the elements of the microgrid have been defined, the records with the desired information for each component must be read at the corresponding addresses. This is also done in the Home Assistant configuration file and it is necessary to have the Modbus frame of each unit (it should be in the manufacturer's manual, but many times it is not and it is necessary to contact the manufacturer to provide it) to know the addresses where the variables to be read are.

In the case of uncontrollable generation elements [11], such as the photovoltaic inverter and the wind generator, and loads (PQube network analyser), it is only necessary to read the instantaneous power since no action instructions can be sent to them. By contrast, in controllable generation elements and storage systems such as Pb-acid batteries in our case, it is necessary to read all the records to develop a SCADA that allows for control of their operation through the control panel, integrated with the rest of the elements.

3.4   Creation of a Control Network Framwork

Once communication has been established with all the equipment, an interface has to be created that allows the user to see in real-time the records collected from the elements that form part of the microgrid and to execute commands to give them instructions (start/stop of generation equipment, loading/unloading of storage systems, etc.).

Using Home Assistant, it is very intuitive to create a control network framework once communication has been established with each element of the microgrid and it has been defined in the configuration file. The starting point is a graphic interface that allows inserting cards with different functionalities. Default cards can be added with maps or weather forecasts to help to estimate the production of the renewable generation systems available in the microgrid. It also allows adding cards with different values of all the registers read numerically (Entities) or to represent graphically those values (Historical graph), or to represent jointly (graphically and numerically) a value using the Sensor card. Home Assistant also allows inserting buttons to send instructions to the different elements that have been monitored.

Figure 5 shows the real-time power values of each of the elements connected to the microgrid under study, indicating a photovoltaic generation of 1320 W and a demand of 9880 W. Wind speed is 5.1 m/s and wind generation is 8020 W. The batteries are stopped, since there is no high demand to provide energy to the microgrid, nor is there a generation surplus to be able to charge them. Moreover, batteries are almost fully charged (SOC 98%).

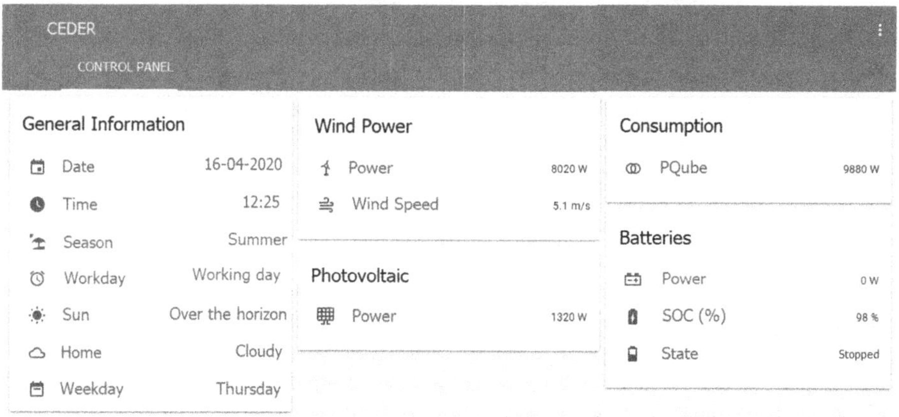

Fig. 5. Control network framework of the CEDER's microgrid in Home Assistant.

The SCADA for the control of the batteries also has to be created, as can be seen in Fig. 6. In Fig. 6 it can be observed how the batteries are in the process of normal charging, the microgrid is injecting them with 1780 W, they are at 96% of their capacity and with a voltage of 266 V.

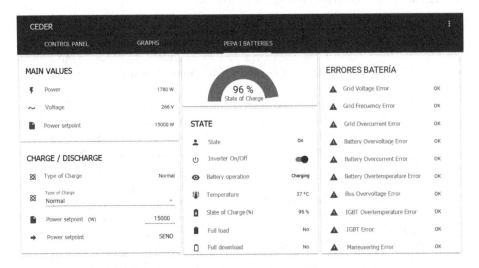

Fig. 6. SCADA of batteries at the CEDER's microgrid in Home Assistant.

Home Assistant allows representing in real-time the value of the variables collected from each of the elements as can see in Fig. 7.

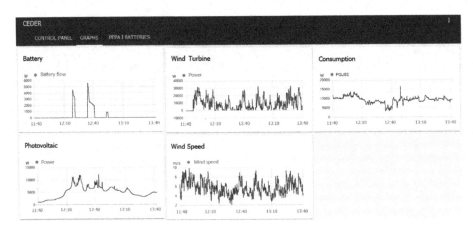

Fig. 7. Power time-series of the CEDER's microgrid elements in Home Assistant.

4   Conclusions

In this paper, a methodology is proposed for the conversion of a network section with generation, storage and loads into a smart electricity microgrid that can be replicated in any network section, based on four steps: 1) identification and description of the elements that make up the network, 2) selection of the hardware and software for monitoring and control, 3) establishment of communication between the elements of the network and 4) creation of a control network framework that allows the management of the electrical microgrid.

The main advantage of this methodology is the use of the free software Home Assistant, installed on a Raspberry Pi 4 to manage the microgrid. Although Home Assistant is a software whose widespread use is for home automation, it offers all the capabilities needed to monitor, manage and integrate into a single HMI and in real-time, all the elements of generation, storage, and consumption connected to a power network to turn it into a smart microgrid, simply and intuitively. It is worth mentioning the feature that this software offers us of unifying all the elements that form the microgrid only in one HMI. This is the main feature that differs from the most known way of monitoring, in which to know the current status of each of the elements it is necessary to access different connection points.

With the application of this methodology, it will be possible in the near future to establish strategies to optimize the operation of the microgrid by taking full advantage of the generation sources and reducing as much as possible the consumption of CEDER microgrid's from the distribution network with the help of storage systems. This could also lead to savings in the energy bill.

References

1. Ton, D.T., Smith, M.A.: The U.S. department of energy's microgrid initiative. Electr. J. (2012)
2. Sachs, T., Gründler, A., Rusic, M., Fridgen, G.: Framing Microgrid Design from a Business and Information Systems Engineering Perspective. Bus. Inf. Syst. Eng. **61**(6), 729–744 (2019). https://doi.org/10.1007/s12599-018-00573-0
3. Warsi, N.A., Siddiqui, A.S., Kirmani, S., Sarwar, M.: Impact assessment of microgrid in smart cities: Indian perspective. Technol. Econ. Smart Grids Sustain. Energy (2019)
4. Yang, J., Guo, B., Qu, B.: Economic optimization on two time scales for a hybrid energy system based on virtual storage. J. Mod. Power Syst. Clean Energy (2018)
5. Kroposki, B.: Integrating high levels of variable renewable energy into electric power systems J. Mod. Power Syst. Clean Energy (2017)
6. Li, Q., Xu, Z., Yang, L.: Recent advancements on the development of microgrids. J. Mod. Power Syst. Clean Energy (2014)
7. Jia, Y., Lyu, X., Lai, C.S., Xu, Z., Chen, M.: A retroactive approach to microgrid real-time scheduling in quest of perfect dispatch solution. J. Mod. Power Syst. Clean Energy (2019)
8. Kaur, A., Kaushal, J., Basak, P.: A review on microgrid central controller. Renew. Sustain. Energy Rev. **55**, 338–345 (2016)

9. Chandak, S., Bhowmik, P., Rout, P.K.: Load shedding strategy coordinated with storage device and D-STATCOM to enhance the microgrid stability. Protection Control Modern Power Syst. **4**(1), 1–19 (2019). https://doi.org/10.1186/s41601-019-0138-0

10. Divya, K.C., Østergaard, J.: Battery energy storage technology for power systems-An overview. Electric Power Syst. Res. (2009)

11. Hernández Callejo, L.: Microrredes eléctricas. Integración de generación renovable distribuida, almacenamiento distribuido e inteligencia, Primera ed. Publicaciones, Ibergarceta (2019)

12. Gharavi, H., Ghafurian, R.: Smart grid: The electric energy system of the future. Proc. IEEE **99**(6), 917–921 (2011)

13. S. Teufel and B. Teufel, "The Crowd Energy Concept," J. Electron. Sci. Technol., 2014

14. Ortega, R., Carranza, O., Sosa, J.C., García, V., Hernández, R.: "Operando En Modo Isla Dentro De Una Microrred", RIAI - Rev. Iberoam. Autom. e Inform. Ind. **13**, 115–126 (2016)

15. Shuai, Z., et al.: Microgrid stability: classification and a review. Renew. Sustain. Energy Rev. **58**, 167–179 (2016)

16. Erice Carbonero, V., López Taberna, J., Marcos Álvarez, J.: Monitorización del consumo eléctrico de un hogar : Procesado de datos mediante Arduino. Universidad Pública de Navarra (2015)

17. Ariel, L., Francisco, C., Jorge, J., María, C.: Algoritmo de control para la administración de una micro red. in Congreso de Investigación y Transferencia Tecnológica en Ingeniería Eléctrica CITTIE (2019)

18. "Compact Fieldpoint." https://sine.ni.com/nips/cds/view/p/lang/es/nid/1199.

19. Franco-Manrique, R., Gómez-Luna, E., Ramos-Sánchez, C.A.: Smart grid analysis and management in colombia towards ETAP real time solution. Ingeniare **26**(4), 599–611 (2018)

20. Etap, "Model-Driven Real-Time Solutions for Power Systems SCADA & Monitoring Power Management Generation Management Transmission Management Advanced Distribution Management Microgrid Master Controller Intelligent Load Shedding Substation Automation"

21. "SOLUCIONES TECNOLÓGICAS PARA MICRORREDES." https://www.acciona-energia.com/es/sostenibilidad/proyectos-innovacion/microrredes/. Accessed 06 Jun-2020

22. "Raspberry Pi." https://www.raspberrypi.org/. Accessed 13 Dec 2019

23. Tridianto, E., Permatasari, P.D., Ali, I.R.: Experimental study of mini SCADA renewable energy management system on microgrid using Raspberry Pi. J. Phys. Conf. Ser. **983**(1) (2018)

24. Goitia-Zabaleta (IKERLAN), N., et al.: Rennaisance - Desarrollo de las comunidades energéticas locales y blockchain (2019)

25. "Home Assistant." https://www.home-assistant.io/. Accessed 18 Dec 2019

26. "MySQL." Available: https://www.mysql.com/. Accessed: 23 Dec 2019

27. Fovino, I.N., Carcano, A., Masera, M., Betta, A.T.: Chapter 6 Design And Implementation of Software, pp. 107–121 (2009)

Analysis of Alternatives for the Acceleration of a Hyperloop System

Luis García-Tabarés[1] , Marcos Lafoz[1(✉)] , Jorge Torres[1] ,
Gustavo Soriano[1] , Daniel Orient[2], and Daniel Fons[2]

[1] CIEMAT, Av. Complutense, 40., 28040 Madrid, Spain
marcos.lafoz@ciemat.es
[2] ZELEROS, Muelle de Nazaret sn, 46024 Valencia, Spain

Abstract. The paper introduces the Hyperloop inspired system by the company ZELEROS and provides a discussion about the alternatives for the acceleration. The ZELEROS system comprises a named propulsion system, based on an air turbine, and an acceleration system based on a linear motor. Different options have been discussed for the linear motor: induction machines, permanent magnet machines and switched reluctance machine, among some other hybrid solutions. Advantages and drawbacks are presented for all of them. For this particular application, where the length of the active side and the speed are really significant, the option of a linear switched reluctance motor results convenient both from the technical and economic points of view. A further discussion about the type of linear switched reluctance motor (LSRM) preferred is also accomplished during the paper, taking into account a particular model of the machine as well as its operation conditions regarding the frequency, dimensions and operation parameters. Three options are compared during the analysis: a single-side horizontal LSRM, a N-side vertical LSRM and a cylindrical LSRM. Qualitative and quantitative (based on the model) arguments are given in favour and against each alternative. Finally, the two-sided vertical switched reluctance machine has been considered as the most adequate for the development of the Zeleros Acceleration System.

Keywords: Railway transportation · Linear motor · Switched reluctance machine

1   Operation of the ZELEROS Hyperloop System

Hyperloop is the commercial name for an ultrahigh speed railway transportation system [1], used both for passengers and cargo, through a tube where the air pressure has been reduced in order to reach speeds up to 1000 km/h. Many technologies have been developed during the last years and one of them belongs to the Spanish company ZELEROS.

The system Zeleros, presented in Fig. 1, is envisioned as suitable for the transportation of passengers and cargo; it aims at being strongly competitive at distances between 500 and 1500 km, still maintaining the ability to be used for shorter distances, and for much longer distances as well, so long the business case works [2]. Therefore, its tactical range falls in the intercity connection, what in the case of Western Europe will mostly mean state capital cities, and large cities such as Barcelona, Frankfurt, or

© Springer Nature Switzerland AG 2021
S. Nesmachnow and L. Hernández Callejo (Eds.): ICSC-CITIES 2020, CCIS 1359, pp. 259–271, 2021.
https://doi.org/10.1007/978-3-030-69136-3_18

Marseille [3]. The station can be potentially brought to the city center, despite this feature is optional, since arriving at an airport or other type of hub can be potentially equally efficient. A case by case analysis needs to be set up. Vehicles will depart and arrive at a minimum interval around of two minutes and a half, keeping this headway during the whole route. Cruise speed will be between 600 and 750 km/h. The pressure level inside the tube will be around 100 mbar, or 1/10th of atmosphere pressure. This is a pressure value similar to that of air at the flight level where the Concorde used to cruise. All the energy needed to fulfill the mission will be carried onboard. Fleets can be composed by vehicles of between 50 and up to 200 passengers. The goods only vehicle equivalent to the 200 passengers vehicle will have a maximum payload of 30 metric tons. In terms of passengers, this means up to 4.800 passenger per hour and per direction per one tube. The capacity can be scaled up by adding further tubes per direction. In case sufficient demand exist and this expansion is deemed necessary, the increment on the infrastructure cost will represent only a fraction of the cost of the works needed to put in place the first tube, especially in the case the tube is placed over pylons, additional cost that what will be largely compensated by the additional traffic.

 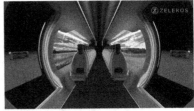

Fig. 1. Technology of the Hyperloop inspired system from ZELEROS.

The system targets a niche of distance that are currently being served by medium size airplanes, since traditional high-speed rails are not fast enough to compete, while maglev solutions seem to be too expensive. The system can be seen as an expansion of the operational envelope of the traditional land transportation, whose current limit is the service provided by high speed rail for well stablished and densely travelled corridors/routes, and can also be seen as a green alternative to airplanes, since the vehicles are fully electrical driven, and the overall energy consumption is substantially lower than that of aircrafts in the above mentioned range.

From a passenger perspective, the user will board as he will normally do on a high-speed rail car. Once inside, a door similar to that of an airplane will close. The vehicle will start motion as driverless people mover. Once the platform deck has been left behind, the vehicle will ingress on an airlock. The vehicle will be quickly depressurized, same as fighter jet on a vertical climb. Then the vehicle will reach the acceleration system. It will provide thrust enough to achieve cruise speed. Once cruise speed is achieved, the compressed air propulsion system will take over and will take care of sustaining the speed.

2   The Propulsion of the ZELEROS System

There are two main propulsion systems included in the solution:

a) *The cruise speed system:*

A compressed air propulsion system, where the air at high pressure is used to generate enough thrust to compensate the overall drag. It can be used to some extend to accelerate it too, particularly for small speed adjustments during the run. This is a system onboard the vehicle. The requirements are: a turbofan like that of airplanes, trained by one or several electrical drives. Depending on the vehicle capacity, mission range, speed profile, and specific pressure value, among others, the electric power needed will be between 7 and 13 MW.

b) *The acceleration system:*

A linear motor commissioned to accelerate from zero speed to cruise speed. It will have a length of between 6 and 15 km that will be placed at the start of the route. This a system that is placed primarily on the track, with some elements placed on the vehicle, depending on the specific type of motor used. The acceleration system can be used at the stations to regenerate the kinetic energy of the moving vehicle, in order to use this energy for the launch of the next vehicle. The requirements are: to be able to provide the power needed to achieve a maximum acceleration of 3 m/s2 to the heaviest vehicle on the fleet, to have adjustable power for vehicles of different mass, a standard acceleration request between 1'5 and 2'5 m/s2, and a jerk (m/s3) limitation in accordance with passenger comfort needs.

3   Options for the Acceleration Systems

As commented in the previous point, the main propulsion system of the vehicle is unable to produce the required force to drive the vehicle bellow a certain speed and this is the reason why an auxiliary impulsion system is needed.

Different alternatives may be considered for this purpose, some of which are based on electrical devices while other use catapults, rockets or any other mechanical system.

While these last options have been used for accelerating different devices in experimental facilities [4], a solution based on an electrical machine for a future commercial ultra high-speed vehicle seems to be much more adequate for different reasons, including controllability, cost, regenerative braking capability, simultaneous operation of different vehicles, etc. Particularly, electrical Linear Machines (LM) are especially suitable and advantageous over rotary ones with gears, because they allow smoother operation with less noise and absence of slipping if the rotational movement is transmitted to a wheel (besides the challenges associated to the use of wheels at very high speeds). So, the first decision was to use a Linear Electrical Machine to accelerate the vehicle.

The second decision was to decide the configuration of that LM. Besides the type of machine to be used (which will be commented in the next paragraphs), the most critical point to consider is whether the Active Side of the LM (the side which includes those coils contributing with the required active power and in some cases with both, the active and reactive power) is stationary (Stator) or moving (Translator).

In order to continue with the decision process, let us consider just as a very simple example, a vehicle with a mass of 10 t, which needs to be accelerated at 700 km/h with an acceleration of g m/s2 (which is well above a commercial value). The required length of the machine should be in the range of 2,000 m, needing a force of 100,000 N.

Common sense advices to choose a moving Active Side located in the vehicle, in order to avoid having a 2 km long Stationary Active Side full of coils. For accelerations closer to commercial values, the length of this Active Side could still increase one order of magnitude.

Nevertheless, having a moving Active Side implies two options with their corresponding challenges:

a) Coils are fed from ground using feedthroughs, catenaries or whatever system requiring physical contact and the corresponding wear. So far, there is no reliable off the shelf system able to be used at affordable conditions of cost and maintenance.

b) Coils are fed from the vehicle, which includes an energy storage system based on batteries (any other would not be able to store the required levels of energy).

Coming back to our previous example, the overall amount of energy needed to accelerate the vehicle would be 52,500 kWh. Considering the highest available energy density batteries (in the range of 160 Wh/kg) an extra mass of 328 t would be required, becoming fully inadmissible.

Previous situation leads to choose undoubtedly a stationary Active Side, which will be fixed to the ground as part of the track.

Next decision would concern the type of LM to be selected, taking into consideration that the Active Side must be long (extremely long in many cases) and stationary, while the Passive Side must be as light and simple as possible in order to maximize the payload of the transport system.

In principle, there are many types of LMs [5] but only a reduced number may be envisaged for this application. The main options that can be considered are [6, 7]:

1) **Linear Induction Machines (LIM)**, the rotary version of the most popular electrical machine (Induction Machine) which is based on the interaction of two travelling magnetic fields, one created by the Active Side and other induced in the Passive Side. In the Linear version, the Passive Side is usually a solid aluminum plate, although a ladder-slit can also be used. There is a conceptual important difference with the rotary version: The existence of "end effects": two additional induced fields at each end of the Passive Side, producing a net reduction of the force and the efficiency. As for other LMs, the machine can be single-sided (one Active Side) or doubled-sided (two Active Sides) but, in any case, there is only one aluminum plate. In the first case, there is a back iron behind the plate to close the field, while in the second one the magnetic flux is closed through both Active Sides. The main advantages of LIMs are its simplicity and robustness, while the drawbacks are related with the low power factor and medium efficiency, as well as the

power which is induced in the Passive Side in the form of Joule losses. End effects can also be very negative.

2) **Linear Switched Reluctance Machines (LSRM)** based on the sequential commutation of coils located in the Active Side creating a magnetic circuit that closes through the Passive Side trying to minimize its reluctance to produce mechanical work from electric power (motoring operation) or to maximize the reluctance to produce electrical power from mechanical work (generating operation). Each group of coils, which are fed in series simultaneously, constitute a phase of the machine. Coils are wounded around iron poles forming the Active Side. Passive Side has only iron poles with no coils. Only certain combinations of Active and Passive Side number of poles are allowed in a LSRM. As for the case of the LIM, LSRMs can be either single-sided or double-sided. Since attraction force between both sides of the machine (normal force) can be much higher than propulsion force, the choice of a double-sided machine is mandatory to avoid non-compensated forces perpendicular to the machine displacement. In this regard, some of the authors participated in the past in the development of the so called Linear Multitranslator Switched Reluctance Machine (LMSRM) [8], a machine with two lateral Active Sides and one or more central Active Sides in between the lateral ones. Between the Active Sides are placed the Passive Sides in an arrangement, which is balanced from the normal force point of view. While lateral Active Sides need back iron to close the magnetic circuit, central Active Sides do not, so as the number of these elements grow, the traction force density (force per unit mass) of the machine increases. Recently, new configurations of LSRMs have been developed like the Mutually Coupled LSRM [9] in which more than one phase are excited simultaneously achieving more force density and less noise and vibrations levels. The main advantages of the LSRMs are its robustness and the low cost derived from its simplicity: Passive Side are simply laminated iron poles while Active Side include simple flat coils that can be manufactured independently and after mounted and connected in their position. In the list of drawbacks, the noise and vibrations due to the big normal force.

3) **Linear Permanent Magnet Machines (LPMM)**, linear machines that include permanent magnets in any of their two Sides. When the magnets are included in the Passive Side, they are in charge of creating the excitation field and the machines are Linear Permanent Magnet Synchronous Machines (LPMSM). Like for the case of the LIMs, this machine presents end effects which cause force ripple. There are also other sources of ripple like the cogging force, a tendency of the two sides of the machine to align due to the presence of the permanent magnets in one side that are attracted by the iron poles in the other side. In a conventional LPMSM, permanent magnets are located in the passive side: they provide the excitation magnetic field but they do not exchange active power.

Active Side only has coils which really deal with the active power of the system, converting mechanical work into electricity or the other way around. It is usual to name "the Primary" the Active Side with the Coils and "the Secondary" the Passive Side.

Besides LPMSMs, there are a number of Synchronous Machines which have Permanent Magnets in the Primary Side (LPPMM) [6] coexisting with the coils, while the Secondary Side is purely Passive like for the case of LSRMs. There are basically four sub-categories of LPPMMs: Linear Switched-Flux Permanent Magnet Machines, Linear Flux-Reversed Permanent Magnet Machines, Linear Doubly-Salient Permanent Magnet Machines and Linear Verneir Permanent Magnet Machines.

The main advantage of LPMM in general, is their high force density and controllability as well as the good power factor while in the side of drawbacks, the most significative is the need of expensive and relative delicate NdFeB magnets and also the presence of ripple in the force and the higher complexity of the coil manufacturing. Other drawback is the existing cogging force due to the permanent magnets.

As a kind of summary, Table 1 shows the advantages and drawbacks for the three previously described families of linear electrical machines, for the particular application that we are considering which is basically characterized by the extremely long Active Side (Primary), a high commutation frequency, low cost requirement and robustness.

Table 1. Comparison of alternatives of Electrical Linear Machine for the Zeleros Hyperloop Impulsion System

Type of machine	Advantages	Drawbacks
LIMs Linear Induction Machines	–Simple & robust –Absence of Permanent Magnets	–Induced currents & heat dissipation in the moving Side –Relatively complex windings –Poor Power Factor –End Effects –Medium Efficiency
LSRMs Linear Switched Reluctance Machines	–Very simple & robust –Low Cost –Absence of Permanent Magnets –Very simple & cheap coils	–Noise & Vibration –High lateral forces –Force Ripple
LPMMs Linear Permanent Magnet Machines	–High controllability & efficiency –Good Power Factor	–High or extremely high number of needed Permanent Magnets –Force Ripple and cogging force –More complex windings

After this analysis, the selected candidate was the Linear Switched Reluctance Machine since some of the drawbacks could be overcome with an adequate drive system while advantages make it especially suitable for this application, especially in real scale systems where the impact of the cost in the overall solution can be decisive. In this regard, Permanent Magnet Machines have to be discarded, especially LPPMMs since they would use this type of magnets along the full accelerating track.

4 Modeling and Selection of a Switched Reluctance Machine Type

Before coming into details regarding the specific type of LSRM that has been selected, we present a short introduction to the working principle of this kind of machine for a better understanding of the methodology, which has been used for its selection and calculation [10]. This introduction is based on Fig. 2, which represent a 3-phase one-sided LSRM with one Active Side with coils and one Passive one with only iron poles.

When working as a motor, one phase (green one for instance) is activated in the moment the iron pole P is entering that phase (fully misaligned. Fig 2.1.a). The pole tries to fully align the phase (Fig. 2.3.a) to minimize the reluctance of the circuit and generates a force in the same sense as the pole moves (motoring operation). When the alignment is achieved, the phase is switched off and the next one comes into operation (the yellow one).

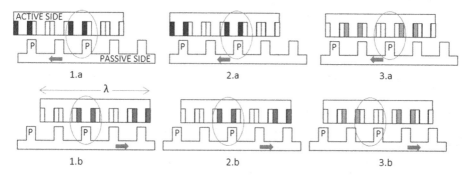

Fig. 2. Working principle of the LSRM: a) Motor Mode b) Generator Mode (Color figure online)

When working as a generator, one phase is activated in the moment the pole P is fully aligned with that phase (Fig. 2.1.b). Then, an external force pulls the pole and tries to take it to the fully misaligned position (Fig. 2.3.b), a force that acts in the opposite sense as the pole moves (generating operation) to maximize the reluctance of the circuit. When misalignment is achieved, the phase is switched off and the next one is switched on (the yellow one).

Switched reluctance machines may present different configurations in terms of number of phases in the active side (m) and number of poles per machine period either in the Active (NA) and Passive (NP) Sides. If λ is the length of a machine period (see Fig. 2), in every commutation the machine advances one stroke (s), given as:

$$s = \lambda/(m \cdot N_p) \tag{1}$$

Since high speeds required high commutation frequencies, "s" must be high in order to minimize that frequency and hence m and NP must be as small as possible.

Calculating the force that the machine is able to produce, requires some knowledge on how it is fed [11, 12]. Figure 3 shows one pole of the Passive Side and the corresponding coil of the Active Side acting over it. The coil is connected to a so-called H-Bridge which is connected to a DC Voltage Source. Positive voltage is applied to the coil when both switches are closed, while negative voltage is applied when the diodes of the bridge are conducting. By closing and opening the switches, the polarity can be reversed and the current controlled. When the switches are conducting, the current goes out the power supply extracting energy from it. When the diodes are conducting the current goes in the power supply injecting energy in it. These two situations are presented in Fig. 3.

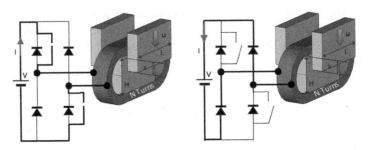

Fig. 3. H-Bridge topology to feed the SRM Coils: a) Conduction of the Switches b) Conduction of the Diodes

The net energy conversion from mechanical into electrical or vice versa is the power flowing through the battery along one period T. If the electrical resistance of the coil is neglected, we can express the total energy W, as a function of the current I and the flux φ:

$$W = \int_0^T V \cdot I \cdot dt = \int_0^T \frac{d\varphi}{dt} I \cdot dt = \oint I \cdot d\varphi \qquad (2)$$

Representing the area enclosed by the closed Flux-Current curve. According to the nomenclature of Fig. 3 and for the pre-dimensioning of the different alternatives of LSRM, the force can be calculated as:

$$F = \frac{W}{T \cdot U} = \frac{K_{mag} \cdot \varphi_{max} \cdot I_{max}}{H} = K_{mag} \cdot B_{max} \cdot I_{max} \cdot L \qquad (3)$$

Assuming the simplification that the value of $\oint I \cdot d\varphi$ is proportional to the product of the maximum values of the current and flux, respectively. The proportionality coefficients are derived from some analytical considerations and also from FEM calculations performed over some benchmark cases.

Equations (1), (2) and (3), along with purely geometrical considerations allowed us to develop a simple universal model to perform the selection of the optimum machine for a given vehicle. These geometrical considerations are based on easy relationships like imposing that the pole width must be twice the width of the coil, or that the pole area must be the same as the return yoke area to avoid saturation in that yoke and obviously from the overall dimensions of the machine to fit in the available space.

Table 2. Analyzed topologies of LSRMs for impelling the vehicle

Single-Sided Horizontal LSRM (1SH)
One Active Side all along the track and one Passive Side attached to the vehicle

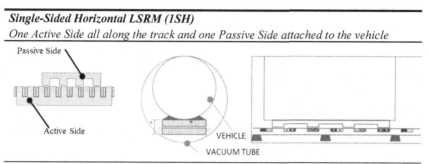

N-Sided Vertical LSRM (NSV)
N Active Sides (2 lat. & (N-2) cent.) along the track. N-1 Passive Sides at the vehicle

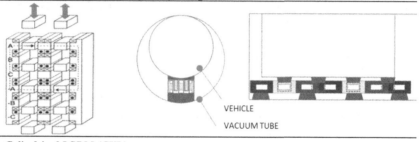

Cylindrical LSRM (CYL)
One tubular Active Sides all along the track and one Tubular Passive Side at the vehicle

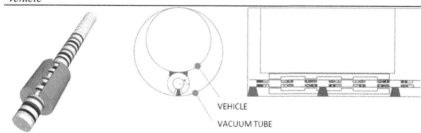

In this application, we can define a so-called Unit Machine consisting of the portion of machine, which repeats sequentially every λ meters and the Traction Modulus, which comprises the number of Unit Machines to produce the required force.

Regarding the optimization criteria, the first approach has been to choose a Unit Machine that maximizes the electromagnetic force produced in it. Once it is defined, the number of Units Machines of the Traction Modulus is decided according to the overall forced requirements.

4.1   Three Configurations of LSRMs

The next step is to choose the most suitable machine topology for this application. In this regard, we have concluded that there are three possible options, which a priori, would fulfil the requirements. Table 2 summarizes these three options in terms of their description, appearance and situation in the vehicle. Left hand side column shows the configuration of the machine while the right hand side corresponds to its location in the vehicle.

Single-Sided Horizontal LSRMs seem to be more adequate to the shape of the available room. They are also simple and easy to adjust with only one airgap but they present the tremendous disadvantage of the non-compensated transversal forces tending to attract the vehicle to the Active Side.

N-Sided Vertical LSRMs present a much higher force density, but they have the drawback of the adjustment of the several airgaps. When N = 2 we have the case of the conventional Double-Sided LSRM.

Cylindrical LSRMs are fully compensated and have the great advantage of avoiding the coil ends so that every meter of the coil is producing thrust. The major drawback when working at high frequency is the difficulty for laminating the iron in the convenient direction all along the magnetic circuit.

4.2   Comparison and Selection of the Three Configurations of LSRMs

The previously described model was adapted to three options of LSRMs to perform individual optimizations for each solution and especially a comparison between the three configurations to select the most appropriate for this application.

Figure 4 and Fig. 5 show some of these results for the Single-Sided Horizontal and the N-Sided Vertical options. X-axis represents the geometrical parameter "A" related to the machine enveloping dimensions, while Y-axes show: the Conductor weight per unit length of Active Side, the same for the iron, the weight of the Passive Side on

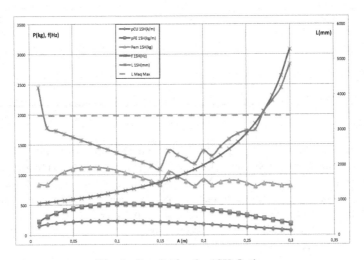

Fig. 4. Results for the 1SH Option

board, the commutation frequency, the required length of the machine and, as a dotted line, the maximum available length to place the machine (machine length must be bigger than that value). Intersection of the Active Side length curve with the dotted line provides the two limits for parameter "A". Working at low values of "A" imply higher conductor weights but much lower commutation frequencies. Although not shown, results for the Cylindrical machine are similar: there is a limit value for the parameter "A" but the smaller its value, the smaller the commutation frequency.

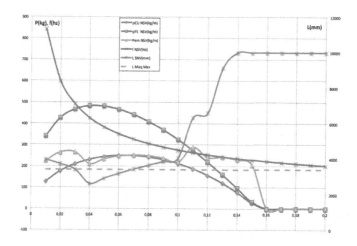

Fig. 5. Results for the NSV Option

Finally, Table 3 summarizes the qualitative and quantitative (given by the model) arguments in favour and against each alternative. For the case of the N-Sided Vertical machine, and for the sake of simplification, "N" has been set to two.

Table 3. Comparison of the topologies of LSRMs

1SH Option	2SV	SRM Ci
Advantages		
–Lower weight/meter of conductor & Iron –Reduced onboard weight	–Reduced weight /meter of conductor & iron –Min. Weight onboard –Min. Commutation frequency –High force density –Balanced lateral forces	–Moderate weight/meter of conductor –Easy coils manufacturing –No coil ends (all the coil length contributes to generate force)
Drawbacks		
–Very high commutation frequency –Non-balanced vertical force higher than the traction force	–Worse fitting to the available space –Need for precise adjustment of the two airgaps	–High weight/meter of Iron –High onboard weight –Difficulty for laminating the iron in the adequate directions

According to the previous considerations, the two-sided vertical switched reluctance machine has been considered as the most adequate for the development of the Zeleros Acceleration System.

5 Conclusions

The paper describes the concept of the ZELEROS Hyperloop Inspired system and the impelling system which is required to accelerate the vehicle up to the needed speed for operating the main propulsion system, which is based on a turbine driven by an electric motor.

Clearly, the option of an electric linear motor is preferred for this application to any other mechanical system due to its better controllability, capability of simultaneous operation for various vehicles, efficiency, etc.

A decision sequence is described along the paper: First, the choice of a Linear Electrical Machine, second to place the Active Side stationary on ground in spite its big length, as supplying the required power and energy to a moving Active Side would be unfeasible. The third decision is to choose the type of Linear Electric Machine among realistic candidates which have been identified and reduced to the following three options: The Linear Induction Machine, the Linear Switched Reluctance Machine and the Linear Permanent Magnet Machine. A justified rationale leads to choose for this application the Linear Switched Machine, basically for cost and robustness reasons.

In the category of Switched Reluctances Machines, three topologies have been identified as potential candidates: The singled-sided horizontal arrangement, the N-sided vertical one (with particular attention to N = 2) and the cylindrical configuration. In order to evaluate and compare the three of them, an analytical model based on simplified equations and geometrical relationships, has been developed and run. Considering both, qualitative and quantitative arguments, we have concluded that a double-sided vertical switched reluctance machine represents the best option for this application.

The selection of the linear motor type for the acceleration system can be complemented with the analysis of the power supply of the motor, already accomplished in a previous publication [13].

References

1. Musk, E.: Hyperloop Alpha (2013). https://www.spacex.com/sites/spacex/files/hyperloop alpha-20130812.pdf. Accessed 1 Nov 2019
2. Kale, S.R., Laghane, Y.N., Kharade, A.K., Kadus, S.B.: Hyperloop: advance mode of transportation system and optimize solution on traffic congestion. Int. J. Res. Appl. Sci. Eng. Technol. (IJRASET), 7 (2005). ISSN 2321-9653
3. https://en.wikipedia.org/wiki/Hyperloop. Accessed 18 Jan 2020
4. Factor Lambda. Holloman High Speed Test Track Design Manual. Research Summary, vol. 1, p. 2 (2005)
5. Chevailler, S.: Comparative Study and Selection Criteria of Linear Motors, January 2006. https://doi.org/10.5075/epfl-thesis-3569

6. Eguren, I., Almandoz, G., Egea, A., Ugalde, G., Escalada, J.A.: Linear Machines for Long Stroke Applications-A Review. IEEE Access. https://doi.org/10.1109/ACCESS.2019.2961758

7. Kumar, P., Geetha, K., Madhavi, K.: Design, modeling and analysis of linear switched reluctance motor for ground transit applications. IOSR J. Electr. Electron. Eng. **10**(1), 2278–1676 (2015)

8. Switched Reluctance Linear Motor/Generator P200602943(OPEM)

9. Azer, P., Berker, B., Ali, E.: Mutually Coupled Switching Reluctance Motor: Fundamentals, Control, Modeling, State of the Art and Future Trends. IEEE Access. https://doi.org/10.1109/ACCESS.2019.2930895

10. Miller, T.J.: Switched Reluctance Motors and Their Control. Magna Physics Publishing and Clarendon Press, Oxford (1993)

11. Kolomeitsev, L., et al.: Control of a linear switched reluctance motor as a propulsion system for autonomous railway vehicles. In: 2008 13th International Power Electronics and Motion Control Conference, Poznan, pp. 1598–1603 (2008). https://doi.org/10.1109/EPEPEMC.2008.4635495

12. Torres, P.M., Lafoz, M., Blanco, M., Navarro, G., Torres, J., García-Tabarés, L.: Switched reluctance drives with degraded mode for electric vehicles. modeling & simulation for electric vehicle applications. Chapter 5. In: INTECH 2016, pp. 97–124. https://doi.org/10.5772/64431

13. Lafoz, M., et al.: Power supply solution for ultrahigh speed hyperloop trains. Smart Cities **3**, 642–656 (2020). https://doi.org/10.3390/smartcities3030033

Prototype System for Remotely Monitoring and Managing Second-Hand Clothing Collection Containers

Ismael Martin Martín[1]([⊠]), Gregorio López López[1]([⊠]),
Sergio González Jiménez[1]([⊠]), and Brice Corrieu[2]([⊠])

[1] Departament of Electronics, Automation and Communications,
Universidad Pontificia Comillas ICAI-ICADE, Madrid, Spain
ismael.martin.1996@gmail.com, gllopez@comillas.edu,
sgjimenez@icai.comillas.edu
[2] Sigfox, Madrid, Spain
brice.corrieu@sigfox.com

Abstract. The current collection of second-hand clothes containers that Cáritas has distributed throughout the Community of Madrid presents some inefficiencies. Through the remotely monitoring of these containers, this project intends to address and reduce them. To do this, a study of the different alternatives on the market is carried out and a prototype is developed to check the functionality of the system. The system is composed of three different parts: a hardware or device composed of an ultrasound sensor that sends the free capacity of the container through the communications network of Sigfox to its own back-end. By creating a callback this message is redirected to the Microsoft Azure cloud platform where it is processed, stored and displayed. In addition, the user can know the capacity of the containers through a web application or front-end and create optimized routes based on this information.

Keywords: Arduino MKRFox 1200 · Azure IoT Hub · Azure Blob Storage · Azure Maps · Azure Time Series Insights · Back-end · Cáritas · Digitalization · Front-end · Monitoring · Sigfox

1 Introduction

This study is part of the Moda Re-project of Cáritas Madrid, whose objective is the recycling of second-hand clothes through a network of containers distributed throughout the Community of Madrid.

Right now the clothes collection system has many inefficiencies caused mainly by the lack of knowledge about the real volume of the containers. This causes containers that are not yet full to be collected or others to get overflow, with bags of clothes accumulating on the outside. This creates a problem of clothing theft and bad image for the organization that can be solved by implementing a system to know the capacity of the containers in real time.

© Springer Nature Switzerland AG 2021
S. Nesmachnow and L. Hernández Callejo (Eds.): ICSC-CITIES 2020, CCIS 1359, pp. 272–284, 2021.
https://doi.org/10.1007/978-3-030-69136-3_19

For this purpose, a collaboration project between Cáritas Madrid and the Fundación Ingenieros ICAI has been set up to monitor the free capacity of the containers. The aim is to provide the organization with a system to improve efficiencies through the optimization of the collection routes. The system will consist of sensors placed in each container that will measure the space available. This data will be sent through an IoT communication network to a *back-end* platform where it will be processed and stored in order to be represented in a *front-end*.

This paper presents a first analysis of the system and the implementation of a prototype to validate results useful for future massive deployments. The developed system combines currently leader technologies such as Arduino, as hardware platform, Sigfox, as communication network, and Microsoft Azure, as Cloud platform.

The remainder of the paper is organized as follows. Section 2 presents the analysis of the different technologies and solutions available for this kind of systems and justify the technology selection in this case. Section 3 describes the design and development of a proof of concept for the target system. Section 4 presents the validation of the developed system. Finally, Sect. 5 draws conclusions and discuss future works.

2   Analysis of the State of the Art

Currently there are a large number of companies in Spain and around the world that are dedicated to the implementation of container monitoring systems. Although depending on the content and the application in particular there are many variations, all the systems are characterized by being supported by the three key pillars shown in Fig. 1:

- a set of devices placed in each container that are in charge of evaluating the free capacity;
- a communications network that is used to send the data from each device to the back-end;
- a back-end where the data are processed, stored, analyzed, and represented though a dashboard.

A study of each of the parts of the system has been carried out, analysing which of the different options are optimal for the application of the project, considering both technological and economic parameters.

The first element to be decided is the communications network, since it will condition both the development of the device and the back-end. For the communication system, LPWAN (Low Power Wide Area Networks) technologies are chosen over others since they perfectly fit the application requirements (i.e., low data rates, very low consumption, high coverage) [1]. Emitting at fairly low frequency allows them to cover large areas, being able to reach all containers. On the contrary, there is a penalty in the bandwidth being able to send only a limited amount of information. Anyway, it is foreseen that one or two daily

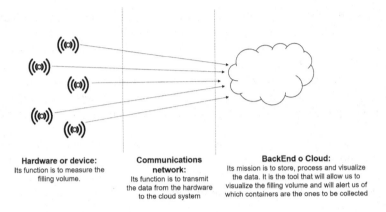

Hardware or device:	**Communications network:**	**BackEnd o Cloud:**
Its function is to measure the filling volume.	Its function is to transmit the data from the hardware to the cloud system	Its mission is to store, process and visualize the data. It is the tool that will allow us to visualize the filling volume and will alert us of which containers are the ones to be collected

Fig. 1. Overview of the system operation

measurements will be made with very little weight each, so this would not be a restriction for the application of the containers.

Within these networks there are two groups depending on whether the frequency band used has its use restricted or not. The MNO (Mobile Network Operator) networks use an existing telephony network and include NB-IoT and LTE-M. They provide security and reliability at the expense of higher cost [2]. On the other hand, the main non-MNO networks are Sigfox and LoRaWAN, which have cost advantages but lose reliability [3].

Despite the fact that the characteristics of all the networks are very similar for the development of the project, we have chosen the Sigfox network, which has advantages when it comes to implementation and development, since its operation is not based on SIM cards such as in the case of NB-IoT or LTE-M.

Once the communications network has been chosen, the Arduino platform was chosen for the development of the prototype due to its simplicity and cost. Among other options the purchase of a device that was too expensive for the prototype or the development of an ad-hoc board which would entail a high time and cost were considered. Therefore, the Arduino MKR 1200 was selected because it comes with a Sigfox communications chip, which facilitates communication without adding an extra communication module and is affordable. A measuring sensor is incorporated to fulfil the functionality of reading the capacity value. In addition, the battery consumption is quite low.

Finally, for the development of the visualization platform you can choose between an own development or the use of a cloud service. The latter option is chosen for its advantages in terms of cost, maintenance, commissioning time, reliability, security, and scalability. Most of the companies that sell these services have specialized services in IoT. Among the three main ones are Amazon Web Services, Microsoft Azure and Google Cloud, but the use of the Microsoft Azure platform is chosen for the development of the prototype due to its wide range of tools specialized in IoT [4].

3   Description of the Developed System

After analyzing the different possibilities of implementation, it is determined that a prototype of the system based on the Sigfox communications network will be developed. The objective is to send the free capacity data from a device to a backend where it is processed, stored, analyzed and represented in a web application.

To make a correct volume measurement it is necessary to analyze the type of sensor that best fits this application. Among the three evaluated ones (i.e., weight sensor, infrared, and ultrasound) the ultrasound sensor is chosen due to its good performance and robustness of the measurement. Its main advantage is the conical shape of the wave with which it is possible to sweep the entire volume of the container in a precise manner, as opposed to the infrared sensor which has a linear wave. For the design and development of the prototype, we have chosen to use the SRFO4 model [5]. This sensor has been connected to an Arduino MKRFox 1200 board whose function is to interpret the sensor reading and send it to the backend through the Sigfox communications network (the board itself includes a chip to facilitate communications with the network [6]).

Two tests are carried out to check the correct operation of the device. In the first one, the ultrasound sensor is calibrated by making different measurements at known distances. It is checked that the theoretical formula 1 to obtain the distance as a function of the time between sending and receiving the wave [7] fits the obtained results, with a small measurement error that can be considered negligible as it does not affect the application.

$$D(m) = \frac{t(s)}{2 \times 343 \, \text{m/s}} \tag{1}$$

In the second test the device is subjected to real conditions inside a container. The aim is to determine whether there is interference with the walls due to the conical shape of the wave. It is observed that there is a small maximum error margin of 6 cm when the distance is less than 70 cm. Despite this, the operation is considered correct for the application as no high accuracy is required.

For the communications part, the network used is Sigfox, as it has already been mentioned. This network is characterized by working in the ISM band at 868 MHz and being a UNB (Ultra Narrow Band) technology having low transfer speeds, of the order of 10 to 1000 bits per second, but being able to cover large areas (reaching 25 km in open field) [6].

Being in a free band one of the main problems that appear is the security and reliability. To guarantee this, each message is repeated three times with different serial numbers, thus ensuring its correct reception [8], and limiting the maximum number of messages sent to 144 per day. [9]. Another of the main advantages of the network is that it allows the location of the containers geographically by means of triangulation, obtaining approximate coordinates in the Sigfox backend. As it has been proved during the development of the prototype, the location is obtained with too much margin of error (around 1 km) so the containers cannot be located based on Sigfox's triangulation.

The flow of information of the developed system is shown in Fig. 2. The Arduino MKRFox 1200 sends the data to the Sigfox backend. Then, the information is forwarded to the Microsoft Azure cloud platform that allows processing and visualization options. This will be done by means of a customised callback available in the Sigfox backend for connecting it to the Microsoft Azure IoT Hub. This callback is created by a HTTP Request of type 'text post' which sends a JSON file with the predefined variables to the IPs defined by the connection string of the previously created IoTHub device [10].

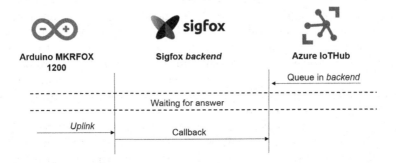

Fig. 2. Flow of information of the system

The variables sent in this callback are the capacity value received from the device, the real coordinates obtained by triangulation of the signal on the Sigfox platform, and the assumed coordinates where the container has to be found.

Finally, this information has to be processed, stored and analyzed. To do this, the Microsoft Azure platform will be used, which has tools that allow the data to be processed in a simple, secure, and scalable way at different levels. In addition, it enables the creation of a web application in which the user is able to see the real state of the free capacity of the containers as well as their representation on a map.

Figure 3 shows the flow of information at the back-end, as well as the tools used within Azure for the development of the web app. The information is ingested in the Azure platform through the specialized tool Azure IoT Hub, from where the message is forwarded to the tool Azure Time Series Insight, which allows a temporary display and processing of information. In addition, the tool Azure Blob Storage is also used to perform cold storage (timeless but slow access) and hot storage (with a duration of 7 days but fast access) which is fed by Azure Time Series Insights. Finally, using an API, Azure Maps makes a request for the information stored and processed in Azure Time Series Insights which will then use the visualization app developed.

The Azure IoT Hub tool acts as a message center between the application and the devices, allowing the ingestion of large volumes of telemetry data from the devices [11]. Its operation is based on the creation of virtual devices with their IP address that will be connected to the real devices.

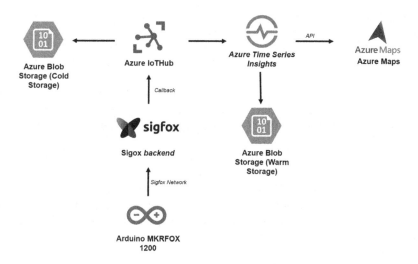

Fig. 3. Flow of information in the system (Color figure online)

Two different devices are created for the prototype: a real device that corresponds to the device previously created by means of the Arduino board; and a simulated device that will be used to facilitate the testing tasks and that will be created by means of a virtual machine inside Azure.

This virtual machine has a Python file that simulates the operation of the container device, sending random capacity values and predefined geographic coordinates. Using the connection string of the device created in Azure IoT Hub, it is possible to send the data every time the file is executed, achieving an identical behaviour to the real device.

Once the information has been received in Azure, it has to be stored. To do this the platform has the tool Azure Blob Storage that stores the information in the form of so-called blobs (data structures that do not adhere to any particular data model or definition like text or binary data [12]). Within this tool, two types of storage will be used. On the one hand, a cold storage will be used, which allows a timeless use of the information, although it has a slower access to it. The routing of this information will be done by means of a text message brokering, which consists of assigning a text endpoint to the container for storing the information [13]. On the other hand, all the information is going to be stored in a hot storage for a period of 7 days, since the tool Azure Time Series Insights needs a quick access to the data that is only achieved with the hot storage.

To perform temporary processing and to be able to view the data, the use of another Azure tool is required: Azure Time Series Insights. This module is responsible for the collection, processing, analysis and consultation of data obtained from the containers. It is designed mainly for the needs of the industrial IoT, with tools such as multilayer storage, time series modelling, or low-cost queries [14].

For the configuration of this tool, it has been taken into account that the environment used is PAYG (Pay-as-you-go) [15], where the payment is based on the data input, the time series are identified based on the device ID of each device and a hot storage will be created to store the information so that it can be processed efficiently.

The last tool used is Azure Maps that provides geospatial functionalities by using maps with the objective of providing a geographic context for the application of the container [16]. The subscription is free and only has a cost when the number of requests is very high.

The final objective of the system is to be able to know the volume status of the containers in real time in order to optimize the collection routes. That is why it is necessary to develop a front-end or web application through which the user is able to visualize the information and manipulate it in a simple way. The development of it has been based on the Microsoft project Azure IoT Workshop: Real-Time Asset Tracking [17]. The web application is developed in an HTML environment to which several functionalities have been applied using Javascript. Many of these functionalities have been based on Azure Maps' Microsft SDK examples' [18]. To obtain the data, both spatial and temporal, an API call to the Azure Time Series Insights and Azure Maps is used.

The main functionalities of the application are the obtaining of the capacity data, the location of the containers in a map, the visual representation of the state by means of a colour code, the representation of temporal graphics that show the evolution, and the creation of routes between the points that need to be collected (Fig. 4).

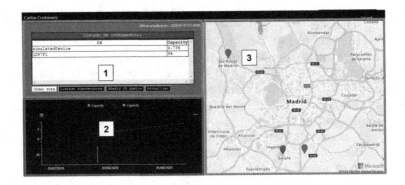

Fig. 4. Web application

In the web application shown in the Fig. 3, three different areas can be distinguished:

- a user interface in which the containers and their capacity are visualised and some buttons that allow access to the different options of the application (zone 1 - green);
- a zone where the temporal evolution of the different containers is shown (zone 2 - blue);
- and a map in which the containers and their capacity are geographically represented based on a colour code (zone 3 - yellow).

The basic functioning of the application is shown in the diagram represented in Fig. 5. When the application is executed, the capacity and location data are obtained from Azure Time Series Insigts and with them the marks are created on the map, the values are written in the user interface table, and the time series are drawn. At this moment the program remains in a waiting position until a button is pressed in the user interface that executes some functionality of the application.

If the button 'Create route' is pressed, a route is created going through all those containers whose free capacity value is lower than 20%, starting and ending in the Getafe base ship. This route is represented on a map and in the table of the user interface the containers appear in order of collection. Pressing the button 'container list' will return to the initial table showing all containers regardless of whether they have exceeded their capacity limit or not.

To check the correct operation of the application the option to 'Add 20 points' has been added which creates 20 bins with a random capacity. Finally, the 'Update' button repeats the reading process and executes the application with the last values obtained.

4 Validation of the Developed System

The aim of this paper is to carry out an initial analysis of the viability of the Caritas project to monitor the clothing containers that are distributed throughout the Community of Madrid. The final objective is, therefore, to validate the future implementation of a system that will allow the organization to improve the efficiency in the collection of clothes from the containers through digitalization. In this section, a functional validation of the prototype will be carried out by analysing the possible areas of improvement for the different components of the system.

For the design of the hardware device, the choice of the ultrasound sensor is considered correct since it carries out measurements with sufficient precision and the conical geometry of the wave makes it ideal for the container. It has also been proven that the 3 m range of the sensor used [5] is sufficient for the 2 m height of the container and in the tests carried out it has been shown that there is no negative influence of the container. There is a margin of error when the distance is less than 70% that can reach an absolute error of 6 cm. In order to improve the device, an ultrasonic sensor with better precision can be used, although this would increase the cost of the device.

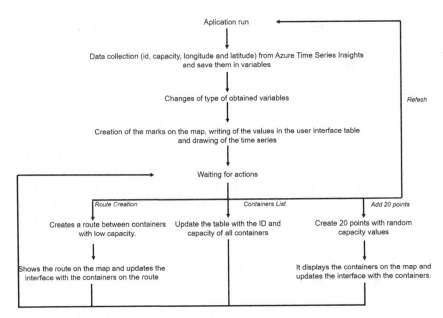

Fig. 5. Diagram of how the web application works

As communication network we have chosen to use LPWAN networks that offer a long range at the cost of decreasing the bandwidth. For the application of the project, where it is intended to make one or two shipments per day of little weight, this is not an impediment. We have opted for the use of the LPWAN Sigfox network. The main problem found during the development has been the loss of messages. In areas where there is good coverage the message was sent and received, but in other trials where coverage has been reduced there has been loss of messages. This is a very serious error to be taken into account as it can cause serious problems for the organization by overlooking containers that are full on the collection routes, making the system unusable. To solve this problem there are several possible solutions. On the one hand, it is possible to opt for the creation of a downlink communication when a message is expected but not received, thus ensuring a re-sending of the data when it has not been sent correctly, ensuring the correct communication. Another option consists in the implementation of signal repeaters near the containers where the coverage is low in order to ensure a good communication.

On the other hand, it has also been purchased that the device coordinates obtained during the development of the prototype by the platform are very inaccurate in cases of good coverage (obtaining an error of more than 1 Km) and null in areas where coverage is low. This makes it impossible to use the location of the network to determine the position of the containers. As a solution to this problem, the prototype has been developed so that each container ID is associated with a geographic coordinate. In this way the location obtained by

Sigfox is only used in case the container is stolen and the distance has been much higher.

Anyway, the network meets the system requirements in terms of bandwidth and coverage in all areas and has the advantage of allowing a two-way communication (although more limited [9]) in case it is necessary to communicate with the device. It also has a lower cost associated with the rest of the communication networks. The Sigfox back-end itself receives all the messages and is able to redirect them automatically to the Azure back-end. It has been verified that there is a certain delay of 1 min between the sending of the Sigfox back-end and the Azure platform, which does not exist when the sending is done from the virtual machine with the simulated device. Anyway, this delay is not an important issue and during the tests carried out no message was lost.

For the storage and processing of the data, the use of a cloud platform has been chosen over the development of an own back-end because of its advantages in terms of reliability, maintenance, and scalability. The tools Azure IoT Hub, Azure Time Series Insights, Azure Blob Storage and Azure Maps from Microsoft Azure have been used and integrated to receive, process and store the capacity data sent both from the developed device and from the device simulated with the virtual machine. The results obtained are very good as they are tools that allow easy integration at a low cost and high scalability.

The core of the project is the web application since it is the tool that the user is going to use to know the volume of the containers in real time and to be able to plan routes accordingly. To check the correct functioning, a test mode has been developed that creates 20 containers with a random capacity between 0 and 100%. In this mode the program is also capable of creating routes by selecting only those containers whose free capacity is less than 20%.

Among the necessary future extensions required by the application is the development of optimal routes. The routes obtained in this first version follow an order of creation based on a list that is not optimal, since this would need the algorithms that go beyond the scope of a first validation of the project.

Finally, it is checked that the prototype meets the project requirements of being able to provide the organization with a system to monitor the free capacity of the used clothing containers in order to create optimal routes and improve the efficiency of the collection system. This system has a low economic cost since the associated costs of the hardware, communication network and back-end have been optimized. It has a user-friendly user interface so that the application is accessible to staff in the organization with any type of qualification. In addition, it is highly adaptable and scalable thanks to the use of cloud platforms that allow modifications to be made easily without the need to alter the system.

5   Conclusions and Future Work

Cáritas Madrid currently has around 165 containers distributed throughout the Community of Madrid in which second-hand clothes are collected for people at risk of social exclusion. In order to achieve greater efficiency in the collection of these containers, a system has been developed to monitor the free capacity for the remaining clothes. In this paper an initial analysis of this system is carried out.

Two phases have been followed in order to carry out this analysis: from an analysis of the technological state of the system to the development of a small-scale prototype and its functional validation for the application.

At first, an exhaustive study has been made of the technological state of this type of technology. For this purpose, the different suppliers of this type of system have been compared, determining what characteristics they have in common (mainly battery power and the use of an ultrasonic sensor to measure the free capacity). An analysis has also been made of what the different technologies are, in the case of a system developed ad-hoc, which are suited to the project at the level of hardware, communications system and backend. Finally, the use of the ultrasound sensor and the Sigfox communications network is determined.

A prototype is developed that has the three functional parts of this system: a device that performs the measurement, a communications network through which to send this information, and a platform on which to process, store and display the information in real time.

The objective of the development of the prototype is the creation of a test environment in which to test the functionality of this system with a view to future massive deployment. It has been proven that the implementation of a technological system that allows the collection of clothing containers in a more efficient way can bring many advantages to a non-profit organization such as Cáritas.

On the one hand, the image of the organization would be improved. Currently one of the main problems they have is that the clothes are not collected in the containers and end up accumulating in bags on the outside of them. This creates a bad image of the organization and the theft of the best clothes. This system would prevent accumulation and improve the image of the NGO.

On the other hand, it would also make more efficient use of the organisation's resources. Another problem they have is collecting containers that are still empty. With the help of the system implemented, the routes could be optimized to collect only those containers whose capacity is equivalent to 80%, achieving a reduction in the number of them. This would imply an economic saving, since it would mean a lower expense in fuel and personnel that carry out the routes, and a redistribution of the human resources to tasks where they can contribute a greater value to the organization managing to create a greater impact to the society.

With this project we want to demonstrate that the impact of digitalization and technological development can be applied to all sectors of society. A non-profit organization can also benefit greatly by applying new technologies to its humanitarian work.

Among the main future works it is the implementation and development of the complete system. In addition, it will be important to develop an algorithm with which to achieve route optimization.

In the long term, it is necessary to study the viability of the project with the company and to begin the development with a pilot phase in which possible problems can be solved. This is when a large scale implementation will be made causing a great benefit for Cáritas.

Acknowledgements. This project has been carried out thanks to the collaboration between the NGO Cáritas Madrid that raises the problem, the Fundación Ingenieros ICAI that channels the problem and tries to give an answer to it and the Universidad Pontificia Comillas with which this master's final project is carried out to give a solution.

It could not have been possible to carry out this work without the support of the director of the Master thesis, Gregorio López López, who has assisted at all times by giving technological and creative support to the work. We also thank Sergio González Jiménez for his collaboration as co-director.

We would also like to thank Marta Reina, manager of Fundación Ingenieros ICAI, for her actions to achieve the project and her role as a mediator between the student and the NGO.

References

1. Mekki, K., Bajic, E., Chaxel, F., Meyer, F.: A comparative study of LPWAN technologies for large-scale IoT deployment. Technical report, The Korean Institute of Communications and Information Sciences (2018)
2. Ligero, R.: Diferencias entre NB-IoT y LTE-M. In: Accent Systems, May 2018. https://accent-systems.com/es/blog/diferencias-nb-iot-lte-m/
3. Ray, B.: Sigfox vs. LoRa: a comparison between technologies = Business models. In: Link Labs, May 2018. https://www.link-labs.com/blog/sigfoxvs-lora
4. Miguel, J., Vañó, Á.: Modelo Comparativo de Plataformas Cloud y Evaluación de Microsoft Azure, Google App Engine y Amazon EC2. Trabajo de fin de grado, Grado en Ingeniería Informática. Escola Tècnica Superior d'Enginyeria Informàtica, Universitat Politècnica de València (2018)
5. Documentación del sensor de ultrasonidos SRF04. SRF04. http://www.robotelectronics.co.uk/htm/srf04tech.htm
6. Aprendiendo Arduino: Sigfox. https://www.aprendiendoarduino.com/2018/03/05/arduino-y-sigfox/. Aprendiendo con arduino. March 2018
7. Llamas, L.: Medir distancia con Arduino y sensor de ultrasonidos HCSR04, June 2015. https://www.luisllamas.es/medir-distancia-conarduino-y-sensor-de-ultrasonidos-hc-sr04/
8. Todo lo que necesitas saber sobre la seguridad de Sigfox. https://www.wndgroup.io/2017/02/17/todo-lo-que-necesitas-saber-sobre-la-seguridad-de-sigfox/. WND Group
9. Sigfox: Asses your project's needs. https://build.sigfox.com/study
10. Sigfox documentation: Callback Api. https://backend.sigfox.com/apidocs/callback
11. Microsft Azure Documentation: Azure IoT Hub: Qué es Azure IoT Hub? https://docs.microsoft.com/es-es/azure/iot-hub/about-iot-hub. Microsoft Azure. August 2019
12. Microsft Azure Documentation: Introducción a Azure Blob Storage. https://docs.microsoft.com/es-es/azure/storage/blobs/storage-blobs-introduction. Microsoft Azure. August 2019

13. Jiménez, S.G.: Azure IoT Hands on Lab. IoT - Universidad Pontificia Comillas ICAI, Madrid, November 2020. https://github.com/SeryioGonzalez/azure-iot

14. Microsft Azure Documentation: Azure Time Series Insights: Qué es la versión preliminar de Azure Time Series Insights? https://docs.microsoft.com/es-es/azure/time-series-insights/time-series-insights-update-overview. Microsoft Azure. August 2019

15. Documentación Microsoft Azure: Detalles de precios de Azure Time Series Insights. https://azure.microsoft.com/es-es/pricing/details/time-series-insights/. Microsoft

16. Microsft Azure Documentation. Azure Maps. Qué es Azure Maps?. https://docs.microsoft.com/es-es/azure/azure-maps/about-azure-maps. Microsoft Azure. January 2020

17. Microsft Azure Documentation. Azure IoT Workshop. Real-Time Asset Tracking. https://github.com/Azure/iot-workshop-asset-tracking. Microsoft Azure

18. Azure Maps Web SDK Samples. https://azuremapscodesamples.azurewebsites.net/. Microsoft

Smart City Tools to Evaluate Age-Healthy Environments

Irene Lebrusán[1]([⊠])(iD) and Jamal Toutouh[2](iD)

[1] Universidad Complutense de Madrid, TRANSOC, Madrid, Spain
ilebrusa@ucm.es
[2] Massachusetts Institute of Technology, CSAIL, Cambridge, MA, USA
toutouh@mit.edu

Abstract. The urban population is aging and the elderly people desire to *age in place* and to continue in the environments chosen by them. Accordingly, the environment should be healthy-age orientated, improving health and fulfilling the United Nations Global Goals, including the aging-related ones. Using the case study of Madrid, the biggest city in Spain, this research analyzes the quality of the spaces to grow old in terms of environmental health. To do so, we have selected a number of variables, drawing on open data provided by the city council, using an age-oriented perspective. We propose a comparative analysis of the 21 districts in Madrid in terms of air pollution, noise, urban fitment adapted to moderate physical activity, and green spaces in the city, as those are very important aspects for healthy aging. According to our results, central areas of the downtown of Madrid offer a worse potential quality of life in terms of the environment than peripheral areas.

Keywords: Smart governance · Elderly · Aging in place · Environmental analysis

1 Introduction

The increase of life expectancy, along with a series of economic and social improvements, has led to changes in both the meaning and the manner of experiencing old age. Among the manifestations of these changes, one of the most relevant is the desire to remain independent in the known environment until a very advanced age [6,9,13]. The idea of *aging in place* comprises the continuity of the elderly in society, and more specifically, in the social environment known and chosen by them. However, for this to be possible, the environment has to fulfill several characteristics, allowing their participation into society, not posing barriers and, above all, in healthy conditions.

Ensuring an enabling and supportive environment to achieve the highest possible level of health and well-being for the elderly was pointed out in the Madrid International Plan of Action on Aging and in the Political Declaration adopted at the Second World Assembly on Aging in April 2002 [25]. More recently, specific attention to age in cities was taken as part of the Sustainable

© Springer Nature Switzerland AG 2021
S. Nesmachnow and L. Hernández Callejo (Eds.): ICSC-CITIES 2020, CCIS 1359, pp. 285–301, 2021.
https://doi.org/10.1007/978-3-030-69136-3_20

Development Goal. The *target 11.7* points that, by 2030, cities will provide universal access to safe, inclusive and accessible, green, and public spaces, for vulnerable population groups, specifically including the elderly among them. Besides, the *target 11.6* notes the commitment to reduce the adverse *per capita* environmental impact of cities by paying special attention to air quality by 2030, that, as we exposed before [11,12] is especially harmful to the elderly. This international commitment is a great advance, as the environment plays an important role in determining how we age and how we respond to disease, loss of function, and other forms of loss and adversity that we may experience at different stages of life, and particularly in later years [29].

But, could cities fulfill this road map? Are our cities a healthy space to grow old? And, how can we evaluate this? The use of digital technologies allow the design of smarter cities, addressing numerous challenges, such as environmental pressures, energy efficiency, and sustainability, or improving urban mobility, among others. But, besides, smart cities can provide a series of tools to advance knowledge of the well-being of the different age groups needs, and especially, the urban lacks as their inhabitants grow older, i.e., Open Data, Smart Governance, and the Internet of Things.

We selected Madrid as a case study to measure the capacity of Spain to achieve the referred international commitments. While it is not the most aged municipality in the country, it is the biggest city and so, it has the largest amount population over 65 years old. Since Madrid city has a greater number and amount of resources than other cities, it would be expected a high level of compliance with age-friendly environments. As there are not recognized specific guidelines of what an age-friendly environment should accomplish, or even explicit indicators with an age perspective to measure the quality of aging in cities, this research raises its own proposal. We use open data gathered by different sensors and other variables provided by the Council of Madrid to evaluate how adequate an environment is for aging, and thus, detect in which areas will be necessary to implement measures leading to healthy aging.

Thus, the main contributions of this work are: *i)* evaluating the possibility of using the provided open data to assess elderly people well-being in our cities, *ii)* assessing different variables that allow observing which districts are healthy for the elderly people; and *iii)* using such information to review the situation of Madrid in terms of age-friendly environments.

The rest of the paper is organized as follows: In the next section, we describe the importance of aging in place, paying especial attention to the effect of the environment for healthy aging. Section 3 introduces the context of our use case and the materials and methods used in this analysis. The evaluation of the air quality and noise based on the shared open data is shown in Sect. 4. Finally, Sect. 5 presents the conclusions and the main lines of future work.

2   Towards Healthy and Inclusive Aging: Spaces Matters

Older adults' well-being is strongly linked to the residential environment, where the older population generally spend more time than the younger population [4]. Accordingly, cities should create healthy and age-friendly environments. A space is age-friendly when they are accessible, equitable, inclusive, safe and secure, and supportive. Besides, we consider they should be healthy in terms of pollution and offering active mobility and moderate exercise possibilities.

2.1 The Importance of *Place* and Place Attachment while Aging

Place attachment is explained as a set of feelings about a geographic location that emotionally binds a person to that place as a function of its role as a setting for the experience [21]. Attachment to space has a strong connection with the *identity of place*, which implies the incorporation of place into the broad concept of self [17].

The place and the known environment are fundamental in the processes of identity and self-definition of the self [17,26], becoming part of the social representation [14]. It acquires a great influence in old age, being a key element in the quality of life and well-being [15,20] that contributes to situate identity in old age [16,19]. This explains why elderly people desire and choose to live in their environment, where they feel they *belong*, as long as they can, and if it is possible, until their death. Thus, the environment has to provide minimum health conditions. Otherwise, problems such as the absence of green spaces or pollution will have an even more negative effect during old age, when the influence of the environment on well-being is greater [8].

2.2 Environment Influence on a Healthy Aging

Older adults are often at risk for increased vulnerability to noise pollution due to slower mental processing and sensory changes that take place in the aging process [2]. They are also more vulnerable than other age groups to the exposure to air pollutants, which may even be fatal [22]. As we have pointed out in previous works, the elderly are more susceptible to suffer from urban pollution (as NO_2) and lack of public space [11,12]. Specifically, air pollution, which caused more than 400,000 premature deaths in 2016, is considered the top health hazard in the European Union (EU) [5] affecting all ages, but being some groups more vulnerable, as the older population. It is considered carcinogenic and causes infertility and diabetes Type 2 [18] and it is linked to obesity, systemic inflammation, aging, Alzheimer's disease, and dementia [5]. It affects the brain in the same way that Alzheimer's does as it causes changes in the structure of the brain [30].

Noise pollution, which causes annually at least 16,600 cases of premature death in Europe [28], is the major preventable cause of hearing loss [1]. It also affects the cardiovascular system and causes hypertension [1,23]. Finally, sound pollution can also cause a range of non-auditory problems, like annoyance, sleep disturbance, and cognitive performance [23].

In relation to this, nature can contribute both directly and indirectly to control pollutants, as the green infrastructure has a natural capacity to directly act as a barrier and remove air pollutants from the atmosphere through gaseous absorption or dry deposition. Vegetation can impede noise propagation by absorbing or diffracting [3]. Accordingly, a bigger presence if green areas would be positive for the elderly.

2.3   The Compromise with Sustainable Development Goals in Terms of Urban Aging

The Sustainable Development Goals (SDGs) were adopted by all United Nations Member States in 2015 as a universal call to action to end poverty, protect the planet, and ensure that all people enjoy peace and prosperity by 2030. Preparing for an aging population is vital to the achievement of the integrated 2030 Agenda, with aging cutting across the goals on poverty eradication, good health, gender equality, economic growth and decent work, reduced inequalities, and sustainable cities [7]. Regarding the people aging in cities, the SDGs establish that: "By 2030, provide universal access to safe, inclusive and accessible public spaces and green areas, in particular for women and children, older persons and persons with disabilities". More specifically, *target 11.7* focuses on access to green spaces and safe public spaces. Regarding the air quality, the *target 11.6* establish that, by 2030, reduce the adverse per capita environmental impact of cities, including by paying special attention to air quality, municipal and other waste management

These applications can make all the difference in the quality of life for elderly patients who want to continue living at home independently and provide peace of mind for their family members [27].

Finally, the consideration of the environment and urban space in terms of age is fundamental to evaluate the capacity of potential integration and adaptation of cities to the needs of their inhabitants.

3   Materials and Methods

In this section, first, we introduce Madrid as our case study and, second, we present the methodology applied to evaluate the quality of the urban space in the city of Madrid to grow old in terms of environmental health. Since there are no specific guidelines to operationalize what an age-friendly environment should accomplish, we propose our definition of it. To do so, and after considering the theoretical definition summarized in Sect. 2 and the information available, we have selected different indicators applicable to the dimensions of environmental well-being from an old-age perspective.

3.1   Madrid Information

The city of Madrid has 21 districts which are further subdivided into 131 neighborhoods. The districts are territorial divisions of the municipality, equipped with decentralized management bodies in order to facilitate the governance of such a big city. These administrative bodies have the purpose to promote and develop citizen participation in the management of municipal affairs. These districts are very different from an urban perspective (as a result of different construction stages) but also in terms of wealth and quality of life. We are specifically interested in analyzing if there is also a difference in the quality of the environment to age in place.

Table 1 summarizes some demographic information and the surface area data (in hectares) of the 21 districts of Madrid. Figure 1 shows the territorial divisions of the city of Madrid into districts. Regarding the distribution of the densities by districts, Madrid reflects a high dispersion (see Fig. 1 and Table 1) with a central area more densely populated and a peripheral area with lower population density. Specifically, the most densely populated districts are Chamberí, Tetuan, Salamanca, Centro, and Arganzuela. These districts are older and more consolidated in urban terms. The group of districts that present a density well below the Madrid average are Fuencarral-El Pardo, Moncloa-Aravaca (both including protected green areas) and Villa de Vallecas, Vicálvaro, and Barajas (spaces with growth expectations in terms of urbanization).

Table 1. Total population, population older than 65 years old, population older than 80, and district surface in ha. per district

Id.	District name	Population	Older than 65	Older than 80	Surface (ha)
1	Centro	140473	22006	7249	522.82
2	Arganzuela	155660	30411	9863	646.22
3	Retiro	120406	31227	10332	546.62
4	Salamanca	147854	35151	12707	539.24
5	Chamartín	147551	34443	12081	917.55
6	Tetuán	161313	30723	11365	537.47
7	Chamberí	140866	33855	12025	467.92
8	Fuencarral-El Pardo	249973	52164	1536	23783.84
9	Moncloa-Aravaca	121683	26543	9108	4653.11
10	Latina	242139	58967	2158	2542.72
11	Carabanchel	260196	48920	18149	1404.83
12	Usera	142894	23853	9352	777.77
13	Puente de Vallecas	240867	42270	16109	1496.86
14	Moratalaz	95614	24822	9768	610.32
15	Ciudad Lineal	219867	49803	18871	1142.57
16	Hortaleza	193264	35788	10926	2741.98
17	Villaverde	154318	26063	9805	2018.76
18	Villa de Vallecas	114512	14406	4139	5146.72
19	Vicalvaro	74048	10639	3594	3526.67
20	San Blas-Canillejas	161222	28034	10942	2229.24
21	Barajas	50010	8955	2231	4192.28
	Madrid	3334730	669043	235556	60445.51

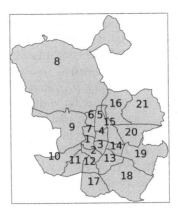

Fig. 1. Map of Madrid with the districts ids.

Regarding the aging of districts, they are also clearly different (see Fig. 2.a). In general terms, the core area and bordering zone is more aged (in some districts, as Retiro, almost 26% of population is over 65 years old, being Moratalaz the district with the highest percentage of people over 65 years old in the city). In the face of this, the districts in the periphery, less populated and with newer buildings, present a higher volume of young couples with children (Villa de Vallecas and Vicálvaro) and where, accordingly, the older population has a lower demographic weight. The case of the demographic pyramid of Centro is a deviation as is characterized by a young immigrant population. In each district, the older population is feminized, as women's life expectancy is higher (87.16 years).

When analyzing "the aging of the aging" or the over aging (the proportion of people older than 80 years over the total population older than 65 years) in Fig. 2, we can see that Moratalaz, Usera, and San Blas-Canillejas are the districts with a bigger percentage of "old-elderly". In comparison, Barajas, Villa

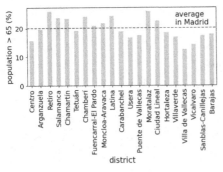
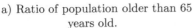
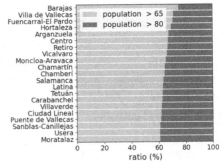

a) Ratio of population older than 65 years old.

b) Ratio of elderly older than 80 over the population older than 65 years old.

Fig. 2. Madrid main demographic information by district.

de Vallecas, and Fuencarral-El Pardo have a smaller proportion of people over 80 years old. In terms of needs and health frailty, the demographic composition can be important for our analysis, as the areas with the oldest population would have a greater need of an age-friendly environment.

3.2 Methodology Applied

One of the aims of this research is to prove how useful are Smart City tools, such as Smart Governance and open data, to assess how healthy are our cities to grow old. In this case, we use the data provided by the Open Data Portal (ODP) offered by the Madrid City Council (https://datos.madrid.es/). This data source has shown be useful for different kinds of studies [10, 24].

To evaluate and compare the quality of the districts to grow old, and considering the aspects highlighted in Sect. 2, we have selected four key dimensions: the availability of green areas, the availability of urban fitment areas to optimize physical activity in old age, the air quality (considering NO_2) and the pollution in terms of noise.

Availability of the Green Areas. The ODP provides the surface in hectares (ha) of the green spaces in the districts. Green spaces, including community gardens, allotments, and forests are an important factor in community identity and can strengthen people's attachment to their communities. Green infrastructure and accessible green space are important factors for individuals and communities to establish a 'sense of place' and 'ownership' of their local landscape [3]. Thus, we evaluated the number of ha per 10000 inhabitants and the number of ha per 10000 elderly people. This allows the analysis of whether there are a fair distribution and access to green areas for all age groups in the city.

Urban Fitment for Old Age. This refers to different facilities and furniture to practice moderate physical activity, as equipment to exercise fingers and wrists or arms, pedal, for waist movement, stairs, and ramp, among other fitments more complex. All those are adapted to different needs and to optimize mobility in later life. The data used for our analysis provide the number and the location of the urban fitment. Thus, we have evaluated the access to those urban elements as the number of urban facilities per 10000 elderly people.

Air Quality. OPD provides the hourly mean concentration of several air pollutants: sulfur dioxide (SO_2), nitrogen dioxide (NO_2), ozone (O_3), carbon monoxide (CO), particulate matter (PM_{10} and $PM_{2.5}$). However, there is no information about all the pollutants in the 21 districts. The pollutant with information that covers more districts is the NO_2, there are sensors in 18 districts. The other pollutants have much less data, e.g., $PM_{2.5}$ is sensed just in six locations of Madrid. Thus, as NO_2 has been proven the major health concern in our cities and it is the one that provides more spatial information, we evaluate NO_2 concentration as a metric of air quality.

Noise Pollution. WHO puts traffic-related noise as the second most harmful environmental factor in Europe, right after air pollution. Thus, we include it in our analysis. The noise pollution data provided by the OPD includes the daily mean of the equivalent sound pressure levels. These data are gathered by sound-meters installed in 31 locations covering 19 districts (excluding Ciudad Lineal and San Blas-Canillejas). Regarding the equivalent sound pressure levels (measured in A-weighted decibels, dBA), we take into account: L_{eq}, that averages the noise measured during the whole day (24 h); L_d, which is evaluated during the day (from 7:00 h to 19:00 h); L_e, which asses the noise during the evening (from 19:00 h to 23:00 h); and L_e, which measures the noise at night (from 23:00 h to 7:00 h). We evaluated these noise levels because noise at different periods of time may have different impacts on the well-being of the elderly.

4   Results and Discussion

This section evaluates the quality of the environment of the different districts of Madrid in terms of the availability of green areas, urban fitment for old age, air quality and, noise levels, based on the data available. These aspects cannot be ignored in the analysis of the individual well-being of the elderly.

4.1   Availability of the Green Areas

Table 2 ranks the evaluated districts according to the number of ha of green areas available per 10000 elderly (green area ratio). The third column takes into account the whole population. The second column express which proportion would be available for the elderly having in consideration the total potential green space users in the district. Figure 3 illustrates the spatial evaluation of this metric. In this case, darker green indicates more ha per elderly (better districts according to that metric).

As we can see in Fig. 3, the *central almond* offers less green space to the elderly, while newer areas, less dense in terms of urbanization, offer a better rate. It is important to remark that the three best districts in terms of this metric are not the ones that provide the largest green area per inhabitant (see Table 2). Villa de Vallecas is the district that provides the largest green area per inhabitant, but the fifth if we take into account just the elderly. Finally, it is noticeable the differences between the best and the worst district, since Barajas provides about 20 times more green areas for the elderly than Chamberí.

Madrid has a rich and extensive green heritage, highlighting its parks and gardens, both historical and advanced garden design. Central areas are not offering enough green areas to their (older) residents, while this lack of green spaces seems not to be a problem in the peripheral areas.

Table 2. Ranking taking into account the availability of the green areas.

Ranking	District	ha/10000 elderly	ha/10000 inhabitants
1	Barajas	3.54	19.76
2	Moncloa-Aravaca	3.45	15.80
3	Moratalaz	3.25	12.53
4	Vicálvaro	3.24	22.55
5	Villa de Vallecas	3.14	24.92
6	Hortaleza	3.02	16.30
7	Fuencarral-El Pardo	2.97	14.23
8	Latina	2.77	11.39
9	Villaverde	2.36	13.97
10	Puente de Vallecas	2.04	11.65
11	Usera	1.95	11.71
12	San Blas-Canillejas	1.74	10.00
13	Carabanchel	1.67	8.87
14	Ciudad Lineal	1.36	6.02
15	Arganzuela	1.12	5.74
16	Chamartín	0.87	3.73
17	Retiro	0.79	3.07
18	Tetuán	0.75	3.92
19	Salamanca	0.57	2.41
20	Centro	0.38	2.42
21	Chamberí	0.19	0.77

4.2 Urban Fitment for Old Age

Table 3 ranks the evaluated districts according to the number of ha of fitment elements available per 10000 old people. Figure 4 illustrates the spatial evaluation of this metric. In this case, darker blue indicates more (better) fitment equipment per old people.

As it happens with the previous index (availability of the green areas) the peripheral districts are in better-compared position. Barajas, Usera, and Villaverde are in better positions, all over 67 facilities per 10000 older citizens. The difference between the best positioned and the worst positioned districts is noticeable because the first ones have about three times more elements than the worst ones. Salamanca, Ciudad Lineal, Latina, Retiro, Chamberí, Fuencarral-El Pardo, and Chamartín are all below 20 per 10000 people over 65 years old.

Given the importance of enhancing physical activity in old age, most districts should invest in this type of facility. There is a clear inequality in the number of fitment elements per elderly an in some districts are really scarce.

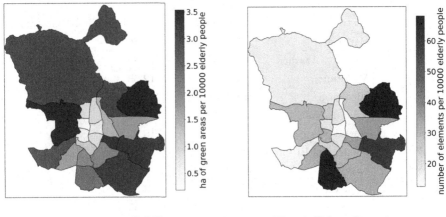

Fig. 3. Green areas availability map.   **Fig. 4.** Urban fitment map.

Table 3. Ranked according to the number of fitment elements per 10000 elderly.

Ranking	District	Number of urban fitment facilities per 10000 elderly
1	Barajas	68.12
2	Usera	67.50
3	Villaverde	67.14
4	Vicálvaro	59.22
5	Moratalaz	34.65
6	San Blas-Canillejas	34.60
7	Villa de Vallecas	31.93
8	Carabanchel	31.68
9	Centro	30.90
10	Moncloa-Aravaca	30.14
11	Puente de Vallecas	29.81
12	Tetuán	26.04
13	Hortaleza	25.71
14	Arganzuela	21.05
15	Chamartín	18.58
16	Fuencarral-El Pardo	17.83
17	Chamberí	17.72
18	Retiro	17.61
19	Latina	15.09
20	Ciudad Lineal	13.45
21	Salamanca	12.52

4.3   Air Quality

Table 4 ranks the evaluated districts regarding the air quality (less NO_2 concentration). Figure 4 illustrates the spatial evaluation of this metric and the dots locate the sensors. NA in Table 4 and white shape in Fig. 5 indicates that there is not open data about pollution in that districts, i.e, Latina, and Vicálvaro .

Table 4. NO_2 concentration levels in terms of $\mu g/m^3$.

Ranking	District	NO_2 concentration
1	Moncloa-Aravaca	20.59
2	Retiro	24.85
3	Fuencarral-El Pardo	25.60
4	Hortaleza	31.00
5	Barajas	33.14
6	Arganzuela	33.65
7	San Blas-Canillejas	34.29
8	Ciudad Lineal	34.29
9	Puente de Vallecas	35.90
10	Moratalaz	35.99
11	Chamberí	36.16
12	Tetuán	36.82
13	Villa de Vallecas	36.83
14	Centro	37.95
15	Chamartín	38.04
16	Villaverde	39.23
17	Carabanchel	42.87
18	Salamanca	51.40
19	Usera	53.47
20	Latina	NA
21	Vicalvaro	NA

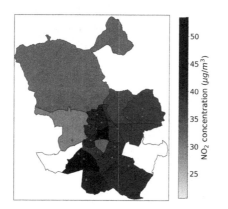

Fig. 5. NO_2 concentration levels map. The dots illustrate the sensors locations.

The results in Table 4 show that there is an important difference among districts. The best air quality is presented Moncloa-Aravaca, followed by Retiro, i.e., the north-west area (see Fig. 5. This could be seen as the (comparatively) best districts to the elderly in terms of air quality. Those are coincident with the presence of the so-called *lungs of Madrid* as *Parque del Retiro*, *Parque del Oeste* or the *Dehesa de la villa*, among others.

The south-east and the central area, as Usera, Salamanca, Carabanchel, or Villaverde districts, register a much worse air quality, with more than twice NO_2 concentration than Moncloa-Aravaca.

In general, Madrid presents a health problem regarding NO_2 concentration in the air [11]. Thus, measures should be taken to improve the air quality to avoid health problems for the population of that city.

4.4   Outdoor Noise Levels

Table 5 summarizes the information about the outdoor noise pollution gathered by the sensors installed in the city. Fig. 6 a, b, and c illustrate the noise pollution by showing the L_d, L_e, and L_n levels, respectively. As there are no information about the levels of noise in Ciudad Lineal and San Blas-Canillejas, they are shown in the table as NA and in the maps, their shape is in white.

Table 5. Noise levels evaluated in terms of dBA. The districts are ranked according to the noise level (L_{eq}).

Ranking	District	L_{eq}	L_d	L_e	L_n
1	Moncloa-Aravaca	53.54	54.81	53.82	48.68
2	Arganzuela	54.36	54.88	56.44	49.06
3	Vicalvaro	56.25	57.75	55.94	50.80
4	Villaverde	56.80	57.24	58.96	51.23
5	Fuencarral-El Pardo	57.60	58.89	58.19	51.83
6	Puente de Vallecas	58.35	59.33	58.20	52.32
7	Barajas	59.06	60.28	59.52	54.76
8	Carabanchel	60.14	61.20	61.06	55.17
9	Tetuán	60.17	61.06	61.90	54.34
10	Moratalaz	60.39	61.81	60.36	53.63
11	Hortaleza	61.38	62.83	62.92	52.64
12	Centro	61.67	62.68	62.66	56.88
13	Latina	62.57	63.95	63.19	57.18
14	Chamberí	62.80	63.92	63.43	58.70
15	Villa de Vallecas	62.90	64.05	63.55	59.04
16	Usera	63.35	64.36	64.23	59.79
17	Salamanca	64.31	65.12	65.12	60.58
18	Chamartín	65.84	66.94	66.46	61.88
19	Retiro	68.77	69.53	69.40	66.23
20	Ciudad Lineal	NA	NA	NA	NA
21	San Blas-Canillejas	NA	NA	NA	NA

As we can see in Table 5 and Fig. 6, noise levels during the day, evening, and night follow a pretty similar behavior in each district, with slight variations in some districts. This means that even at night inhabitants suffer from high levels of noise, which negatively affects their health. The noisiest areas are in the city center, with some exceptions (and some noisy districts) in the south area.

It is important to note that most of the evaluated districts suffer from noise levels higher than 55 dBA, which is the threshold of being considerate harmful for humans [28]. Thus, as it happens with air pollution, measures should be taken to improve such a hazardous situation [12].

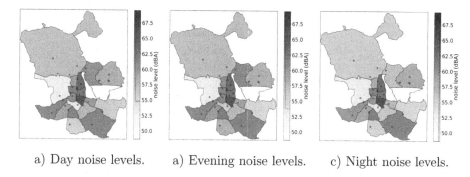

a) Day noise levels.   a) Evening noise levels.   c) Night noise levels.

Fig. 6. Maps showing noise levels. The dots illustrate the locations of the sensors.

4.5 General Overview

Table 6 shows the districts ranked according to the four index evaluated. Analyzing the positioning of each district in each of the rankings, we can clearly see that some are generally better positioned than others. While there is more variability regarding the better positions (most of them located at the peripheral areas of the city), it is clear that some districts are worse prepared to age in place, and according to our definition, they are not age-friendly areas. The central zone and the surrounding areas are more prone to offer an insufficient quality of life in terms of environmental health, with the worst punctuation's in green areas, facilities, air quality, and noise pollution. It is also difficult that these districts can fulfill the measures promised before the UN in the SGDs. Other districts, such as Barajas, offer good quality in green areas and facilities. However, the location (in the airport area) contributes to a worsening of results in terms of pollution and noise.

Table 6. Districts sorted according to their ranks in the four variables evaluated.

Green areas	Fitment equipment	Air quality	Noise
Barajas	Barajas	Moncloa-Aravaca	Moncloa-Aravaca
Moncloa-Aravaca	Usera	Retiro	Arganzuela
Moratalaz	Villaverde	Fuencarral-El Pardo	Vicálvaro
Vicálvaro	Vicálvaro	Hortaleza	Villaverde
Villa de Vallecas	Moratalaz	Barajas	Fuencarral-El Pardo
Hortaleza	San Blas-Canillejas	Arganzuela	Puente de Vallecas
cre Fuencarral-El Pardo	Villa de Vallecas	San Blas-Canillejas	Barajas
Latina	Carabanchel	Ciudad Lineal	Carabanchel
Villaverde	Centro	Puente de Vallecas	Tetuán
Puente de Vallecas	Moncloa-Aravaca	Moratalaz	Moratalaz
Usera	Puente de Vallecas	Chamberí	Hortaleza
San Blas-Canillejas	Tetuán	Tetuán	Centro
Carabanchel	Hortaleza	Villa de Vallecas	Latina
Ciudad Lineal	Arganzuela	Centro	Chamberí
Arganzuela	Chamartín	Chamartín	Villa de Vallecas
Chamartín	Fuencarral-El Pardo	Villaverde	Usera
Retiro	Chamberí	Carabanchel	Salamanca
Tetuán	Retiro	Salamanca	Chamartín
Salamanca	Latina	Usera	Retiro
Centro	Ciudad Lineal	Latina	Ciudad Lineal
Chamberí	Salamanca	Vicálvaro	San Blas-Canillejas

Finally, it is important to remark that are districts that do not provide pollution data (air quality or noise). This hardness the evaluation of the quality of the health of the inhabitants of these districts. Thus, it would be important to install sensors to gather data from these districts. Besides, having a large number of sensors located in different areas would help to gather information with better resolution in this regard.

5   Conclusions and Future Work

Given the aging of the urban population, the challenge for cities lies in achieving a healthy and safe environment for the elderly. It means creating inclusive and accessible urban environments to benefit their aging population, enhancing health and well-being during old age. Environmental factors are interrelated and have a positive bearing on maintaining the capacities of the elderly.

In this work, we evaluate open data to assess the capacity of Madrid districts to offer a quality environment to age in place, as well as its capacity to accomplish with UN SDGs goals in terms of aging.

According to the evaluated data, we can see that central areas are less adequate to aging, meaning that they offer fewer possibilities for healthy aging in place. The elderly living there are exposed to more noise, more pollution, less green space, and in general, less urban facilities adapted for the elderly. This contrasts with the peripheral areas of Madrid that are (comparatively) more age-friendly. However, it seems difficult for this city to comply with the commitments referred to the UN if a large investment is not made from now to 2030.

Smart city tools proved their usefulness to analyze the environment quality. Smart cities can allow the elderly to age in society, preventing health frailty, and evaluating and foreseen needs and if there is a risk of not complying with an international agreement, as the UN commitments. Smart cities can be the tool to not leave vulnerable population behind.

Among the limitations of this paper, most important is data availability related. There is a shortage of information to evaluate other aspects of an age-friendly environment. The lack of use of open data standards in ODP and the poor documentation found hardness the analysis capacity for this type of studies. Obtaining and producing data with an age perspective is needed to reach an egalitarian society. For example, the lack of consistency in terms of urban fitment reduces the comparability of data.

The future research lines are: *i)* include socioeconomic aspects and housing new multivariable analysis taking into account new data (e.g., socioeconomic aspects, housing quality); *ii)* using machine learning approaches to evaluate more complex correlation of this results with health outcomes; and *iii)* assessing other cities in terms of comparison, considering new dimensions (such as, morbidity, economic impact, use of spaces).

Acknowledgements. J. Toutouh research was partially funded by European Union's Horizon 2020 research and innovation program under the Marie Skłodowska-Curie grant agreement No 799078, by the Junta de Andalucía UMA18-FEDERJA-003, European Union H2020-ICT-2019-3, and the Systems that Learn Initiative at MIT CSAIL.

References

1. Basner, M., et al.: Auditory and non-auditory effects of noise on health. The Lancet **383**(9925), 1325–1332 (2014)
2. Brandom, P.: Noise Pollution and Older Adults - A Real Health Hazard (2018). http://www.ageucate.com/blog/?p=1377. Accessed 08 Aug 2020
3. Brink, P.T., et al.: The health and social benefits of nature and biodiversity protection. A report for the European Commission (ENV. B. 3/ETU/2014/0039). London/Brussels: Institute for European Environmental Policy (2016)
4. De Keijzer, C. S.: Green Spaces and Healthy Ageing. https://www.isglobal. org/en/healthisglobal/-/custom-blog-portlet/green-spaces-and-healthy-ageing/ 6113078/0 (2019), Accessed: 2020
5. European Environment Agency: Air quality in Europe - 2018 (2018). https://www. eea.europa.eu/publications/air-quality-in-europe-2018. Accessed 07 Jul 2019
6. Fernández-Carro, C., Evandrou, M.: Staying put: factors associated with ageing in one's 'lifetime home'. Insights from the European context. Res. Ageing Soc. Pol. **2**(1), 28–56 (2014)

7. Help Age International: Ageing, Older Persons and the 2030 Agenda for Sustainable Development (2020). https://www.un.org/development/desa/ageing/news/2017/07/ageing-older-persons-and-the-2030-agenda-for-sustainable-development/. Accessed 1 Jan 2020

8. Lawton, M.P., Nahemow, L.: Ecology and the aging process (1973)

9. Lebrusán, I.: Las dificultades para habitar en la vejez. Documentación Socia 6(1) (2020)

10. Lebrusán, I., Toutouh, J.: Assessing the environmental impact of car restrictions policies: Madrid central case. In: Nesmachnow, S., Hernández Callejo, L. (eds.) ICSC-CITIES 2019. CCIS, vol. 1152, pp. 9–24. Springer, Cham (2020). https://doi.org/10.1007/978-3-030-38889-8_2

11. Lebrusán, I., Toutouh, J.: Car restriction policies for better urban health: a low emission zone in Madrid, Spain. Air Qual. Atmos. Health 1–10 (2020)

12. Lebrusán, I., Toutouh, J.: Using smart city tools to evaluate the effectiveness of a low emissions zone in Spain: Madrid central. Smart Cities 3(2), 456–478 (2020)

13. Lebrusán Murillo, I.: La vivienda en la vejez: problemas y estrategias para envejecer en sociedad. Consejo Superior de Investigaciones Científicas (2019)

14. Milgram, S.: Cities as social representations. In: Social Representations, pp. 289–309 (1984)

15. Oswald, F., Kaspar, R.: On the quantitative assessment of perceived housing in later life. J. Hous. Elderly 26(1–3), 72–93 (2012)

16. Peace, S., Holland, C., Kellaher, L.: 'Option recognition' in later life: variations in aging in place. Ageing Soc. 31(5), 734 (2011)

17. Proshansky, H.M., Fabian, A.K., Kaminoff, R.: Place-identity: physical world socialization of the self. J. Environ. Psychol. (1983)

18. Raaschou-Nielsen, O., et al.: Air pollution and lung cancer incidence in 17 European cohorts: prospective analyses from the European study of cohorts for air pollution effects (escape). The Lancet Oncol. 14(9), 813–822 (2013)

19. Rowles, G., Oswald, F., Hunter, E., Wahl, H., Scheidt, R., Windley, P.: Aging in context: socio-physical environments. Ann. Rev. Gerontol. Geriatrics 23, 110 (2004)

20. Rowles, G.D.: Evolving images of place in aging and 'aging in place'. Gener. J. Am. Soc. Aging 17(2), 65–70 (1993)

21. Rubinstein, R.I., Parmelee, P.A.: Attachment to place and the representation of the life course by the elderly. In: Place Attachment, pp. 139–163. Springer (1992). https://doi.org/10.1007/978-1-4684-8753-4_7

22. Simoni, M., Baldacci, S., Maio, S., Cerrai, S., Sarno, G., Viegi, G.: Adverse effects of outdoor pollution in the elderly. J. Thoracic Dis. 7(1), 34 (2015)

23. Stansfeld, S.A., Matheson, M.P.: Noise pollution: non-auditory effects on health. Brit. Med. Bull. 68(1), 243–257 (2003)

24. Toutouh, J., Lebrusán, I., Nesmachnow, S.: Computational intelligence for evaluating the air quality in the center of Madrid, Spain. In: International Conference on Optimization and Learning, pp. 115–127. Springer (2020). https://doi.org/10.1007/978-3-030-41913-4_10

25. United Nations: Report of the Second World Assembly on Ageing: Madrid, 8–12 April 2002. Technical Report, United Nations, April 2002

26. Valera, S., Pol, E.: El concepto de identidad social urbana: una aproximación entre la psicología social y la psicología ambiental. Anuario de psicología/The UB Journal Psychology, 5–24 (1994)

27. Woetzel, J., et al.: Smart cities: Digital solutions for a more livable future. McKinsey Global Institute: New York, NY, USA, pp. 1–152 (2018)

28. World Health Organization: Environmental noise guidelines for the European region (2018). http://www.euro.who.int/en/health-topics/environment-and-health/noise/publications/2018/environmental-noise-guidelines-for-the-european-region-2018. Accessed 07 Jul 2019

29. World Health Organization: Age friendly environments (2020). https://www.who.int/ageing/projects/age-friendly-environments/en/b. Accessed 27 Aug 2020

30. Younan, D., et al.: Particulate matter and episodic memory decline mediated by early neuroanatomic biomarkers of Alzheimer's disease. Brain **143**(1), 289–302 (2020)

Experimental Comparison of Visual Inspection and Infrared Thermography for the Detection of Soling and Partial Shading in Photovoltaic Arrays

Leonardo Cardinale-Villalobos[1]([⊠]) (iD), Carlos Meza[1] (iD),
and Luis D. Murillo-Soto[2] (iD)

[1] Electronics Engineering School, Instituto Tecnológico de Costa Rica,
Cartago, Costa Rica
lcardinale@tec.ac.cr
[2] Electromechanic Engineering School, Instituto Tecnológico de Costa Rica,
Cartago, Costa Rica

Abstract. Soling and partial shading of solar panels are two of the most common conditions that affects the power yield of a photovoltaic (PV) installation. Even though human inspection can easily identify such situations, in the case of large power plants covering thousands of hectares it is not practical. In this regard, unmanned areal systems (UAS) represents a useful tool to gather images in a short time for the inspection of thousands of PV panels. Using RGB and infrared cameras, UAS can be used to perform visual inspection (VI) and infrared thermography (IRT) to detect failures in PV arrays. The present paper presents the results of an experiment designed to evaluate the effectiveness of VI and IRT for detecting soiling and partial shadowing. It has been found that for the aforementioned conditions VI are more effective. Also, the methodology presented can be used as a reference for future research for other techniques and other failures. The results provide technical-scientific information for those in charge of operation and maintenance to make an objective choice of failure detection techniques.

Keywords: Solar PV system · Fault detection performance · Partial shading · Soiling · Thermography

1 Introduction

A photovoltaic (PV) power plant is capable of operating for more than 25 years and due to its low energy density the installations can occupy thousands of hectares [38]. A group of PV panels are connected in series to form strings and, in some cases, in parallel to form arrays injecting the generated energy through a power inverter. Weather, soling and obstacles that produces shadows yield suboptimal conditions in the PV array, i.e., the group of PV panels produces less power than expected. In the case of soling or obstructing elements the suboptimal

© Springer Nature Switzerland AG 2021
S. Nesmachnow and L. Hernández Callejo (Eds.): ICSC-CITIES 2020, CCIS 1359, pp. 302–321, 2021.
https://doi.org/10.1007/978-3-030-69136-3_21

condition can be corrected if detected. In this regard, strategies related to the operation and maintenance of PV modules acquired greater importance. Even though such conditions can be identified by human operators, as reported in [12], expert visual inspection and fault analysis in a 3 MW installation take 60 days. Thus, developing techniques that detects such suboptimal conditions in shorter time becomes a necessity.

There are several techniques to identify faults and suboptimal techniques, e.g. [4,5,9,12,17,20,22,29,30,32,37]. Two of the most promising are based on imaging, given that these techniques do not require to intervene the PV power plant circuit, does not require contact with the element of interest and generates a large amount of qualitative and quantitative information for each image. Such images can be taken in a relative short time if unmanned aerial systems (UAS) are used. UAS also known as drones with onboard thermal cameras enable inspections from the air and through digital photogrammetry techniques it is possible to detect failures in an agile way (e.g., [15,36]).

The camera attached to the UAS can be of the type that captures the red, green, blue (RGB) band or the infrared band. With an infrared band detection camera it is possible to obtain thermal images of solar panels which allows the identification of temperature gradients or hot spots that can be associated with panel failures [2,23]. Such technique is referred as infrared thermography (IRT).

The present paper compares two drone image-based fault detection techniques: (1) visual inspection (VI) based on RGB images and (2) a strategy based on IRT through infrared images. An experiment has been designed to measure the performance of the aforementioned techniques for partial shadowing and soiling, which represents two of the most common suboptimal techniques. The rest of the paper is structured as follows: firts the suboptimal conditions considered are described, then the material and methods are presented. Section 4 presents the main results and Sect. 5 gathers the main conclusions.

2   Suboptimal Conditions Considered

For the comparative analysis we consider the following suboptimal conditions:

- Partial shadowing: The power generated by a series of solar panels will suffer a decrease in the power generated when they are partially shaded [27]. Partial shading can be caused by objects located in the surface on the panel or by objects not in contact with the panel. The power affectation depends on the portion of the module that is shaded and on the degree to which it is shaded [24,31]. An example of a shadowed panel is shown in Fig. 1.
- Soiling: can be caused due to the presence of a thin layer of particles such as soil, dust, leaves, pollen or bird droppings [24]. The PV power affectation is greater as the soiling increases. A dirty PV module is shown in Fig. 2. Soling can be uniform or non-uniform. Dirt due to dust consists of particles of different sizes and materials that cover the entire PV module, which, over time, will form uniform layers of dust and regions with greater accumulation

of dirt [18]. Non-uniform dirt covering only some cells of the PV module, due to leaves, bird droppings or patches of soil have a severe power loss effect, this type of failure is associated with both soiling and partial shading. PV cells that capture less irradiance have a lower short circuit current than the rest, causing the entire module to deliver less current. In addition, dirty cells will cause a hot spot that can be detected with IRT [24].

Fig. 1. Partial shadow on a PV panel (left) and strange object on a PV panel (right).

Fig. 2. Soiled PV module.

3   Materials and Methods

3.1   The PV Installation Analyzed

The data used to compare VI and IRT suboptimal detection techniques consisted of images from a ground mounted PV installation located in Santa Clara, Costa Rica. The details of the PV installation are shown in Table 1.

Table 1. Information about the PV installation analyzed

Longitude	−84.51
Latitude	10.36
Azimut angle	0° with respect to the South
Inclination angle	15°
Peak DC power	19.4
Number of PV panels	72
PV panel models	Canadian Solar CS6k-280M and HANWHA Q-Cells QPRO BFR G4.3
Total surface (m²)	125
Performance factor (%)	77.7
Annual Yield (MWh)	28.69
Date of commissioning	May 31st, 2017

Figure 3 shows an aerial view of the PV installation considered, where it can be seen that the site consists of six well distinguished sections. Each section has a string of 12 PV modules connected to an inverter SMA Sunny Boy 3000TL-US. In this analysis only strings 2, 4, and 6, shown in Fig. 3, were used. The aforementioned strings have a direct current STC power of 3380 W.

Fig. 3. Picture of the PV installation. Strings 2, 4 and 6 were used in this research.

3.2 Image Capturing

The data used to determine the suboptimal conditions in the PV installation consisted of images taken from an (UAS). The following considerations have been considered to take the images:

– The drone is always flown at a height greater than 5 m to avoid that it causes shadows on the panels [20].

- The flight height depends on the detail that is necessary to observe in the PV modules for proper fault detection, thus, the size of the fault has been taken into account to determine the spatial resolution require for the images taken in a drone mission (ground sampling distance (GSD) [8]). A GSD of 3.0 ± 0.5 cm/px is required for deep inspections [9], allowing to detect possible hot spots at cell level [4].
- The measurements were made at a time with sufficient irradiance to allow the capture of thermal contrasts, with a correct angle and without wind currents that generate convection cooling [40], constant sunlight conditions with a clear sky are also desirable so that solar panels in good conditions have a homogeneous thermal distribution [36].
- The images were captured with an angle between 5° and 60° with respect to the perpendicular of the panel (see Fig. 4) [40] and the irradiance was always greater than $700\,W/m^2$ [16]. The camera's emissivity was set to 0.85 for crystalline cells as indicated in [17].
- The drone was set to consecutive image capture as recommended in [37,40] for fault detection in PV installations.

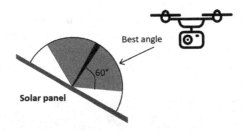

Fig. 4. Recommended orientation of the thermal camera with respect to the panel position.

A commercial Phantom 4 Pro multirotor drone was used as the UAS platform (see Fig. 5). The characteristics of the RGB and thermal infrared camera are shown in Table 2 and 3, respectively.

Table 2. Characteristics of the RGB camera used

Parameter	Value
Sensor	1″ CMOS/Effective pixels 20M
Lens	FOV 84° 8.8 mm/24 mm
PIV image size	4096 × 2160
Photo	JPEG
Image size	3:2, 4:3, 16:9
ISO range	100–3200 (Auto)

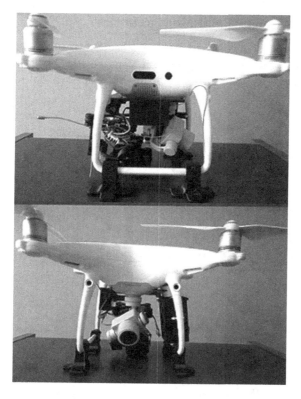

Fig. 5. Drone with RGB and thermal camera used in this research.

Table 3. Characteristics of the FLIR VUE PRO R 336 thermal camera [10,11]

Parameter	Value
HFOV × VFOV	25° × 19°
Sensor (width × height)	5.764 mm × 4.351 mm
Focal length	13.00 mm
Image width × height	336 × 256
Frequency	9 Hz
Accuracy	+/−5 °C o 5% from reading
Thermal sensitivity	40 mK
Sensor	Uncooled microbolometer

3.3   Other Instruments and Measurements

On-site irradiance was measured with a Spektron 210 sensor and the ambient temperature and relative humidity from a Vantage Pro 2 weather station. The power from the inverters was taken from the built-in SMA data logging system. A schematic of the system is shown in Fig. 6.

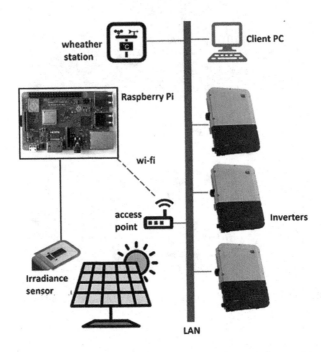

Fig. 6. Schematic diagram of communication links to information sources.

3.4   Experiments

The research was developed through a case study applying an experiment. Pre-defined temporary suboptimal conditions were induced to the PV installation in operation which allowed collecting and processing quantitative information to compare the IRT and VI techniques through statistical analysis. Taking as reference [14, 39] the following stages were used:

- Selection of the sample and information sources.
- Design of the experiment.
- Definition of protocols and criteria for the interpretation of results.

The experiment used a repeated measurement design because multiple treatments had to be applied to the same subjects [35]. A total of 28 experimental units were analyzed from the 8 treatments applied to the 2 subjects (Strings 4 and 6). String 2 was used as a control subject to establish a reference condition in each experimental unit for the normal operation of the PV strings, i.e. without applying failures. The factors and levels evaluated are shown in Table 4.

Table 4. Factors and levels used in the experiment to generate the diverse treatments.

Failure	Factor	Level
S1	Soiling	10 months of natural soil
S2		30 months of natural soil
S3		12 cells with white spots
S4		12 cells with dry leaves from the site
S5		21 cells with white spots
S6		21 cells with dry leaves from the site
PS1	Partial shading	Shading of approximately 70% of a panel's area
PS2		2 shadows, each approximately 30% of the area of a panel

The treatments were applied to the subjects without interaction between factors. Each level was applied in both subjects making two repetitions in each one. The selection of the modules of each string to which the failure was applied was chosen at random. The partial shadows were limited to the modules on the right margin due to site conditions. It was considered that there is an independent relationship between the treatments, because they were randomized and do not generate a residual effect in the subject [13], i.e., the PV string return to their normal state once the treatment is removed.

3.5   Description of Each Factor and the Levels of the Experiment

– A. Soiling

Table 4 describes the dirt conditions used for faults S1–S6. Faults S1 and S2 allowed the generation of soil conditions that cause weak shading [24]. Natural dirt accumulated in the solar panels over time was used as suggested in [18] which states that it is possible to take as an indicator of soiling the exposure time that the module has been under natural conditions.

Failures S3 and S5 were made to generate a strong obstruction of the irradiance due to some strange object on the solar panel. Samples of glass of 480 mm × 160 mm × 5 mm were prepared in which white paint was placed to simulate dirt on the PV module (see Fig. 7); this allowed to replicate the treatments in multiple moments in different positions of the PV array. The experiment took as a reference the methodology used in [34] to study the effects of dirt on solar modules.

Faults S4 and S6 are a variation of S3 and S5 to evaluate soiling. In this case, dry leaves and seeds were used, where to achieve repeatability in the experiment the objects were adhered to the glass with cold silicon (see Fig. 8).

Fig. 7. Glass with white circles used to simulate dirt obstructing the path of radiation in three PV cells.

Fig. 8. Glass with dry leaves and seeds to simulate dirt obstructing the radiation path in three PV cells.

– **B. Partial shading**

The experiment was developed by applying shadows to the solar modules in operation. The methodology took as reference experiences of previous investigations, in which, they placed an object to obstruct the solar radiation of a portion of the solar module, allowing that it influences diffuse radiation [26]. The two partial shading levels (PS1 and PS2) applied were made by placing an object next to the PV string to create the shadow (Fig. 9).

3.6 Protocol for Missions with UAS

As mentioned previously, for each treatment a flight was performed with the UAS capturing RGB and infrared images of the PV strings of interest ensuring that the requirements indicated in Sect. 3.2 were met. The flight height was 25 m according to the GSD equation presented by [21] to obtain a maximum GSD of 3.0 cm/pixel in thermal images and even less in RGB images.

The thermal images were configured to contain the radiometric information in RJPEG format. Thermographs were taken every 1 s and RGB images every 2 s during each test. The orientation of the cameras with respect to the perpendicular plane of the module was around 20 °C.

For each test, the irradiance, ambient temperature and relative humidity were recorded. Each treatment was applied 15 min before the measurement was taken to ensure that thermal equilibrium existed [17].

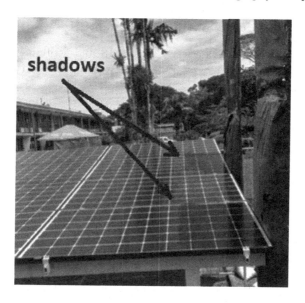

Fig. 9. Example of partial shadows generated on the PV modules.

3.7   Fault Detection Criteria

The temperature variation due to a hot spot is an indicator of the severity of the fault, where less than $10\,^\circ\mathrm{C}$ is considered within the normal operation tolerance [16,28] however, at lower irradiance, the temperature variation of a fault will decrease [7].

Fault detection in PV installations by VI can be done following the detailed guidance of [32]. For example, it is possible to identify soiling by evaluating the appearance of the solar modules so that it is classified as: clean, slightly dirty or very dirty. Furthermore, the dirt can be classified according to its location as: close to the frames or located somewhere on the glass (e.g. bird droppings). Partial shadows can be identified by observing the glass surface of the PV module.

According to the literature review, the criteria for the detection of the failures of interest for the applied techniques were determined. The criteria used are shown in the Table 5.

Table 5. Criteria used for the determination of failures

Technique	Criteria for fault detection
IRT	Hot spot with a delta $\geq 10\,^\circ\mathrm{C}$
VI	Presence of radiation attenuation on the panel due to shade
	Appearance of light or heavy soiling

3.8   Date and Conditions of the Experiment

All measurements were made between august 18 and september 2, 2020. The average ambient temperature was $30\,^{\circ}\mathrm{C}$, the relative humidity 60% and the reflected temperature $22\,^{\circ}\mathrm{C}$.

3.9   Measurement Normalizing

The three mono-crystalline strings are equivalent, however, their output power may vary slightly, so the power of the strings under test (String 4 and String 6) were compared with the control String 2 to set a reference level. Table 6 shows the variation in the average output power under non-fault conditions after two hours of operation with an irradiance greater than $700\,\mathrm{W/m^2}$.

Table 6. Power comparison of the string under test with respect to the control string

String	Power (W)	Variation (%)
2 (control)	2549	–
4	2566	0.67
6	2534	−0.59

4   Results and Discussion

The results of the induced suboptimal conditions are shown in Table 7. Each one of the induced condition was considered as a fault because it caused a decrease of at least 4% in the power of the array [1].

Table 7. Power effect of the faults studied

Fault (String)	Power in control string (W)	Power in string under test (W)	Estimated power without fault (W)	Losses (%)
PS1 (4)	2224	1920	2239	14.2
PS2 (6)	3133	2746	3115	11.9
S1 (4)	2137	1879	2151	12.7
S2 (6)	2137	1461	2124	31.3
S3 (6)	2421	1994	2407	17.1
S4 (4)	2421	1749	2437	28.3
S5 (6)	2094	1648	2082	20.8
S6 (4)	2094	1573	2108	25.4

4.1   RGB and IR Images Analysis

The most representative images that identifies suboptimal conditions are shown in Fig. 10, 11, 12, 13, 14, 15. For each experimental unit, a discrete output variable was generated to indicate whether or not the technique detected failure; the results are shown in Table 8.

Slight soiling identified at the edges   Hot spot with delta >10 °C

Fig. 10. RGB (left) and IR image (right) analyzed for experimental unit 1.

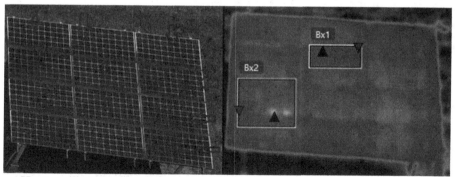

Heavy soiling identified at the edges   Temperature delta < 10 °C

Fig. 11. RGB (left) and IR image (right) analyzed for experimental unit 2.

Figure 16 shows the summary of the failures detected with each of the techniques. It can be seen that VI identified more failures than IRT. The VI was able to detect all the failures, on the other hand, the IRT detected only 68% of the evaluated test, missing 45% of the cases of soiling.

The results of soiling failures for IRT are shown in the Fig. 17. IRT was not able to detect the 30 month natural soiling (S2). Also the types of soiling with

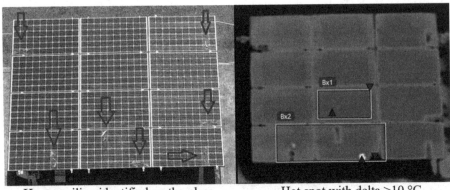

Heavy soiling identified on the glass   Hot spot with delta >10 °C

Fig. 12. RGB (left) and IR image (right) analyzed for experimental unit 6.

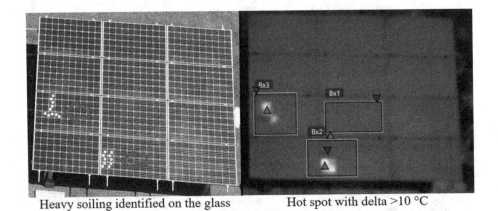

Heavy soiling identified on the glass   Hot spot with delta >10 °C

Fig. 13. RGB (left) and IR image (right) analyzed for experimental unit 18.

Heavy soiling identified on the glass   Temperature delta < 10 °C

Fig. 14. RGB (left) and IR image (right) analyzed for experimental unit 19.

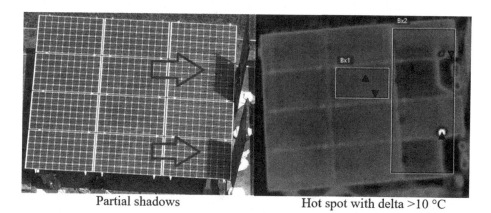

Partial shadows   Hot spot with delta >10 °C

Fig. 15. RGB (left) and IR image (right) analyzed for experimental unit 22.

Table 8. Output variable of the experiment for IRT and VI. D = Detected, ND = Not detected

Experimental unit	Treatment	IRT output	VI output
1	S1	D	D
2	S2	ND	D
3	S1	D	D
4	S2	ND	D
5	S4	ND	D
6	S6	D	D
7	S4	D	D
8	S6	D	D
9	S4	D	D
10	S6	ND	D
11	S4	D	D
12	S6	D	D
13	S5	ND	D
14	S3	ND	D
15	S5	ND	D
16	S3	D	D
17	S5	D	D
18	S3	D	D
19	S5	ND	D
20	S3	ND	D
21	PS1	D	D
22	PS2	D	D
23	PS1	D	D
24	PS2	D	D
25	PS1	D	D
26	PS2	D	D
27	PS1	D	D
28	PS2	D	D

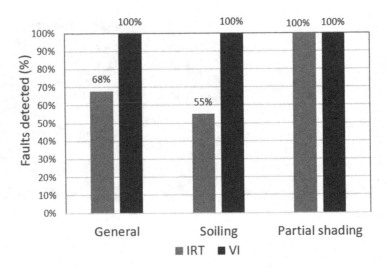

Fig. 16. Percentage of failures detected by each technique in the experiment.

white spots (S3 and S5) were the least detected. Finally, for the soiling with dry leaves (S4 and S6) there was one case of each that the failure could not be detected. Therefore, IRT is able to detect all types of soiling evaluated, however, there are levels of soiling that were not detected in some cases.

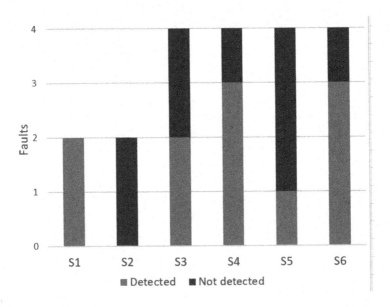

Fig. 17. Failures detected and not detected by the IRT under soiled conditions.

The detection of the failures was done strictly following the criteria of Table 5. However, in Fig. 11 it can be seen that through the IRT it was possible to appreciate a distortion in the thermal distribution of the PV array. In addition, in Fig. 14 it was possible to identify specific regions of lower temperature on the PV modules and temperature gradients lower than $10\,^{\circ}C$, even though none of these cases met the requirement to be cataloged as failures, this suggests that, to detect soiling suboptimal conditions a lower threshold for the temperature gradient might be required.

4.2 Statistical Analysis

To determine if one method performed significantly better than the other, a hypothesis test was done using Fisher's exact test [3, 19] as follows:

$$H_0 : N_i = N_j$$

$$H_a : N_i \neq N_j$$
$$\forall i \neq j$$

Where N is the number of identified failures, i and j are IRT and VI techniques respectively.

The test yields a p-value of p $= 0.002$ and odds ratio (OR) $= 27.8$, therefore, considering a significance level of $\alpha = 0.05$ it fulfills the alternative hypothesis $(p < \alpha)$, i.e. significant differences were found between both methods [6]. In addition, when evaluating the hypothesis tests for each of the failure factors (soiling and partial shading) with the contingency tables shown in the Table 9, significant differences were obtained for soiling (S) with $p = 0.001$ and an OR $= 33.87$. The OR coefficient obtained in both cases indicate that there is a high probability that a fault will be not detect using IRT instead of VI, specifically detecting soiling [25]. That is, the VI is associated with a greater capacity for dirt detection compared to the IRT.

Table 9. Contingency table separating the factors (types of failures) of the experiment

Factor	Technique	Result		Total
		Not Detected	Detected	
S	TI	9	11	20
	VI	0	20	20
	Total	9	31	40
PS	TI	0	8	8
	VI	0	8	8
	Total	0	16	16
Total	TI	9	19	40
	VI	0	28	40
	Total	9	47	56

Another way to compare both methods is by the sensitivity in the effectiveness of fault detection, this is based on the analysis of true positives achieved by each technique [33]. The results show that IRT had a sensitivity of 68% while VI had 100%.

5   Conclusions

The present paper has analyzed two image-based fault detection technique (IRT and VI) for photovoltaic arrays for two of the most common temporary faults or suboptimal conditions, i.e., soiling and shading. Partial shadows were correctly detected with both techniques, however, IRT did not perform as well as VI for the detection of soiling. Nevertheless, IRT did detect at least once all the types of faults evaluated. The results also suggest that soling with IRT might be detectable if a temperature difference threshold smaller than $10\,^{\circ}C$ is used.

The methodology used allowed a quantitative comparison from experimental data between two techniques for failure detection in PV systems. This can be used for future experiments with other configurations of PV arrays and other types of failures, making it possible to validate theoretical models that are still being studied and to generate quantitative indicators of the effectiveness of each technique. Including treatments of conditions that are an apparent failure but without a significant affectation on power will allow studying the capacity of each technique to discriminate between true and false failures; this is pending for future research.

Acknowledgement. This paper is part of a project 5402-1360-4201 "Identificación de Fallas en Sistemas Fotovoltaicos" financed by the Costa Rica Institute of Technology. In addition, the first author is part of the Master of Science: Maestría en Ciencia y Tecnología para la Sostenibilidad of DOCINADE. Thanks to the Electronics students at TEC Dalberth Alberto Corrales Alpizar and Jose Eduardo Zuñiga Ramirez for their contribution in the development of the data acquisition system and John Martin Chacon Zambrana for the support in the data collection of the experiment.

References

1. Acciani, G., Falcone, O., Vergura, S.: Typical defects of PV-cells. In: IEEE International Symposium on Industrial Electronics, pp. 2745–2749 (2010). https://doi.org/10.1109/ISIE.2010.5636901
2. Alsafasfeh, M., Abdel-Qader, I., Bazuin, B.: Fault detection in photovoltaic system using SLIC and thermal images. In: 2017 8th International Conference on Information Technology (ICIT). IEEE, May 2017. https://doi.org/10.1109/icitech.2017.8079925
3. Bolboacă, S.D., Jäntschi, L., Sestraş, A.F., Sestraş, R.E., Pamfil, D.C.: Pearson-fisher chi-square statistic revisited. Information 2(3), 528–545, September 2011. https://doi.org/10.3390/info2030528

4. Cardinale-Villalobos, L., Rimolo-Donadio, R., Meza, C.: Solar panel failure detection by infrared UAS digital photogrammetry: a case study. Int. J. Renew. Energy Res. (IJRER) **10**(3), 1154–1164 (2020)
5. Chaudhary, A.S., Chaturvedi, D.: Thermal image analysis and segmentation to study temperature effects of cement and bird deposition on surface of solar panels. Int. J. Image Graph. Sig. Process. **9**(12), 12–22 (2017). https://doi.org/10.5815/ijigsp.2017.12.02
6. Cohen, H.W.: P values: use and misuse in medical literature. Am. J. Hypertens. **24**(1), 18–23, January 2011. https://doi.org/10.1038/ajh.2010.205
7. Cubukcu, M., Akanalci, A.: Real-time inspection and determination methods of faults on photovoltaic power systems by thermal imaging in turkey. Renew. Energy **147**, 1231–1238, March 2020. https://doi.org/10.1016/j.renene.2019.09.075
8. Felipe-García, B., Hernández-López, D., Lerma, J.L.: Analysis of the ground sample distance on large photogrammetric surveys. Appl. Geomatics **4**(4), 231–244 (2012). https://doi.org/10.1007/s12518-012-0084-2
9. FLIR: A guide to inspecting solar fields with thermal imaging drones (2019). https://thermalcapture.com/wp-content/uploads/2019/08/pv-system-inspection-thermal-drones-07-15-19.pdf
10. Flir: Flir Vue Pro and Flir Vue Pro R (2019). http://www.flir-vue-pro.com/wp-content/uploads/2016/10/FLIR-VUE-Pro-R-Datasheet-TeAx.pdf
11. Flir.com: Adjusting Sensitivity and Gain On The FLIR Vue Pro R (2019). https://flir.custhelp.com/app/answers/detail/a_id/3134
12. Gallardo-Saavedra, S., Hernandez-Callejo, L., Duque-Perez, O.: Image resolution influence in aerial thermographic inspections of photovoltaic plants. IEEE Trans. Ind. Inf. **14**(12), 5678–5686, December 2018. https://doi.org/10.1109/tii.2018.2865403
13. Gutiérreza-Pulido, H., De la Vara-Salazar, R.: Análisis y diseño de experimentos, 2nd edn. McGraw-Hill Interamericana, México D.F. (2008)
14. Hernández Sampieri, R., Fernández Collado, C., Baptista, L., Del Pilar, M.: Metodología de la investigación, 5th edn. Mc Graw Hill, México (2010)
15. Higuchi, Y., Babasaki, T.: Failure detection of solar panels using thermographic images captured by drone. In: 2018 7th International Conference on Renewable Energy Research and Applications (ICRERA). IEEE, October 2018. https://doi.org/10.1109/icrera.2018.8566833
16. International Energy Agency: Review of Failures of Photovoltaic Modules. Technical Report July, Performance and Reliability of Photovoltaic Systems (2014)
17. International Energy Agency: Review on Infrared and Electroluminescence Imaging for PV Field Applications. Technical Report, Photovoltaic Power Systems Programme (2018)
18. Javed, W., Wubulikasimu, Y., Figgis, B., Guo, B.: Characterization of dust accumulated on photovoltaic panels in Doha, Qatar. Solar Energy **142**, 123–135, January 2017. https://doi.org/10.1016/j.solener.2016.11.053
19. Jones, J.B., Schropp, M.A.: Research fundamentals: statistical considerations in research design: a simple person's approach. Acad. Emerg. Med. **7**(2), 194–199 (2000). https://doi.org/10.1111/j.1553-2712.2000.tb00529.x
20. Leva, S., Aghaei, M., Grimaccia, F.: PV power plant inspection by UAS: correlation between altitude and detection of defects on PV modules. In: 2015 IEEE 15th International Conference on Environment and Electrical Engineering (EEEIC). IEEE, June 2015. https://doi.org/10.1109/eeeic.2015.7165466
21. Linder, W.: Introduction. Digital Photogrammetry, 4th edn., pp. 10–12. Springer-Verlag, Berlin (2016). https://doi.org/10.1007/978-3-662-50463-5

22. Köntges, M.: Reviewing the practicality and utility of electroluminescence and thermography (2014). https://www.nrel.gov/pv/assets/pdfs/2014_pvmrw_33_kontges.pdf

23. Madeti, S.R., Singh, S.: A comprehensive study on different types of faults and detection techniques for solar photovoltaic system. Solar Energy **158**, 161–185, December 2017. https://doi.org/10.1016/j.solener.2017.08.069

24. Maghami, M.R., Hizam, H., Gomes, C., Radzi, M.A., Rezadad, M.I., Hajighorbani, S.: Power loss due to soiling on solar panel: a review. Renew. Sustain. Energy Rev. **59**, 1307–1316, June 2016. https://doi.org/10.1016/j.rser.2016.01.044

25. Mchugh, M.L.: The odds ratio: calculation, usage, and interpretation. Biochemia medica **19**(2), 120–126 (2009). https://hrcak.srce.hr/37593

26. Mekki, H., Mellit, A., Salhi, H.: Artificial neural network-based modelling and fault detection of partial shaded photovoltaic modules. Simul. Model. Pract. Theory **67**, 1–13, September 2016. https://doi.org/10.1016/j.simpat.2016.05.005

27. Mellit, A., Tina, G., Kalogirou, S.: Fault detection and diagnosis methods for photovoltaic systems: a review. Renew. Sustain. Energy Rev. **91**, 1–17, August 2018. https://doi.org/10.1016/j.rser.2018.03.062

28. Moretón, R., Lorenzo, E., Narvarte, L.: Experimental observations on hot-spots and derived acceptance/rejection criteria. Solar Energy **118**, 28–40, August 2015. https://doi.org/10.1016/j.solener.2015.05.009

29. Murillo-Soto, L., Meza, C.: Fault detection in solar arrays based on an efficiency threshold. In: 2020 IEEE 11th Latin American Symposium on Circuits Systems (LASCAS), pp. 1–4 (2020). https://doi.org/10.1109/LASCAS45839.2020.9069046

30. Murillo-Soto, L.D., Meza, C.: Photovoltaic array fault detection algorithm based on least significant difference test. In: Figueroa-García, J.C., Garay-Rairán, F.S., Hernández-Pérez, G.J., Díaz-Gutierrez, Y. (eds.) WEA 2020. CCIS, vol. 1274, pp. 501–515. Springer, Cham (2020). https://doi.org/10.1007/978-3-030-61834-6_43

31. Mäki, A., Valkealahti, S.: Power losses in long string and parallel-connected short strings of series-connected silicon-based photovoltaic modules due to partial shading conditions. IEEE Trans. Energy Convers. **27**(1), 173–183, March 2012. https://doi.org/10.1109/tec.2011.2175928

32. National Renewable Energy Laboratory: Development of a Visual Inspection Data Collection Tool for Evaluation of Fielded PV Module Condition (2012). https://doi.org/10.2172/1050110, http://www.osti.gov/bridge

33. Pintea, S., Moldovan, R.: The receiver-operating characteristic (ROC) analysis: fundamentals and applications in clinical psychology. J. Cogn. Behav. Psychotherapies **9**(1), 49–66 (2009)

34. Sisodia, A.K., Mathur, R.: Impact of bird dropping deposition on solar photovoltaic module performance: a systematic study in Western Rajasthan. Environ. Sci. Pollution Res. **26**(30), 31119–31132 (2019). https://doi.org/10.1007/s11356-019-06100-2

35. Tango, T.: Repeated Measures Design with Generalized Linear Mixed Models for Randomized Controlled Trials. Taylor & Francis Group, Tokyo, Japan (2017)

36. Tsanakas, J.A., Ha, L., Buerhop, C.: Faults and infrared thermographic diagnosis in operating CSI photovoltaic modules: a review of research and future challenges. Renew. Sustain. Energy Rev. **62**, 695–709, September 2016. https://doi.org/10.1016/j.rser.2016.04.079

37. Tyutyundzhiev, N., Lovchinov, K., Martínez-Moreno, F., Leloux, J., Narvarte, L.: Advanced PV modules inspection using multirotor UAV. In: 31st European Photovoltaic Solar Energy Conference and Exhibition, Hamburg (2015). https://www.researchgate.net/publication/283087341

38. Watson, J.J., Hudson, M.D.: Regional scale wind farm and solar farm suitability assessment using GIS-assisted multi-criteria evaluation. Landscape Urban Plan. **138**, 20–31, June 2015. https://doi.org/10.1016/j.landurbplan.2015.02.001
39. Wohlin, C., Runeson, P., Höst, M., Ohlsson, M.C., Regnell, B., Wesslén, A.: Experimentation in Software Engineering. Springer, New York (2012). https://doi.org/10.1007/978-3-642-29044-2
40. Zefri, Y., ElKettani, A., Sebari, I., Lamallam, S.A.: Thermal infrared and visual inspection of photovoltaic installations by UAV photogrammetry—application case: Morocco. Drones **2**(4), 41, November 2018. https://doi.org/10.3390/drones2040041

Author Index

Printed in the United States
By Bookmasters